CW00544532

Victoria Wright and Denise Taylor

Cambridge IGCSE®
ICT

Coursebook

Revised second edition

CAMBRIDGE
UNIVERSITY PRESS

CAMBRIDGE
UNIVERSITY PRESS

University Printing House, Cambridge CB2 8BS, United Kingdom

One Liberty Plaza, 20th Floor, New York, NY 10006, USA

477 Williamstown Road, Port Melbourne, VIC 3207, Australia

314–321, 3rd Floor, Plot 3, Splendor Forum, Jasola District Centre, New Dehli – 110025, India

79 Anson Road, #06–04/06, Singapore 079906

Cambridge University Press is part of the University of Cambridge.

It furthers the University's mission by disseminating knowledge in the pursuit of education, learning and research at the highest international levels of excellence.

www.cambridge.org
Information on this title: education.cambridge.org/9781108698061

© Cambridge University Press 2019

This publication is in copyright. Subject to statutory exception and to the provisions of relevant collective licensing agreements, no reproduction of any part may take place without the written permission of Cambridge University Press.

First published 2010
Second edition 2016
Revised edition 2019

20 19 18 17 16 15 14 13 12 11 10 9 8 7 6 5 4 3

Printed in Dubai by Oriental Press

A catalogue record for this publication is available from the British Library

ISBN 978-1-108-69806-1 Paperback with CD-ROM

Additional resources for this publication at education.cambridge.org

This book acknowledges the limited reuse of some materials from Cambridge IGCSE® ICT, by Chris Leadbetter and Stewart Wainwright, Cambridge, 2010

Cambridge University Press has no responsibility for the persistence or accuracy of URLs for external or third-party internet websites referred to in this publication, and does not guarantee that any content on such websites is, or will remain, accurate or appropriate. Information regarding prices, travel timetables, and other factual information given in this work is correct at the time of first printing but Cambridge University Press does not guarantee the accuracy of such information thereafter.

....

NOTICE TO TEACHERS IN THE UK
It is illegal to reproduce any part of this work in material form (including photocopying and electronic storage) except under the following circumstances:
(i) where you are abiding by a licence granted to your school or institution by the Copyright Licensing Agency;
(ii) where no such licence exists, or where you wish to exceed the terms of a licence, and you have gained the written permission of Cambridge University Press;
(iii) where you are allowed to reproduce without permission under the provisions of Chapter 3 of the Copyright, Designs and Patents Act 1988, which covers, for example, the reproduction of short passages within certain types of educational anthology and reproduction for the purposes of setting examination questions.

....

All questions and answers provided have been written by the authors. In examinations, the way marks are awarded may be different.
* IGCSE is the registered trademark of Cambridge International Examinations.

Contents

Introduction   iv

Chapter 1   Types and components of computer systems   1

Chapter 2   Input and output devices   16

Chapter 3   Storage devices and media   33

Chapter 4   Networks and the effects of using them   41

Chapter 5   The effects of using IT   55

Chapter 6   ICT applications   64

Chapter 7   The systems life cycle   91

Chapter 8   Safety and security   105

Chapter 9   Audience   122

Chapter 10   Communication   130

Chapter 11   File management   139

Chapter 12   Images   146

Chapter 13   Layout   160

Chapter 14   Styles   175

Chapter 15   Proofing   185

Chapter 16   Graphs and charts   194

Chapter 17   Document production   204

Chapter 18   Data manipulation   218

Chapter 19   Presentation   240

Chapter 20   Data analysis   251

Chapter 21   Website authoring   278

Glossary   297

Index   305

Acknowledgements   308

Introduction

When we wrote this book our main aim was to provide material to cover the new Cambridge IGCSE ICT syllabus (0417), but we also wanted to include current interesting examples of ICT usage to invite you to find out more by carrying out your own research. The constant change in the field of ICT has made this edition of the textbook imperative. There are many overlooked aspects of the subject that are clarified by examples shown in the screenshots of the practical chapters. In addition, there are new perspectives on familiar aspects of ICT in this edition.

Content

The book is entirely based around the 0417 syllabus, which it follows in the same order chapter by chapter. The first 11 chapters contain the theory, research topics and some exercises that you can carry out either on your own or with your class. Chapters 12 to 21 are the practical chapters to help you to carry out tasks that include creating a variety of publishing documents, modelling using spreadsheets, writing websites and using a database. Practical exercises for chapters 12 to 21 have been supported with examples from the CD ROM.

Focus of the book

This book will help you to work through your course and give you the opportunity and the support to carry out research, use independent thinking and gain new skills following a structured path.

Throughout this book you will gain background knowledge to help you to answer the types of questions and understand the practical techniques that you will meet in your studies.

To support your learning, many of the chapters include examination-style questions.

Focus on you

One of the advantages of this book is that it does not contain anything outside the syllabus for your course so you will know that everything in the book is important for your study. The discussion topics suggested for you will also encourage you to think independently and to arrive at your own answers after studying the issues and listening to others.

This book is therefore aimed at teaching you underlying skills, which you will be able to apply during your course and afterwards in your subsequent studies.

We hope that you will enjoy using this book to help you throughout your course.

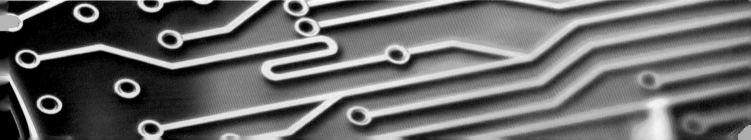

Chapter 1:
Types and components of computer systems

Learning objectives

When you have finished this chapter you will be able to:

- define the physical components of hardware for a computer system, including identifying internal hardware devices
- identify external hardware devices and peripherals
- define software as programs for controlling the operation of a computer or processing of electronic data
- define applications software
- define and describe system software and describe operating systems which contain a command line interface (CLI) and a graphical user interface (GUI)
- describe the central processing unit and its role
- describe internal memory, i.e. ROM and RAM and the differences between them
- define input and output devices and describe the difference between them, as well as secondary/backing storage
- describe and compare the characteristics and uses of a personal/desktop computer and a laptop computer, as standalone and networked computers
- describe the characteristics and uses of tablet computers and smartphones, including their ability to use wireless technology or 3G/4G technology
- describe how emerging technologies are having an impact on everyday life.

Overview

Information and communication technology (ICT) is used almost everywhere. This chapter will help you to learn and to understand what different ICT systems can do and what their effects on society are.

First, you will learn about hardware and software and the difference between them; next you will look at the hardware components of a computer system, then at some of the different operating systems. Finally you will consider emerging technologies and the type of impact they have on everyday life.

Figure 1.01 Typical computer system

1.01 Hardware and software

There are two main components of any computer system, such as the typical system shown in Figure 1.01: the hardware, and the software. In this section you will identify the physical parts of the hardware and explore the difference between application software and system software.

Computer hardware consists of the physical parts of a computer system, the parts that are tangible, (that you can touch). This includes the computer case, screen, keyboard, mouse, printer, pen drive, and also all the parts inside the computer case, for example components such as the hard disk drive, motherboard or video card.

KEY TERMS

Motherboard: a printed circuit board that allocates power to the CPU, RAM and other hardware components, and allows them to communicate with each other.

There are many different types of hardware components, even inside a mobile phone. Just because it is inside the phone casing, doesn't mean that you couldn't touch it if you took off the case off! Therefore it is still hardware.

Computer software is the opposite: you cannot touch it. Software is a set of instructions for a computer to make it perform certain specific operations. You need hardware *and* software for a computer system to work.

Desktop and laptop computers

A desktop computer usually has a computer case and a separate monitor, keyboard and mouse. It is called a desktop as that is normally where it is placed. There are also desktop computers, known as 'all in ones', where the computer part is in the same case as the monitor. Neither type is very portable.

A laptop computer has the same components as a desktop, but the computer, monitor, keyboard and a touchpad are integrated into a single, portable unit. In Section 1.04 later in this chapter this will be discussed in more detail.

Hardware components

The computer case contains many of the other hardware components; it can come in various shapes and sizes, but typically as a tower.

The computer case contains the **motherboard** on which other components are mounted, such as the CPU, the main memory and expansion slots for other hardware components, and the internal hard disk drive, which is a mass storage device that is used to store data files and software applications; there can also be an optical disk drive which makes it possible to read from and write to CDs and DVDs.

Other hardware components typically found inside a computer case are a sound card, a video card and a cooling mechanism, such as a fan.

A computer system also needs input devices, such as a keyboard and a mouse or a touchpad (also known as a trackpad) so that the user can interact with the computer via the interface. A display device such as a monitor is also needed.

Most computer hardware is divided into several types of device:

- An input device is used to put data into the computer. Input devices can also be referred to as peripherals and the more common ones are: keyboard, mouse, touchpad, microphone, bar code readers, scanner, digital camera, joystick.

- A **processor** does something with the data given by the input device.

- An output device is used to show the processor's results. Output devices may also be called peripherals and examples would include printers, speakers, plotters, projectors and display screens.

- A storage device keeps all the data and the software.

KEY TERMS

Processor: called CPU, short for central processing unit.

Internal hardware devices

The hardware inside the case of a computer (see Figure 1.02) includes the **processor** or CPU which is a chip attached to the motherboard. The processor makes complex calculations and logical decisions, executing computer programs, and also sends instructions to other parts of the computer.

What does the CPU do?

A CPU is fitted into a socket on the motherboard and it contains various components:

- the arithmetic logic unit (ALU), where the calculations occur:

  - logical operations, including AND, OR, NOT, etc.

  - bit-shifting operations, which means moving or 'shifting' the positions of bits left or right (which is how multiplication is performed)

  - arithmetic operations to add and to subtract (because addition can be used to multiply and subtraction can be used instead of division).

- the control unit (CU), to manage the various components of the computer; the control unit reads and interprets the instructions from memory and changes them into signals which activate other parts of the computer calculations.

- the cache, to act as high-speed memory where instructions and data can be copied to and retrieved.

In order to understand how these calculations actually get carried out, a little bit of knowledge about the binary number system is needed.

3

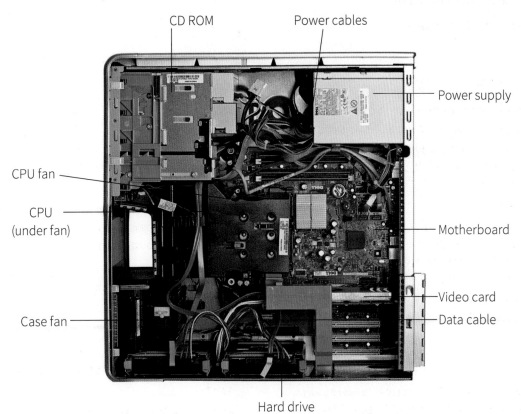

Figure 1.02 The internal hardware components of a computer

The binary number system is made up of only 0s and 1s and is used in computing to represent whether a switch is 'on' or 'off'. Think of a light switch with a '0' written on the top and a '1' written on the bottom; when you turn on the light switch, it goes from '0' to '1'.

Computers store and process data using binary numbers. For example, a computer stores the letter 'B' as 01000010. The data is stored as a series of zeros and ones because the computer cannot immediately understand words like 'hello' or 'teacher', or numbers such as '49'; it can only understand electrical signals being turned on or off. These signals can stand for 0 (no signal being sent) or 1 (an electrical signal). Everything else has to be made up of combinations of the presence or absence of electrical signals. The name for a single signal unit (a 0 or a 1) is a bit, which is short for **b**inary dig**it**.

By putting a number of these bits together the computer can represent many different types of data. For example, 01000001 stands for 'A' and 01000010 stands for 'B'.

Notice that the examples of A and B that were given both contain eight bits. This is because quite often eight bits are grouped together like this. A group of bits like this is called a byte.

KEY TERMS

Sound card: this enables the computer to send audio information to an audio device, such speakers or headphones.

Video card: this is an internal circuit board for displaying images from a computer onto a screen.

Other hardware components

A **video card**, also known as a graphics card, can generate images, translate them and output them to a display.

A **sound card** lets you hear, record and play back sounds.

The **power supply** converts alternating current (AC) electricity from the mains supply to direct current (DC) electricity, and then supplies it to the other components.

A **hard disk drive** (see Figure 1.03) is for storing programs and data. The computer can read from and write to it. (When we say 'read from', it means being able to open a file from the hard disk and load its contents into memory; 'write to' means that we can save to the hard disk.) There are different types of disk drives but they generally work by spinning a disk and using a drive head to read/write. For hard drives a magnetic head is used.

Figure 1.03 Hard drive

External hardware devices

There are many external devices available; the ones usually encountered are keyboard, mouse, trackpad, printer, scanner.

QUESTION 1.01

Make a note of all the external hardware devices your group can think of.

Now explain what the devices on your list do, and make a note of whether they are input or output devices.

Software

The set of instructions that make a computer system work is called the software. However advanced or expensive the hardware of a computer system is, it cannot do anything unless it has instructions that it can follow that make it work. There are two main types of software:

- **Systems software** is essential to keep the computer working.

- **Applications software** lets you do your day-to-day tasks on the computer. Applications software needs the operating system to be able to work.

KEY TERMS

Applications software: programs that carry out operations for specific applications such as word processing, spreadsheets or presentations. Applications software cannot run on its own without systems software.

System software

System software may be classified as operating system, **device drivers** and utility software.

KEY TERMS

Device driver: a program that controls devices such as printers.
Command line interface: a way of interacting with a computer via keyboard input at a prompt on the screen.
Graphical user interface (GUI): an intuitive way of communicating with a computer through a colourful screen by clicking on icons using a mouse or trackpad.

KEY TERMS

Linker: a computer program that takes files generated by a compiler and then combines them into a single file that can be executed.
Compiler: a computer program that converts source code into a language that can be understood by a computer.
Utilities: part of the system software that can analyse, configure, optimise and maintain a computer.

An operating system, therefore, provides a platform for application programs to run. As a user, one of the ways you can interact with the operating system is through a **graphical user interface** (**GUI**), such as Windows; it allows you to enter commands by pointing at icons or objects that appear on the screen, and then clicking on them.

A different way of interacting with the operating system is by using a **command line interface** (**CLI**). This allows the use of commands such as COPY and RENAME for copying files and changing their names. The commands are accepted and executed by a part of the operating system called the command processor or command line interpreter.

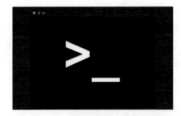

Figure 1.04 Command line interface showing prompt

Now you know that the operating system creates an interface between you and the hardware, here is a list of some of the things that the operating system might also include:

- The ability to load programs.

- Device drivers to run hardware peripherals such as printers.

- **Linkers**: in most programming languages you can break down a large program into different pieces of code (or modules), to make the task simpler; the linker puts these modules together so that the program can run.

- Utility software, which is programs that help make your computer work more efficiently or that add functionality. **Utilities** may include programs such as antivirus software, backup facilities, disk repair such as a defragmenter, file management, security and networking programs.

- Graphical user interface.

- A shell, which is an interface to allow you to access the services contained in an operating system.

- BIOS (basic input and output system). The BIOS translates the operating system commands into action by the hardware. Without the BIOS the operating system cannot communicate with the hardware.

- A hypervisor to let you install more than one operating system on a computer if you wish. It can divide the resources such as the CPU, RAM and so on in the physical computing environment into two or more smaller independent 'virtual machines'; each virtual machine can run its own operating system, where it appears as if the virtual machine has its own CPU and RAM.

- A bootloader, which is a little bit of code that is the first thing to run when you switch on. It then 'boots up' or starts the operating system.

General purpose software
Here are a few examples of general purpose software applications that you may use in your daily work, and how they can be used:

- Word processing applications are used to produce letters, reports and memos.

- Database programs are used to store and retrieve information.

- Spreadsheet applications are used for tasks that involve calculations or graphs and charts.

5

- Presentation applications are used to create slide shows and presentations.
- Desktop publishing (DTP) packages are used to produce posters, newsletters and magazines.
- Photo-editing software used with photographs from a digital camera or a scanned image to edit the image.
- Video editing software
- Graphics programs are used for artwork.
- Computer aided design packages are used to produce detailed designs and plans.
- Communications software such as web browsers and email programs are used to access the internet and send and receive email.
- Web page editors are used to create web pages.
- Audio production and editing programs are a common way of producing high quality music at low cost.
- Applet is a little program that can perform interactive animations or other simple tasks.
- App. (which is short for application) and is usually associated with use on a smartphone, tablet, or other mobile device.

Sometimes, general purpose programs (also known as off-the-shelf software) are combined into one integrated package so that they can be bought together. Word processing, spreadsheet and presentation programs are often bundled together in this way.

Some organisations prefer to have software specially written for them so they can have the exact software features that they need. This type of custom-made software may include applications for payroll, accounts, stock control, route planning, the travel industry or weather forecasting.

QUESTION 1.02

a When you are on the internet, you are using a specific type of software. What is its generic name?

b Make a list of the advantages of custom-made software over off-the-shelf software.

1.02 The main components of computer systems

In this section you will learn the roles that different hardware components perform in a basic computer system, in order to understand the differences between them.

Input and output devices

Input and output devices are looked at in more detail in Chapter 2, but to help you start thinking about them, try the following question.

QUESTION 1.03

a Create two columns with the labels 'Input' and 'Output'. Now enter each of the following devices into the appropriate column.

Monitor	Projector	Digital camera
Scanner	Touch screen	Gamepad
Webcam	Modem	Joystick
Touchpad	Trackerball	Keyboard
Microphone	Cameras	MIDI keyboard
Printer	Speakers	Mouse
Plotter	Bar code reade	Burglar alarm

b Now you have done that, draw a circle around two of the words that could be both input and output!

Processor

People often use the word 'processor' to refer to the **central processing unit** (CPU) of a computer. A **microprocessor** is a single integrated circuit (chip) that performs the functions of a CPU. Microprocessors are used to control devices such as washing machines, video players and burglar alarms.

EXTENSION ACTIVITY 1.01

a Try to list as many other home devices with a microprocessor as you can.

b Investigate the use of microprocessors in household devices. In what way do they help? What are the disadvantages?

Main or internal memory

A very important part of a CPU is the main memory. This is used to store all the data and instructions currently being used. The main memory is sometimes called other names, such as internal memory, primary memory or immediate access store (IAS).

The **random access memory** (RAM) is attached to the motherboard; it is where software currently in use and documents that you are currently working on are stored whilst you are using them.

Read-only memory (ROM) stores instructions for your computer to start up when you switch on. The contents of ROM can't be changed.

KEY TERMS

Random access memory: known as RAM, stores data and applications while they are being used. It only stores them while the computer is on, but when you turn the computer off, everything in the RAM is lost. This is known as being volatile.

Read-only memory: known as ROM, this has data preinstalled onto it that cannot be removed. Unlike RAM, ROM keeps its contents when the computer is turned off. It is therefore known as being non-volatile.

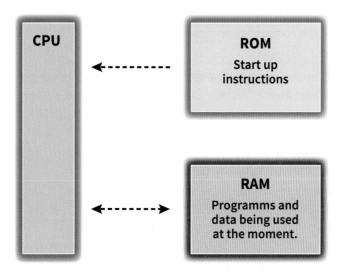

Figure 1.05 ROM and RAM

The main memory is volatile. This means that when the computer is switched off, it will forget everything. So when you next switch on nothing will happen until you have reloaded all the programs and the document you were working on. In order to reload the programs and data, the computer must be switched on and running. This means that when you switch it on, the computer must already have some software in it so that it can start up. That startup software is stored in a special type of main memory called **read only memory** (ROM; see Figure 1.05). ROM cannot be changed, even by switching off the power.

ROM would be useless for doing work or running programs, though, because we normally want to change things. If you use a word processor to type up a piece of coursework for school, then want to check your emails or play a game, it becomes necessary to change the set of instructions used by the computer. This couldn't be done

if there was only ROM, because we could not change its contents. So another sort of memory is needed.

This other form of memory is called **random access memory** (RAM). All the programs in current use are stored here, as well as all the data currently in use.

Think of RAM as a worktop or desk. Before you start work you may get out your laptop, your textbook, a notepad and a pen and put them all onto your desk. This is like starting the program you want by clicking on its icon to put it into RAM; you may then open the file you want, which means you click on its name and the drive where it is stored to also put it into RAM. As with the example of the desk, you now have everything out that you need to do your work.

Normally a computer's RAM is much bigger than its ROM because it needs to hold far more. However, the ROM is bigger in some computer systems; these include everyday microprocessor-controlled devices such as washing machines.

NOTE: Don't confuse main memory ROM with a CD ROM or DVD ROM; they are different.

QUESTION 1.04

ROM and RAM are types of memory found in computers.

a What does ROM stand for and what does it do?

b What does RAM stand for and what does it do?

c What is the main difference between ROM and RAM?

d Write an explanation of the difference between volatile and non-volatile computer memory.

Backing storage

A **storage device** is used to store programs and data when the processor is turned off. The programs and data must be put back into the processor's memory when needed for use.

Storage devices are sometimes called **backing store**, **secondary storage** or **external storage**; these all mean the same thing.

KEY TERMS

backing store: a secondary storage device for data.

External storage device: data storage that is separate from the computer, it usually plugs into a USB port on the computer.

Secondary storage device: sometimes called external memory, this is non-volatile memory (does not lose stored data when the computer is switched off); an example would be a pen drive.

1.03 Operating systems

You have read that the software programs are what 'bring the computer to life' and that the software that controls your computer is called the operating system (OS) or system software.

The OS manages all of the software and hardware of the computer system. However, there are many different types of OS. The three most common are Microsoft Windows for PCs, Apple OS X for Macintosh (Mac) computers, and Linux.

MS Windows comes preloaded on most personal computers; OS X comes preloaded on all new Mac computers; Linux is an open-source operating system which means that it can be modified and redistributed.

User interfaces

The operating system is the set of programs that do all of the things needed to make a computer work. One of its programs controls what users see on the screen. This is called the interface or (in full) the human–computer interface (HCI).

There are many different types of interface. Which one is chosen depends on:

- the jobs that the computer has to do
- the type of user and their abilities.

You will have seen that a GUI uses graphics to stand for more complicated actions that the user wants the computer to carry out (see Figure 1.06).

Figure 1.06 A graphical user interface

Typically, GUIs use icons to represent things that can be done. You can point at the icon on the screen with the cursor you control with the mouse. The screen can be divided into different areas which can have different things in them; these areas are called windows. Put the four elements (windows, icons, mouse, pointer) together and

you get WIMP. Graphical user interfaces are sometimes called WIMPs.

Pointing using a mouse and clicking on icons is simple to do and requires little IT knowledge, so a GUI is an interface that can be used by a young child or by someone who knows little about computers.

A command line interface (CLI) is also an interface for communicating with a computer (see Figure 1.04). However, this time you have to type in specific commands to tell the computer what to do. This is far more difficult to use for two main reasons:

- The user must know all the commands.
- The user must be careful not to make any typing errors, otherwise the computer will not be able to understand the commands and carry them out.

CLIs are used by people like technicians looking after computer systems. The technicians know the commands and are able in this way to access the whole of the system. However, someone using a GUI can normally only get to places on the system that they have been given icons for.

QUESTION 1.05

Many other types of user interface can be used on computer systems.

a Find out about menu-based interfaces and form-based interfaces. For a menu-based interface, find an information system at a local train station or bank. For a form-based interface, look at a typical website for booking a hotel room.

b Write down what you have found for each one, explaining why they are used in that situation.

c Discuss with members of the class what experience they may have of different user interfaces.

d What types of user interfaces are used by different people in school? Discuss why they are needed.

EXTENSION ACTIVITY 1.02

a Try to find out about some more types of interface. What, for example, is a 'natural language' interface?

b Are the type of user and the job that is to be done the only factors dictating what a computer interface will look like?

c A washing machine uses a computer processor to control the wash cycle. What does the user interface look like? Why is it not a GUI?

d What kind of user interface does a camera have?

1.04 Types of computer

There are different types of computers that perform a huge variety of roles. In this section you will learn about a variety of computers and you will compare the roles that they can perform.

In the 1990s, portable computers became popular and became known as laptops. Because they are more portable than desktops they have many advantages for mobile work but they are not as portable as tablets. Laptops have the power and flexibility of desktops, but because of the weight and size of a laptop, tablets are far more portable.

Desktop computers are generally used at fixed locations. Both desktop and laptop computers can be connected to a network. Imagine if you had one or more computers or laptops, you could create a home network so that you would only need one printer; it would also mean that you can share files with other computers on the network. You will read much more about computer networks in Chapter 4.

Tablet computers became a mass-market product in 2010. A tablet is a computer that is internet-enabled and small enough to be handheld. It has a touch screen display with the circuitry and battery together in a single unit. It can also have sensors, cameras, a microphone and a speaker. Tablets can run application software, generally known as 'apps'. Tablets are simple to use as well as being light to carry around; they provide you with access to the internet and apps very quickly after turning on.

Although all tablets can connect to the internet using WiFi, you can also get tablets that let you use 3G or 4G mobile internet connections. This type of tablet is often described as cellular. The disadvantage of this is the added cost: the initial price to buy the tablet will be greater, as well as having to pay a monthly amount for the service.

If you have WiFi at home then you can browse the internet on your tablet, as you can anywhere else that WiFi is available. For many, WiFi-only tablets are sufficient because you can download content onto your tablet that you can use if you are going to be away from a WiFi connection. If, however, you need to keep up to date with emails when you are out and about, a 3G or 4G version will be necessary. Then you can browse the internet even when you cannot find any convenient WiFi hotspots.

A smartphone is a multifunctioning mobile phone. Packed into its tiny case can be a camera, a web browser, a high-density display, a lot of storage space, a micro SD card slot and a touch screen. Like the tablet, you can download apps and access the internet quickly; you can use a smartphone for email, browsing the internet, playing music and watching movies (even though the screen is rather small). You can also use it for GPS (Global Positioning System) navigation, and speech recognition (which helps the fact that the keyboard is rather small to use quickly); it also has a camera and camcorder capabilities.

A smartphone, like a tablet, uses cut-down applications, known as apps, which are available for almost every subject area you can think of: medical and fitness monitoring, star recognition, word processing, spreadsheets and charting, playing games; the list is endless.

a

b

Figure 1.07 Portable computing: (a) a laptop (b) a tablet

Not all tablets, smartphones and laptops have the same specifications but the table below shows possible advantages and disadvantages that they may have.

Devices	Advantages	Disadvantages	Main uses
Tablets	Quick to turn on Portable Easy to use Lots of apps to choose from Ability to transfer data	Can be expensive Not all have expandable memory. Some lack cellular connectivity or have expensive contracts Amount of battery life Speed of data transfer and compatibility	Portable entertainment Web browsing Games Reading Email Video calls
Smartphones	Pocket sized Can make calls, and send texts and emails 3G/4G connectivity to access the web from most places Lots of apps available Ability to transfer data	Small screens can make reading difficult Web browsing can drain the battery quickly Typing on a small touch screen may be slow Amount of battery life Speed of data transfer and compatibility	Multifunctional device you can easily keep with you
Laptops	Excellent for work functions Full-size keyboard Very large storage capacity	Larger and heavier than a tablet or smartphone Slower to start than tablets Amount of battery life	Using applications software of all types
Personal computers	Easy to upgrade Usually have a larger screen than a laptop	Not portable Take up a lot of space	Work and home applications Watching TV and films

Table 1.01 Summary of computer types

The advantages and disadvantages of each type of computer are summarised in Table 1.01.

QUESTION 1.06

a Look at Table 1.01 and make a note of any more advantages or disadvantages you can think of for smartphones and for tablets.

b Explain the context where each of the four computer types discussed above would be used, and who would use it.

1.05 Impact of emerging technologies

Artificial intelligence

Artificial intelligence (AI) refers to computer systems that are able to perform tasks that would normally be carried out by humans or where a task is too dangerous or boring and repetitive to be done by humans. Therefore AI needs to be able to react like humans. Examples of this are voice recognition and language translation, but there are many more applications to consider.

Machines that are programmed to think and act in part as human beings are already affecting our lives in many ways. There are already robotic cleaners available for home use that can clean floors and carpets and manoeuvre themselves around furniture and other obstacles. Some of the other examples of emerging technologies described in this section also include aspects of artificial intelligence.

Driverless cars

Driverless cars are guided by GPS, WiFi and spatial laser sensors (see Figure 1.08). A car without a driver? What

Figure 1.08 A driverless car

would the advantages be? They are probably safer because there isn't a driver to make the errors that cause accidents! Sensors are used to communicate with other driverless cars, so if all cars were driverless, they could go faster safely, giving people more time to carry on with other things, meaning that the economy could benefit. Also there may be less congestion on the roads if cars could interact with each other. In 2011, Google brought out a version of a driverless car. It can be seen driving around the streets in parts of the USA.

The logistics industry, which manages the movement of goods from their source through all of the stages of travel until they reach their destination, would benefit too. Time limits are often placed on the drivers of lorries and freight trucks by their company. These limitations could be avoided as driverless transport would be able to travel 24 hours a day; the journey would not need to include rest time for the driver either, or food breaks. This could result in reduced costs. Another area to benefit from the use of driverless cars is by disabled people who cannot drive as they would gain some degree of mobility and independence.

There are some disadvantages to this innovation: some people may lose their jobs, for example people who depend upon driving to make a living; the software would have to be robust and safe from hackers; there may also be privacy concerns as self-drive cars depend on collecting and sharing location data. If something went wrong and a crash occurred there is no legal precedent yet to determine who would be responsible.

EXTENSION ACTIVITY 1.03

Discuss in your class: 'It may be worrying to trust your safety on the road to a computer, but do the benefits of a self-drive car outweigh the disadvantages?' In your discussion, consider what it would mean for people with sensory or physical disabilities.

Computer-assisted translation

Computer-assisted translation (CAT) is not the same as machine translation!

Machine translation is text translation by a computer, without any human involvement. However, human translators can use CAT software to support them during translation.

A CAT system creates and manages a translation memory (TM) which means that translators can reuse existing strings of previously translated text. The TM's database keeps collecting content as it is translated. When the TM is large, the translation process is faster.

3D and holographic imaging

Holography refers to the creation of 3D images that can change as the position of the person looking at them changes. This is, in fact what would happen if the object was actually there and not a 3D image.

A holographic imaging system for the operating room has been developed for surgery in hospitals. A 3D holographic image of body structures can 'float in the air' and a surgeon can move around it and touch it without needing any special glasses. This means that the surgeon can plan and evaluate surgical procedures.

This sort of capability could be developed for many other applications such as architecture, virtual gaming and training in work that needs carrying out to exacting standards.

Vision enhancement

There is an implant available that can be placed into the retina of a blind person. They then wear glasses that have a video camera mounted on them. Data flows from this camera either to a pocket computer where it is processed or to a visual processing unit mounted on the glasses. The resulting visual information is sent along the optic nerve to the part of the user's brain called the visual cortex, allowing partial sight to be restored.

There are disadvantages, though: for increased accuracy the implant would need more electrodes, and currently it could be a problem to fit these into the implant.

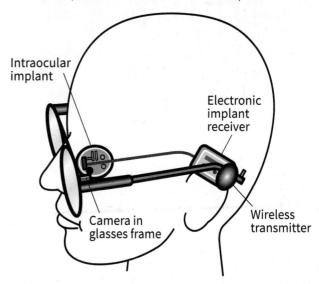

Figure 1.09 Retina implants can allow a degree of sight for blind people

11

Robotics

Robots are able to copy the movements and actions of human beings when they perform certain tasks, but to become more useful to us, robots are now being taught to think for themselves and to react to situations as a human would. Work is being carried out so that robots, using artificial intelligence, can think analytically.

Robots can be categorised into two different types: fixed and mobile. Some are fixed to a single point in the factory and the work that needs to be done is brought to them. This type of robot is usually called a robot arm because, like our arm, it is fixed at one end and yet has a large degree of movement available.

Robots are used in production lines because they:

- produce more consistent results than human workers

- are more precise than a human being

- can work continuously without a break

- do not require heat or light

- do not need to be paid, although they do cost a lot to buy in the first place

- can work in areas or with materials that would be dangerous for a human being.

Figure 1.10 A robot at work in a factory making a car

A production line is used to create an end product from raw materials or other components. Computers can be used to control the flow of materials along the whole production line.

Artificial intelligence can also use a form of robot to help to clean up the environment and reduce pollution effects from air or water. Very advanced software programs are needed to run these machines because they need to be able to distinguish the difference between biological organisms and something that could be a pollutant, such as any form of hazardous waste.

Many factories burn fuel of some sort. This means that byproducts are released such as carbon dioxide or other gases. Artificial intelligence programs can capture the different patterns that these gases make during combustion; the manufacturing process could then be modified to cut down on pollution.

Biometrics

You will read about **biometrics** in Chapter 8, where you will see that biometrics provide strong authentication that is unique based on physical traits such as fingerprints, retina scans or DNA, and behavioural traits such as voice patterns or handwriting and signatures.

> **KEY TERMS**
>
> **Biometrics:** in information communication technology, biometrics refers to technologies that analyse unique personal characteristics such as fingerprints, eye retinas and irises, voice and facial patterns, and hand measurements.

At present, biometric systems are mainly used for:

- verification: to make sure a person is who they say they are

- identification: to identify a person in a crowd

- screening: to match a person who may be on a 'watch list' for security purposes.

Quantum cryptography

Quantum cryptography uses physics to generate a key that relies on the properties of light, in particular, photons. A photon is a tiny particle of light that is too small to be seen individually. All light is made up of photons; not only visible light, but also radio waves, television broadcasts, x-rays, ultraviolet and so on. The difference between all of these applications is the wavelength of the radiation involved.

Photons have no mass and travel at the speed of light. They have another property known as polarisation which, though difficult to imagine, through quantum mechanics enables a secret key to be sent from the sender to the receiver. This key can then be used to decrypt an encoded message sent over a public channel such as the internet.

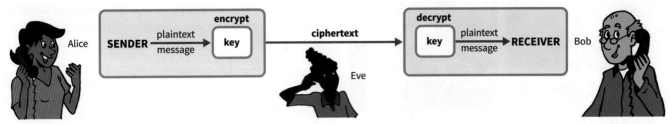

Figure 1.11 Eavesdropping

The particular quantum properties of photons mean that if an eavesdropper looks at the secret key, a change occurs to the particles of light being observed. The receiver would then know that something had changed and that their communications might be compromised.

So the main advantage of quantum cryptography over conventional cryptography (Chapter 8) is the completely secure transmission of the secret key, with eavesdropping detection.

Devices already exist for quantum key distribution (QKD) but work is being carried out to make the process more usable.

3D printers

Printers are now able to actually make many different objects in three dimensions, using different materials such as metal, plastic, resin, ceramic, fabrics and more. This means that they can replace other machines such as those in a factory production line, and one 3D printer could replace more than one machine.

They work by printing over and over again many thousands of times, building up layers on top of each other, eventually creating a 3D model.

You could design a 3D object on your own computer, connect it to a 3D printer and wait for it to be printed (or built). You could print a bicycle for yourself because these printers are capable of making moving parts. First you would have to design every part of your bicycle, including the wheels, the handlebars and so on, and then you could print them all out!

The printer manages this by turning a whole object into many thousands of microscopically thin slices, then it makes it slice by slice, sticking the tiny layers together until it forms the object.

Figure 1.12 3D printer

Figure 1.13 Items created by 3D printers

Drones

A **drone** is an aerial vehicle that crosses the boundaries between robotics, aeronautics and electronics. It is controlled by remote control systems from the ground; you can even control them from a smartphone or tablet.

Figure 1.14 (a) Drone (b) Control box

A typical drone would be made of light composite materials so that it is manoeuvrable and lightweight so that it can fly at high altitudes. Drones can be equipped with infrared cameras and GPS.

Drones are used by the military, and also for search and rescue, weather analysis, deliveries, spotting poachers and much more.

Virtual reality

Virtual reality (VR) is a computer-generated environment, sometimes called a virtual world, where a person can immerse themselves and interact to perform a wide variety of actions. It is often associated with gaming but it can also have other, more serious purposes; there are many ways in which VR affects our everyday lives.

To take part in a controlled VR environment, you would wear goggles to give you a slightly different view in each of your eyes; this would give the scene a 3D effect that makes images of objects seem solid. You may also wear gloves that are able to detect finger movements, as well as headphones to control what you hear.

Some examples of VR in everyday life are:

- You can take a virtual walkthrough of a museum, a virtual model of a new house being designed or the inside of a new car.

- Car manufacturers can use VR to create prototypes of a new vehicle so that it can be tested and altered before being developed.

- Astronauts, pilots or medical students, for example, can use VR for training before going into difficult situations. Surgeons can also carry out surgery remotely in a VR environment by using robotic devices.

EXTENSION ACTIVITY 1.04

Carry out some research to find two other uses of virtual reality.

Summary

- The physical parts of a computer system make up its hardware.

- The instructions are given to a computer system by its software.

- Software is necessary for computer hardware to do anything.

- A computer consists, generally, of devices for input, processing, output and storage.

- As well as the main processor (CPU), a computer contains two types of memory: RAM and ROM. RAM stores data and software while processing is occurring, but not when the computer is switched off; ROM stores essential software needed when the computer is first switched on, and retains this data when the computer is switched off.

- Backing storage is different from memory.

- Storage devices store software and data when the computer is switched off.

- There are different types of operating system user interfaces, two examples being a command line interface (CLI) and a graphical user interface (GUI).

Exam-style Questions

1.01 Which of these are true and which are false? [4]

	True	False
Hardware consists of computer programs		
A linker is an example of applications software		
A graphical user interface is part of an operating system		
A device driver is part of the hardware of a computer system		

1.02 Circle **two** items that are used as an output device: [2]

Scanner   Touchpad

Temperature sensor   All-in-one printer

Slideshow presentation   Joystick

Multimedia projector

1.03 Define an operating system (OS): [1]

....

....

1.04 Describe **three** features of a graphical user interface (GUI). [3]

....

....

....

1.05 Describe a command line interface. [1]

....

....

1.06 You are going out for the day but need to be able to carry on working. You need to decide whether to take your smartphone or your tablet with you. Discuss the advantages and disadvantages of each. [6]

....

....

....

....

....

....

1.07 List the capabilities available to a networked computer that a standalone doesn't have. [3]

....

....

....

1.08 There have been many advances in computer memory in recent years. Describe the changes that these advances have made to tablet computers. [4]

....

....

....

....

....

....

....

....

....

15

40181 700982

Chapter 2:
Input and output devices

Learning objectives

When you have finished this section, you will be able to:

- identify input devices and their uses, including types of keyboards, pointing devices, digital cameras and sensors
- describe direct data entry and its associated devices and identify their advantages and disadvantages
- identify output devices and their uses, including types of display screens, printers, speakers, motors, heaters, buzzers and lights
- describe the advantages and disadvantages of output devices.

Overview

In Chapter 1, you saw how the hardware of most computers can be divided into several types of device (see Figure 2.01).

Input devices are used to put data into the computer; a processor does something with the data given by the input device; output devices are used to tell someone or something the results that the processor came up with and backing storage keeps all the data and the software that is used.

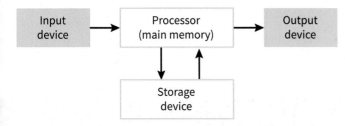

Figure 2.01 The main components of a computer system

Because any computer system has a method of putting data in and for getting information out, you need to be able to identify and to describe the devices associated with input and output.

We will look first at input devices, then at output devices. You will also see how input and output devices can be integrated in a system.

2.01 Input devices and their uses

There are two different categories of **input device**. They are:

- **Manual input devices** which are the devices used by people to enter data into a computer themselves;

- **Direct data entry (DDE) devices** such as optical mark readers or a bar code reader, which enable data to be entered directly, without a human having to input it manually.

KEY TERMS

Input device: transfers data into a computer so that it can be processed.

Different types of manual input devices

- Keyboards, including numeric keypad and musical keyboards

- Pointing devices, such as a mouse, a touchpad or a trackerball

- Joystick or driving wheel

- Touchscreen

- Scanners

- Sensors

- Remote control

- Digital cameras, including webcam, video camera

- Microphone

- Graphics tablet

Keyboards and keypads

Keyboards

Keyboards are input devices used to enter fixed values, often characters, into the computer system. There are many different types of keyboard. This section looks at qwerty keyboards, concept keyboards and numeric keypads.

17

Figure 2.02 Qwerty keyboard

A qwerty keyboard is still the most common type, and is used to type letters, numbers and punctuation into a computer. It gets its name from the arrangement of letters on the top line of keys: Q W E R T Y (see Figure 2.02).

Keyboards are used for everything from writing an email to writing a book.

EXTENSION ACTIVITY 2.01

a   Investigate different layouts of keys on keyboards. For example, look at the Dvorak keyboard and keyboards designed for use with languages other than English.

b   Find out about keyboards that are qwerty keyboards but are not the normal rectangular design. These are sometimes called ergonomic keyboards.

Concept keyboards, unlike qwerty keyboards, allow the user to decide what each of the keys should stand for and they can be changed as necessary.

A concept keyboard looks like a flat sheet with pressure pads all over it. If a sheet of paper, sometimes called an overlay, is placed on top showing different symbols then the computer can be programmed to show that particular symbol when the key is pressed. If the program is changed then the same pad can stand for different symbols.

Concept keyboards can be used when the normal symbols are inappropriate or when the person who is to use it would find difficulty in using an ordinary keyboard.

The number of different symbols can be very restricted, and this can also be a disadvantage because it makes it difficult to produce any input outside a very limited group.

You may have seen an overlay sheet for a concept keyboard in a fast food restaurant. The sheet is laid on a fixed grid of pressure pads. Each pressure pad is linked to a computer and programmed with whatever data the user wants; in this case a food or drink item (and its price) from a set menu.

QUESTION 2.01

Find out about the use of concept keyboards in your school. Alternatively, find a retail outlet (fast food outlets are good places to start) where a concept keyboard is used at the counter.

a Why is this a good type of input device to use?

b If there is a concept keyboard in a café or restaurant, what outputs do you think would be generated by the inputs?

Numeric keypads

Most qwerty keyboards have a section on the right with a group of keys representing the digits from 0 to 9 arranged in a rectangle. This is a **numeric keypad**. Numeric keypads on their own are used by shoppers to input their PIN numbers when they pay for something by card. Numeric keypads are small, easy to use and language independent.

Pointing devices

Mice

A **mouse**, as you probably know, is a device that allows you to move the pointer on the screen and to make choices by clicking the mouse buttons. A typical mouse has a small ball underneath. As the mouse is pushed around on a desk, the ball rolls against the flat surface. The movement of the ball is detected and sent to the computer, which works out how the mouse has been moved and then moves the pointer to match.

The advantages of using mice as pointing devices are:

- they provide a fast method of input

- they are intuitive to use because they simply involve pointing at things.

The disadvantages are:

- mice can be easily damaged or vandalised

- some people, particularly if they have physical disabilities, find mice difficult to use

- overuse of a mouse can lead to repetitive strain injury (see Chapter 5)

- mice need a flat surface to be moved around on.

QUESTION 2.02

There are other types of mouse apart from the mechanical one described here.

a Find out about optical mice. Explain how an optical mouse works. Then explain the advantages that an optical mouse has over a mechanical mouse.

b Some mice do not need a wire to connect them to the computer. Explain how they work and what advantages they have.

c If you need to select an icon or menu item shown on screen using a mouse, the mouse needs to do more than just sense how it's being moved around. List the other features needed to let you select particular things using a mouse.

Touchpads

A mouse is sometimes not a suitable way to control the pointer. A laptop computer is designed for use in places other than on a fixed surface. This means that there is often no surface for the mouse. A laptop is designed to have all the necessary peripherals in one case and a mouse would have to be carried separately.

Laptops come with a variation on a mouse for a pointing device. It is called a **touchpad** and is a flat area next to the keyboard (see Figure 2.03).

Figure 2.03 A laptop computer with a touchpad

Most touchpads have the ability to let you use the corners of the pad for particular functions, such as a right-click.

QUESTION 2.03

Find out about other gestures that you can use on a pad such as a swipe, and describe how to do them.

Trackerballs

These are a little like upside-down mechanical mice. They have buttons like those on a mouse.

The ball is rolled around directly by the user rather than being moved by the whole mouse being pushed. Trackerballs have the following advantages over a mouse:

- A trackerball is stationary and does not need a surface to be moved around on.

- It can be built into a machine like an information system and is not as likely to get damaged as a mouse. It can also be used by disabled people who may not have the freedom of movement necessary to use other pointing devices.

A disadvantage is that trackerballs can be difficult to use for some applications needing fine control.

Joysticks

A **joystick** can carry out the same tasks as a mouse as well as other functions such as controlling the movement of a motorised wheelchair (see Figure 2.04).

Figure 2.04 Wheelchair operated by a joystick

As a pointing device, a joystick might move a character in a game or a spaceship or a car or any other shape, as a pointer. The joystick might have buttons with specific uses such as picking up an object in the game. Individual actions depend on how the joystick's software has been programmed.

Joysticks are used in many practical applications, not just as a pointing device in a computer system.

Because of their advantages, joysticks are used in applications like the following:

- to play many games because they give the user the impression of being in control, and there is a direct and immediate result of the player's actions which adds to the enjoyment of the game

- to control aircraft because of their simplicity in a very complex environment

- to control motorised wheelchairs because they allow the user to give many different commands with very little physical movement.

The disadvantage of using a joystick as a pointing device is that it is more difficult to control the fine movement of the pointer on the screen than with a mouse.

Touch screens

A **touch screen** can be found on personal computers, laptops, tablets and smartphones. It is a display screen that is both an input and an output device.

A touch screen can determine where on the screen the user has touched and sends that information to the processor.

There are two main types of touch screen:

- **resistive**, which means it is sensitive to pressure from your finger

- **capacitive**, which means that the screen is sensitive to your body's electric field.

Traditionally, most touch screens were built using resistive technology but now the industry has moved towards capacitive technology.

Resistive touch screens work by detecting a small amount of force applied to the screen. They are made with two surfaces that are separated by a resistive material. Because the top surface is slightly flexible, when you touch it the two sheets will be pressed together, thus changing the resistance between the two surfaces.

The advantage of a resistive touch screen over a capacitive one is that they are relatively inexpensive to produce and you can use it with your finger, a stylus or anything you can point with.

Capacitive touch screens work differently as they are sensitive to your body's electric field. They simply 'sense' the presence of your finger electrically so you don't need to push down on the touch screen.

The advantage is that they tend to be much more responsive, allowing you to glide a finger along the screen, and to use different multi-finger gestures, which isn't possible with a resistive touch screen.

Disadvantages are that you cannot use them with a traditional mechanical stylus and they can be expensive.

20

QUESTION 2.04

If you have a touch screen device that uses capacitive technology, such as a smartphone, and a pair of gloves, put the gloves on and try to use the device. What happens and why?

An advantage for touch screens as a whole is that they are very easy for people to use. That's why touch screen technology is used a lot for applications such as ticket machines at railway stations and self-service checkouts at a supermarket.

QUESTION 2.05

a Investigate different finger gestures that can be used with touch screens and what they do.

b A touch screen may be used when you arrive for an appointment at a university or a doctor's surgery (see Figure 2.05). Describe how this might work and what its advantages and disadvantages might be.

Figure 2.05 A touch screen computer in a reception

Touch screens are common in information systems in places like train stations where they are often used to buy train tickets because:

- they are difficult to vandalise compared with something like a mouse

- they are largely weatherproof so can be in the open air, such as on a station platform

- they need no computer knowledge at all to be able to operate them

- fewer staff are needed if customers can serve themselves.

A disadvantage is that disabled people can find them difficult to use.

Many touch screens are basically on/off switches in that they rely on a particular area of the screen being touched; the input is simply whether or not that area has been touched. In this way the ticket machine inputs the type of ticket simply by interpreting the area of the screen that has been pressed.

QUESTION 2.06

a   List the advantages and disadvantages of using touch screens as input devices.

b   Touch screens are often used as the input device attached to information systems like those at train stations, but they are used in many other situations, particularly where there are only a limited number of options to choose from. Can you think of other examples?

c   Most touch screen applications have two areas of the screen always reserved for two important commands. Try to discover what they are and decide why they are important.

Graphics tablets

A **graphics tablet** is like a very large touchpad that accepts input from its associated pen or stylus. It uses motion detection technology to capture writing digitally. To do this, it senses the progress of the pen moving over its surface and sends this information to the computer. A graphics tablet can be used to 'draw' diagrams and illustrations.

Usually, a graphics tablet's active surface is treated as though it was the computer's screen; touching the top left of the tablet will move the pointer to the top left of the screen, for example, and touching the bottom right will move the pointer straight to the bottom right. Unlike a mouse or touchpad, there is no need to move the pointer across the screen: it moves straight to where the user touches the tablet.

Graphics tablets are used for copying drawings on paper by allowing the user to trace over the top of the drawing. They are also used for creating original drawings and even writing, particularly for languages such as Chinese and Japanese. The ease of drawing and writing like this is the main advantage of using a graphics tablet.

A disadvantage of using a graphics tablet is that it can sometimes be difficult to relate the position and movement of the stylus on the tablet with the position and movement of the pointer on the screen.

Sensors

A **sensor** is a device that collects data. A keyboard does nothing until someone presses a key, but a sensor is collecting data all the time on its own.

There are a lot of different types of sensor, but most have something in common. They measure some physical property that can have any value (within limits); it could be temperature, pressure or another measurable physical property.

Although there are many different types of sensor, you will study three types in this section: temperature, pressure and light.

For all of these sensors, it is important to realise that the sensor does not make a decision.

KEY TERMS

Sensors: collect data automatically by measuring some property of their environment.

The advantages of using sensors as devices to collect data are:

- They are more reliable than a human being because a human may forget to take readings.

- A human may take inaccurate readings.

- It is not possible for a human to go to some places where readings need to be taken, like the inside of a reaction vessel, where chemical reactions take place.

A disadvantage of using sensors is that they need a power source. If there is a power cut or their battery dies, they will stop working.

Temperature sensors read the temperature of their surroundings and send the readings to the processor. The processor may then do something according to the input.

For example, think about how an automatic washing machine works (see Figure 2.06). When a washing machine is turned on to do the wash, the tub will fill with water. The processor in control of the wash cycle will need to ensure that the water is hot enough to do the wash. If it is not hot enough, the processor will turn on the heating element until the temperature sensor reports that the water is hot enough. If the water is too hot then the processor may let in some cold water to cool the water down until the temperature sensor reports that the water is cool enough.

Note that this device is called a 'temperature sensor'. It is not called a 'heat sensor', because heat is not a measurement. It is not called a 'thermometer' because that is something designed for human beings to look at.

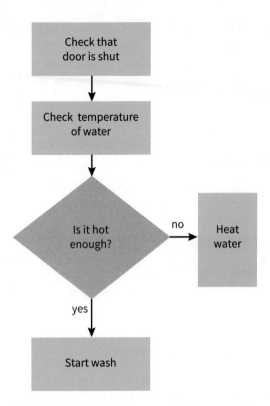

Figure 2.06 Using a temperature sensor in a washing machine

Temperature sensors are also used in many other applications, including:

- regulating the temperature of a room in a centrally heated or air-conditioned house

- controlling temperatures in greenhouses

- controlling the heat in reaction vessels in a scientific experiment.

Figure 2.07 Temperature sensors are used in systems that control the temperature in a commercial greenhouse

22

QUESTION 2.07

Explain the role of a temperature sensor in controlling the temperature in a greenhouse.

Pressure sensors measure pressures and send the results to the processor, where the decision is taken as to what to do.

A pressure pad could be used under the carpet in a house as part of a burglar alarm system. If something presses on the pad and that makes a contact which sets the alarm off then it is not a sensor. It is just a switch.

However, if measurements of the pressure are sent to a processor then a decision can be made. The processor can decide whether it is enough pressure to indicate a human being or whether it is the cat and so the alarm should not go off. If the processor can make a decision like this then the device that reads the pressure is a sensor.

Light sensors measure the amount of light falling on them.

This could be used for something simple like a sensor in a car to decide whether or not to turn the dashboard lights on because it is getting dark. Or in a burglar alarm system, if a beam of light is shone onto a light sensor then someone walking through the beam will reduce the light hitting the sensor. This information sent to a processor would indicate to it that there was something moving in the room.

QUESTION 2.08

Some school geography departments record the weather in their area using an automatic weather station. How could the three types of sensor mentioned in this section be used to record the weather? Find out if your own school has a weather station like this.

Inputting images: scanners and cameras

Scanners

A **scanner** is a device that shines light at a drawing or a photograph and can interpret the reflected light so that the image can be stored in a computer system. Most scanners have a flat sheet of glass on which the **hard copy** (a photo or printed piece of paper) is placed.

The advantage of scanning documents is that hard-copy material can be changed into a form that can be edited or stored on the computer system.

Scanners are often used for three different types of input:

- images from hard-copy material
- optical character recognition (**OCR**) from hard-copy text
- optical mark reading (**OMR**) from specially prepared hard-copy forms.

While scanners make it possible to put images of hard-copy photographs and printed illustrations into a computer, there may be a reduction in the quality of the image, and scanned diagrams can sometimes appear distorted.

KEY TERMS

OMR: Optical Mark Recognition enables data marked by a human, such as surveys and tests, to be captured during a scanning process.

OCR: Optical Character Recognition scans a typewritten document and translates the images into an electronic format that the computer can understand.

QUESTION 2.09

a Give an example of when OCR would be used.

b Give an example of when OMR would be used.

Digital cameras

Digital cameras take pictures using a series of sensors that are arranged in a grid; when all of the individual pin-pricks of colour are put together they make a picture. These little areas of colour are called **pixels** ('**pic**ture **el**ements'). The more pixels that are used, the better the quality of the picture.

The camera records the pictures either in flash memory or on a removable media card (see Chapter 3 for what this means). This card can be used to upload the picture into the computer; alternatively, most cameras can be connected to the computer using a USB cable, or via WiFi, to upload the images directly.

The advantages of digital cameras over traditional film cameras are:

- the picture can be seen immediately and erased if it is not good enough
- digital images can be manipulated more readily than those on film
- the image can be used in other electronic documents.

EXTENSION ACTIVITY 2.02

Investigate the number and colour of printer inks found in different types of printer. Why will there be more colours in a photo printer than in an ordinary printer? What will the colours be?

Video cameras and webcams

Video cameras are used to make electronic motion pictures.

A video camera can be linked to a computer in order to feed the video directly into the computer. Once stored in the computer, the video can be edited directly and incorporated into websites or stored on a portable storage medium.

Video cameras are used for leisure and also for security purposes. Video footage can also be taken using digital cameras and mobile phones.

Webcams are a special category of video camera that have no storage capacity but are connected directly to a computer. Laptops may have a webcam built in to the lid, just above the screen. Another type of webcam can be plugged into a desktop computer and used that way.

Webcams are often used to provide live video pictures when chatting with friends and family members using applications such as Skype.

They can also be used to provide pictures to accompany a meeting held by people who are talking to each other over the internet. Such a meeting is called a **video conference**.

The live images provided by a webcam can be added to a website. For example, some webcams show street scenes; others might show wildlife habitats.

Webcams are dedicated devices so they can be left on permanently if necessary. This means that they can be used for remotely watching a property for security reasons or remotely monitoring elderly people while allowing them to maintain their freedom. A disadvantage is that they need to be connected to a computer because they have no storage.

Inputting sound and music

Microphones

Microphones can be used to allow a computer to convert sounds into data that it can handle. This can be used in a number of different applications, for example in adding speech to a presentation that has been produced using a piece of presentation software. Microphones also allow people's speech to be translated into text that can then be used by a word processor.

Microphones can be used by disabled people; they use them to input data when using a more common input device is not possible for them.

A disadvantage is that the software used to translate the spoken word into text to be used in a word processor can be unreliable and has to be trained.

MIDI keyboards

A music or **MIDI keyboard** can act as an input device (Figure 2.08).

Figure 2.08 Midi keyboard and interface

It needs to be connected to the computer system using a MIDI interface, a special type of interface that translates the signal coming from the keyboard into electronic data that the computer can handle. For example, when a key is pressed on the keyboard, the MIDI turns that input into the pitch, duration and so on of the note, which can be used to reproduce the note electronically.

The disadvantage of this form of input is that the user needs to have musical ability! However, storing MIDI data this way takes less space than storing sound samples. This technology is widely used for digitally recording and editing music. It also lets one musician play many instruments on the same recording.

Remote controls

A **remote control** is a small, handheld device that can be used to operate equipment such as a TV or stereo. It has a number of buttons. When a button is pressed, the remote control sends an infrared signal to the equipment. Each signal contains a code; there are enough different codes to allow all the buttons to have their own code so that the equipment knows what to do. Remote controls are used to control home entertainment systems, satellite boxes, lighting and shutters, for example.

Their main advantage is convenience; for example, you do not need to stand up to change TV channel. A disadvantage is that the signal can interfere with other equipment and can be blocked by objects between the remote control and the equipment it controls.

QUESTION 2.10

a Why do you have to point the remote control directly at the TV in order to change channels?

b Investigate other types of remote control, then explain how one of them works.

2.02 Direct data entry and associated devices

Most of the input devices discussed so far in this chapter have required a person to enter the data using **manual input devices**, but there are other methods that allow data to be entered directly, without human intervention. These are **direct data entry** methods, used when large amounts of similar data need to be entered, often in commercial or business applications.

OCR and OMR

If you have a hard copy of a text document you can scan it into your computer where you can use special software to turn it into text that can be used by a word processor. This is known as optical character recognition (**OCR**) because it attempts to recognise each character in the text.

OCR software compares the shape of each character with the shapes that it knows and, when it is matched, the computer stores the fact that it is a letter 'R', for example. This can make the input of data from hard-copy documents much quicker than retyping them. OCR software can also be used to read data from passports or identity cards directly into a computer.

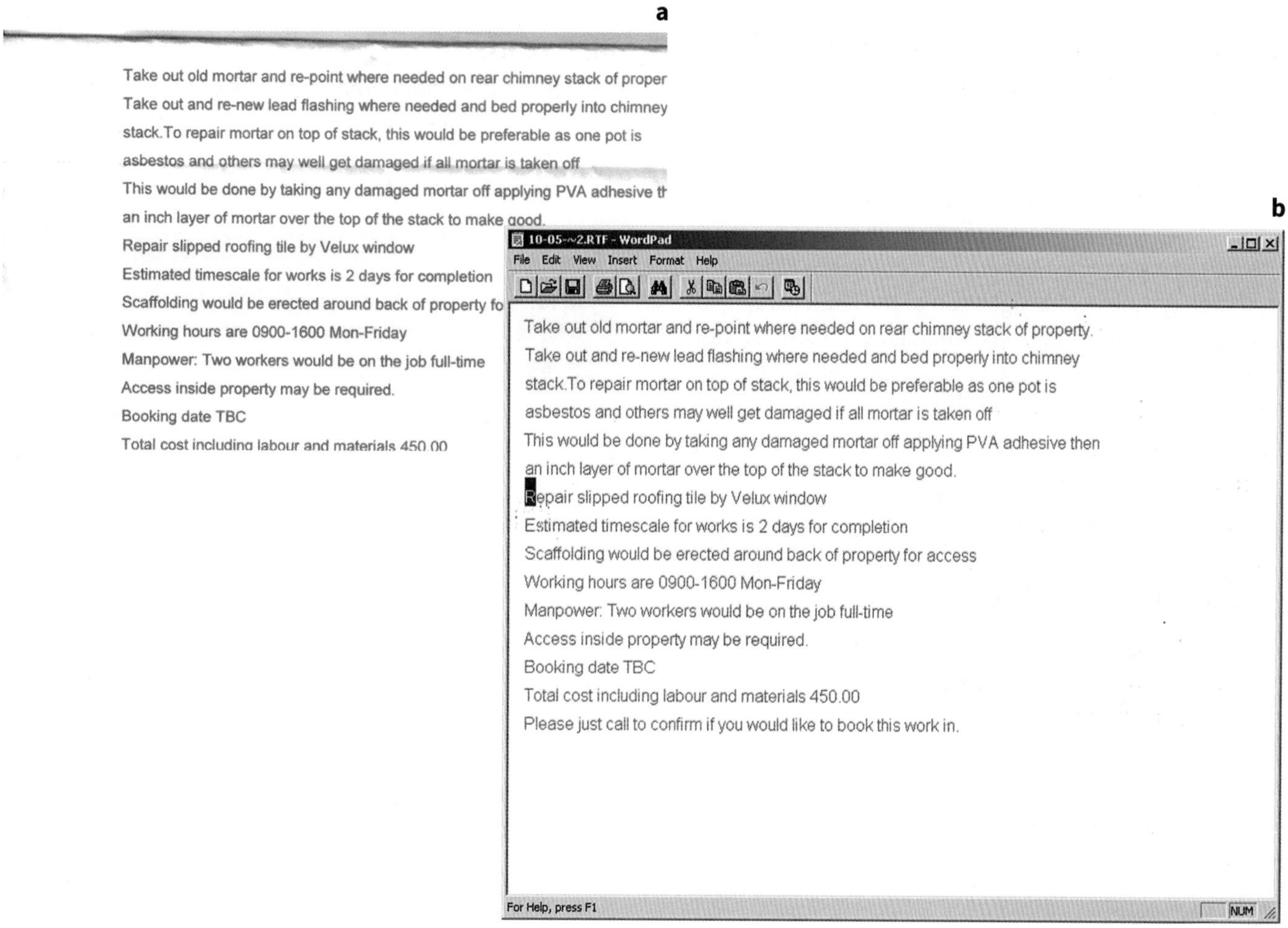

a

Take out old mortar and re-point where needed on rear chimney stack of proper

Take out and re-new lead flashing where needed and bed properly into chimney

stack.To repair mortar on top of stack, this would be preferable as one pot is

asbestos and others may well get damaged if all mortar is taken off

This would be done by taking any damaged mortar off applying PVA adhesive th

an inch layer of mortar over the top of the stack to make good.

Repair slipped roofing tile by Velux window

Estimated timescale for works is 2 days for completion

Scaffolding would be erected around back of property fo

Working hours are 0900-1600 Mon-Friday

Manpower: Two workers would be on the job full-time

Access inside property may be required.

Booking date TBC

Total cost including labour and materials 450.00

b

10-05-~2.RTF - WordPad _ | □ | ×

File   Edit   View   Insert   Format   Help

Take out old mortar and re-point where needed on rear chimney stack of property.

Take out and re-new lead flashing where needed and bed properly into chimney

stack.To repair mortar on top of stack, this would be preferable as one pot is

asbestos and others may well get damaged if all mortar is taken off

This would be done by taking any damaged mortar off applying PVA adhesive then

an inch layer of mortar over the top of the stack to make good.

Repair slipped roofing tile by Velux window

Estimated timescale for works is 2 days for completion

Scaffolding would be erected around back of property for access

Working hours are 0900-1600 Mon-Friday

Manpower: Two workers would be on the job full-time

Access inside property may be required.

Booking date TBC

Total cost including labour and materials 450.00

Please just call to confirm if you would like to book this work in.

For Help, press F1   NUM

Figure 2.09 Example of a document suitable for OMR

A disadvantage is that the text produced is not always reliable, particularly if the hard-copy original is unclear or has smudged text.

A scanner can also be used to scan a sheet of paper looking for marks on the paper, such as answers to multiple-choice exam questions or even votes in an election. This is known as optical mark recognition or optical mark reading (**OMR**). OMR scanning aims to find the marks on the paper; it is not interested in their shape, only *where* they are (see Figure 2.09).

The advantage of this method of input is that it is extremely fast because there is only a small amount of data on a sheet and it is far more accurate than other methods for this type of data. The disadvantages are that the sheets will not be read accurately unless they are properly lined up, and that dirty marks on the paper might be misinterpreted by the system as marks to be input. Many school registers use this sort of data capture.

MICR

MICR stands for **magnetic ink character recognition** or **reader**. This technology is used by banks to add data to the bottom of bank cheques so that it can be read into a computer quickly and accurately.

Figure 2.10 Magnetic ink characters on the bottom of a cheque

An example can be seen in Figure 2.10, where the automatically read numbers include the bank number, account number and cheque number.

The ink used to print the characters has magnetic characteristics that can absorb and emit a magnetic signal. When the cheque passes through a special scanner, the part of it with the magnetic ink goes over a magnet to charge the ink before it goes on to the MICR read head. The read head reads the magnetic signal emitted by the magnetic ink on the cheque because each character produces a unique waveform. But have you noticed that the numbers can be read by humans as well?

QUESTION 2.11

Explain the differences between OCR, OMR and MICR and give one possible use for each.

Bar code readers

A **bar code** is a set of short parallel lines in contrasting colours, often black and white. The dark lines are thick, medium or thin. If they are taken in pairs of dark and pairs of light lines they can stand for the digits 0 to 9. These can then be read as a code number.

Supermarkets, other retail outlets and services such as libraries read bar codes to enter the details of a product.

Bar codes are read by devices that shine a laser at them and then read the reflection to tell how thick the lines are. Using a bar code for data entry is much faster than using a keyboard. It is also more accurate because a human can make mistakes.

The information contained in a bar code on a typical supermarket product is:

- country of origin number
- manufacturer number
- item number
- check digit.

The price of the item is NOT in the bar code.

EXTENSION ACTIVITY 2.03

a Find out what a check digit is.

b Write out an example of how a check digit works.

RFID readers

RFID stands for Radio-Frequency Identification, and an RFID reader will typically consist of a small chip and an antenna.

 KEY TERMS

RFID: radio frequency identification. An RFID reader will take data from an RFID tag attached to an item when it is within range.

An RFID device has similar uses to a bar code or the magnetic stripe on the back of a credit card in that once it is scanned it provides a unique identifier for the object it is attached to.

Almost anything can have an RFID tag, for instance merchandise in supermarkets or stores, shipping containers, train carriages, expensive musical instruments and so on.

RFID has three elements: a scanning antenna, a decoder to interpret the data and the RFID tag itself which will have been programmed with information.

An advantage of RFID is that the chips do not need to be positioned precisely on the scanner like a barcode does because RFID devices work within a few metres of the scanner. For instance, if you went to a supermarket where all of the goods had an RFID chip, you could put all of your groceries in a bag, and then put the bag onto the scanner and total your purchases straight away.

Sometimes the chips can clash: a reader collision is when a signal from more than one reader reads the chip or tag; a tag collision is when lots of tags are together in a very small space.

Magnetic stripe readers

On credit cards, bank cards, library cards and hotel room card keys you may see a black **magnetic stripe** (Figure 2.11). This cannot store much information, but many tasks do not require very much.

Imagine a hotel room key card. When the guest checks in, the receptionist writes information onto the stripe using a machine. The information includes a unique code for the room so that when the user puts the card into the reader on the hotel room door, the code is read and the door is unlocked.

An advantage of this compared to using an ordinary key is that if the card is lost there is no way of identifying which room it is coded to open because all the cards look the same.

A disadvantage is that the information can easily be read or altered by using a small device that can be bought over the internet!

Figure 2.11 A credit card, showing the chip (on the front), and the magnetic stripe (on the back)

QUESTION 2.12

Some colleges issue cards to their students to gain access to the different areas of the college.

a What information might the college be able to learn from the use of these cards?

b Find out what is recorded in the three sections of the magnetic stripe on the back of a credit or debit card.

Chip and PIN readers

Credit and debit cards have always had a magnetic stripe on the back in order to store information that needs to be kept secret in order to maintain the integrity of the card and the account. However, to make credit and debit

cards more secure, they now include a small circuit with a number of computer devices all stored on a thin sliver of silicon, i.e. a **chip**. The chip can be seen on the surface of the card.

When making a payment using a chip and PIN card, the user puts the card into an input device called a **chip and PIN reader**, which reads the information stored in the chip (Figure 2.11). The most important piece of information in the chip is the **PIN** (personal identification number), which is a digit code that the user must know to be able to use the card. The user types the PIN on the numeric keypad attached to the reader. That PIN is checked against the PIN stored on the card's chip, and if the two match then the payment goes through.

An advantage of this technology is that the information held is secure because the chip is difficult to read. A disadvantage is that people tend to be careless when using their PIN.

Smart cards and contactless payment

Contactless card payments involve using a debit or credit card to make payments without having the need to put the card into a reader or to enter a PIN. Their use is usually limited to small purchases (Figure 2.12).

Figure 2.12 A contactless payment card

A smart card is a card that can be preloaded with money. It is like a sandwich with a filling containing an embedded microprocessor. The microprocessor replaces the magnetic stripe that you see on a credit or debit card.

A smart card is used for convenience and speed. For instance, if you used it to pay at the till in a school café, it would speed up the process because all you have to do is to swipe the card over the reader to pay and go (which is useful when there is a queue of people behind you!).

Device	Advantages	Disadvantages
OMR	Fast and accurate	Forms have to be accurately designed and accurately filled in. The OMR reader can only read shaded areas.
OCR	Fast and accurate as it avoids typing errors and is less expensive on labour.	Possible difficulty when reading handwriting. Has to be checked for errors.
MICR	Fast processing and greater security because the special ink characters cannot be changed.	The amount of characters that can be read is limited. The device and the ink are expensive.
Barcode reader	Saves time when product prices change as only the price data in the database will need updating once for each product. Quick and easy to get data into the system. Updates stock-control automatically so saves time. Very accurate.	The technology is expensive. Barcodes must be undamaged.
Chip and pin reader	Secure. Hard to clone. Chips hold more data than magnetic stripes. Portability.	Security: you may forget your PIN or people may see what your PIN is as you enter it.
Magnetic stripe reader	Very fast data entry. No data entry errors as nothing to type in. Robust. Cannot be read by human.	The magnetic stripe can only hold a small amount of data. Cards need to be in physical contact with the reader to work. Data will be lost if the stripe becomes damaged. Easy to duplicate.

Table 2.01 Advantages and disadvantages of direct data entry

2.03 Output devices and their uses

Output devices comprise items such as monitors, printers and control devices.

Display screens (monitors)

A **monitor** is a device that displays information from the computer on a screen.

The main types are:

- CRT (cathode ray tube)
- TFT/LCD (thin film transistor)
- IPS/LCD (in-plane switching)
- LCD (liquid crystal display)
- touch screen.

CRT monitors

These are generally the cheapest form of monitor. They are also the oldest type and are extremely bulky, which is why they have been superseded almost entirely by TFT monitors. They work by firing a beam of electrons at a fluorescent screen.

These screens have a similar size display area, but the TFT monitor is far thinner and lighter than the CRT monitor. One advantage of CRT monitors is that you do not have to be directly in front of the screen to be able to see what is on it.

TFT monitors

These use a different technology to CRT monitors. TFT monitors don't use a beam of electrons. Instead, they have a white light behind the screen that is blocked by tiny coloured windows. When the window is opened, light shines out. By opening and closing these tiny windows many times each second, the monitor makes a sharp, coloured, moving image. This technology means that the units can be very thin.

Because they are so much smaller and lighter than CRT monitors, TFT monitors can be easily and safely wall mounted. If they need to be placed on a desk, they take up very little space. TFT monitors are used in laptop computers and mobile phones; they produce far less glare on the screen which makes them more restful on the eye. TFT is not significantly different from LCD but a modern version of LCD giving it a much improved image quality.

IPS/LCD monitors

> It is helpful to note that LCD is the type of technology and IPS is the type of panel being used in the LCD screen. Also that LED is the type of lighting used. It is possible therefore to have an LCD screen with an IPS panel and LED backlighting.

IPS displays have good viewing angles and colour reproduction, and they also have good contrast and black levels.

A disadvantage could be that their response times (the time it takes for them to form an image on the screen) may be slower than other types of display.

Multimedia projectors

These are devices that can project an image from a computer onto as large a surface as is necessary (Figure 2.13). The only limit to the size of the projection is the power or brightness of the light produced by the projector. In all other respects the device is the same as an ordinary monitor screen.

Figure 2.13 Multimedia projector

The device can be totally portable or fixed, but a disadvantage is that it relies on a powerful and expensive bulb to provide the pictures. These bulbs are fragile, particularly if the projector is moved while it is still hot.

EXTENSION ACTIVITY 2.04

Some classrooms in your school may have interactive whiteboards. Find out how they work and make a list of the input devices that work with them.

Printers and plotters

Printers and plotters are output devices that produce characters and/or graphics on paper and on other materials.

As you probably know, there are different types of printer (see Figure 2.14).

Laser printers

Laser printers work by using a laser to 'draw' the required outputs onto a drum. This puts a positive electric charge on those parts of the drum which have been hit by the laser. An ink powder (called toner) is then sprayed on to the drum and it sticks where there is an electric charge. This drum is then pressed against a piece of paper and the ink is transferred to the paper. The paper is then heated by a 'fuser' so that the toner binds to the paper, producing a printed copy. If there are four drums with four different colours of toner then coloured printouts can be produced.

Laser printers are used when quality and speed of output are important.

One disadvantage of using laser printers is that the toner is toxic (poisonous) and the cartridges that it comes in must be disposed of carefully. Other disadvantages with laser printers are that the reproduction of colour is not always as precise as it is with an inkjet printer, and laser printers tend to be more expensive to buy than inkjet printers, but other factors may make them cheaper in the long run.

EXTENSION ACTIVITY 2.05

Discuss as a whole class what may make a laser printer less expensive in the long run than an inkjet printer.

Inkjet printers

Inkjet printers work by squirting ink at the page out of different nozzles for different coloured ink. A stepper motor advances the paper while the print head with the nozzles scans across. They produce high quality output and are relatively inexpensive to buy.

One disadvantage of inkjet printers is that they often use water-soluble ink, so if printouts get wet, the ink will run. This does not happen with printouts from laser printers.

Inkjet printers are commonly used in home computer systems and small offices where most printing is of single copy outputs. They are also often used in machines that print out photographs directly from digital cameras.

29

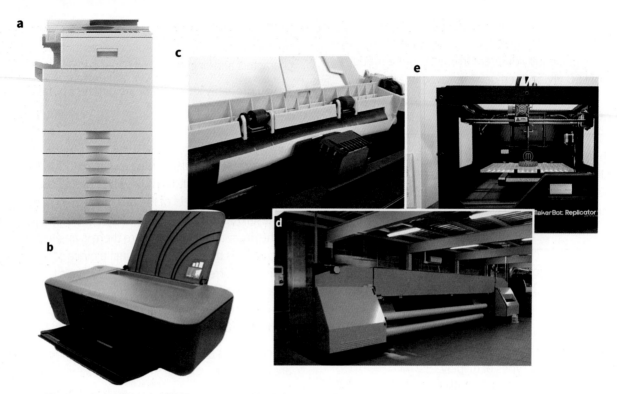

Figure 2.14 Different kinds of printer: (a) laser printer (b) inkjet printer (c) dot matrix printer (d) wide format printer (e) 3D printer

Dot matrix printers

Dot matrix printers use a set of pins to press an inked ribbon against the paper. Where the pin hits against the paper a coloured dot is left. These dots can be arranged in patterns to produce the required output on the paper.

Dot matrix printers are slower than other types because the method used in printing is mechanical. This also makes them very noisy.

Wide format printer

Some offices have a use for a wide format printer, possibly to print out a huge spreadsheet. For graphic arts use they are also important in order to output layouts, posters and more. Individuals may also want to print out their photographs in a wide format.

QUESTION 2.13

a Discuss the possible disadvantages of a wide format printer.

b Research the possible sizes of wide format printers to find out how wide is wide!

3D printers

You will have familiarised yourself with 3D printers in the discussion of emerging technologies in Section 1.05 of Chapter 1.

Plotters

A **plotter** is an output device for printing vector graphics. A vector graphic, unlike normal image formats (.jpeg, .bmp or .gif, for example), is not made up of pixels; vector graphics follow a path with a start and end point that may create a line, square, triangle, curve or other shapes.

A plotter uses pens to draw the vectors, giving a hard copy of the output that is sharp and clean and therefore ideal for being used to print designs of ships, machines, plans for buildings, for engineering or for architecture.

Plotters used to be used with applications such as computer aided design (CAD). However, this work is being taken over by wide format conventional printers.

There are two basic types of plotter (see Figure 2.15). **Flatbed plotters** have the paper lying flat under the pens. The pen itself is attached to a motor in a very similar way to the print head of an inkjet printer.

A **drum plotter** lies the paper on a drum that spins to drive the paper under the pen while the pen itself moves across the drum. They are very similar in principle to the flatbed plotter but take up less space. They can occasionally still be found being used for applications where a different tool is used rather than a pen, such as vinyl cutting for sign making.

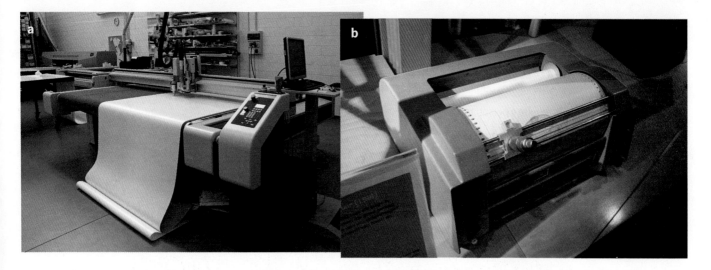

Figure 2.15 Different kinds of plotter: (a) flatbed plotter (b) drum plotter

Speakers

If you had a computer you would probably want to be able to listen to multimedia presentations, films, music and more. To enable you to hear sounds or music your system would need to have **speakers**.

An important use of speakers is as an output device for some disabled people, particularly blind people who cannot see the screen. The speakers allow special software (a screen reader) to describe aloud what is shown on the screen. Also, if a computer user has difficulty in using a keyboard or mouse, then there is dictation software that can be used as input, and input can be checked by listening to it being played back through the speakers.

Headphones and earpieces are personal speakers, and are often used in environments where other people should not hear the sounds produced. For instance, if there is a presentation to people from different countries, they could each listen to a translation by an interpreter into their first language.

Control devices

It is important to understand the links between certain types of input and output devices. We have just been talking about speakers and headphones as output devices; they naturally pair up with a microphone as an input device.

The next type of output device is an **actuator** (see Figure 2.16). Actuators are used in control applications and match up with sensors as input devices because both sensors and actuators are automatic devices which do not need any human involvement.

Earlier you saw how sensors collect data automatically as input. This section is about control devices, which work in

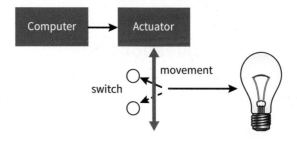

Figure 2.16 Using a computer to control turning on a light

parallel with sensors. **Control devices** are used to change some physical value in response to a command from a computer.

Sensors and control devices together with the controlling computer make up a **control application**.

Heaters can be controlled by actuators. They are used in central heating systems and to ensure that greenhouses do not fall below a certain preset temperature.

Motors can be used by a computer system to control elements of many household devices from washing machines to DVD players or air conditioners. If a device follows a set of specific rules, it can be controlled by a processor. Similarly, if a device uses motors to carry out actions, those motors can be controlled by a processor.

Buzzers or beepers make a single sound and are often used to inform a user that a particular thing has happened. For example, when the cooking time is up on a microwave, the microwave may make a beeping noise. Such devices are usually used in a quiet environment because they will then be heard clearly. Other devices use **lights** or **lamps** as signals to the user. If the device is controlled by a processor then the light can be considered to be an output device.

31

Summary

- You need to recognise the various input devices and be able to explain how they are used.
- You need to recognise the various output devices and be able to explain how they are used.
- Manual input devices require a person to enter data.
- Direct data entry requires no human intervention.
- MICR is used for the account numbers on a cheque.
- Sensors are automatic input devices that send data to the CPU.
- Control devices are used to change a physical value in response to a command from a computer.
- A temperature sensor is not a 'heat sensor', because heat is not a measurement. Neither is it a 'thermometer' because that is something designed for human beings to look at.

Exam-style questions

2.01 Tick **one** box in each row to show whether the item is for input or output.

Item	Input (✓)	Output (✓)
Bar code reader		
Touchpad		
Microphone		
Speakers		
RFID		
Plotter		

2.02 If you have a paper photograph that you want to digitise, which of the following would you use? [1]

   a scanner

   b joystick

   c touch screen

2.03 What is magnetic ink character recognition often used on? [1]

   a till receipts

   b cheques

   c bar codes

2.04 Describe the advantages and disadvantages of a supermarket using a bar code reader and an RFID reader. [4]

....

....

....

....

2.05 Describe two ethical issues associated with the use of a 3D printer. [2]

....

....

....

....

Chapter 3:
Storage devices and media

Learning objectives

When you have finished this chapter you will be able to:

- identify optical, magnetic and solid-state storage devices, their associated media and their uses
- describe the advantages and disadvantages of these devices.

Overview

Storage devices are peripheral devices to the main computer system and are used to hold data whether the computer is on or off. The **storage medium** is the part that holds the data and the **storage device** is the machine that lets you store data on the medium, and then read data from it. For instance, a CD RW disk is the medium because that is the part that has the data on it; the CD RW drive is the machine that you insert the CD RW disk into in order to read from it or write to it. There are both internal and external CD RW drives.

In this chapter we are going to look at the different storage devices and media so that you will be able to identify them and understand their advantages and disadvantages.

3.01 Storage devices and media

There are three different types of storage device, and each type stores the data in a different way:

- **Magnetic storage media** hold data magnetically. The surface of the media is made of magnetic material, and data is written to it by changing the local magnetic polarity to represent either a 0 or a 1. A magnetic device can then read the magnetic state of the disk, extracting the 1s and 0s, to retrieve the data from the disk.

- **Optical storage media** store data on their surface by little 'pits' burnt by a laser into the surface representing 0s and 1s. The laser can then be shone onto the surface more gently and, where it hits the pits, the reflection is different to that coming from a flat surface. These differences can be used to store digital data.

- **Solid state storage** is different from magnetic or optical storage because it has no moving parts and fits directly into the computer. The device and the medium are the same thing.

Magnetic storage media

KEY TERMS

Magnetic storage media: store data magnetically.
Optical storage media: store data on their surface.
Solid-state media: storage media with no moving parts, based on electronic circuits and using flash memory.

Fixed hard disks and drives

A **fixed hard disk** is the main storage on most personal computers (see Figure 3.01). The data is stored on one or more disks. The hard disk is fixed into its **drive** inside the computer so the hard disk drive tends to refer to both the disk and the drive at the same time.

Disks

Figure 3.01 A hard disk

Each disk has a device called a **read/write head**. This can write data onto the disk so that it can be stored, and can read data from the disk when it needs to be used.

The advantages of fixed hard disks being used as the main storage are:

- they can store very large amounts of data

- access to the data is fast

- there is no limit to the number of times the medium can be reused (i.e. the data can be deleted and new data written).

A disadvantage is that fixed hard disks can be fragile, and because they are stored inside the computer's case, data held on them should be backed up to ensure its safety.

Fixed hard disks are used to store three types of data:

- the operating system of the computer

- the user's applications

- the user's data, including any work that the user has done on the computer and any files like videos and music that have been downloaded.

These three types of data are all stored on the hard disk and then sent to the computer's RAM when they need to be used.

The data is organised on the disk so that **direct access** to it is possible. The disk has an index on its surface. If the user sends an instruction to read a particular file of data, the read/write head will look in the index to find out where it is and then go straight to that part of the disk. This is called **direct access to data** and means that there is no need to read through the whole disk to find just one piece of data, which speeds up the process a lot. This type of direct access to data is important when it is necessary to access data quickly.

Portable and removable hard disks

These are very similar to fixed hard disks and they use the same technology. The only difference is that they are not connected inside the computer case and will usually have a different type of interface to the computer, for instance via USB (see Figure 3.02). They can easily be connected to the computer to either have the data read from them or to have data written onto them. After this they can be removed and taken somewhere else.

They need to be more carefully protected than a fixed hard disk because they are likely to get knocked as they are moved about. Despite the protection, they are still fragile. They cost more than other forms of portable storage but can hold far more data so they are particularly useful for making a backup of all the data in a system.

Figure 3.02 A portable hard disk

The advantages of a portable drive are:

- It does not require an external power source, unlike a fixed hard drive, so you can connect it to a USB port and start using it immediately.

- If you are on the move, it is small enough to carry with you; some of them, even though quite slim, have a tough outside casing to help to minimise possible damage.

- It can be easily used by multiple PCs for file sharing, particularly for large files.

- It allows scheduled automatic backup of files which is easy to set up; then it won't matter if you forget to backup.

- It allows for quick archiving of data.

A disadvantage could be that it is not recommended that you switch between Macs and PCs once a disk has been formatted.

> **QUESTION 3.01**
>
> What does the disk drive use to find a particular file on the hard disk?

Magnetic tape drives and tapes

Magnetic tapes store data in a similar way to how data is stored on magnetic disks. The only difference is that the data is stored in a long line on the tape rather than being scattered over the surface of a disk. The **magnetic tape drive** is the device that drives the tape around the read/write heads (see Figure 3.03).

Magnetic tape

Figure 3.03 Inside a data cartridge showing the magnetic tape

The tape is read and written by a read/write head similar to those used on magnetic disks. However, in the disk device, the read/write head moves to the correct position to access the data. In a magnetic tape reader, the read/write head stays still and the tape moves past it. This means that data that is at the far end of the tape will take a long time to get to because all the other data will have to be read first. This sort of storage is called **serial storage**. Serial storage means that the data is stored one piece after the other (see Figure 3.04).

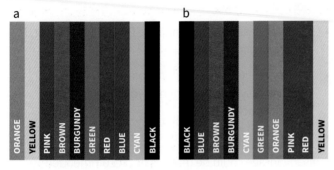

Figure 3.04 The difference between (a) serial and (b) sequential storage

In (a), the colours (data) are in a random order so the read/write head has to move along the tape until it finds the requested colour. In (b), the colours (data) are stored in alphabetical order, which means the read/write head can fast-forward to the correct part of the tape.

If the data is arranged in some sort of order, perhaps alphabetical order, this would speed up finding a particular data item because the device could fast-forward through the unwanted bits. This form of storage is called **sequential storage**, and it gives faster access to data than serial storage, but is still very slow compared with the direct access to data on hard disks.

Magnetic tapes are used where there is a need to store large amounts of data and where the speed of access is not important, for example for storing backups where a lot of data needs to be stored. Tape storage is also cheaper than disk storage and is less likely to be corrupted.

Sometimes the sequential way that data is stored on a tape is very useful. For example, the payroll for a large company is processed once a month. It is important that everyone gets paid. If the data is stored on a tape then everyone's data has to be read and there is no danger of missing someone out. The same is true of utility bills. These need to be sent to every customer on particular dates.

QUESTION 3.02

a Which type of storage device will be used by a large organisation with large volumes of data where speed of access is not important?

b What kind of data access will be used by this device?

Optical storage media

A **CD** (short for 'compact disk') can hold quite large files but has limited data storage size. This makes CDs ideal for holding data like music files. However, when the file becomes larger, as for a movie, they may too small.

For larger files it is necessary to use a **DVD** (short for 'digital versatile disk'). DVDs can hold much more data than a CD, though Figure 3.05 shows that they look very similar.

Both CD drives and DVD drives use a laser to read and to write the data, but a DVD drive uses a more precise laser. Because of this, the data on DVD media can be closer together and therefore more data can be squeezed onto the surface.

 KEY TERMS

Storage media: something onto which data is written for safe keeping, like a tape or a disk.

Figure 3.05 Left to right: CD, DVD and Blu-ray™. CD ROMs, CD RWs, DVD Rs and Blu-rays look similar but hold different amounts of data. Also, some can be written to (recorded on) whereas others cannot

Throughout this section on optical storage media, it is vital for you to distinguish between disks that you can write to and those that can only be read. A good principle is never to use 'CD' or 'DVD' on their own; they should always have some letters after them to say what type they are. The main types are as follows:

- ROM stands for 'read-only memory'; these cannot be written to, only read from.

- R stands for 'recordable'; these can be written to just once and then can only be read from.

- RW stands for 're-writable'; these can be written to multiple times.

The uses for the different types of optical storage media

CD ROMs and **DVD ROMs** cannot be written to, only read from. This means that the contents of the CD or DVD can never be changed. This is a big advantage if the contents need to be protected from being corrupted in some way. Examples include using them to sell music or movies. Software companies use them to distribute software and data files, and publishers to distribute reference material like encyclopedias.

This form of storage is robust because the media are not easy to damage and yet they store large amounts of data and are fairly inexpensive. They also have the advantage of protecting the data that is stored on them, because it cannot be changed.

What is an advantage at some times is a disadvantage at others; for instance, when you no longer like the music or have watched the film as often as you want to, it would be nice to be able to change the contents but it is not possible.

CD Rs and **DVD Rs** can be written to just once, but after that the contents can no longer be changed. They can be used to store music or movies, or to make a copy of files at a particular time, for an archive, for example. However, once they have been recorded onto, no further changes can be made to the data, which makes them less useful for making regular backups of files because every time a backup was needed a new disk would have to be used.

The advantage of CD Rs and DVD Rs is that you can write what you want on to them and then the material on them is protected. Disadvantages are that they can be written to only once, and not all CD/DVD devices (e.g. music CD players) can play them.

CD RWs and **DVD RWs** are ideal for moving files from one computer to another, perhaps for taking work into school that you have been doing on your computer at home. They are not easy to damage and can store large amounts of data. Because they are rewriteable, they can be used over and over again. This quality also makes them ideal for taking backups of the files on a system.

If a business decides that it is sensible to back up all the files on their system each evening in a form that can be removed from the building overnight, DVD RW would be the ideal format. It is robust, it is portable, it can hold a lot of data and it can be rewritten each evening.

A **DVD RAM** is very like a DVD RW but the data is stored in a different way on the surface of the disk. The different form of storage means that the surface can be written to far more often than the surface of a DVD RW. It also means that access to the data is faster. Reading and writing can take place simultaneously: if a DVD RAM were used as the storage in a television recording machine it would be possible to record one television programme while watching a different one from the disk at the same time. This means that they can be used in household recorders for recording and watching TV programmes and can also be used as a subsidiary system to support the memory of a computer. Despite being more expensive than other forms of DVD, they have a greater capacity, though they cannot be used in an ordinary DVD player.

Blu-ray disks have very much larger storage capacities than other optical storage media and at the same time can perform high-speed transfers. These two advantages mean that it is now possible to record and play back hours of high-definition video. The disadvantage is the cost, which is much higher than that of standard DVDs.

QUESTION 3.03

a Is it a good idea for a small company to use DVD Rs for backing up every day?

Give a reason for your answer.

b Name four different types of optical storage.

EXTENSION ACTIVITY 3.01

The difference between HD DVD and Blu-ray devices is in the type of laser used. Different lasers use different wavelengths of light. The shorter the wavelength used, the more data can be squeezed onto the disk surface.

Investigate this and try to explain why this type of disk is called 'Blu-ray'.

Solid-state storage

Solid-state storage devices have no moving parts. This makes them more robust than other types of storage. They use similar technology to RAM and ROM memory chips, but don't need electricity to maintain the data.

They are small and extremely portable, and can store large volumes of data. They are also straightforward to use since many of them are designed to fit straight into a computer port. Examples of devices that use solid-state storage are given below.

Memory sticks and pen drives

These are two names for the same thing; they are small storage devices, with a lot of storage space. They are ideal for storing data and software that needs to be transported from one computer to another. They can be used for backups of the main files on a computer system.

Figure 3.06 Memory card and memory stick

Flash memory cards

These are similar to memory sticks as they are a form of portable memory (see Figure 3.06). The distinctive difference is in their shape and the way that they connect to the parent device. A memory stick or pen drive fits into the USB port in a computer, while a memory card gets its name from the fact that the device is flat and looks like a card. Because of this it is not practical for the connector to be a USB, so the card slots into a port which is a different shape. Such cards are also called computer flash (CF) cards or secure digital (SD) cards.

Flash memory cards are used in small electronic devices that need large volumes of storage, such as digital cameras to store photographs; mobile phones to store photographs, telephone numbers and other data; and MP3 players to store music files. They can be slotted into a computer case so that their contents can be downloaded quickly.

Solid-state devices have two main disadvantages. First, they are more expensive than other forms of secondary storage. Secondly, their lifespan is more limited as they only have a lightweight protective cover in order to keep them as small as possible.

There are other types of memory cards which are smart media cards, memory stick and multimedia cards.

The advantages of memory cards are that they:

- have non-volatile memory so there is no danger of data loss if the power source fails
- are solid state, hence are free from mechanical problems or damage
- are small, light and compact so are very easily portable
- need very little power
- are available in many sizes
- can be used in different devices such as cameras, computers or mobile phones.

Disadvantages of memory cards are that:

- they can break easily
- they can be lost, misplaced or smashed
- cards may be affected by electronic corruption which can make the entire card unreadable.

3.02 Advantages and disadvantages of different storage mechanisms

The advantages and disadvantages of the various storage media discussed in this chapter are summarised in Table 3.01.

Type of device	Storage capacity	Data access speed	Portability	Robustness	Cost
Fixed hard disks	Very large	Fast	Low	Fragile if moved	Expensive
Portable hard disks	Very large	Fast	Medium	Robust	Expensive
Magnetic tapes	Very large	Slow	Medium	Robust but needs care	Expensive
Memory sticks / pen drives	Large	Very fast	High	Very robust	Medium
Flash memory cards	Large	Very fast	High	Very robust	Medium
Blu-ray	Large	Fast	High	Robust	Medium
CD	Large	Fast	High	Robust	Low
HD DVD DVD ROM DVD R DVD RW DVD RAM	Limited	Fast	High	Robust but needs care	Low to medium

Table 3.01 Storage media advantages and disadvantages

Summary

- Memory sticks and pen drives (two names for the same thing) are small, with a lot of storage space.
- Solid-state storage devices have no moving parts.
- CD Rs and DVD Rs can be written to just once.
- CD ROMs and DVD ROMs cannot be written to, only read from.

Exam-style questions

3.01 Describe sequential storage on a magnetic tape. [2]

....

....

....

....

3.02 Name two advantages of using solid-state storage instead of magnetic or optical storage. [2]

a ....

b ....

3.03 Name three types of data stored on a computer's hard disk. [3]

a ....

b ....

c ....

3.04 Describe the differences between RAM and ROM. [4]

3.05 There are two main types of hard drive available to a computer. State what they are and describe their use. [4]

1 ....

....

....

2 ....

....

....

Chapter 4:
Networks and the effects of using them

Learning objectives

When you have finished this chapter, you will be able to:

- understand what a router does and how it works
- understand the use of other common network devices, including network interface cards, hubs, bridges, switches, modems
- understand the use of WiFi and Bluetooth in networks
- understand how to set up and configure a small network, including access to the internet, the use of a browser, the use of email, access to an ISP
- understand the characteristics and purpose of common network environments, such as intranets and the internet
- define the terms LAN, WLAN and WAN
- understand the advantages and disadvantages of using different types of computer to access the internet
- describe security issues regarding data transfer
- describe network communication.

Overview

In this chapter you will discover different methods of linking computers together into a network to enable them to communicate with each other and to share information. You will look at the devices associated with computer networks and how they are used, also at the advantages and disadvantages of the different types of computer that can be used to access the internet. The next logical step is to find out how to set up a small network yourself. Finally, you will be able to describe different methods of network communication.

4.01 Networks

Networks are usually described as a type of **area network**. The types of network that you will have come across most frequently are **Local Area Network** (LAN), **Wide Area Network** (WAN) and **Wireless Local Area Network** (WLAN).

A LAN enables a group of computers that are in close proximity to each other to be networked. Typically, a LAN would be used in a school, in an office or at home. A LAN is useful because it allows resources such as files, printers, games and other software applications to be shared by the computers on the LAN.

A WAN normally connects LANs together to cover larger geographic areas. Typically, a WAN will connect cities, a country or many countries. The internet is an example of a WAN; it joins local area networks across most of the world. Imagine an organisation that has offices in more than one town; they would probably each have a LAN set up in each building and then connect them all together into a WAN.

> **KEY TERMS**
>
> **WAN:** a Wide Area Network consists of two or more LANs which are geographically separated and are linked by telephone lines or radio waves.
>
> **WLAN:** a Wireless Local Area Network covers short distances, using radio or infrared signals.

A WLAN covers short distances, like a LAN. It connects wirelessly using radio or infrared signals instead of the traditional method of network cabling.

Routers

A **router** provides a link between two or more networks; routers work together to direct **data packets** to their correct destination. It is said that they provide this link intelligently, because all routers can:

- make decisions about whether a message should be passed between the networks

- make the format of the message suitable for the new network

- read the information about the message and decide not only where the message should be going but also decide the best route that can be taken for it to get there.

> **KEY TERMS**
>
> **Router:** a device that is used to forward data packets along networks; it will select the best route for each data packet so that data travels as quickly as possible to its destination.
>
> **Data packet:** data sent over the internet is broken down into small parts called packets. A router will then use the best possible route to the receiver for each packet; they will be reassembled upon arrival.

A router is often used to provide a connection between a network and the internet because of its ability to join together two dissimilar networks.

How routers store computer addresses

Because a router, as its name suggests, decides on the route that a data packet should take, it needs a list of addresses; this is called a routing table, and is a data file in the router's RAM. The table on each router or node keeps the address of the next router or node along the path.

The main function of a router is to forward a data packet toward the destination address of the packet. This means that it will need to know where to send it, so the router will search the routing information to find the address of the next destination along the path. Not only that, it will also decide which particular route will be optimal in the journey of the data packet.

Routing data packets

When you send an email or ask for a web page, the message or information is broken into small parts called packets. Each packet has a header that contains the packet's individual identification number and its position in the overall message, the sender's internet address and the receiver's internet address. The rest of the packet contains part of the data of your message (see Figure 4.01).

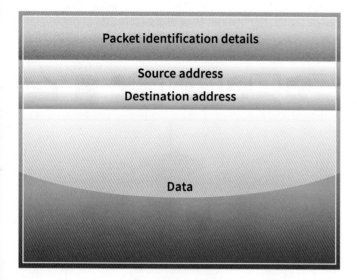

Figure 4.01 An internet protocol data packet

A router works by first deciding if the destination address for a packet is on the LAN or outside it; it gets the address from the field in the packet header. If the destination is on a WAN or the internet, the router uses its internal routing table to choose the best route for the packet to take in the next step of its journey.

Each packet travels separately by the best available route at any particular millisecond (see Figure 4.02), so they may not all travel together. Upon arrival, the packets are reassembled into the original message.

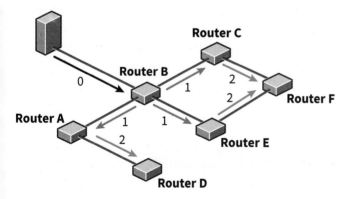

Figure 4.02 Possible paths to a destination through different routers

Network devices

Network devices are the hardware components that connect computers and other devices together in a

network. Once they are connected, they can share files and resources within the network.

The most common devices used to set up a LAN are a hub or a switch, a router, cabling, **WiFi** technology, network cards and a **modem**.

In a network, one computer acts as a server, and the other computers are called clients. The server connects to a hub or a switch to which the client computers are also connected. They use the hub or switch to pass signals to each other and the signals are directed by the router.

Network interface cards

Each computer on a network needs a network interface controller (NIC) to provide the hardware interface between the computer and the network, which can be wired or wireless. This can be provided by a separate network interface card, though newer computers come with an **Ethernet** NIC already built in to the motherboard of a computer. For wireless networks the NIC provides the radio communication to the network access point.

KEY TERMS

Modem: changes or 'modulates' digital data sent from a computer into analogue waves so that it may travel along telephone lines; the modem at the receiving end changes or 'demodulates' the analogue data back into a digital form that the receiving computer can understand.

Ethernet: the most common standard defining the wiring and signalling in a LAN.

WiFi: wireless network technology that allows communication via radio waves to connect devices to a local area network, which can then allow them to connect to the internet. The term WiFi is used for communications meeting IEEE 802.11x standards.

Hubs

Where a network has a central point to which all the signals from individual computers are sent, a particular kind of network device, either a **hub** (Figure 4.03) or a **switch**, is needed. The cables from all the computers on the network are plugged into this device.

Although hubs and switches look similar, when signals are received from the network, hubs and switches treat the signals differently.

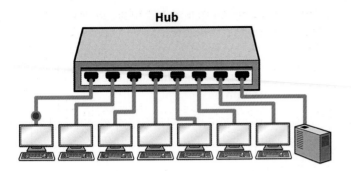

Hub

Figure 4.03 A network hub

If a computer needs to send a signal to another computer on the network, the signal is sent to the hub or switch. A hub will then broadcast the data to all the connected devices (including back to the device that sent the signal in the first place!). This creates a lot of needless network traffic. If the hub can have 16 devices connected to it the amount of traffic will be 16 times greater than it needs to be. The message will be sent to all the devices on the network, but only the device for which it was intended will accept it.

Switches

A **switch** handles messages more intelligently than a hub, by inspecting the address of the device to which they should be sent. The switch knows the addresses of the different devices on the network and only sends the message to the correct device.

A switch is a better choice than a hub because it reduces the number of packets that are needlessly transmitted within the network, thereby increasing the performance of the network. One disadvantage is that switches are more expensive than hubs.

Bridges

Sometimes, different networks need to be joined together. For example, if office workers using a star network need to access information from a different office where the computers are arranged in a bus network, this becomes a situation where two different types of network need to be joined together.

The device which allows two dissimilar networks to send messages from one to the other is called a **bridge**.

A bridge can only connect networks that use the same rules for handling the messages. They can change the form of a message so that it is suitable for a different physical type of network like the star and bus networks in the example

shown in Figure 4.04. If the star network uses a hub at its centre then all messages will be sent to all devices connected to it. This will include the bridge, so the bridge will have to be able to decide which messages should be passed on to the bus network and which should not.

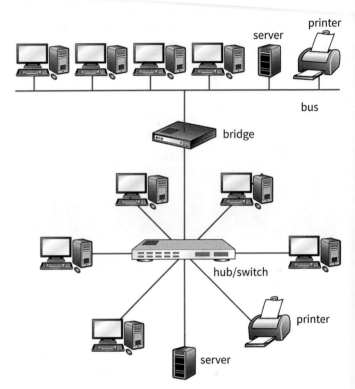

Figure 4.04 Using a bridge to join two networks together. In this example, a bus network is joined to a star network

Modems

A modem is used to connect a computer or a network to the internet. A modem changes the digital signal from the computer into an analogue one (called **mo**dulating) that can be transmitted down telephone lines. When the message reaches the other end of the telephone line, another modem changes the signal back to a digital one for the computer at the other end to understand (called **dem**odulating; mo + dem = modem!).

EXTENSION ACTIVITY 4.01

Research different types of network configurations, then draw a diagram of a star network and a bus network.

The use of WiFi and Bluetooth in networks

A wireless router enables you to set up a wireless local area network (**WLAN**).

The WLAN uses **WiFi** technology. WiFi-enabled devices can network with each other. If a laptop has a WiFi network card it will be capable of sending and receiving radio signals over a relatively short distance such as within a house or office building. The transmission rate is high, so you can work normally anywhere within range and are not tied to a specific location within your house or office.

KEY TERMS

WLAN: a Wireless Local Area Network that enables users of mobile technologies such as laptops, smartphones or tablets to connect to a LAN through a wireless connection.

Bluetooth: a wireless technology used in computers, phones and other devices; it enables these devices to communicate with each other over short distances using radio waves.

Bluetooth is a less powerful form of wireless transmission than WiFi; Bluetooth was developed to provide a wireless communication method between specific devices that are close together.

Bluetooth can be used to do the following:

- wirelessly connect and use a Bluetooth mouse, which gives more freedom of movement than with a wired mouse

- wirelessly connect to a printer, meaning that fewer wires need to be used, which makes it safer around the computer (fewer wires to trip over; see Section 8.01)

- wirelessly synchronise contact details such as phone numbers between laptop and phone

- use games controllers with a games console, or connect two consoles so that two people can play games against each other.

All of these uses of Bluetooth have two things in common:

- the range of the transmissions needs to be small

- the volume of data to be transmitted in a given amount of time is small.

These facts mean that there is no need for the more complex WiFi with its more expensive hardware requirements.

Bluetooth and WiFi are methods of wireless communication that use different standards: Bluetooth is based on a wireless radio system designed to connect peripherals at short range, whereas WiFi networking enables surfing the internet at broadband speeds.

Bluetooth is mainly intended for peripherals such as a cordless mouse, keyboard or hands-free headset, and WiFi is mainly for computer-to-computer connections instead of using cables to enable users to surf the internet at broadband speeds.

Bluetooth, being best suited to low-bandwidth applications, is useful if speed is not an issue, such as when transferring information between devices that are nearby.

WiFi is suited for networks because it is faster and can be used at a greater distance. It also has better security than Bluetooth.

EXTENSION ACTIVITY

Investigate ways that a Bluetooth connection can be used by a mobile phone.

Connecting to a network with WiFi

With a wireless broadband connection you can connect to the internet without cables. To do this you would need a WiFi router (Figure 4.05) and a computer with a WiFi adaptor.

Figure 4.05 Most ISPs supply a WiFi router when you register with them

To connect to a wireless network you click on the WiFi icon to see a list of available networks. You should see the name of your home network. Your **internet service provider** (ISP) will have supplied you with a password that you need to enter. This password can also usually be found on a sticker on the bottom of your router.

If it is the first time that you are connecting to a network you will need to choose whether it is a home, work or public network.

KEY TERMS

Internet service provider: a company that provides internet services for a monthly fee; you need an ISP in order to connect to the internet.

Connecting to a network with Bluetooth

Bluetooth is a wireless standard for connecting peripherals and for wireless networking.

To connect a Bluetooth device to a computer, first you check that the device to be connected is switched on and that you have made it 'discoverable'. This means that the device is broadcasting itself as available to be 'discovered' by the computer.

Select the Bluetooth icon on your computer then choose to 'Add a Device', or 'Pair with a Wireless Device'.

After a few seconds you should see the device you want to pair with. If the device needs a passkey, you will be asked to type a number on the screen.

Your device should now be paired with your computer.

KEY TERMS

Internet connection sharing: ICS is a way of connecting more than one computer in a LAN to the internet using only one connection and IP address.

How to set up and configure a small network

If you plan what you need to do, then proceed step-by-step through the plan, you should be able to set up your own network without too much difficulty. An example of such a plan is shown in Table 4.01.

1	Make a list of all of the existing hardware.	Draw a rough diagram of the hardware showing where it is. You should include here a note of the networking hardware that each computer in your network already has.
2	Decide which computer will be your ICS host.	If you plan to have each computer sharing one internet connection and IP address, **Internet Connection Sharing** (ICS), then you need to know which computer will be the host. That computer will have a direct internet connection and provide it to the other computers in your network.
3	Decide on the type of network technology to use.	For instance, will it be a WLAN?
4	Now make a list of all the hardware you will need and check against the list/diagram you created in Step 1. You may need to buy some items.	If you have decided on a WLAN you will need a NIC for each computer. Check what else you might need, for instance you may need to set up an account with an ISP if you haven't got one already.
5	Install the network adaptors and install your modem on the host computer.	This will create your network connections to each computer.
6	Switch on!	Turn on all of the computers, printers and other peripherals to be connected to the network.
7	Check that the host computer is connected to the internet.	To establish the internet connection on the host computer, run the New Connection Wizard.
8	Run the network setup wizard on the host computer.	This will configure the network adaptors (NICs) and configure the computers to share the one connection. Each of the computers will require a name to identify it. A shared files folder will be set up so that any files put into that folder can be accessed by each computer. The printer sharing facility will be set up, as will the internet connection firewall.
9	Run the network setup wizard on the other computers in your network.	This needs to be done on each computer on your network. You must ensure that the active internet connection on the host computer is maintained during this process.

Table 4.01 Network setup plan

QUESTION 4.01

a Looking Table 4.01, discuss with your class which tasks may be different for an Ethernet connection, rather than for a WLAN connection as described.

b Together, draw up a similar table to show the stages for an Ethernet connection where they differ.

Using a browser

There are different software applications for browsing the internet.

QUESTION 4.02

a As a class, do some brainstorming to list as many internet browsers as you can.

b Which one do you mostly use? Why?

You can choose which browser to set up as your default browser; for Windows 7 or 8, you would open the current default browser and then select Tools > Internet Options > Connections (Figure 4.06). If you have installed another browser already, its name will appear in the list you should now see. If it isn't there, choose Select, click on the browser you want to use and click the select button.

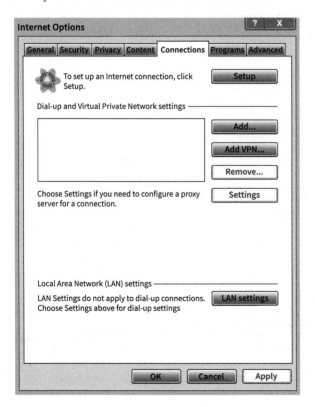

Figure 4.06 Windows Connections tab showing all the tabs available to change settings

If you have Windows 10, you set your default browser by selecting the following steps: Start menu > settings icon > System > Default Apps (in the left pane) > Scroll down and click Web browser > Click the name of the browser you want to set as default from the list that opens of available browsers.

You can also go through each tab to make changes: you can turn on or off your pop-up blocker, change the appearance of the browser, turn off the browser history, customise all of your privacy settings, and much more.

Figure 4.07 Address bar of a typical browser

The address used to access a website is called a Uniform Resource Locator (URL). Every page, image or file on every website has a unique URL as above.

Consider the URL http://www. cloudschool.ac.uk/ This takes you to the front page of the Cloud School site; the following URL takes you to a particular location on that site: http://www. cloudschool.ac.uk/school-books/maths/algebra. The different elements of this URL are explained in Table 4.02.

http	This indicates the **protocol** to be used in the communication between the browser and the web server (in this case, the hypertext transfer protocol). A protocol is a set of rules used for communication so that browsers and web servers can understand each other.
:	The colon is just there to separate the protocol information from the rest of the address.
//	Indicates that contact with a server is needed.
www	Name of the server to be contacted using the http protocol.
cloudschool	The domain name, which is like an address to get to a specific place on the internet.
/	This indicates that you want to go to the root folder (the folder where all other folders are kept) on the Cloud School site.
school-books/	This indicates which folder in the root folder to go to.
maths/	This indicates which sub-folder in the school-books/ folder to go to
algebra	Indicates which file in the maths folder you want to view.

Table 4.02 Deconstructing a URL

Access to the internet

To connect to the internet, you will need the following hardware and software:

- a computer
- a modem and telephone line
- an internet service provider (ISP)
- software to connect you to your ISP
- internet browsing software.

The modem is necessary if you are using a telephone line to access the internet. The ISP provides you with a gateway to the internet, a wireless router, an email service and access to the internet. When you have an account with an ISP it means that you will be paying them monthly to access the internet through their service.

There are two types of software that you will need:

- software to connect you to your ISP; this is different for each ISP
- browsing software, which you use to find and look at information on the World Wide Web. There are many browsers to choose from including: Microsoft Internet Explorer, Safari, Firefox, Chrome and many more.

Email

Email is short for electronic mail; it is a program that lets you send and receive emails over the internet and over electronic networks. Emails are convenient and they typically arrive at their destination within seconds of being sent, but this doesn't always guarantee that they will be read straight away! You can also send a file to someone by attaching it to an email message.

Such attachments may be a file of any type; when you receive the email to which it is attached, you will need to click on the attached file name or icon, and it will open up in the application in which it was written. This could be a disadvantage if you do not have that application on your computer. (There is more about email in Chapter 10.)

The internet and the intranet

The **internet** is a global network of interconnected computer networks. The internet is used to connect people, communities and countries worldwide, with the advantages and disadvantages shown in Table 4.03. Businesses can use the internet for information retrieval, communications, marketing and sales to distant customers, and banking.

An **intranet** is a private computer network within an organisation, such as a school or a business. Even though an intranet uses internet technologies, it is safeguarded from the global internet.

It is a private area so it will require a username and password to access it. This makes it a secure area for storing, accessing and working on electronic documents relating to the organisation. However, not all employees or users of the intranet will have access to every area of it. It will usually have folders on the network that can be accessed by employees and an internal email system. Advantages and disadvantages of using an intranet are discussed in Table 4.04.

Advantages of the internet	Disadvantages of the internet
The internet is a global system than can be accessed by users all over the world	Lack of security causes risks of hacking, loss of data, lack of privacy and theft of personal information
Enables research using a huge volume of information on almost every subject. Has powerful search engines to find the most relevant sites for your search term or key word	Information on the internet has no quality control, so not all the information is reliable; it could be inaccurate or biased
Instant news available from many different viewpoints	Age-inappropriate content
Fast communication worldwide	Spamming and malware threats (see Chapter 8)
Entertainment	Cyberbullying
Staying connected	Addiction
Online services and e-commerce	

Table 4.03 Advantages and disadvantages of access to the internet

Advantages of an intranet	Disadvantages of an intranet
Security of information and encrypted access to sensitive information	Users need to keep their passwords secure as different levels of access to information are used
Information only available to people inside the organisation	Unauthorised access or abuse of access
Secure communications between employees	Costs of implementation
Collaboration and teamwork is facilitated because authorised users can all access the same information	Costs of maintenance
It can strengthen the corporate culture	
Productivity should be enhanced because intranets can help users to find and view information faster and use applications relevant to their roles and responsibilities	

Table 4.04 Advantages and disadvantages of access to an intranet

Advantages and disadvantages of different types of computers for accessing the internet

You could carry a smartphone or a tablet in your pocket, if you wanted, or carry an ultra-light laptop from which to access the internet anywhere. If you wanted the full capabilities of a PC, with a larger display, when you are using the internet then a desktop computer or a laptop would be best.

Laptop, desktop computer, tablet or mobile phone?
There are three main questions to consider:

- Do I want to use my device to access the internet wherever I am?
- If so, what type of internet connection will I want to use?
- Do I only want to access the internet from school, work or home?

Device	Advantages	Disadvantages
Mobile phone	Instant access everywhere using wireless technology. Portable internet access. Can keep private or business separate. Can be used as a wireless modem for your laptop instead of paying access fees in an internet café.	Extra cost of data plan to access internet. Small screen area.
Tablet	Portable internet access. Can connect from anywhere using wireless technology. More comfortable to use than a laptop when out and about. Has a lot of functions as your PC has. Better for taking notes in a meeting than a smartphone.	Can't work with massive amounts of data. Will need to pay for a cellular device or access limited to hotspots. Larger screen size than smartphone.
Laptop	Can connect to the internet using wireless technology. Has more storage capacity and memory than tablet or smartphone so better for large downloads.	Portable internet access but heavier than a mobile phone or tablet.
Desktop	Can have a larger memory and storage space for downloading from the internet than other gadgets. Not portable as other devices are.	Not portable so internet can only be accessed. Needs a separate keyboard screen (unless it is an all-in-one), and usually a mouse.

Table 4.05 Advantages and disadvantages of different devices

WiFi hotspots

Hotspots can be found in public locations such as train stations, airports, hotels, coffee shops and restaurants. In such places, you can connect your smartphone, tablet or laptop wirelessly to the establishment's internet service.

The advantages are that a lot of hotspots are free and you can locate them fairly easily.

The disadvantages are that some of these 'free' hotspots require you to buy a coffee, or a meal if you are in a restaurant.

Internet café

Another place where you can connect to the internet is to use the computers provided in an internet café (see Figure 4.08). Although this is useful if you have no other way of accessing the internet, it is not free and there are security concerns when using computers used by lots of others (see Chapter 8).

Figure 4.8 An Internet café

Tethering

If you have a smartphone, you can use it as a modem for your laptop. This process is called tethering.

QUESTION 4.03

a Research tethering to find out how it works.

b Either try this out yourself, if you have the hardware, or describe the steps needed either in writing or orally to your class.

4.02 Network issues and communication

Security of computer networks

You will have read about some security issues in Chapter 1 and earlier in this chapter; it is also dealt with in much more detail in Chapter 8.

Network security is about the policies that the network administrator uses to prevent issues arising.

QUESTION 4.04

What other WiFi devices may be connected to your home network?

Security isn't just about hackers, viruses and malware; a security issue could arise from an unintentional human error, for instance. A network security problem isn't always about outside threats but may be something as simple as legitimate users of the network making a simple mistake, maybe by keying in something incorrectly; maybe due to inexperience or lack of training. The infringement of copyright is also a security issue. There are other, deliberate acts of trespass onto a network system to collect data that, in an organisation, would be termed 'industrial espionage'.

Other network security issues could be caused by lightning, or other natural occurrences. However, a more common problem could be the use of outdated or failing equipment, software failures and errors.

It is always worth remembering that the internet is not policed (see Chapter 9 section 9.2).

Network security can be maintained through physical means, such as ID cards or biometrics (for biometrics, please see Chapter 8 section 8.03) and are used to keep the location of the network server secure.

Avoiding password interception

If a person has access to your network they may be able to intercept the network traffic and access sensitive data. Therefore your router's default login information should be changed; you should also set a password for your local WiFi network.

If a person does not have direct access to your computer they could hack into the system through the internet connection, often via an open network port, but using a correctly configured firewall can prevent this.

Spyware is unwanted software that records a user's actions and can therefore be used to steal passwords; it is generally designed to be very difficult to remove. For instance, if you try to uninstall this software as you would any other program, you would probably find that it reappears when you restart your computer. **Anti-spyware software** offers protection against such intrusions if you keep it up to date.

In Section 8.03 there is a lot of information on security issues such as effective security of data as well as security of data online, much of which also applies to networks.

Principles of data protection legislation

Increasing demand for personal information to be securely gathered, processed and stored has resulted in the need for international data privacy legislation. There are now numerous laws globally to govern how personal information is handled. Such a global requirement has resulted in the laws varying greatly from country to country. However, there are various common themes running through them:

- how the data may be used and who it can be shared with
- individual choice about what information is collected about them and how it may then be used
- individuals' access to information stored about them and whether it can be amended or deleted
- the requirement for organisations handling personal information to protect it
- the requirement that personal information should not be sent to a different country unless that country has equivalent legislation in place that is at least as robust as the originating country.

QUESTION 4.05

a   For the country where you live, research data protection to determine any rules that are in place.

b   Working in pairs or small groups, list the principles you would like to see in data protection legislation.

Network communication

Facsimile communication

A **fax** machine is a device that sends and receives a facsimile copy of a paper document using the telephone network. Fax is short for facsimile; the machine scans the paper document and converts the light/dark areas into sound that can travel over a telephone network to another, receiving fax machine. The receiving machine then converts the sound back into light/dark areas on a piece of paper, thus creating a copy of the original document. Since this relies on actual pieces of paper, it is known as **physical faxing**.

In contrast, **electronic faxing**, sometimes called e-faxing, is when the internet is used to send a fax instead of using a fax machine.

E-faxing has many advantages:

- it doesn't require any extra hardware, software or telephone lines
- it offers paperless communication so is more environmentally friendly
- it can send and receive faxes as easily as sending or receiving emails from anywhere in the world
- it means that you can use a smartphone or a tablet to access faxes.

Email communication and attachments

Electronic communication (email) is messages that are both sent and received by computers; the message itself is text-based, but other file types can be sent as 'attachments' to the message.

Advantages and disadvantages of using email or faxing

Table 4.05 gives a comparison of the two communication mechanisms.

Fax	Email
Data can be kept private	Encryption needs to be used for data to remain private
Faxes cannot be blocked	Messages can be blocked
Cannot filter faxes as junk mail	Filtering junk mail out is simple
Documents sent as a fax message do not contain viruses	Attachments may have viruses

Table 4.05 Comparison of faxing and emailing

QUESTION 4.06

Discuss the differences between using fax or email, and try to fill in the missing cells in Table 4.05.

Video-conferencing

A video conference allows people at different locations to see and talk to each other whilst sitting in front of a camera and a microphone (see Figure 4.09). This can save on time and travel costs.

Figure 4.09   A video conference in progress

To support a video conference, the following hardware will be needed:

- video camera
- display screen
- microphone
- loudspeakers
- high-speed network / internet connection.

Audio-conferencing

Audio-conferencing is a meeting that is held between separate callers using a telephone instrument. Therefore it allows people in different locations to talk to each other as a group.

As telephones are generally accessible and easy to use, audio-conferencing is a simple method of holding business meetings. There is a variety of methods and technologies to support audio-conferencing. Many telephone companies offer the ability to use three-way calling. This would allow you to call two other people on separate lines, then to join them together to form a group. This means that each person in the group who has the three-way calling facility, can expand the meeting by adding another two people.

Audio conferencing can also be conducted using a computer and the internet making the service available to all sizes of businesses as well as individuals.

Web-conferencing

Web-conferencing is a live meeting that can have many different purposes such as training, collaborating or marketing, or it could just be a meeting via the internet. It is interactive because you can use multimedia tools such as presentations, video, file sharing or applications; whiteboards, with annotation tools, can also be used. In fact, you can do almost anything that you could do if everyone were present in the same room.

You can decide which features you want to use, such as:

- switching your webcam on or not
- clicking an icon to represent a raised hand to indicate that you want to say something
- the room notes feature that allows you to make notes during the conference and then email them to yourself
- the mute facility so that you don't get interrupted whilst you give a presentation
- the lock to ensure a meeting is kept private.
- opting for the 'Leave Meeting' option.

Summary

- Hubs and switches look similar but they handle signals differently.
- A LAN is easy to set up, is inexpensive, faster than a WAN or a WLAN and more secure. It is limited to a small geographical area.
- A WLAN works without cables, so is useful where computers and devices are moved around quite often. They are a bit slower than a LAN, are inexpensive to set up but the setup is easy.
- A WAN is costly and far less easy to set up than a LAN or a WLAN; it is slower than a LAN but isn't limited to any geographical area.
- Network hardware devices include hubs, bridges, switches and routers.
- Networks are valuable because they allow hardware like printers to be shared, as well as the sharing of software and of files.
- Browsers, email software and an ISP make communication over the internet possible.
- WiFi and Bluetooth are wireless forms of communication on a network.
- Fax, email and video-conferencing are methods of communication.
- The internet is open to all.
- Intranets are set up by organisations and access to them is strictly controlled.
- IDs, passwords and authentication techniques are used to identify users to networks.
- Data can be protected by passwords, firewalls and encryption techniques.

Exam-type questions

4.01 a An organisation uses standalone computers and wants to connect them to a local area network. Name two items of hardware that would enable the computers to be connected to a LAN. [2]

1 ....

2 ....

b Two dissimilar networks need to be joined together. Name the device that would you use to join them. Please explain your choice. [2]

....

....

....

....

4.02 Describe fully the benefits of using an intranet rather than the internet. [3]

....

....

....

....

....

....

4.03 List four items of hardware needed for video-conferencing. [4]

a ....

b ....

c ....

d ....

4.04 Describe a local area network (LAN).   [3]

....

....

....

....

4.05 A restaurant business has several computers already and they are considering joining them together into a network. They may want to open other restaurants in the future. They need to decide which type of network is best for them: a LAN, a WLAN or a WAN.

Describe the differences between these types of networks and recommend one of them, giving your reasons.   [6]

....

....

....

....

....

....

....

....

Chapter 5:
The effects of using IT

Learning outcomes

When you have completed this section, you should be able to understand:

- the effects of IT on employment
- the effects of IT on working patterns within organisations
- the effects of IT on microprocessor-controlled devices in the home
- the effects of IT on potential health problems related to the prolonged use of IT.

Overview

In this chapter we look at how ICT has affected us.

Since the advent of computers, our ways of working have changed drastically. There have been many positive effects as a result of the use of IT in our daily lives but there are also a few negative aspects that should be highlighted.

One area that has seen enormous changes is employment; many types of jobs have changed and some have disappeared completely. In addition, the patterns of working hours have also changed and this has had an impact on the quality of life for many people, such as creating much more free time to engage in more social interaction.

However, the hazards associated with the use of IT equipment, such as eye-related health problems, and muscular-related problems, such as repetitive strain injury (RSI), are becoming more prevalent with the overuse of particular IT equipment. RSI in particular can cause problems as it occurs when one action is repeated many times, such as when you use a keyboard, mouse or screen for long periods. RSI can be thought of as an overuse injury.

The wonders of the microprocessor will also be explored in this chapter because they are found in almost every household all over the world.

Finally, we look at how ICT and using it can affect our well-being. We identify some of the major health risks and offer some ways to prevent them; we look at some of the safety issues that present themselves in computer systems, from cables, to electrical supplies, to positioning devices.

Microprocessors are the small programmable processors found inside computers. They accept digital data as input and process the instructions stored in memory to produce the output as required. They require input and output devices to be connected to them to make them useful as computer systems.

5.01 The effects of IT on employment

Change in work patterns

There has been a reduction of employment in offices, as workers' jobs have been replaced by computers in a number of fields, such as payroll workers, typing pools and car production workers.

Payroll workers

Salma worked in the Finance department's payroll section. When computer systems were introduced to her department she applied to go on a course about using the specialist applications software used for calculating the salaries and wages of the workers. Most of the workers in her department were made redundant, but she had finished her course and was therefore able to continue working at the factory. She changed her job by learning the skills necessary for a different role. This is called **reskilling**.

KEY TERMS

Reskilling: when people change their jobs by learning the new skills necessary for another job.

Payroll clerks should be proficient in using spreadsheet software and competent with computers and automated systems. Companies may also subscribe to an outside payroll service, and the payroll clerk would use this service's specialised software; therefore they must be comfortable and confident in learning new software.

The workers who are still employed in administration have had to learn to use the new technologies and their jobs have changed a lot. However, a positive benefit has been that jobs often no longer have to be done at precise times, so the workers may have the opportunity to plan their working hours around their family commitments.

Typing

IT has helped to change the old-fashioned notion of a typing pool (Figure 5.01) so that now, instead of most documents being written using a typewriter, they have become much more professional-looking because they are word processed or produced on computers using

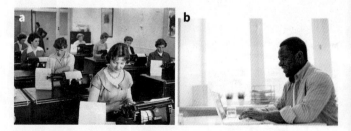

Figure 5.01 (a) An old-fashioned typing pool (b) The way most typing is done today

specialist software. Almost anyone who uses a computer is able to produce these very professional-looking documents. Therefore the job of typist has been made redundant by the use of computers and printers.

EXTENSION ACTIVITY 5.01

Discuss the possibility that handwriting may soon become a thing of the past.

What other types of job can you think of that may be under the threat of becoming redundant in the near future?

Car production workers

The concept of an assembly line was evident before the Industrial Revolution, where individual workers would take responsibility for an area of expertise in making one part of the whole product by hand using simple tools.

a

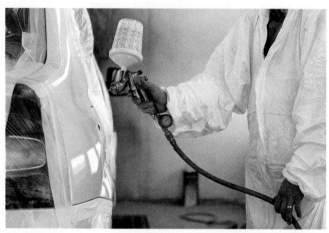

b

Figure 5.02 (a) Car production using assembly line workers (b) A modern production line using robots

Building or assembling the different parts of a car required different skills and knowledge depending on which part of the line you were working on. Each expert worker would have had to train in their specific field, and on the assembly line that's basically all they would do, though to a high standard.

Azad trained as a spray painter and this was what he specialised in. It is a very skilled job but also hazardous because prolonged exposure to the chemical toxins in the paints used on a daily basis could have had a detrimental effect on his health in the long term. His expertise would guide him to knowing when the job was done to a satisfactory level before moving on to paint the next car on the assembly line. Sometimes he would have to repaint if the results were not so good.

He was forced to retire when the company introduced robots to do his job (Figure 5.02). The company is very happy with the robots because they get the timing right every time. This means that the finished car is as perfect as it can be and the costs are lower because the robots are automated, which means that fewer people have to be employed. Sales are up because the quality of the car's bodywork is very high and it is cheaper.

However, there are no longer any people left who have the skills that Azad had. Soon, there will be nobody left who remembers that the job can be done by human beings simply by using their sight and manual dexterity. What will happen if the machines can no longer do the job properly? This loss of skills is known as **deskilling**. Deskilling means that skilled people are replaced by technology that can be operated by people who require fewer skills. However, where robots are completely replacing skilled workers is slightly different from the concept of deskilling.

Azad is happy in one way: his son was going to follow him as his apprentice in this very skilled yet hazardous job. Azad is grateful that his son has instead got a job in the control room, managing the robots that manipulate the containers of paint. This job is just as skilled as Azad's used to be and also requires training to be able to do it. Azad's son is said to be skilled. Azad's son works alongside a technician who is not as skilled as he is but might be learning from him in an apprenticeship role. He is semi-skilled.

58

KEY TERMS

Deskilling: when people who have been doing a skilled type of job are replaced by technology requiring operators with less skill, thereby saving the company money.

IT specialisms in the workplace

Today's IT systems demand ever more specialised computer skills and capabilities in the workplace. Over 80% of the jobs that are in the greatest demand globally are IT related. The range of jobs is increasing exponentially because each type of job requires very specialist IT skills and capabilities. Some of these are no longer a 'job for life' but have become short-term contract work. In addition, some specialist IT skills can take an individual from one end of the globe to another over short periods of time. It is not uncommon for young entrants to the job market to have more than one job contract with several different companies and organisations simultaneously. An example would be an individual who may have studied for a degree in computing but specialised in databases and not in web applications. Each of these is a very specialised skill, and individuals in each field would not necessarily be able to do each other's job despite both having studied computing at tertiary level. Alternatively, individuals do not necessarily have to have studied a whole qualification, such as a degree in computing, but might perhaps studied a single course in web applications or databases through one of the free (massive open and online courses) MOOCs.

Smart working styles

Online collaboration using technologies such as video-conferencing and VOIP have changed some of the working styles of the past. Training events can now be moved online via webinars, and synchronous telecommunications using video-conferencing applications and internet telephony allow colleagues meet in real time online or asynchronously, using applications similar to social networks to conduct training, host conferences or meetings. Some companies use automated telephone messages to answer frequently answered questions. Many customers do not like these impersonal telephonic communications but it does save companies a lot of money by reducing the number of staff needed to answer calls. Similarly, automated telephone marketing has also replaced many jobs by constantly calling telephone numbers randomly and automatically without any human intervention. Viral marketing encourages friends to forward marketing materials to each other, thereby causing a reduction in jobs for some traditional marketing methods, such as handing out brochures and leaflets.

KEY TERMS

VOIP: Voice Over Internet Protocol.

Increase in employment due to IT

While there has been a reduction in some kinds of jobs as described above, there has also been an increase in employment in other fields, such as website designers, computer programmers and delivery drivers.

Website designers

The job of web designer only began when the internet began and so is a relatively new type of job on the job market. Initially, only people with advanced computer technology skills were able to design websites. Nowadays, a much larger proportion of computer users are able to design and create their own websites because the software is much more user-friendly and intuitive. In addition, there are many more free resources and software packages for making websites than were available a few years ago.

Millions of websites are being added to the internet every minute of the day and this means that millions of people are now designing websites. Learning how to design and create websites was not taught at school about fifteen years ago, but nowadays there are many courses on how to design and create websites at secondary and tertiary educational institutions (Figure 5.03).

Figure 5.03 Students designing a website

Websites can range from simple to very complex types, for example a social club may only require a simple website that allows users to access information such as the dates and times of events and to inform potential members of the club's history and development. It may also allow users to contact key people within the club by displaying their contact details. These types of website do not require a high level of technical skill and could be designed and created by people who would not necessarily earn their living as a web designer. However, the more complex types of website, such as those used by large companies like banks, the public services and big retail businesses, require the expertise and skill of qualified web designers. Web designers should be able to create more interactive websites, whereby users can enter data, receive the results of their queries in real time (e.g. when booking tickets) and send emails. The more sophisticated websites allocate users an area on the main website to keep track of their own interactions with the company. E-commerce websites require the web designer to create a backend database to store all their clients' or customers' details and record all their transactions. Security is another extremely important aspect when designing websites because hackers are also computer programmers and so the technical skill of the website designer will determine the level of security of the websites they build.

EXTENSION ACTIVITY 5.02

Create a list of all the new jobs that have been created to support website designers. Describe the extent to which the new job of website designers has increased employment in other fields.

Computer programmers

The job of computer programmer involves using a specialised coded language that helps humans to communicate with machines. There are hundreds of different computer programming languages in use today. Many computer programmers can use more than one language to develop specific computer systems. People from all walks of life, both young and old, who did not specifically study computer programming, can program nowadays. There are numerous online tutorials that teach people how to program.

The job of computer programmer is also a relatively new type of job that did not exist before computers did. Computer programmers create computer systems for education, entertainment, health, finance and a host of other fields. Some companies hire computer programmers to develop computer systems specifically for their needs. In such cases, bespoke software is being produced. Sometimes, you can buy generic software off-the-shelf packages, such as your regular 'office suite' with a word processor, spreadsheet, presentation and desktop publishing software sold as a group. These computer programs were created by computer programmers and they continually improve these pieces of software (Office 2007, Office 2010, Office 365, etc.).

QUESTION 5.01

Can you think of other types of jobs that are needed to support the jobs of computer programmers?

Delivery drivers

As online shopping and e-commerce is becoming very popular, the need for delivery services is increasing. You can order almost anything online and it can be delivered to your doorstep in a very short space of time. You can order goods from all parts of the world and your goods can sometimes travel long distances before you receive them. There are an increasing number of online shopping facilities that offer delivery services, with the result that more delivery drivers are needed by the many courier companies that are operating now.

Figure 5.04 Delivery of goods ordered online is becoming a lot more common

5.02 The effects of IT on working patterns within organisations

In the past, most traditional jobs started early in the morning and ended by around five o'clock in the afternoon from Monday to Friday every week. Now, though, IT has become a huge driver for change in the ability to work remotely and to be in communication with the office wherever you are. It means that work does not have to be the place you turn up to every morning, but it is increasingly something that can be done anywhere, and at any time, as long as it suits both the employee and the employer. For instance, software can be used that enables virtual meetings to take place via high-speed broadband and mobile networks. Universities can offer online courses where the tutor and the students may all be in different countries, using university forums to communicate asynchronously. Communication software means that you may log into your employer's LAN remotely to work on projects or other documents, contracts and documents may be exchanged via email, or synchronous meetings may be held using a variety of available software.

Another change in working habits is that companies can offer **job sharing** whereby the workload and the hours are shared between two or more people. **Flexible working** also allows individuals to work **compressed hours**, which means that they can complete their normal 40 working hours per week over a shorter period of time.

60

KEY TERMS

Part-time working: working fewer hours per week than people usually do.

Flexible working: doing a job at times that suit the worker and not necessarily during the traditional 9 a.m. to 5 p.m. hours.

Job sharing: when one job is shared between two or more workers.

Compressed hours: extending the number of working hours in a day in order to decrease the numbers of days spent at work during a working week or two.

All these flexible working patterns have enabled more people from different walks of life to enjoy the benefits of working, for example more parents can return to work if they have flexibility around the times they need to be at home to take care of their younger children. More students can do **part-time work** outside of their study times to help support themselves while studying. Job sharing can be flexible

enough for the job sharers to arrange their own working hours between themselves. Self-employment has also been made easier because people can work from home and advertise their goods and services around the country, and even throughout the whole world, through websites.

5.03 Microprocessor-controlled devices in the home

The positive effects microprocessors have on lifestyle

Microprocessors can be found in many household appliances, such as washing machines, TV remote controllers, dishwashers, microwave ovens, refrigerators, burglar alarm systems, robotic vacuum cleaners and so on. The proliferation of microprocessor-enabled appliances enables people to enjoy more leisure time as household chores using these devices can be done in less time than if they were done manually. You can even program your television to record your favourite TV programme while you are away.

Figure 5.05 A modern kitchen

The low cost of microprocessors has increased their use exponentially and this is evident as they appear in an ever increasing number of gadgets and appliances that make our lifestyles easier and creating more leisure time for social interactions (Figure 5.05).

The negative effects microprocessors have on lifestyle

Before the advent of these household gadgets, people spent more time having to wash dishes, sweep floors, brush carpets and hand-wash laundry, and these activities helped to keep people healthier and fitter. Exercise was much more a part of people's daily routines because of the lack of technology.

Figure 5.06 How washing had to be done before washing machines

Microwave cooking is much quicker compared to cooking food the traditional way, when it took much longer to prepare and cook everything from scratch. However, the modern way is often not as healthy. These technological advancements began to change women's lives in particular as it was usually women who had to do these tasks. This meant that as their tasks in the home became easier they were freed to work outside the home more (this was also helped by other more general and political factors).

5.04 Potential health problems related to the prolonged use of IT equipment

There are reportedly many hazards in using IT equipment. However, much has yet to be proved, such as the threat of the small amounts of radioactive materials found in them. Health problems relating to overuse of thumbs, wrists, eyes, neck and back muscles are common. Other health hazards relate to stress caused by the constant

need to be chatting or messaging others, even to the extent that some people experience 'phantom' calls, imagining they've received a text or a call when they have not. Many users keep their laptops in their bedrooms or on their beds, and the artificial light from the screen affects their sleeping pattern because it causes a decrease in the amount of melatonin in the blood which helps you to sleep better.

Repetitive strain injury (RSI)

RSI can be caused by the exertion of your wrist muscles, particularly when using a keyboard or mouse to carry out repetitive actions that strain the wrist muscles. It can be painful, and legislation now encourages companies to employ strategies to reduce the incidence of RSI. As a result of the health and safety regulations, many companies ensure that their employees are not prone to RSI by introducing job rotation strategies where possible. Employees following a job rotation strategy will be able to change to another job every few hours to avoid constantly repeating the same type of work which could cause them to develop RSI.

Other health problems

Back problems can be caused when you sit for too long in a 'hunched up' position while using a computer that is positioned too low or too high. Eyesight problems can be caused due to the direction of lighting and the problems of glare.

Simple strategies for overcoming some of these potential health hazards include being aware of your own usage patterns and assessing whether you are causing any health problems by of the way you use IT. Muscular-related problems that can lead to RSI indicate that you should decrease the amount of time you spend using the IT device in the same position: change your position, use comfortable, adjustable chairs or take short breaks to give your thumbs, wrists, neck and back some time to recover from working in one position. You can also position your screen so that the lighting is at the right angle, thereby limiting the possibility of damage to your vision or eyesight. You can also use anti-glare screens or personalise your screen to enlarge the size of the text or images according to your own personal needs.

61

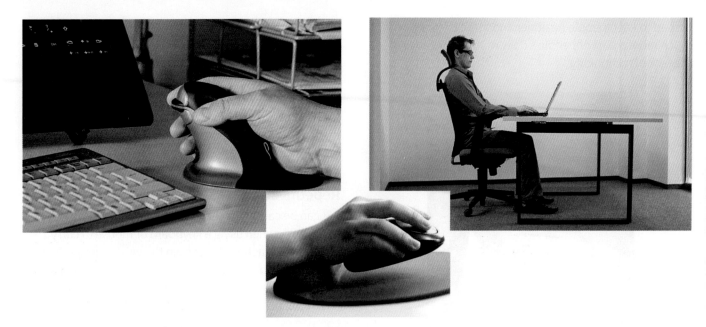

Figure 5.07 Equipment for health problems associated with IT use: mice for RSI sufferers, special chairs for back problems and wrist support mouse pad

Ideally, you need to have the computer screen positioned at eye level. You could use an adjustable chair and special ergonomically designed keyboards to help you to avoid back problems. Other sensible practices when using a computer for prolonged periods of time is to take regular short breaks, and to exercise and eat sensibly as well.

Physical safety issues related to IT use, such as trailing cables and where to locate devices, are covered in Chapter 8.

Summary

- Many new types of job are emerging due to the increased use of IT in our everyday life. However, there are also many types of job that are being lost because the skills required to produce some goods and services have become redundant.

- Changing working patterns and more flexible working hours are creating more free time for people to socialise more frequently or to further their career goals through further studies, or simply to take more control of their own time.

- The impact of the microprocessors found in most household devices and appliances is creating more free time for people. However, a major disadvantage is lack of exercise, as the machines take over doing most of the strenuous physical tasks.

- New threats to health and safety have arisen due to the proliferation of computer-based equipment used in everyday life.

Exam-style questions

5.01 Distinguish between the terms deskilling and reskilling. [2]

....

....

....

5.02 Complete the table below: [8]

Working pattern	Explain what each means	Example
Part-time working		
Flexible hours		
Job sharing		
Compressed hours		

5.03 The use of IT affects people's health and well-being in many different ways. Discuss three possible health problems and how they can be minimised. [6]

....

....

....

....

....

....

....

....

....

5.04 Ben and Jill are a young couple who both work full-time. They have two young children who attend a day-time crèche. Their lifestyle is hectic and they struggle to find time for leisure activities. Discuss the types of microprocessor-enabled household appliances they should use to help create more free time for them. [5]

....

....

....

....

....

....

....

Chapter 6:
ICT applications

Learning objectives

When you have completed this chapter, you should be able to understand:

- applications for communications, data handling, measuring and modelling
- the use of microprocessors in control applications
- applications in manufacturing industries
- school management systems
- booking systems
- banking applications
- computers in medicine, libraries and the retail industry
- expert systems
- recognition systems
- monitoring and tracking systems
- satellite systems.

Overview

Fifty years ago, people did not use ICT in their everyday lives. Nobody had a computer at home and devices that were used in the home did not contain computers or microprocessors.

Nowadays, most people have a mobile phone and live in houses with many devices that use ICT to make their lives easier. The workplace, whether it is your school or the organisation that you work for, will probably use many computer-controlled devices.

In this chapter we will look at the ICT applications in everyday life that have caused lives to change so dramatically.

6.01 The range of communication applications

Traditionally we have communicated mainly via letter-writing, written reports, newsletters, telephone and face-to-face meetings, but the use of ICT has brought about major changes in the way we communicate with each other on a personal level, and also on the way that organisations communicate. We will look at a number of different applications, including hardware and software, the effects on the people concerned and how organisations have been affected.

Newsletters

Organisations like schools, universities and clubs have always produced newsletters for parents or for students or for their members (Figure 6.01).

The use of word processing software enables easy editing to correct errors, and spell checkers and grammar checkers help to improve quality.

Using a word processor and/or a desktop publishing (DTP) application it is very easy to click a button to format a document in very clever ways:

- using columns
- altering the margins and the spacing
- changing the character size
- using different typefaces (fonts) like **Arial** or `Courier`
- different effects, like *italic*, **bold** and ^super^scripts
- indenting of text
- automated bullet points and numbering
- justification of text.

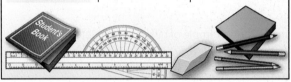

Figure 6.01 A school newsletter showing text in columns, with headlines, text boxes, use of margins, and colour images; ICT applications have made this easy to produce

There is a skill in producing a newsletter, and part of the skill is to ensure that the document looks impressive while remaining readable without too many distracting effects.

QUESTION 6.01

a Look at the newsletter in Figure 6.01 and the text above and try to spot as many uses of simple word processing techniques as you can.

b Decide whether you think the newsletter is effective. How could it be improved?

EXTENSION ACTIVITY 6.01

a Imagine that you have produced a newsletter that has five different typefaces with different font sizes. Why do you think your teacher will not think it suitable?

b You want to put an image of your school logo over the top of text so that you can still read the text underneath. How can you do this with a DTP application? You can get some hints about this in Chapters 13 and 14.

DTP applications allow for many different publishing formats with very little effort (Figure 6.02), and many people can now contribute to the production of a school newsletter. The people who receive the newsletter are now better served: there is more information and it is better presented.

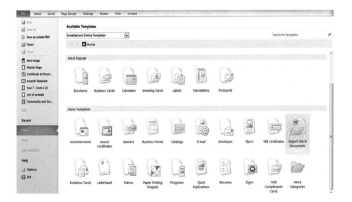

Figure 6.02 An example of different templates in a typical DTP application (this example is from Microsoft Publisher)

When it comes to printing, multiple pages are now easy to process, especially double-sided (**duplex**) pages. Duplex printing requires a duplex printer (unless the paper is manually turned over). A large print run would not be suitable for an inkjet printer because of the time taken to do the printing and the cost of the ink. Consequently, a colour laser printer is probably the most suitable option to consider for this job.

KEY TERMS

Duplex: a feature of printers that enables automatic printing on both sides of a sheet of paper.

Flyers and posters

Although flyers and posters look very different to newsletters, the same sorts of considerations apply, so it is not the features of the DTP application that will tend to alter, or the methods of production. The difference is in the design of the finished product (Figure 6.03).

Figure 6.03 An example of a flyer; its design contains more text than a poster but it is eye-catching and more illustrative than a text-heavy newsletter

QUESTION 6.02

Find out how very large posters, such as for the side of a building, are printed.

Applications used for publicity and corporate image publications

Examples of publicity and corporate image publications include business cards, letterheads, flyers and brochures, among others (Figure 6.04).

Figure 6.04 Different types of personal and corporate publicity

Websites

A website is a collection of web pages, text, graphics, video and sound. A website is hosted on a web server on the internet. The information on the website can be viewed by internet users using a **web browser**. Websites are used to raise the profile either of a person or an organisation and to communicate with others.

In order to produce a website you either have to write code or a use a web authoring application (see Chapter 21). The application's features are similar to those found in DTP software: the designer just needs to design the layout for the web pages on the website. Hyperlinks can be provided to jump to other web pages on the website or to other websites.

For example, a school website is used to show information about the school, and to communicate with parents and other interested people to ensure that they feel fully involved with the school. The website is also used to advertise the school to people who currently have no connection with it, potential new parents in particular, and it is also used to advertise school events.

Of course, the internet is used for advertising in a wider sense in all kinds of organisations. Consequently, some old-style advertising is now no longer done and the advertising industry has suffered because of it. But many advertisers have moved some of their business across to the internet – it's just another medium for them to use.

Multimedia presentations

Multimedia presentations use a mixture of different media to present information effectively and to maintain the interest of the viewer. The normal screen image containing text and graphics is supplemented by animations, video and sound. Sound can be synchronised with what is happening on the screen.

Changes from one screen to another can use complex **transitions** to catch attention.

Hyperlinks can be included as part of a single-user presentation to give the user a choice of path through it. Typical examples of multimedia presentations would be a presentation on a website or, in education, a computer assisted learning (CAL) package.

CAL presentations are interactive and give you the opportunity to manage your own learning by allowing you to:

- learn at your own pace
- repeat sections that were difficult
- omit sections that you already know and understand.

This sort of presentation, using different media and allowing control over your own work, should help you to maintain interest in what you are doing.

EXTENSION ACTIVITY 6.02

If you wanted to give a user the option of repeating a CAL presentation, how could you do it?

A multimedia presentation can also be in the form of a slide show to be shown to an audience using a data projector.

Many chain stores use multimedia presentations on large screens. The presentations run in a loop while the store is open. They will typically use a lot of colour, fast cuts from one image to another and intricate transitions in order to keep the viewer's attention.

Now that organisations communicate in so many different ways, it is important for each of their documents to bear the same corporate identity so that it can be recognised immediately as coming from that organisation, whatever type of document. For instance they will always use the same logo, font, colours and style; this is known as their 'corporate image' or 'house style'. This will project their corporate identity or overall image of the organisation.

Cartoons

Computers can be used to create cartoon animations. You can scan or create an image on screen with a graphic application. Then, if you use computer-generated imagery software (**CGI**) to give instructions of how the image should move and where it should end up, the software can calculate the intermediate stages and automatically produce copies of them. These copies can be displayed in sequence to produce the moving image. This type of CGI imagery is widely used in the film industry.

> **KEY TERMS**
>
> **CGI:** Computer-generated imagery software for creating cartoons.

Music scores

Music is written by a composer who then writes it on a 'staff' or 'stave', which is a series of parallel horizontal lines. The position in which a symbol is placed tells you what note to play. A music score is when the separate instrumental and vocal parts for a piece of music are printed together (Figure 6.05).

Figure 6.05 A music score

Software can also be used to write music. It relies on the idea that if an instrument is connected up to a computer then the software can read the notes as they are played. The standard way of connecting computers and electronic musical instruments is with MIDI (Figure 6.06).

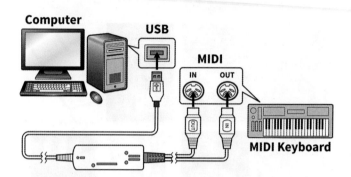

Figure 6.06 A MIDI interface translates signals from the attached instrument into electronic data, which can then be stored and manipulated by the computer

Sometimes music needs more than one instrument to play at the same time in order to produce the desired sounds. A piece of music can be played on one instrument and the score recorded by the software to a 'track'. If the composer is satisfied, the new accompanying part can be saved as another track. The composer builds layer upon layer of tracks in the same manner.

The computer can also print the score for all the parts.

There are major benefits to composing in this way. The composer can hear their music immediately and can edit the composition immediately or send it anywhere in the world electronically. Composers can collaborate with people all over the world on the same piece of music.

The use of mobile phones for communication

Mobile phones have many purposes and some mobile phones are more sophisticated than others. You will be able to make and receive telephone calls and to use short messaging service (SMS), better known as text messaging on all mobile phones as basic functions, however, mobile phones are used as digital cameras, for playing computer games, for navigation using GPS (Global Positioning System), for playing music, surfing the web, accessing emails and doing a host of other things using different apps.

Most mobile phones are able to connect to the internet by using third generation (**3G**) or fourth generation (**4G**) networking technology. These refer to networking standards that deliver high-speed data service to mobile devices. Faster internet access is possible with 4G compared to 3G.

KEY TERMS

3G and 4G: communication protocols used by smartphones to connect to the internet, 4G being much faster than 3G.

Text messaging

Text messaging is the least expensive way of communicating using mobile phones, using what is called the Short Messaging System (SMS). It is useful as it makes it quick and simple to send short messages.

Mobile phone screens have developed to form a larger proportion of the total interface to allow for better use when watching movies or playing computer games. Keyboards have now become integrated into the screen as touch screens which disappear when the screen is being used for another function.

The use of internet telephony

The **Voice Over Internet Protocol** (VOIP) allows the use of the internet to carry voice data when making phone calls. When using VOIP technology, the voice data is broken into packets of data that are sent along different routes to arrive at the same destination where they are reassembled in the right order (see Chapter 4). This technology is referred to as packet switching. VOIP telephony is generally free, except for the initial cost of connecting to the internet; the actual call itself is mostly free. VOIP telephony can be between a computer and a landline telephone and not only just between two computers.

6.02 Data handling applications

Data tracking, data mining and data analysis are some of the most important tasks that most organisations are required to do. Data analytics (DA) is a relatively new science that analyses large amounts of raw data so that conclusions can be made which can influence decision-making more accurately.

Data is being collected using ever more sophisticated methods about almost every aspect of your life. Schools get data every year about how many children will require places at their schools depending on birth statistics. Schools then share their data with job agencies to ensure they attract the right numbers of teaching staff, and if shortfalls are predicted, higher education authorities are alerted and university students are encouraged to consider a career in education. If this fails, then teachers

may have to be recruited from other countries. The results of such analyses are important for countries because it informs governments of priorities that they will need to focus on well in advance.

However, there can also be a more sinister side to collecting so much data about individuals; this topic is covered in Chapter 8 on safety and security.

Surveys

The starting point, whatever the data-handling application, is data collection. This can be done automatically, but another method is to use surveys. In computer terms surveys are conducted using **data capture forms**. In general terms it is important to decide what data needs to be collected and then to decide what questions should be asked. Data capture forms can be on paper, or they can be electronically based and filled in directly onto the computer.

Address lists

Sometimes a form asks for an address or an email address or phone number. Why would this be needed?

Address lists or contact details are very valuable. Organisations that deal with mail orders need to be able to send brochures to potential customers, so a list of names and addresses is something they can use for their business.

As an example, imagine a business which specialises in publishing science fiction novels and selling them by mail. The first and most valuable list of addresses is that of all the people who have bought books from the company in the past. This list is particularly valuable because everyone on the list has already proved that they are interested in the type of books that are being sold by the company because they have bought them in the past.

EXTENSION ACTIVITY 6.03

Lists like these are very important to organisations, and contact lists gathered in this way are often put up for sale by the organisation for whom the survey is being conducted. Do you think that this is ethical?

Club and society records

Clubs and societies need to keep data on their members. This data can be searched for specific members of the club so that they can be contacted. It can also be searched for specific data: all the members who are in a particular age group, so that a team can be chosen to represent a school, for example.

School reports

To understand the use of ICT in producing school reports you need to consider what information is on the reports:

- **Student-specific data**. This would include the student's name and the name of the class they are in. This information is already on the computer system. It is stored in the 'student file'. If the template for the reports is stored on the computer then the system can be told to produce a set of reports for every student in the school, or just for a year group, or even for all the girls in the hockey team. Any subset is possible. These reports will be stored electronically and await further information being imported to them.

- **Student progress**. The name of the class teacher who writes a report on the student's progress will need to be on the report.

- **Absences and late arrival**. This data will be stored in the attendance register, and the computer can quickly calculate how often a student has been absent or late to classes and insert the figures on the report.

- **Teacher comments**. The teachers will have to write a comment for each of the students that they teach. These comments tend to be repeated many times for different students as there is a limit to the number of appropriate comments that can be made. A set of responses can be stored on the computer system and the teacher then simply chooses the comments that apply to that student, which are then added to the report by the computer. This set of comments is called a comment bank.

- **Date of the report**. This is easy for the computer to add to the form; alternatively, it may just say which term the report is for, in which case the same information will be on every report.

When the reports are completed they can be printed out for distribution to parents.

School libraries

A small example, with only five books and six students, will be enough to show how a large library system might work in a school library.

First, apart from looking to see whether or not a book is owned by the library and checking to see whether a particular student is allowed to take a book from the library, there is little else that they can be used for. The system will need to keep track of the students who can use the library (the Students file, Table 6.01) and the books that they can borrow (the Books file, Table 6.02).

Name	Form	Geography group
Boparra	6DY	Mr Singh
Broad	6FT	Ms Williamson
Flintoff	6DY	Mr Singh
Harmison	6FT	Mr Singh
Shah	6FT	Ms Williamson
Strauss	6DY	Mr Singh

Table 6.01 School library Students file

ISBN	Book title	Author
9782489768734	Economic Geography	Daniel Bedori
9781453624561	Geography for A Level	Akira Itoko Wicksamaringhe
9781123498764	Glacial Valleys	Jean Percy
9789123456785	Meteorology	Samira Jordani
9780234567895	Volcanoes	Paolo Fernandez

Table 6.02 School library Books file

The main thing that computers need to be used for in libraries is to keep a check on which books are out on loan and who has them. In order to do this another file must be included in the library database. At the moment there is nothing that links a particular book to a student because there are no foreign keys. In order to keep track of the books, yet another file is needed, called the Loans file (Table 6.03), to contain the student names and also the **ISBN** of the books. This means that the three files are now linked together using the Name field and the ISBN field as **foreign keys**.

KEY TERMS

ISBN: International Standard Book Number, which consists of 13 digits. ISBNs include a check digit calculated using a mathematical formula to validate the number.

If the teacher wants to know where a particular book is and how to get it back if it is still on loan, they only need to know the title of the book. For example, a teacher wants to know where *Meteorology* by W. Akram is. The books file is searched for the title and author. The ISBN is taken from the Books file. The ISBN is then used in the Loans file to find out firstly whether or not the book is in the library or out on loan. In this case it is out on loan; Flintoff has it. Using this name the teacher can then ask the computer to search the student file to discover that Flintoff is in 6DY. The teacher can then go to the correct form room to speak to the student.

ISBN	Name	Returned?	Date due back
9782489768734	Flintoff	yes	16/05
9781453624561	Shah	yes	23/05
9781123498764	Boparra	no	29/05
9789123456785	Flintoff	no	29/05
9780234567895	Strauss	yes	30/05

Table 6.03 School library Loans file

Notice that in order to be useful it is necessary to have three files with two sets of foreign keys.

EXTENSION ACTIVITY 6.04

a   Why is it necessary to have the third table of loans? Can the problem of keeping a track of the books and the loans be solved in another way? (Can the loan be added to either the Books table or the Student table? Try both methods with the data given in the Loan table here and see what happens.)

b   Find out what system is used in your school library. Is it a manual, paper-based system? Is it a computerised system? Try to decide how it works and think about the way that the three tables of information that are in this solution would be used in your library. What are the special items of hardware that would be needed in a library system? Would it be reasonable to type in the ISBN of a book every time it was taken out on loan?

6.03 Measurement applications

A measurement application has something to do with measuring a value or a set of values. A computer can be used to display the values to the user by displaying a representation of the magnitude of the thing being measured. The computer needs to be given some data to describe the measurement that needs to be taken. These measurements will be taken by devices that can automatically take measurements and return the values to the computer. These devices are called sensors. Most of the data that is measured will be analogue data. Throughout this work we should remember that any analogue data that is measured will need to be changed into digital data so that it can be used by a computer system. See Chapter 2 for more details about sensors as input devices.

ICT is much better than a human at providing great precision in taking measurements. It is very important to be precise when measurements are taken by a weather station (see Figure 6.07) because they are used in making weather forecasts. Similarly, the temperature within a reactor vessel during a chemical reaction may need to be accurately measured. If the temperature gets too low the reaction will stop, but if it gets too high the pressure could make the whole vessel dangerous. These temperature points may be very precise.

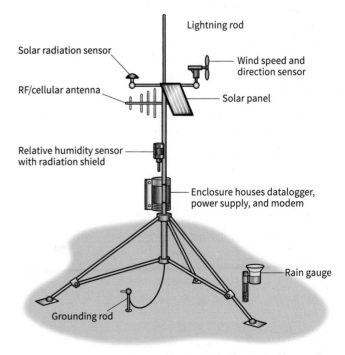

Figure 6.07 An automatic weather station; these typically consist of a rechargeable battery, a data logger and various sensors

QUESTION 6.03

a If you want to measure barometric pressure and use this data on a computer, what would you use?

b Where would you use it?

Precision and safety are not the only reasons for using ICT in measurement. If measurements need to be taken over a long period of time, a human being may forget to take them or may not be available at the right time. So ICT systems have a number of advantages over humans when taking measurements:

- Precision: ICT can provide more accurate measurements than a human, and more frequently.

- Reliability: ICT can be relied upon to take the measurements every time, all the time.

- Accuracy: ICT will ensure that the measurements are taken at exactly the right time.

- Non-interference: measurements can be taken without disturbing the thing that is being measured.

- Computer-recorded data can be analysed more easily and quickly than human-recorded data.

- Automated systems can operate where humans cannot, and free up humans for other tasks.

Scientific experiments

There are many different scientific experiments that need to be controlled by processors which can take measurements and then make decisions based on the measurements that have been taken. Why is the use of sensors to take measurements during scientific experiments so important?

- Often the experiment being done will be dangerous to human beings. Sensors can be used where human beings cannot.

- The findings from scientific experiments are based on the accuracy of the measurements that are taken.

- There is a need for the measurements not to be missed or the results of the experiment will begin to be questioned.

- It is important to ensure that nothing interferes with the experiment that may change the results.

Temperature sensors can be used to measure the temperature of the chemicals that are reacting in a vessel; they may be used to measure the temperature of an engine part in an engineering workshop to ensure that the friction in the engine is not excessive. There are many instances where temperature sensors are used.

The use of light sensors is less obvious. They may be used, for example, in a biological experiment about plant growth. The computer can be used over long periods of time to take measurements at regular intervals of the levels of light. The data can then be used as part of an experiment to determine growth rates of different plant types in different growing conditions.

Experiments may also need a pressure sensor. Pressure sensors are very important in chemical experiments. Some reactions will only work if they are done at particular pressures and the computer must ensure that the correct pressure is used. Also, chemical reactions often involve the chemicals changing their state and creating large volumes of gas. If kept in the same reactor vessel, there will be large pressure build-ups, which can be very dangerous if the pressure becomes too great.

Analogue data and digital data

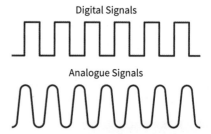

Figure 6.08 Analogue signals vary continuously; digital signals are either on (1) or off (0)

Analogue data refers to audio or video signals and such like that vary continuously, but digital data is based on binary form (Figure 6.08). A good example is a light switch: being on or off is digital because it only has two states, but if a dimmer switch is used instead, then that is analogue.

All natural signals are analogue, such as the human voice, animal sounds and notes played by instruments. In order

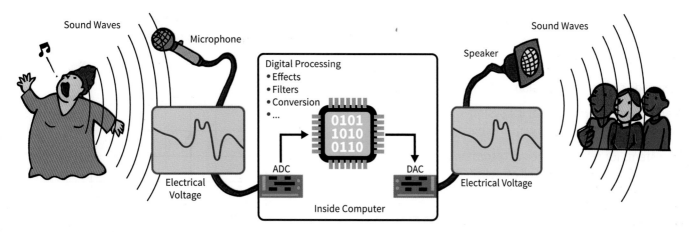

Figure 6.09 Analogue to digital conversion

for these to be recorded and processed by a computer they need to be converted into digital signals (bits, which are 1s and 0s; see Figure 6.09).

When the data has been collected it needs to be sent to the computer. This will be via an analogue to digital converter so that the signals that arrive at the computer can be understood by it.

The use of microprocessors and computers in pollution monitoring

Pollution monitoring is concerned with monitoring the quality of the environment. Frequently, it is about measuring the levels of pollution in the environment and reporting the levels over long time periods. Computers are often used for this purpose.

Figure 6.10 Exhaust fumes being released from a vehicle

Particularly important are levels of gases like carbon monoxide and nitrogen dioxide that are produced by vehicle exhausts (see Figure 6.10). These can be monitored

by installing specialised sensors that will detect the levels of the particular gas and report back to the computer via an analogue to digital converter. The computer can be used to:

- draw graphs to show the recent levels in an understandable form

- store the data over a long period and report the findings when the user asks for the results

- store the results in a spreadsheet to allow the user to predict future levels

- produce information in table or graph form for importing into a report for publication.

The atmosphere near busy road junctions is one type of pollution monitoring; there are many others. Any part of the environment in which we live can be monitored.

> **EXTENSION ACTIVITY 6.05**
>
> There are two timings to be set in any experiment. The first is the time interval between the readings being taken; the second, for how long the experiment will run.
>
> In pollution monitoring, discuss what the two critical timings are that need to be decided.

The use of microprocessors and computers in hospital intensive care units

The intensive care unit in a hospital produces and uses a lot of data. It is here that ICT can enhance patient care. It can:

- improve access to the clinical data of a patient

- reduce errors

73

- ensure that compliance with quality standards is observed

- monitor a patient's vital signs

- provide support for decision-making.

It can be seen, therefore, that ICT systems in an intensive care unit can be associated with improved care.

ICT systems for managing health records in local doctors' practice settings are often well established.

6.04 Microprocessors in control applications

'Computer control' is about applications where the computer is not only taking measurements from the world around it, but has been given command over some devices which will allow decisions to be made and actions to be taken that will have a direct bearing on the results that are taken the next time.

Control applications use preset values to determine when something should happen. For instance, a greenhouse heater should come on when the temperature drops below a preset value.

Turtle graphics

Turtle graphics are an example of computer control, and have many built-in commands that allow you to perform actions by giving the computer a set of clear instructions to follow.

In each of the following diagrams the turtle is represented by a triangle shape. The shape that is used to show the position of the turtle does not really matter except that it needs to show the direction in which it is pointing. The turtle is normally considered to be located at the position where the triangle is pointing.

Moving forwards

Most turtle graphic commands are made up of two parts: the first is the name and the second gives a value which tells the computer how much needs to be done. For example, FORWARD 5 would tell the turtle that it must move forwards and that it needs to move 5 units (Figure 6.11). This is not always true, as we shall see later, but it is a good place to start. The actual command word is FORWARD but it can become very annoying to have to write it in full every time it is used, so each command

word has a shortened form. The short form will be put in brackets after each of the commands given.

FORWARD 5   (FD 5)

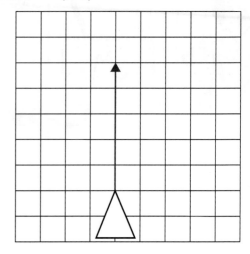

Figure 6.11 Moving forwards

Moving backwards
BACK 5   (BK 5)

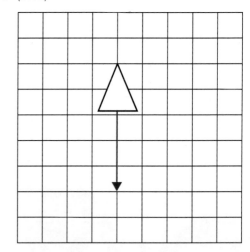

Figure 6.12 Moving backwards

This makes the turtle go backwards (Figure 6.12) but is very rarely used as it is possible to turn around completely and then go forwards instead.

Turning sideways
There are two commands that make the turtle turn to face another direction. The command must tell the turtle which way to turn and then tell it how much to turn. The number is the number of degrees in the angle that has to be turned. You can ask the turtle to turn left (Figure 6.13) or right (Figure 6.14).

LEFT 90 (LT 90)

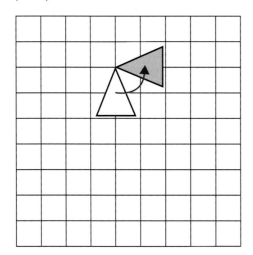

Figure 6.13 Turning left

Notice that it looks as though the turtle has moved to the right, but if you imagine the line that will be drawn by the turtle if it goes forward now, you will see that it has moved to the left. Be careful with turns, it is easy to get mixed up.

RIGHT 90   (RT 90)

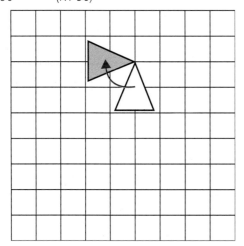

Figure 6.14 Turning right

Sometimes you want the turtle to move without leaving a line behind it. If this is the case then before you move the turtle it is necessary to tell it to lift the pen off the paper. The command is PENUP. This does not need a number after it. The turtle will now move around without drawing anything until it is told to put the pen back onto the paper. The command for this is PENDOWN.

Imagine you want to draw a square of side 4 units. The commands would be:

| FORWARD 4 | (FD 4) | FORWARD 4 | (FD 4) |
| RIGHT 90 | (RT 90) | RIGHT 90 | (RT 90) |

| FORWARD 4 | (FD 4) | FORWARD 4 | (FD 4) |
| RIGHT 90 | (RT 90) | RIGHT 90 | (RT 90) |

The result would be as shown in Figure 6.15.

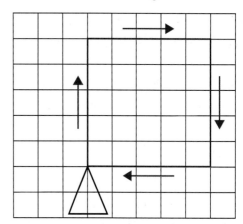

Figure 6.15 Moving the pen

QUESTION 6.04

Is the final command necessary? How would the diagram be different if it was not there? How would the diagram change if the RIGHT 90 commands had been before the FORWARD 4 commands? How would the diagram have changed if the turn commands had been LEFT 90 instead of RIGHT 90? What would the diagram look like if the turn commands had alternated between RIGHT 90 and LEFT 90?

When using turtle graphics, it is very easy to become confused between RIGHT and LEFT as the turtle moves around the page. Always make sure that the turtle is pointing away from you before you try to do the next command. You can do this by moving the paper around as the diagram is drawn.

Repeating

The set of commands that drew the square were a bit tedious because they are the same commands done over and over again. This can be shortened to make it easier to write down.

Consider the commands for drawing the square; there were four pairs of:

FORWARD 4   RIGHT 90

If these are going to be put on the same line we need to make sure that they are kept separate, so a comma is put in between them:

FORWARD 4, RIGHT 90

Now, this pair of commands needs to be done more than once:

REPEAT FORWARD 4, RIGHT 90

We don't need the gap, but we do need to make it clear what commands we want to be repeated, so these commands are put in brackets:

REPEAT (FORWARD 4, RIGHT 90)

This will certainly draw the square, the problem is that it will go round and round the square for ever because there is nothing to stop it. We need to tell the computer the number of times that it should do the commands in the bracket. The answer in this case is 4, because a square has 4 sides:

REPEAT 4 (FORWARD 4, RIGHT 90)

The REPEAT command is the last of the commands that are needed for the exam work.

QUESTION 6.05

a A student has been asked to write a command for drawing an equilateral triangle. The command produced is REPEAT 3 (FORWARD 5, LEFT 60). Draw the diagram which this command will produce and explain why it does not work. What should the correct command be? Try to produce a command to draw a regular hexagon.

What would be the result of running the following command?

REPEAT 4 ((REPEAT 4 (FORWARD 4, LEFT 90), RIGHT 90)

Try to produce some simple drawings and the commands that will produce them.

b LOGO is a very powerful programming language. Investigate how it can be used. If your school has a copy of it, investigate the commands that are available for producing sounds.

Control of automatic cookers

In Chapter 2, automatic washing machines were discussed; now consider a cooker with an automatic function. An automatic cooker has two inputs made by the user: the desired temperature and the length of cooking time. A sensor measures the temperature in the cooker and the microprocessor controls a heating element to keep the temperature constant. The microprocessor controls a light or a buzzer to inform the user when the cooking time is up.

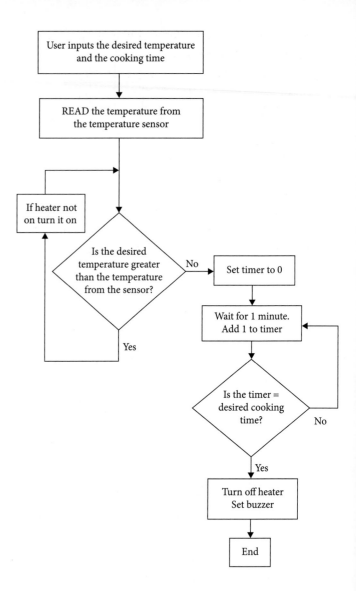

Figure 6.16 Flowchart illustrating the questions asked and decisions made by the microprocessor in an automatic cooker

Central heating and air conditioning controllers

You need to consider six factors for control applications. Here they are in the context of keeping a room warm (or cool) enough for its occupants:

1 What inputs are needed? Inputs from the user: room temperature required; time system turns on; time system turns off. Inputs from the system: temperature sensor will input the actual room temperature; clock gives the time of day.

2 The desired outcome: in this case, the heating or cooling of the room to the temperature input by the user. This should only be carried out at the times when the system should be switched on.

3   The item under control. The microprocessor will need to control a boiler (for the heating system) or an air conditioner (for the cooling system).

4   Normal operation. The microprocessor will first check the time on its clock against the time that the user has input that it should be switched on. When the system reaches that time and is switched on, the microprocessor compares the time against the time that the user has input for the system to be switched off. When it reaches that time, it switches off and goes back to comparing time to see if it should be switched on.

When the system is on, the microprocessor reads the temperature from the temperature sensor and compares it with the preset, desired temperature. If the temperature is too low (heating system) it will turn the boiler on until it is warm enough. If the temperature is too high (cooling system) it will turn the air conditioner on until the room is cool enough.

5   Measurement interval. The microprocessor will need to monitor the temperature sensor on a continual basis while the system is switched on, but a boiler or an air conditioner takes time to alter the temperature of a room so the time delay will need to be about five minutes between taking measurements.

6   Error conditions. If the temperature is not changing then it may mean that a window is open, that the boiler is not lighting properly or that the air conditioner is broken. The microprocessor needs a method of informing the user that the system is unable to control the temperature.

Most devices that are computer controlled follow these rules in much the same way. In a typical controller for a central heating system the user sets the required temperature as well as the on and off times of the system. The microprocessor makes decisions based on the user inputs and the readings from the sensors.

Computer-controlled glasshouses

The temperature in a glasshouse will be controlled just like the central heating controller. The humidity in the glasshouse must also be controlled. A humidity sensor tells the computer how humid it is and the computer can then make a decision to turn on the water supply to the sprayers.

The windows can also be opened or closed by the computer.

Glasshouses may also have blinds on the glass that can be computer controlled. A light sensor measures the light intensity. When the sun is at its strongest the computer actuates electric motors which draw the blinds down so that the plants are shaded.

Computer control can be used for a single glasshouse in a garden, but it is more likely to be used in commercial areas and large glasshouse complexes where it is simply not feasible for human beings to carry out the large number of necessary adjustments to maintain optimal growing conditions.

Burglar alarms

A simple burglar alarm detects when a door or window is open using a simple magnet and contact switch. A signal is sent to the control application which sets off the alarm. One sensor not mentioned yet is a movement sensor. These use infrared light to detect when there is movement within the range of the sensor. The radiation of infrared light from objects in the sensor's field of view should be constant. If there is something moving in range then the pattern of the infrared light changes and the sensor detects this change. These sensors are called **passive infrared** (PIR) sensors.

> **QUESTION 6.06**
>
> Research how movement sensors ignore small animals. (You could start by looking at how an automatic floor clearer works, or how an automatic lawnmower works; they both need to avoid small animals.)

6.05 Modelling applications

Computer modelling uses mathematical formulae to describe something. The formulae are used to analyse or predict how something will behave in different conditions. For example, a computer model of a building could test how it will react to an earthquake or to hurricane force winds.

There are two obvious reasons for modelling a situation: to test situations without endangering anybody; to test their feasibility without spending large sums of money (building a prototype to find that it doesn't work is expensive).

If a computer model is produced of a new design of car, the individual parts of the car can be studied in great detail in specific conditions. However, the 'thing' being modelled can be anything from an atom to a rear suspension system to a reservoir to a planet!

Spreadsheets

Spreadsheets are very valuable for simple computer modelling because they allow 'what if . . . ?' questions to be asked.

A family can store their family finances in a spreadsheet. A school tuck shop can store the records of the shop in a spreadsheet. This allows questions to be asked like: 'Apples are preferred to other types of fruit but students do not buy them because of the price we are charging. What would be the effect of cutting the profit we make on every purchase?'

If our assumption about the preference for apples is valid then we should be able to reduce the cost of an apple in the spreadsheet model and increase the number sold. We would need to factor into our spreadsheet the likes and dislikes of students. The spreadsheet should then be able to predict the increase or the decrease in the profits.

6.06 Applications in manufacturing industries

Robotics

Robotics were discussed in Chapter 1 as they have a major role within the manufacturing industry. You should look back at Chapter 1 to remind yourself about the use of robots and then remind yourself of their advantages and disadvantages below.

Advantages and disadvantages of using computer controlled systems rather than humans

Although the initial costs of robots can be high, they can reduce costs in manufacturing industries through increased speed, being able to work continuously (no need for breaks), reduced labour costs (no need to train and re-train or hire new staff), higher product quality and the ability to carry out work in areas that may be too dangerous, too repetitive or too physically demanding for humans.

Some disadvantages of robots include the fact that they cannot make independent decisions. If something happens that was not programmed for, they cannot

change their actions to accommodate the new situation. The initial setup costs can be very high and they create unemployment for humans. They sometimes break down and then there is no one to carry on their work while they are being repaired.

6.07 School management systems

School registration systems

School registration systems are based on OMR system technologies. This type of input was described in Chapter 2. Sheets are printed with ink that is readable by human beings but not by the scanning process. These inks tend to be blue or pink pastel shades. Instructions are given to the user using these inks on the paper and areas are assigned in which the user can make marks. The positions of the marks rather than the marks themselves are the important thing. When the page is scanned the only thing input to the computer will be the coordinates of the marks and the computer can then tell which areas have been shaded in and hence what the user intended to be input.

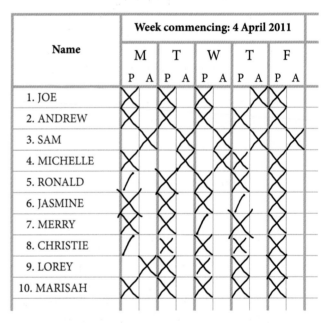

Figure 6.17 Part of school registration form for a class. The form has been designed for use with an OMR system. The teacher marks the appropriate box for a given student: P = present, A = absent

Recording learner performance

Most school management systems typically allow staff to record student grades and then automatically calculate the final grades to appear in the reports that go home to parents. The built-in functions enable teachers to filter student data in order to track student performance. Some more sophisticated systems will automatically alert staff to potential underperformers so that no underperforming students go undetected and all students can receive the assistance they may require when they need it the most.

Examinations are organised on demand by some examination boards. The school management system is capable of carrying out all the tasks associated with this based on the data input into the system. Automated emails will be sent to examination boards, staff, students and parents to remind everyone of an impending examination. Students only have to login to a computer with the secure login details to take the examinations. In some cases they are informed of the results as soon as they have completed the examination. However, not all examinations are conducted online and on demand yet.

Similarly, creating timetables and organising teaching cover or substitution timetables are also handled by the school management system simply by inputting some important information into the system. The formulas and functions built into the system produce error-free timetables. When staff had to create similar timetables themselves, it often took several revisions before they managed to create a perfect version. Changes to the timetable are also effected much more efficiently, and the system can inform all those concerned instantaneously using electronic communications such as email and mobile phone alerts.

6.08 Booking systems

Consider a concert being held in a theatre. It is necessary to sell the 1000 tickets that are available to people who want to buy a ticket in advance. The promoter of the concert decides that instead of just selling the tickets at the theatre they will be on sale at a number of different shops in the area. Each shop needs to be allocated blocks of seats to sell otherwise the same seat may get sold twice. The promoter decides to let each of the ten shops have 100 tickets to sell. The problem of the same ticket being sold twice will not happen now because each of the tickets is unique. However, there is now another problem. Some of the shops might sell out and have to send people away without a ticket, while other shops do not sell all their allocation and this will mean empty seats on the night of the concert. This would not happen if there was a way of allowing the popular shops to sell the unwanted tickets from the other shops. This could be done by

physically moving the tickets from one shop to another, or it could be done by leaving the tickets in one place and allowing the individual shops to have access to them via computer communications.

Theatre booking systems

Theatre booking systems allow booking agents in different locations to be in communication with a central computer system which stores details of the available seats for shows.

When a customer rings or goes into the agency or shop:

- The customer states their requirements, which will include the name of the show or concert, the date for which tickets are required and the number and type of tickets that are wanted.

- The agent will then go online to the computer system and search for suitable tickets. While this is being done no other customers can be serviced because of the danger of selling the same ticket twice. This is called locking the file so that no one else can change anything. More sophisticated systems just lock individual seats to avoid jamming the system up.

When the tickets are agreed:

- The customer pays by card (or cash if the shop has that facility agreed with the theatre).

- The seats that have been bought are changed to show 'sold' on the computer system.

- The file of seats is unlocked so that other customers can make bookings.

- The ticket is printed out at the shop or a receipt (an eticket) is printed out which will be exchanged for the full ticket at the theatre.

This is an example of a real-time computing application.

This system can be extended to allow the same sort of booking on the internet.

The advantages and disadvantages of an on-line booking system.

Advantages:

- Online booking saves time

- There is no need to discuss with another person

- You can get immediate information about availability

- Online booking systems can send an automatic email to you to confirm your booking.

79

Disadvantages:

- The system is expensive to install initially

- Cost of staff training

- An online database and a website would both need to be created and have the ability to communicate with each other, in order for a customer to be able to search online for availability of the booking they require.

- In order to ensure absolute reliability, time and cost will need to be expended to keep the database up to date and the system functioning correctly.

> **QUESTION 6.07**
>
> Think about the advantages and disadvantages of an online booking system and try to add to the lists above.

Cinema booking

Cinema bookings can be done in much the same way. Customers can book over the internet; they can also book using the keypad on a mobile phone. The payment may be made immediately. When the customer gets to the cinema they go to a ticket machine, type in their reference number and feed in their credit or debit card. The machine debits the card and prints out the ticket.

This allows the owners of the cinema to reduce their costs by employing fewer people than they would otherwise have to without the automated system.

Travel applications

The travel industry allows bookings to be made by individual customers using the internet, or by travel agents. It is just as easy for customers to do their own bookings as it is to use a travel agent, but many customers

continue to use travel agents to book holidays. The reasons are:

- Some customers do not have internet access.

- Travel agents give insurance against the travel company going out of business. If the customer books the holiday themselves they may find it difficult to get their money refunded or may have difficulty if they are actually on holiday when it happens.

- The process is rather harder than booking a cinema ticket and it may prove too daunting for some people to contemplate if they are not very ICT literate.

Airlines commonly encourage passengers to book over the internet. Internet booking allows the costs of tickets to be reduced. The passenger is issued with a reference number, which is emailed to them after a successful booking has been made. This can be used to check in online, which saves time at the airport.

6.09 Banking applications

Electronic funds transfer

Part of the process for producing a payroll for a company is that after calculating the amount that a worker has earned during the week, the computer arranges for the money to be paid into the worker's bank account. This does not involve cash being taken to the bank and paid in over the counter. This movement of funds is called **electronic funds transfer** (EFT). An EFT message is sent to the company's bank asking that the money be taken out of the company account. An EFT message is then sent to the worker's bank stating that the correct amount of money should be added to the worker's account. The flow of the data is shown in Figure 6.18.

> **KEY TERMS**
>
> **EFT:** Electronic Funds Transfer.

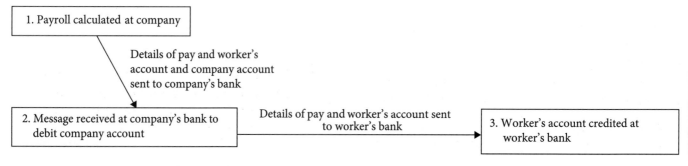

Figure 6.18 Using EFT to pay workers

EFT is used at checkouts in supermarkets; although it is still possible to pay with cash, the preferred payment method is either a debit or credit card. The card is inserted into the card reader at the point of sale (POS) terminal, and the funds are then transferred electronically from the card holder's account to the supermarket's account in the same way as the worker's pay is transferred.

Individual customers can also use EFT while carrying out their banking requirements using internet banking. The customer is asked for their identification checks and is then allowed to state specific accounts to which they want to transfer money from their own accounts. The only other details needed are the bank code and the account number that the funds should be sent to. The transfers are then carried out immediately.

ATMs

An automated teller machine (ATM; sometimes called the hole in the wall) is the machine outside banks and in other locations that allows you to carry out transactions such as withdrawing and depositing cash or cheques, checking your balance and paying bills without actually going into the bank. There are many other services available at an ATM, such as topping up a mobile phone or selecting a language to use.

The customer needs to provide identification by using a plastic card provided by the bank and a PIN (personal identification number).

These processes are all real-time processes because the account needs to be checked and updated without delay.

> **KEY TERMS**
>
> **ATM:** Automated Teller Machine.

Telephone banking

Telephone banking is a service offered by banking institutions. When it first became available a customer could make a telephone call to the bank and the bank employee would ask a series of security questions before carrying out the requested transaction for the customer.

When touch-tone telephones became generally available, a customer could call the bank, and using the keypad on a touch-tone telephone would respond to automated questions, before carrying out transactions without the need for intervention by a bank employee.

A typical customer of telephone banking can access their account(s) check their balance and latest activity, transfer funds between accounts, order a new cheque book, make payments on a loan or request information on other services offered by the bank.

Before touch-tone telephones, it was labour intensive for bank employees, but now it offers the customer a baking service night and day that they can access from home.

Credit/debit cards

You will remember that the use of bank cards was discussed in Chapter 2. When a card is used, the same sort of funds transfer is carried out as described in the EFT example at the start of this section. There are slight differences over where the funds come from.

If the card used is a credit card the message is sent to the credit card company. The credit card company then arranges for funds to be sent to the account of the organisation which has accepted payment using the card.

The credit card company then stores the information that the card has been used, where it was used and how much was spent in the transaction. This information is collected together once a month and a statement is sent to the card holder showing them how much they owe. Notice that the use of a credit card requires both real-time processing for payments and batch processing for the production of statements.

Debit cards are used in the same way but the customer is dealing with their bank when they use their debit card rather than a credit card company. The bank will debit the customer account immediately (a real-time process) rather than waiting to produce a statement at the end of the month. The transaction will simply be shown as a payment on the normal bank statement.

> **QUESTION 6.08**
>
> **a** Research internet banking to find out how it operates.
>
> **b** Using a word processor and writing using your own words, describe the process of internet banking; then list its advantages and disadvantages.

6.10 Computers in medicine

The study and practice of medicine is an enormous subject and continually growing. Computer technology is important in helping health professionals provide as reliable and efficient a service as possible and also in keeping them aware of medical advances.

Diagnostic systems

When a patient goes to see a doctor they may have symptoms of an ailment. They go to see a doctor because of the doctor's expertise and experience, but no doctor can be expected to be an expert in every part of medicine.

The problem is that there is so much information about diseases and symptoms that doctors need help to make sure they have not missed anything. They used to get this extra information from books but nowadays this has been superseded by information held on computer systems.

Computer systems can hold more information, can be updated regularly and can use computing techniques to aid searches for information. In order to produce a system which will be useful for doctors, the accepted knowledge about diseases and conditions and their symptoms are collected together. This means interviewing expert doctors to collect their knowledge and using information from books. This knowledge is all collected together and stored in the computer. There needs to be some way for the doctor to interrogate the data that is stored and also for the computer to output answers to the doctor's questions. There needs to be a set of rules which tell the computer how different parts of the data fit together and interact with each other. Finally, there needs to be a program which is able to apply the rules to the data to come up with sensible results. When all these parts are put together a system is created which in some respects is more expert than the doctor. It is called an expert system.

There are many types of expert system. We will consider here an expert system for medical diagnosis. On its own, used by a non-expert, it is not reliable for diagnosis. Diagnosis needs experience and the human ability to relate to individual patients. However, it is a powerful tool for the doctor.

The four parts of a medical expert system are:

- the facts about illnesses and conditions – the knowledge base

- the means of asking questions and getting responses from the system – the user interface or human – computer interface (HCI)

- the set of rules that the data has to abide by – the rule base

- the program that can apply the rules to the data in order to get sensible results – the inference engine.

All expert systems have these four parts (Figure 6.19).

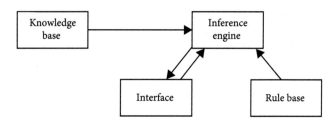

Figure 6.19 Flowchart representing an expert system

Pharmacy records

When a doctor has diagnosed a patient's problem they may prescribe medicine. There are thousands of medicines available, each of which has possible side effects and lists of other medicines that they should not be mixed with. All this information can be found in large reference books which doctors use.

What the doctor needs is all this information stored on the computer. Information stored like this is an **information system**. The doctor can search the system for possible medicines to prescribe and can see the information that is available on each one. This sounds very like an expert system. The difference is that the emphasis in the diagnosis system is on the expert system making decisions. When considering the medicines information system the emphasis is on providing information.

Patient records

Your doctor, and the team of health professionals who care for you all keep records about your health and any treatment and care you receive from them. For example, when someone is admitted to hospital, their details are entered into the patient record system. Once this information is on record, whenever that patient is admitted in the future, their records can be found very quickly. The typical information held on record for a patient could include:

- Name, address and next of kin

- History of contact with the hospital, clinic or surgery

- Notes and reports about health, treatment and care given

- X-rays and laboratory tests

- Relevant information from other health professionals

- Relatives or people who care for the patient

Monitoring patients

Computerised monitors are used for patients in hospital who need close monitoring because doctors and nurses are not able to do this continuously. Sensors can be attached to a patient to monitor their pulse rate, temperature, breathing rate per minute, their blood oxygen levels and blood pressure. The sensors send the information to a computer where the data is checked for problems, such as the breathing or pulse rate being too high or too low; can be logged for checking later. Outputs from this type of system can be displayed in the form of graphs on a screen display; a loud alarm can be sounded to attract the attention of a nurse or a doctor if there is a sudden problem.

Security of patient records and systems

There is reason for concern about the implications of security, access and use of electronic patient information. Some of the concerns are:

- Hacking which can lead to the altering of patient data or destruction of the systems

- Misuse of health information records by authorised users of the systems

- Long term data management concerns about keeping data secure in the future

- The possibility of intrusion into personal healthcare matters by the police, insurers, social workers, other government or corporate institutions

3D printers for medical aids

You read about 3D printers in Section 1.05, but did you know that most hearing aids are already created using 3D printers, and that scientists have also worked out the theory of how to print blood vessels and skin, and even embryonic stem cells?

In medicine, 3D printers are having most success with prosthetics such as dental work and hearing aids (as mentioned above). These may all be made from either plastic or pliable materials. They need to be made for a specific patient, so each will be individual, rather than mass produced.

The categories of healthcare where 3D printing can be applied are for body parts or prosthetics, medical devices and human tissues.

Medical 3D printing is expanding quickly in areas such as the creation of: tissues and organs; customised prosthetics, implants, anatomical models and more. The benefits of 3D printing for medical tools and equipment include: customising and personalising medical products drugs and equipment; cost-effectiveness; increased productivity; the democratization of design and manufacturing; and enhanced collaboration.

> 3D printers have been taken to war-torn areas where many people have had to have limbs amputated.

Unlike inkjet printers, 3D printers have an additional axis, called the z-axis. They have a mechanism called an elevator that moves a platform up and down to achieve printing on the z-axis. Also unlike inkjet printers, its cartridge is filled with substances other than ink. If the cartridge were filled with plastic, it would output a three-dimensional plastic appliance according to the instructions given; if the cartridge were filled with cells, then it would output a mass of cells. In a similar way that an inkjet printer uses cartridges filled with different colours, so a 3D printer can have cartridges filled with different types of materials. If a drawing is carried out using CAD software for example, and the cartridges filled with the correct substances, then it is possible to print items as prosthetic hands, arms, legs, etc.

6.11 Computers in libraries

The use of computers in school libraries was covered earlier in this chapter (Section 6.02). The same points that were made then will apply to the uses made of computer systems in larger libraries. However, in a larger library there will be a different form of input. This will almost certainly be by bar code readers. The readers will use the bar code from the book that is being borrowed and will read the member ID from the member's library card.

EXTENSION ACTIVITY 6.06

a Why will the ISBN of the books in the Books file be replaced by a book ID?

b Discuss the other differences between the school library system and a larger, public library system before reading any further. Note that there are no 'right answers' here, because all libraries tend to use similar but different systems.

c What is the Dewey system of classification? What part will that play in a computerised library system?

Note that there will be a need for a member ID to identify the member rather than using the name, as was done in the school library example earlier. The reason for this is that there are far more members of a public library than there are of a school library.

A library database will typically have a minimum of the following tables: a books table, a borrower table and a loans table. The loans table would have a **Book ID**, a **Borrower ID**, the Date of Loan and the Due Date.

Regular checks for loans that are overdue for return can be made by searching for Due date is before Today, or Today is greater than Due Date.

When late records are found, the borrower ID can be used to link to the borrower's record. The borrower's address / email can then be used to issue reminder automatically for overdue books.

QUESTION 6.09

a How will the system know about members who still do not return books despite having been sent a letter?

b How can the tables be slightly altered so that a similar letter is not sent again tomorrow?

6.12 Expert systems

Expert systems were explained above, where an expert system to aid medical diagnosis was described. The same four principles of collecting knowledge from experts in the field apply for the following applications.

Mineral prospecting

Mineral prospecting differs from medical diagnosis because of the types of data that the expert system works with. There is still the knowledge base which is created by using the combined knowledge of as many experts as possible. However, there are other forms of data that can be used:

- Satellite data can be input. This can be in the form of pictures of the Earth's surface, which may show outlines of the ground that are not otherwise visible.

- Sensors can be positioned on the ground to capture tiny movements, which may show that there is seismic activity in the area.

- Data from geological surveys can be input. For example, an explosion is set off on the surface some kilometres away from sensors that are placed on the surface. According to the length of time that it takes the shockwave to reach the sensors and the strength of those shockwaves, it is possible to create maps of what is beneath the surface.

Using all this data, the expert system can then make predictions as to the likelihood of finding particular minerals in that area. Note that what is produced is a prediction; certainty of an outcome is not possible. This type of expert system will predict whether a particular mineral is present by giving a probability of its presence as a percentage.

Car engine fault diagnosis

When you take a car for a service, a diagnostic tool will be used to find problems. Diagnostic software will access the computer system in the car where fault codes for problems are stored. Modern cars have computer processors, microchips and sensors which link to the diagnostic scanner; some vehicles have several units to control areas such as engine management, brakes, suspension, windscreen wipers and so forth.

The advantages are that mechanics can easily identify problems and repair them as quickly as possible; the problem diagnosis is quick and accurate so there can be cost savings as less time is used by a mechanic to identify any problems; small problems can be found and corrected before they can escalate into larger, expensive problems!

EXTENSION ACTIVITY 6.07

Try to find out what types of sensor are used to provide evidence for a car engine diagnosis expert system.

Chess computers

Chess computers are programmed with strategies for playing the game. They are able to quantify how good their position and their opponent's position is. At each turn they work through possible moves, trying to analyse what the outcome will be and hence find the strongest move.

The best machines have a degree of intelligence in that they can learn when they do something wrong. When these computers are beaten they will analyse the moves so that if the same situation arises in a future game they will not make the same mistake again.

Expert systems that 'learn' in the way that the best chess-playing systems do have gone one stage beyond a normal expert system and are said to use artificial intelligence.

6.13 Computers in the retail industry

The stock of a business is the items that it either manufactures or sells or uses. To keep track of their stock as items are bought in, sold or used, a business needs a **stock control system**.

In a supermarket, the stock will include everything on the shelves and in the storerooms.

The advantages are:

- save money on keeping too much stock of any item
- prevent perishable stock from going off before it is sold
- prevents running out of stock.

When items arrive at the store, they are added in to the stock levels in the stock control system, usually using a bar code scanner, and the stock level is increased.

In many stores, the point of sale system at the checkout is linked to the stock control system. This means that as soon as an item is sold the stock levels are automatically adjusted.

With such a system of automated entry when stock is delivered and when it is sold, it is very easy for stock levels to be monitored. This enables stock to be reordered when it is running low.

This is effected by the stock control system checking if the stock level for every item is less than the minimum stock level required to be kept. The appropriate stock is then reordered from the supplier.

This system of reordering as soon as the minimum reorder level is met is a **real-time** system. However, if the manager requires to see all of the necessary orders before they are sent out, they will be collected for them to consider together and to give them approval. This collection of the information is what turns the system into a **batch process**. So this has become a batch system rather than a real-time system.

POS/EFTPOS

Point of sale (POS) terminals are terminals that are set up at the exits of supermarkets that allow shoppers to pay for their goods in the following way:

- The shopper presents their purchases.
- The items are scanned using a bar code reader.
- The stock file is searched for the bar code.
- When it is found:
  - The number in the stock file has one subtracted from it.
  - The number in the stock file is checked against the minimum stock level and the need to order more of this stock is added to the list to be sent to the manager at the end of the day if necessary.
  - The description and price of the article is sent to the terminal.
- The price and description are displayed on the screen.
- The price and description are printed on a till receipt.
- The price is added to the total so far.

This means that shoppers have a printed record of their purchases and are able to check for errors. The system proves to be very popular with shoppers, which pleases the management of the supermarket because more people come to shop in the store.

If there is a chip and PIN reader added to the POS it becomes an electronic funds transfer at the point of sale (EFTPOS) terminal. Not only does the system control stock levels and produced itemised receipts, but it also controls the way that payment is made. Customers are encouraged to pay by card because this will reduce the amount of cash being handled at the tills.

Internet shopping

Internet or online shopping means that you can visit web stores while sitting in front of your computer. Just about anything can be bought online. Products available include

85

books, clothing, household appliances, toys, hardware, software, health insurance, cars and batteries, and these are just some of the many millions of products that can be bought from an online store.

The advantages are:

- there is often more choice

- goods are usually less expensive

- people choose to shop online because of the convenience as you don't have to travel to the store

- disabled or elderly people may find it easier to use online shopping than to go to a town to source their requirements

- when purchasing a book from a bookstore, each household drives separately, but delivery trucks deliver to many customers on a single route so less fuel emissions are created

- buying multiple books online from the same seller results in fewer emissions from transport

- more employment for delivery drivers / delivery companies

- no need to stand in a long line at the checkout

- online stores don't close

- there is worldwide access to online goods

- comparison sites can be used to find the most appropriate or least expensive option

- shopping sites online usually provide reviews from previous customers to assist in decision making

Despite the convenience of online shopping, people do not always choose to use it. The disadvantages are:

- you cannot touch or try the merchandise

- fear of credit or debit card being compromised

- not everyone has a computer or is ICT literate enough to carry out their shopping online.

- not everyone is confident in using the technology to order and pay for goods online

6.14 Recognition systems

MICR, OMR, RFID and OCR were covered in Section 2.02 earlier in this book. You will remember that:

- MICR stands for Magnetic Ink Character Reader and that the numbers on the bottom of a cheque are printed using magnetic ink so that they can be read by a special reader even if they have been written over.

- OMR stands for Optical Mark Recognition, and involves scans from specially prepared hard copy forms that have spaces for a mark to be placed, such as on a register or a multiple-choice answer sheet. An example of a specific use of OMR is multiplechoice examination papers.

- RFID stands for Radio Frequency IDentification and is a device that can scan in a unique identifier for an object that has an RFID chip.

- OCR is Optical Character Recognition because it can read each character in text from a paper document that has been scanned in and reproduce it in a form that can be edited by you in a word processor.

You have seen how RFID (Section 2.02) can be used to purchase goods in a supermarket using contactless payments; it can also be applied to passports or cars.

Passports

Many governments are changing their immigration and migration laws and regulations to combat the forging of passports. When a passport with an RFID chip is presented near a computer with an RFID scanner, the scanner provides enough energy for the chip to broadcast the information held, which is then read into a computer.

The small chip can hold enough information to make it impossible for a person to fake their identity. Information such as photographs, fingerprints and detailed documents can be encoded into the chip. This means that although a person might be able to change the photograph on their passport, they won't be able to change their fingerprints to match those held in the chip.

Processing of cheques

You saw in Section 2.02 how MICR is used to scan in information on a cheque when it is paid into the bank. Once that has been done, a process is started whereby the cheque has to be 'cleared', the proceeds paid into

Figure 6.20 The process of paying by cheque

the recipient's bank account and then the same amount deducted from the payer's bank account (Figure 6.20).

The use of cheques has greatly declined as businesses are now using automated payments and cards. It is still an important payment method though, in particular for small businesses.

After the cheque has been paid in to the recipient's bank and it has been scanned using MICR at their bank, the electronic data is sent to the bank's clearing house. All cheques are sorted and the sort code, account number and bank number from the bottom of the cheque, as well as the amount, are sent to the payer's bank.

The paying bank debits the payer's bank account with the amount written on the cheque and forwards the amount to the recipient's account.

Cheques are paper items and they are also physically transferred between banks at the same time as the electronic data is processed.

Automatic number plate recognition (ANPR) system

Automatic number plate recognition (**ANPR**) technology can be used to help detect and deter criminal activity. It can help to find travelling criminals, organised crime groups and terrorists. ANPR can provide evidence in the investigation and can be used by law enforcement agencies.

KEY TERMS

ANPR: Automatic number plate recognition.

This is how it works: as a vehicle passes an ANPR camera, the vehicle's registration number is read and immediately checked against a database of records of vehicles of interest to the police. The records for all vehicles passing by a camera are stored. The use of ANPR can help in the detection of offences, such as in finding stolen or uninsured vehicles and solving cases of terrorism as well as organised crime.

6.15 Monitoring and tracking systems

These are real-time systems that allow employers to stay connected with their workforce to see where they are at any time. This usually works by every employee having an app on their mobile phone; the employer can then set up an online account to view a web portal where they will be able to check the current locations of their employees.

The app will also usually have a 'send location' button that allows the employee to check in at the current location.

The tracking of members of the public with a smartphone is also possible if the 'send location' facility is activated on their phone. If you are travelling then this would be using data from the allocation in your contract as it will be constantly accessing the internet. This could prove costly and you may not want others to be able to track you so you should consider carefully before this facility is turned on.

Cookies

Many of the websites that you visit use **cookies**. This means that they write a small file called a 'cookie' to your computer's hard drive either without you knowing it or by asking your permission first.

KEY TERMS

Cookie: data put onto your hard disk by the website you are browsing.

A cookie is a unique identifier placed on your computer by a web server and can be used to retrieve your records from their databases. Once a cookie is in your computer, it will track your movement around the website that put it there and the cookie can be read by the site's owners.

Cookies do many different jobs: they let you navigate between pages efficiently and they store your preferences. This can generally improve your experience when you are

87

browsing a website by making the interaction between you and the website faster.

When you purchase goods or services from a website you need to fill in forms with your name and address details and payment information. Cookies remember your information so you don't need to fill in the same form every time you buy something from them.

Unfortunately, some cookies help the websites that put them onto your computer more than they help you. Some websites use cookies to help them to target advertising based on your location and/or browsing history; some provide personal information to others that you may not want anyone else to know. Some types of cookie can discover the type of computer and software that you are using and some may be able to get your email address. They may sell such data to advertisers, marketing firms, those who want to send junk email, and so on.

> **QUESTION 6.10**
>
> Find out how to delete the cookies stored on your computer.

Key-logging

Key-logging is a method of recording all the keystrokes that you make on a computer keyboard. Either hardware or software can be used to do this. Some employers use such a system openly to monitor their employees' computer use; in this case key-logging is a surveillance tool. However, if it is used covertly, then it would be classified as spyware; if the key-logging software hides itself in the system, this would make them fully fledged Trojan programs (see Chapter 8).

As such programs can be used by cyber criminals, detecting them has become a priority for antivirus software companies.

Employee call monitoring

Some employers, who are concerned that their business telephones are being used by their employees for personal calls, monitor employees' calls. On the other hand, some employers may need to monitor phone calls so that they can evaluate their customer service department. The employers could then use the recording of conversations between customers and their customer service department for further training. So employee call monitoring can have advantages for the employer and for the employee, especially for security purposes in case for instance, any verbal abuse occurred.

Electronic tagging devices

Devices for electronic tagging can be used in many situations such as monitoring the well-being of the elderly and tracking offenders.

Some devices allow the monitoring of a patient's disorder to aid early intervention which could help avoid complications. Other tagging devices can detect whether an elderly patient has taken a fall, or it can remind a patient that it is time to take their medication or if they suffer from a type of dementia that could cause them to get lost, they can be traced. Monitors can help those who wear them to keep track of their own health and fitness thereby helping them lose weight or to sleep better.

A tracking device can be worn around the neck of a patient, or elsewhere about their person such as clipped to a belt or carried on their key ring. This type of tag has a button enables the wearer to speak directly to an operator in a 24-hour call centre. This can be useful if the patient has a fall in their home.

The tagging of offenders can be used to help to reduce prison populations because if a person wearing a tag moves out of their designated boundaries, the tag sends a signal to a monitoring centre.

6.16 Satellite systems

Wherever you are at any time, there are several GPS satellites 'visible'. They each send a signal to a GPS receiver such as your smartphone or satnav. They transmit information about the satellite position and also the current time; this information is transmitted at regular intervals and travels at the speed of light. When your receiver intercepts the signals it calculates how far away each satellite is, using data about how long it took for the messages to arrive. Once your receiver knows how far away it is from at least three satellites, it pinpoints your position using a process called **trilateration** (Figure 6.21).

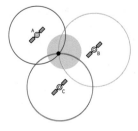

Figure 6.21 Trilateration your GPS receiver picks up a signal from the yellow satellite, you must be somewhere on the yellow circle; if it also picks up signals from the blue and red satellites, you must be at the black dot where the signals from the three satellites meet

If, before you begin a journey, you program your satnav with the information of where you want to go, the satnav will calculate the quickest route to get to your destination. However, you can choose another route if you want, by inputting various **waypoints** that you want the route to take.

Geographic information systems (GIS)

A **GIS** is a computer system for capturing, storing, checking and displaying data that relates to positions on the Earth's surface; it can show data of different kinds on one map.

The system can include data about the population, their income or education level as well as information about the land, such as rivers and streams, types of vegetation, or soil. It can include many different types of information about where there are factories, farms, schools, drains, roads, electric power lines and much more.

KEY TERMS

GIS: Geographic information systems for capturing, storing, checking and displaying data related to the surface of the Earth as a map.

Therefore, GIS gives you the power to create maps and to integrate information (Figure 6.22). It can be used to visualise scenarios and help to develop effective solutions to many problems, such as pollution, or to assess community needs and resources.

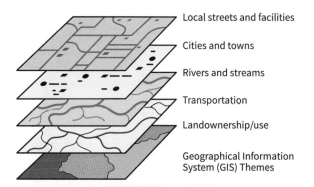

Local streets and facilities

Cities and towns

Rivers and streams

Transportation

Landownership/use

Geographical Information System (GIS) Themes

Figure 6.22 Layers of information that can be used to create a map with GIS

Media communication systems

This term is often used instead of 'mass media' or 'news media'. It relates to the use by specialised communication businesses such as the press, photography, advertising, cinema, broadcasting and/or publishing of outlets or tools that they can use to store and to transmit data.

Therefore, communication media facilitate the communication and exchange of data between a vast number of individuals, across long distances, via email, teleconferencing, internet forums and so on. It is many-to-many communication; it differs from traditional mass media channels of communication such as TV, radio or magazines, which is one-to-many communication.

The worldwide use of the internet and mobile communications, as well as social software tools, has changed communication systems into interactive networks that are connected both locally and globally. Not only social networking sites, but also media such as SMS, blogs, podcasts and wikis enable the flow of messages from many to many. They have provided for alternative mediums for communication between citizens all over the world, and allow them to participate in journalism.

Such communication systems can change and sometimes shape life worldwide.

Summary

- Key-logging is a method of recording all keystrokes that you make on a computer keyboard. Either hardware or software can be used to do this.
- MICR, OMR, RFID and OCR are all automated methods of input.
- Mobile phones are used as digital cameras, for playing computer games, for navigation, for playing music, surfing the web, accessing emails and using a host of different apps.
- Voice over internet protocol (VOIP) uses the internet to carry voice data to make phone calls.
- When using VOIP technology, the voice data is broken into packets of data that are sent along different routes to arrive at the same destination and be reassembled in the right order.
- Data analytics (DA) analyses large amounts of raw data so that conclusions can be made which can influence decision-making.
- A measuring application will measure a value or a set of values that will be processed by the computer.

Exam-Style Questions

6.01 Discuss the types of communication applications that a business might use for publicity and what benefit the use of a corporate image may bring. [3]

6.02 Explain why using computers in measurement may be better than humans taking the measurements. [2]

....

....

6.03 List **five** services offered by an Automatic Teller Machine (ATM). [5]

....

....

....

....

....

6.04 Name the **four** parts of an expert system. [4]

....

....

....

....

6.05 List **three** advantages and **two** disadvantages of online shopping. [5]

....

....

....

....

....

6.06 Describe what an RFID chip consists of. [2]

....

....

Chapter 7:
The systems life cycle

Learning objectives

When you have finished this chapter, you will be able to:

- identify methods of researching an existing system
- record and analyse information about a current system
- identify and justify a specification for a new system
- produce designs to solve a given problem
- describe testing designs, strategies and improvements
- describe methods of implementation
- identify and explain technical and user documentation for an information system
- describe evaluation strategies and why they are needed.

Overview

When an organisation, or a client, considers that one of its systems has problems or is in need of improvement, a **systems analyst** studies the system to determine where the problems are and how the system can be improved. The analyst then plans the implementation of the solution and hands the plans on to a software team to produce the solution and test it. The analyst then plans how the system is going to be imported into the organisation and arranges for continuing maintenance of the system. This whole process is known as the **systems life cycle** and can be summarised as:

- analysis
- design
- development and testing
- implementation
- documentation
- evaluation/maintenance.

KEY TERMS

Systems analyst: an IT specialist responsible for the life cycle of a new/modified IT system, from analysing the problem to implementing an entire system.

Systems life cycle: the different stages in the process of producing a new IT system.

Most software system life cycles are similar, but the names of the stages may differ.

The analyst does not start at the beginning and work straight through to the end. They may reach one stage and realise that they have to go back and find out something else or plan things differently. They may find that something does not work properly, so they have to go back and change the design. This process is called

the **waterfall model** (see Figure 7.01) of the systems life cycle. However, at each level it is possible to go back to any of the previous stages to refine the end product; this is known as **iteration**.

7.01 Analysis

The analysis stage starts with the definition of the problem, and a feasibility study. It involves looking at the problem with the client to find out the client's requirements and needs.

The people in the organisation know how their business works, the nature of the problem and how much they can spend. The analyst knows about computer systems and what is possible. In response to the problem definition, the analyst produces a report that states what is possible. This is called the **feasibility study**. If the feasibility study is accepted then this is when the collection of information begins.

Methods of researching an existing system

The information can be collected in a number of ways:

- **Observation**. The systems analyst can learn from watching what is going on in an organisation. The systems analyst will try to understand how things are done and the relationships between people's work. The advantage is that it only involves the systems analyst(s). The disadvantage is that people tend not to work in a normal way if they know they are being watched.

- **Interviews**. The systems analyst will want to find out how things work and what doesn't work properly in an organisation. The obvious thing to do is to ask

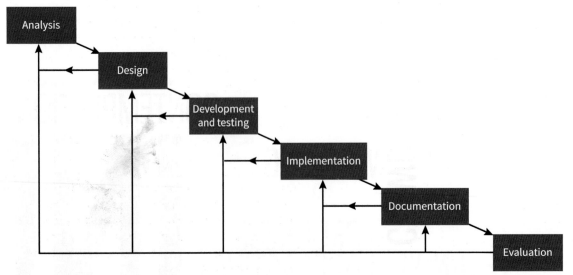

Figure 7.01 Waterfall model of the systems life cycle

the people who operate the system at the moment. Questions do not have to be fixed in advance, but it is helpful if the analyst has a logical, enquiring mind and knows how to probe for information.

- **Questionnaires**. With this method, many people's views can be obtained in a short period of time. Questionnaires are much less time-consuming for the analyst than interviews and everyone feels that their views matter. Each person also has the chance to consider their answers before filling the questionnaire in. The disadvantages are that some of the people may not take it seriously and the questions cannot be changed halfway through as they can in an interview.

- **Document collection**. Documents reveal a lot about an organisation. Some processes and procedures are captured in documents. But input and output documents should also be examined. The analyst will be looking for answers to questions like: How is the data collected? What data is collected? What happens to this data after it has been collected? A disadvantage is that documentation is often difficult to understand for someone who is outside the organisation, so it may be necessary to interview someone to explain it; also, documents do not always reveal all of the processes and procedures about a system. So raw data needs to be collated, studied and recorded. Sometimes it will bring to light areas where there are gaps in the data collected and this would mean that a further interview would be needed to clear up the confusion.

The best way to deal with information like this is to record it in a diagram that shows the passage of data through the system and the different files that are used. It should identify all of the system's inputs and outputs and how data is processed. It would also show details of the storage of files and how the files are related. Other diagrams could be used to show the hardware involved in the system. All the features of the existing system should be identified.

Throughout this stage when you are recording and analysing information about the current system, it is important for you to be able to identify the inputs, outputs and processing of the current system and to identify its problems. It is also important to note that some parts of the old system may be working very well and time and effort spent changing them could not be justified. The need for this sound background information is in order to make decisions about the design of the new system and to ensure that all of the problems with the old system will be addressed at the design stage.

In addition to addressing existing problems, it is essential to identify the requirements of each type of user for the new system so that these requirements may be designed into the new system.

Requirements specification

As the analyst collects data about the existing system and its problems, a list will be forming of what will be necessary in the solution. This list is the **requirements specification** and will include what the organisation wants the system to do, details about the storage requirements, and information about the desired hardware and software.

The requirements specification lists the things that, after consultation, the organisation has decided must be successfully done to satisfy them, and the analyst has agreed that this is what can be delivered. This agreement is extremely important to both parties and the agreement must be clear in what is expected. It is going to provide the 'rules' around which the final evaluation will be carried out.

Once the requirement specification is agreed, it leads to the next stage.

QUESTION 7.01

In your class, discuss how the analyst would best collect information in each of the three applications listed below; also discuss why the methods might differ.

a A small general purpose shop wants to install a computerised stock control system. All stock control has been done manually until now. The owner is the only person who works in the shop.

b A dress shop has used a computerised system for some time for selling items and giving receipts to customers. However, the stock is still controlled manually. The owner looks after all the ordering of stock and record keeping but does not work in the shop. The owner has decided that she wants some help to deal with suppliers and stock control in the shop. There are six shop workers.

c A large supermarket uses a fully computerised stock system together with POS terminals. The owner has decided that the present system needs updating, mainly because a rival supermarket has installed a more modern system. There are in excess of 100 workers who work in different departments in the supermarket. The supermarket stocks in excess of 30 000 items. Some workers work as shop assistants, others as supervisors; some work in the accounts department and others in site management, because it is a very big store.

Method	Advantages	Disadvantages
Observation	Allows the systems analyst to gather first-hand, unbiased information.	Often people won't be working as they normally do if they know they are being watched.
Interviews	A lot of very detailed information can be gathered.	Interviews take a long time so they are not possible if large groups of people are involved.
Questionnaires	A questionnaire is a quick and simple way to gather information.	Information gathered is limited by the questions asked and people may have information in their heads that the questionnaire doesn't ask about thus limiting usefulness. People don't always take time to fill in a questionnaire well.

Table 7.01 Advantages and disadvantages of different methods of analysis

7.02 Design

All computer systems consist of:

- input
- processing
- output
- storage.

Output designs

The purpose of the design stage is to decide what the output will look like. It may seem odd to start from what appears to be the wrong end, but the analyst's job is to produce a system that will do a particular thing. In other words, the really important part is to decide what the organisation wants to happen **in the end**. If the client likes the output, they are likely to accept the whole solution.

Imagine that the client is a mail order company and that the analyst has been asked to produce a system that will allow the telephone receptionists to take orders over the phone. The client wants the receptionists to be able to search to see if stock is available, and then place an order. They are not really interested in how the system does it. The analyst will design what the output screens must look like and then produce what is known as a **prototype**. This prototype will be realistic enough to allow the client and workers to tell whether it will be suitable for the tasks that they want it to do.

Care must be taken when designing the screens that the layout is produced properly. The content of what is output on the screen must be understandable to the people who are going to be using it. At all stages the client and the workers who will be using the system must be able to have a say in the acceptability of the screen designs.

Figure 7.02 Analyst with client workers who have input to the design

The client may decide that the company logo must appear on every screen and that the corporate colour scheme should be used for the backgrounds. One of the workers may be colour blind and consequently some colour schemes should not be used. This sort of detail should have been found out in the analysis stage. Many things that can happen that force the analyst to go back to a previous stage and change the requirements specification, and hence the design.

QUESTION 7.02

What term is used to describe going back to a previous stage which results in an improvement to the end product?

Input designs

Once the output has been designed, it is clear what the inputs should be and it is then possible to design the input screens. These input screens go through the same prototyping process as the output screens. Not all input data will come from input screens, however. The analyst has to decide how that data will be collected and design a method of inputting it. For example:

- Will automatic data collection be used? For example, a sensor tells the system when someone enters a building or what the temperature of a process is.
- Are questionnaires (**data capture forms**) going to be used? If they are, should they be designed so that the answer sheets can be read by a special OMR or OCR machine?
- Is the data going to be input by someone using a keyboard and a screen?

When data is entered into the system it will have to be checked for accuracy because any computer system can only be as good as the data that is used in it. Therefore the input data will need to be validated and verified.

Figure 7.03 Example of a data capture form

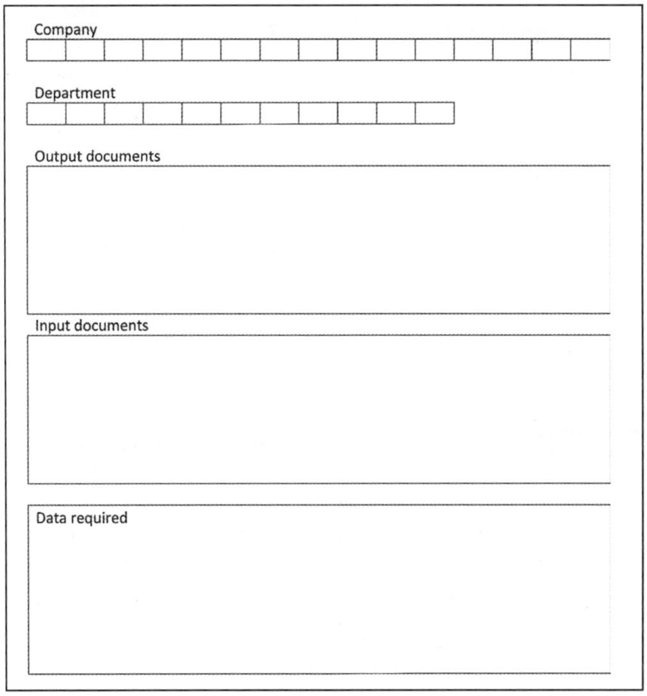

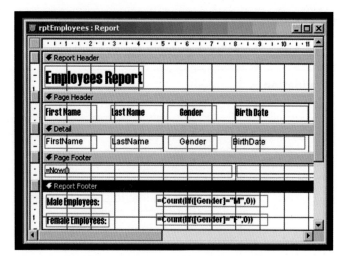

Figure 7.04 Example of report before print

Employees Report

First Name	Last Name	Gender	Birth Date
Manuel	Ortega	Male	24/07/1980
Ingrid	Schmitt	Female	01/10/1974
Nancy	McBride	Female	16/06/1995
Jean-Stephan	Villain	Male	29/08/1985
Dominique	Nayraguet	Male	21/08/1985

Male Employees: 3
Female Employees: 2

25 March 2016

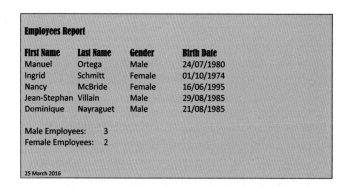

Figure 7.05 Example of an employee report when printed

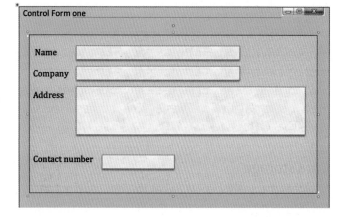

Figure 7.06 Example of a screen layout form

Special routines called validation routines are set up to ensure that the data is valid; some examples are given in Table 7.02.

Validation routine	
Length check	For example, a password may need to be eight letters long.
Type check	This checks that it is the correct type of data, e.g. is it numeric, string, boolean, date, etc.?
Format check	To check that the data is in the correct format; for instance, a telephone number, a national insurance number or a card number may always need a set format.
Presence check	To check that there is an entry in the fields where data has been 'required', such as a key field.
Check digit	The final one or two digits in a code contain a way of checking that the data is correct. An algorithm is worked out that should end up with digits that match the final digits in the code. (Often seen in a bar code, for example.)

Table 7.02 Input validation routines

The verification check will ensure that the data was correctly transferred into the system in the first place. The method for verification will probably be either a visual check or double entry of the data, then a comparison of the two sets of data. See Chapter 20 for further discussion of verification routines.

Data storage

Now that the analyst knows what the input and output will be, it is possible to design the data storage. Among the questions that need to be considered are:

- How much data needs to be stored about each item?
- What is the overall volume of data that needs to be stored and will the volume of data change in the future?
- How often are the different data items going to be accessed? How quickly does the required data need to be accessed?

- Who should have access to the data? How will that access be controlled?
- What sort of hardware is going to be needed for the storage?

Processing

Finally, the analyst can design how the input data is processed to produce the outputs required. At this point there should be a good understanding of the system design and of how the different parts work together to achieve the required results. The system design specification is produced and this is used as the input to the next stage.

QUESTION 7.03

Refer to the earlier question in this module where three example applications were outlined.

For each of these applications, decide what the important points about the input to and output from the system are. What validation and verification of the data input will be necessary? What form will the output take? What data needs to be stored? What are the important features of the data and how will these affect the hardware and the **structure data/files**? What will be the form of the access to the data?

🔑 **KEY TERMS**

Data/file structure: the format in which data are stored and organised.

7.03 Development and testing

The system design now comprises a number of different sections: an input section, an output section, a storage section and a processing section. There may be many more or the analyst may have divided a section into several subsections.

These different sections are called modules and the development of most software is done in modules. Each module can be coded by different programmers to speed up the process. When the modules are completed they can be linked together to form the complete software solution.

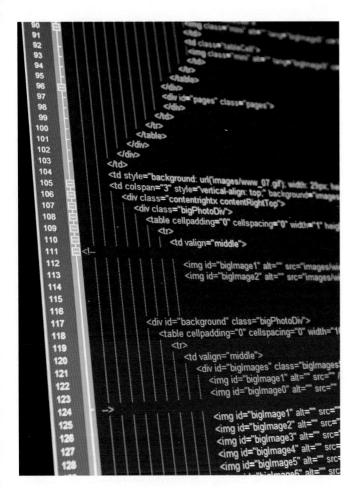

Figure 7.07 An example of the kind of coding programmers would use

Test design

Before the software is produced, it is important to consider how the system will be tested to ensure that it meets the requirement specification.

It is important not to leave the strategy for testing the software until after the software has been produced because there is a tendency to make the testing fit the software rather than the other way around!

To do this, a **test strategy** is needed **before** the software is produced. This involves:

- deciding which parts of the software functions need to be tested

- drawing up a **test plan** that includes:

  - the tests to be performed

  - the data to be used in the tests

  - the expected outcome

  - the purpose of each particular test.

The test strategy will include testing all the different parts of the solution to make sure that the results are as expected. This means testing the input, the output and the storage as well as all of the different functions that the software is meant to be able to carry out; file structures should also be tested and validation routines should be tested to ensure that as much inaccurate data is spotted as is possible.

Testing

The functionality of the individual modules will be tested as standalone units. This is referred to as **unit testing**. Any errors found will be reported back to the module's programmer and it is their responsibility to correct the error. Then, the particular test that failed will be rerun to check that the error has been fixed.

When unit testing is complete, the modules are linked together for **integration testing**. At this point the full functionality and performance of the design can be tested, checking that all the modules coordinate with each other correctly.

Both test data and real data should be used in the testing. Test data is specially prepared to test that a particular part of the processing is working. A good example would be a system which allowed examination marks out of 100 to be entered. A validation check will ensure that marks greater than 100 will be rejected. A test to show that the validation check is working might be to input a mark of 105 and see what happens.

Test data should include some data that could be part of the solution, some that would be right on the edge of being acceptable and some, like 105, which should produce error messages. These sorts of test data are called normal, **extreme** and **abnormal data**, respectively. Real data will be used to ensure that things like the volume of data will not inhibit system performance. For further discussion of test data, please see Chapter 20.

KEY TERMS

Abnormal data: data that should not normally be accepted by the system being tested because the values are invalid and should therefore be rejected.

Extreme data: if normal data is data that would normally be entered into a system, extreme data are values that are at the limits of the normal range of data. Extreme values are used when the testing of a system takes place; they are used to make sure that all normal values will be accepted and processed correctly.

One thing to remember is that you cannot exhaustively test whether a piece of software will always work. Imagine a simple program that will add two numbers together. A sensible test to see if it works would be to input the numbers 3 and 4. If the software gives the answer 7 it has passed the test. What about 5 and 9? What about 7 and 3.5? An infinite number of tests need to be carried out to show that the software always works, but that is impossible. A better approach is to try to think of tests that will prove that the software does not work. If the tests cannot cause a failure, then the assumption is that the software works.

If the testing shows that part of the solution does not work properly then consider the waterfall model that you saw at the start of this chapter. When something does not work properly the analyst needs to go back in the work to find the area of design or analysis which caused the problem, and to have another look at that part of the work in the light of the test results. Changes may be needed to the specification or the design or both.

The client should always be a party to the test plan. They have to be convinced that the software works as agreed. If the testing follows the test plan and the results are satisfactory, then they will accept the product and the next stage can be entered.

> **QUESTION 7.04**
>
> Refer to the first question in this module, where three example applications were outlined.
>
> For each of these applications, consider what test data would be sensible to include in the test plan. What would be the important parts of the test strategy? What areas of the proposed solution will need to be tested? What validation testing will need to be done?
>
> Will the testing of the third application be any more important than the testing done on the first application?

7.04 Implementation

When the system has been produced and thoroughly tested, it then has to be implemented into the client organisation. How this is done will be decided beforehand as there are some choices to be made as to how it will be implemented.

If a completely new system has to be designed, doing something that was not done before, then there is no choice, the system has to be put in place and switched on.

However, most systems are designed to take over a task from an older system, so a changeover plan is necessary to manage the change from one system to the other:

- **Hardware**. The first thing to be done is to buy and install any new hardware that will be necessary for the new system. It is possible that all the old hardware will be good enough, but this is unlikely. The business may need to shut down, although it could be possible to install the new hardware while the business is normally shut (overnight or at the weekend).

- **Data files**. After the hardware has been installed, the files of data have to be loaded onto the new system from a storage device. It may be necessary to employ data-entry staff temporarily in order to ensure that the data is entered properly. Note that it is important that these data files are as accurate as possible when the new system starts to work. Decisions will have to be made about how the data entry should be checked for accuracy.

- **Training**. The staff who are going to be using the new system will need to be trained in how to use it. If they are familiar with a computerised system already then the training may not need to be very extensive. However, if they are not used to a computerised system the training has to be planned. Staff could be trained by having training days where a tutor is brought in to the firm. This has big advantages: there is someone who can answer specific questions that the staff may have; the management can be sure that everyone has actually done the training. A disadvantage is that the staff are not working while the training sessions are held. Another method is to put all the lessons onto a DVD and each member of staff is given a copy so that they can do the training when it suits them. Advantages of this are: the firm can

Figure 7.08 Training taking place

run normally while the staff are learning; staff can learn at their own speed; staff can skip sections they already know or can redo sections that they find difficult. A disadvantage is that the staff have to use their own time to do the training.

QUESTION 7.05

Discuss the advantages and disadvantages of the two types of training for the staff and for the firm. What other forms of training could be used?

System implementation

The implementation of a new system can be carried out in four different ways.

As an example, consider an examinations board that needs to change the system that it uses to store candidate results, collate the results for each candidate from all the subjects, produce all the results for each candidate, and send the results to the examination centres around the world. The old system is proving to be very slow and unreliable because there has been a large increase in the number of candidates taking the examinations recently.

Direct changeover

The old system is shut down and the new system is started up. The old system is no longer available so if something goes wrong it is not possible or very difficult to go back to the old system. Although this sounds like a simple method of implementation, it requires careful planning. All the files must be loaded up and ready to use, all the workers must have been properly trained and the system must have been fully tested.

In the above example of the examinations board, the information stored is too important to be lost during the changeover, and if the part of the system that produces the results does not work properly the results will not be produced in time. This is an example of a time-sensitive process which is very important to the organisation, and hence a direct changeover is not appropriate.

An advantage of a direct changeover is that it is simple and cheap to do, but a disadvantage is that if it is not properly planned and tested the organisation might have to shut down.

Phased implementation

In a phased implementation, one part of the system is changed but the rest of the system continues to use the old methods.

In our example the input of the marks might be done using new input methods from the new computer system while the processing and the production of the results is still done with the old system. This allows the new input system to be thoroughly tested before going on to replace the processing part of the old system with the new processing software from the new system.

A disadvantage is that there are two systems running at the same time so that the staff will need to use two different systems to process one set of data, but in important applications it is often worth the extra work. Notice that all the different results for all candidates in all subjects are treated in the same way at the same time. The system has been split up according to the processing rather than the data used.

At the next phase, another part of the system is changed over, and so on until the whole system has been implemented.

Pilot implementation

This type of implementation is very like a phased implementation except that the division of the tasks is done according to the data rather than the processes.

In the examination results example the decision might be taken to change all the IGCSE results to the new system while the rest of the results, for other qualifications, are still produced on the old system. Note that there are now some results that will be using the whole of the new system while some will be using the old system. In this way the scale of the problem is reduced if the new system is faulty. Again, the workers will need to use both systems until the full changeover is done, but the organisation gets the experience of a live system before introducing it throughout the company.

The example here is based around the data being divided by the different levels of examinations. It could just as easily have been divided according to country; for example, all the Indian results done by the new system and the rest of the world remaining with the old methods. Or it could have been divided by subject, with all the mathematics results produced by the new method and the rest of the subjects using the old system.

Once the pilot is seen to be operating correctly and there are no outstanding problems, the implementation can be extended to full coverage.

Parallel running

This method of implementation involves both systems running at the same time. They will continue to run side by side, producing two sets of results, until the client is satisfied that there are no faults with the new system.

In the example it would mean that the data will be input twice, the results will be stored in two systems, the processing will be done twice and the results will be produced twice. Obviously this is an expensive method of changeover, but it is worth it if the system and its results are very important to an organisation. It provides an excellent way of testing the system using real data, because it is possible to compare the results produced by the two systems; if there is a difference, then there is a fault in the new system.

QUESTION 7.06

Refer to Question 1 in this module where three example applications were outlined. For each of these applications, consider:

- the data files that will be needed and decide how they will be produced and what measures should be taken to try to ensure accuracy of the data held in the files
- the different methods of implementation.

For each of the examples explain why some implementation methods are not sensible and justify a choice of which one should be used.

7.05 Documentation

To maintain an information system the organisation will need **technical documentation** to cover how every part of the system works, and **user documentation** for the users of the information system so that they have a guide to how to use it.

Documentation should be produced while the system is being developed. This is especially important for the technical documentation because there will almost certainly be more than one person producing the solution and each person involved needs to know what everyone else is doing.

Technical documentation

The technical documentation is the information about the solution that a technician needs in order to understand how the system works. It is required when updating or fixing problems with the system. It will include:

- **Purpose of the system**: this is the definition of the problem that the system solves, as agreed with the client. This definition supplies a means of measuring the scope of the solution and leads directly to the next item.

Implementation Method	Advantages	Disadvantages
Pilot implementation: the new system is trialed or piloted in one department of the organisation. Once the pilot system is running successfully, the new system will be implemented throughout organisation.	Every feature in the new system can be fully trialed so if there is a problem with the new system, only one department of the organisation is affected. Staff from the trial can train other staff.	The department where the pilot takes place will not have any back-up system if there is a problem.
Direct changeover: the old system is stopped and new system started.	Very quick to changeover. Little time or effort.	If the new system fails, data can be lost. There is no back-up.
Phased implementation: the new system will be introduced in gradual stages, slowly replacing the old system until it takes over.	Allows users to become familiar with new system in stages. Staff training can be done at each different stage.	If any part of the new system fails, there is no back-up, so data can be lost
Parallel running: the new system is started and the old system runs side-by-side until there is confidence in the new one.	If there is a problem with the new system, the old system will carry on running as a backup. Outputs from both systems can be compared to ensure the new system is running correctly.	Data has to be input to the old and new systems so takes a lot of time and effort, more expensive.

Table 7.03 Advantages and disadvantages of different implementation methods

- **Limitations of the system**: there will have been some limitations put on the system in the initial discussions between the client and the analyst. For example, in the examination board example in the previous section, the client might have intended to have included an electronic method of distribution of the results to centres. But once the analyst had done the feasibility study, it was decided that this would add too much to the final cost, or it would mean that the project would not be ready on time. This is a limitation to the system. It may be reported towards the end of the documentation despite being part of the initial discussions. There may also be an issue with some of the original requirements not being met because they were not possible within the time limits set for the system's completion.

- **System flowcharts**: these show the complete information system, and are sometimes referred to as the **system architecture**.

- **Program coding**: details of any programming done will need to be included, such as the original designs for the program, possibly in the form of **program flowcharts**. The code itself must be fully annotated.

- **Annotations**: explain what each line of code does; is contained within the code itself.

- **List of variables used**: this will include the name of the variable, the reason it is being used and the data type. The reasons for this list are twofold: to help the technician follow the program if some maintenance needs to be done, and to ensure that variables are not duplicated.

- **File structure**: this defines the data types of all the fields in the files used by the system. It also shows the linkages between the files. If the system uses databases, then the database management system will have a view that shows the relationship between the files, which can be included here. This information is needed in case the file structures need to be modified in the future.

- **Hardware and software requirements**: the hardware needed to run the system is listed, including estimated file sizes so that storage choices can be justified. There may be diagrams to show how the servers, peripherals, storage devices, network and user terminals are interconnected. Software requirements should also be listed, including details of software that has been bought in, that has been modified or that has

been specially written. Minimum system requirements for running the software will also be included.

- **Validation routines**: reasons for using validation were given earlier in this chapter, as were the different validation routines that can be used. Details of the different validation routines that are used to check the input data are given in this section of the technical documentation.

User documentation

User documentation is provided for the people who will use the system. Users do not need the technical details of how the system works, but they do need to know its features and functionality. It includes:

- the purpose of the system

- limitations of the system

- its hardware and software requirements

- glossary of terms.

The purpose of the system will be in terms that the user can understand and will simply state what they can use the system for; similarly with the limitations and the hardware and software requirements. This section is about what to use it for and how to use it. The glossary of terms is necessary for users who are not familiar with all the technical terms that the documentation may include.

- **How to use the system**: this will include the sort of data that needs to be input, how to input it, and its format. If a price is to be input, for instance, is it always necessary to have two digits input after the point? What sort of output is required? How is it to be produced and what should it look like?

- **Sample runs**: the outputs from some successful runs of the software should be shown so that the user has a reference of how the system should look if it is used properly. These may be screenshots of input and output screens.

- **Error messages**: things will go wrong with any system and when they do it is important that the system has been designed to output error messages. Users can look these up to find out what has caused the error and what can be done about it. These error messages need to be in non-technical language.

- **Trouble-shooting guide**: there should be some assistance given for minor problems that can arise with the system, otherwise every time things go wrong it will be necessary to call a technician. The trouble-shooting guide tells the user how to identify that certain things have gone wrong and what can be done about them.

- **Frequently asked questions (FAQs)**: there are some things that experience has shown are problems or questions that many users have. These problems are drawn together with the answers that go with them.

EXTENSION ACTIVITY 7.01

Refer to Question 1 in this module, where three example applications were outlined. Then, as a class, discuss for each of these applications who the audience is going to be and what content would be necessary in each of the user and technical guides.

7.06 Evaluation

At some point after the new information system has been operating as a normal business application it is time to review the project.

Evaluation against the requirements specification

Before the solution was produced, the systems analyst and the client organisation agreed a set of things that the finished solution should do. This was the requirements specification, the list of requirements that needed to be met for the system to be a success. If the system does not satisfy these requirements the problem may not have been solved. The solution will be considered a success if all the requirements are met. It may even be considered a success if most of the requirements are met. The test plan was set up to provide the evidence that the requirements have been met and that the software does everything that is required of it. Also, the users must be asked for their view of how the implementation has gone and how well the system works for them, as users tend to discover problems that computer-literate testers do not think of.

Limitations and improvements

As a result of the evaluation, a list of required changes will probably be built up.

Some of the changes are needed to address the limitations – a shortfall between the requirements specification and what has been delivered. This type of testing is known as functional testing. Functional testing

does not prove that the solution is perfect or even that it is carried out in the best way, but it does provide evidence that the solution satisfies all the requirements it was intended to.

Other changes will address improvements identified during operation of the system, perhaps in response to the client's changing needs or to accommodate changes in the external environment.

Continual evaluations of and improvements to the system can be made. Refer back to the waterfall model (Figure 7.01), which shows that you can go back to any previous stage to address problems or to make improvements. Reference to the technical documentation is critically important in making the changes. It is also necessary to update the documentation to record any changes made.

Maintenance

This continual process of changes to the system is known as **maintenance** and will take place throughout the system's operational life cycle. There are three forms of maintenance:

- **Error correction (corrective maintenance)**: all complex software goes wrong sometimes. The errors are called 'bugs' in the software. The system support staff have to be able to find these bugs and fix them.

- **Added functionality (adaptive maintenance)**: things change in any organisation. The original problem that the system was built for may have altered. The system may be required to do something else. For example, suppose the examination board in the example used earlier in this chapter has expanded into a different country. The authorities in that country may want the results to be presented in order of the marks that were awarded rather than according to the centres that the candidate was in.

- **Performance improvement (perfective maintenance)**: Organisations usually want to speed up processes or make them more efficient. Or it may be that the system has simply grown beyond its original capacity, for example with a larger user base or increased number of products being handled. The systems analyst has to consider how to solve these issues. It may be a change to the hardware (higher performance servers, for example; see Figure 7.05) or changes to the software – using a relational database instead of flat files, for example.

Figure 7.09 A computer engineer carrying out maintenance on a server

Any changes will require careful planning and implementation.

EXTENSION ACTIVITY 7.02

Look back to the first question in this module, where three example applications were outlined.

As a class, discuss for each application what sort of evidence the analyst should provide to the management of the organisation so that the performance of the solution can be evaluated. Give examples of the types of event that would mean that the three different types of maintenance would be needed.

Summary

- There are six stages in the waterfall model of the systems life cycle: analysis, design, development and testing, implementation, documentation and evaluation/maintenance.
- System analysis and design is a continual iterative process that refines the solution.
- The analysis stage consists of problem definition and a feasibility study that, on agreement, is followed by information collection, resulting in a requirements specification.
- Designing the output is the first part of the design stage, followed by input, storage and processing design.
- The development and testing stage consists of dividing the coding work into modules that are subsequently tested individually before integrating them together and testing as a whole.
- Implementation starts with installing new hardware and data, and training the staff. The changeover to the new solution can be carried out in four different ways: direct changeover, phased implementation, pilot implementation or parallel running.
- Documentation is important to the future maintenance of the system and consists of technical and user guides, which have recommended formats. Any changes to the system must be reflected in the documentation.
- The evaluation stage looks at how well the solution meets the requirement specification and then defines how the system needs changing.
- Maintenance goes on throughout the system's operational life and consists of error correction, adding functionality and performance improvements.

Exam-style questions

7.01 Put the stages of the system life cycle given below into the correct order using the spaces available. [6]

Design
Implementation
Analysis
Evaluation
Development and testing
Documentation

Stage 1 ....

Stage 2 ....

Stage 3 ....

Stage 4 ....

Stage 5 ....

Stage 6 ....

7.02 Give **two** activities that will take place during the analysis stage. [2]

a ....

b ....

7.03 What are the three different types of test data that should be used when testing the system life cycle? [3]

1 ....

2 ....

3 ....

7.04 Name six items that should be in the technical documentation. [6]

1 ....

2 ....

3 ....

4 ....

5 ....

6 ....

7.05 Explain the waterfall model of a systems life cycle. You should use a diagram to illustrate your points. [6]

....

....

....

....

....

Chapter 8:
Safety and security

Learning objectives

When you have finished this chapter you will be able to:

- describe common physical safety issues and what causes them
- describe some simple strategies for preventing common physical safety issues
- evaluate your own use of IT equipment and develop strategies to minimise the potential safety risks
- explain what is meant by personal data and why personal data should be confidential and protected
- explain how to avoid inappropriate disclosure of personal data by evaluating your own use of the internet and social networking sites and discuss why e-safety is needed
- understand what effective security of data is and what security of data online is
- discuss the effectiveness of different methods of increasing security.

Overview

The use of computers is increasing all the time and a number of physical safety concerns have arisen. There are hazards to the physical safety of computer users such as the cabling connecting computers in a network, the siting of a new printer, electrical overload or having a drink next to a computer, for instance. Most of these safety concerns are temporary and can be easily resolved. There are also the problems associated with online safety and security and security of data. For these reasons we will look at common safety concerns for users of computers, as well as viruses, malware and the dangers of identity theft.

8.01 Physical safety issues

Computers and their peripherals are electrical devices which need to be connected to each other, and this will involve some cables and an electricity supply. Add to that the possibility that several computers may be connected by cables in order to create a network, and suddenly there are a lot of wires around. Simple precautions can be taken to overcome the safety problems that this can cause.

Ideally, the installation of the computers will have been well planned and the cables will all be well hidden and out of the way. In most cases this does not happen. These cables can be very dangerous: someone could trip over them. If cables are trailing and causing a safety issue, cable ties can be used to gather them tidily together and keep them away from people.

Spilling drinks!

Most of the time computers and devices need to be plugged in to an electrical power source. This is why care has to be taken to avoid any risk of electrocution.

If a drink spills into your computer or device you could risk it being damaged and you may be in danger of injury! You will probably have been told not to have drinks near to your computer so that you will avoid accidental damage to the device or injury to yourself (Figure 8.01).

How would a spilled drink cause problems? Data travels between components in a computer via an electrical current; if liquid comes into contact with those components when the power is on it may create an accidental connection between two points, therefore causing damage to the circuit.

What could happen? The keyboard, motherboard, memory or the processor could be affected.

Figure 8.01 Don't risk spilling a drink on your PC!

If a drink is spilled into your keyboard, this is what you should do:

- Don't panic.
- Unplug your computer immediately! (Do not wait to shut down your computer using the software.) If you unplug it quickly, you may prevent the electronics inside the computer from being damaged.
- Using a soft cloth, dry up as much of the liquid as you can.
- Pull out any other cables connected to your computer, such as USB components, cards and any other external devices.
- Hold the laptop or keyboard upside down and very gently move it from side to side to drain it. Don't shake it! A lot of the liquid should drain out.
- Leave it upside down on the desk so that the rest of the liquid can drain out.
- Wait about 24 hours then use a soft, damp cloth to clean the outside.

The best advice is the most boring: don't drink while you work at a computer or near to any devices!

What is electrical overload?

When an extension lead has several sockets for you to plug more than one appliance into, you may find that once you have everything plugged in, together they will add up to more than the maximum current rating stated for the extension lead. This is **electrical overload**, which could cause the plug in the wall socket to overheat and possibly cause a fire.

> ### KEY TERMS
>
> **Electrical overload:** electrical circuit overloads are when too many electrical items are plugged into one socket causing more current to be put across an electrical wire or circuit than it can handle.

The danger signs are if the plugs or sockets become hot, or fuses blow unexpectedly; there may be flickering lights or scorch marks on sockets or plugs.

If this happens, you should check that there isn't any loose wiring, that only one extension lead per wall socket is being used and that there isn't one extension lead plugged into another.

You can calculate amps by dividing the amount of wattage by the voltage. For example, if you have an electrical item that is rated at 1000 watts and it runs on 120 volts, when you divide it you will see that almost half of a 20 amp circuit is already being used. You can usually find the information on the bottom of the device or on a sticky label attached to its cable.

$$\frac{1000 \text{ watts}}{120 \text{ volts}} = 8.33 \text{ amps}$$

Remember that when more than one device is plugged into an extension socket, you will need to add the amps that you have calculated together (Figure 8.02).

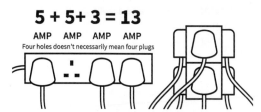

Figure 8.02 Think about overload

Trailing cables

You will probably have noticed that there are usually a lot of cables attached to computers, such as power cables or network cables. When these cables need to go across the floor, there is a risk that people might trip over them.

What could happen if someone trips on a cable? There might be injury or an electric shock to the person; if the plug had been wrenched out during the trip, there could be damage to the lead or plug, and the equipment attached to the cable may be damaged if it was pulled off a desk.

Because of these potential risks of electric shocks or fires, it is good health and safety practice to make sure that when cables need to cross a floor, they are all inside cable ducts, or under the carpet or flooring.

Other risks associated with computer equipment

Because computer equipment is often heavy, there is a risk of injury if you move it, or if an item of hardware falls on someone.

If you get a new printer, it will generally need to be connected to a computer so you will need to decide where to put it. You will probably put it on a shelf near the computer, but before you put it there, ask yourself two questions: Is the shelf designed to carry that much weight? Will the printer fit properly on the shelf without it being precariously balanced?

Devices must be placed in suitable positions. Make sure equipment is placed on tables or shelves that are strong enough for them; the position must be able to support the weight of the device and a check should be made to see if it will be large enough to support the device under each of

107

Figure 8.03 Trailing cables can be tidied up to prevent them becoming a hazard

its corners. Also, devices need to be placed where users can get at them easily. If it is a printer, you will need to add more paper regularly and to change the ink when necessary.

108

QUESTION 8.01

Consider the computer systems in your school. Are all of the safety points followed? Do the users of the computer systems follow the safety guidelines suggested?

What about your computer system at home, if you have one?

Discuss steps that you can take to prevent physical danger to yourself and others when using a computer.

EXTENSION ACTIVITY 8.01

The components inside computers, monitors and printers contain many different toxic materials. These will not affect you or other users when working on a computer, but they can cause problems when computer equipment is recycled or discarded.

If your school were considering upgrading some computers, how should they dispose of the old equipment?

Carry out some research to find out what is inside a PC, screen and printer that may be toxic.

Consider electronic waste and computer recycling and decide what you think is the best way to dispose of discarded computer equipment. Collaborate with others to create some guidelines.

8.02 E-safety

E-safety is a term associated with use of the internet and also with other means of using electronic media to communicate, such as mobile phones. E-safety refers to protecting everyone from harm while they are using new and developing technologies so that they do not put themselves, or others, at risk.

The hazards can be split into two types:

- illegal or inappropriate content
  - copyright issues
  - plagiarism
  - inappropriate images
  - social network software
- contact
  - inappropriate contact with adults
  - bullying
  - financial risks.

So e-safety seeks to protect children, young people and vulnerable adults from the adverse consequences that can be associated with the use of electronic media, including from bullying and from inappropriate sexualised behaviour. Some **search engines** have safe modes to ensure that search results do not bring up inappropriate sites.

KEY TERMS

Search engine: a program that searches for and identifies items in a database to match the keyword(s) that you type in. Google is a search engine for the World Wide Web, but there are many others.

Personal data

Consider what counts as **personal data**, whether it is stored on a computer, on paper, on an IT system, on a CCTV system and so on. You have seen from the key words section that personal data relates to a living individual who can be identified; this could include a variety of types of information.

KEY TERMS

Personal data: data relating to a living individual; it covers any information that relates to an identifiable, living individual.

QUESTION 8.02

What do you think counts as personal data? You could start by talking about the different ways a person could be identified.

Make a list of the physical characteristics that could be used to identify a person. Now add to that list as many other ways as you can to identify someone, starting with their name.

EXTENSION ACTIVITY 8.02

Research 'data protection' in the country where you live and try to find out how 'personal data' is defined. Write down your own definition as a result of this and of your previous discussion.

You may not always need to know a person's name for that person to be identified. You may need to know more than one thing about them though.

> **Example:**
>
> Imagine that someone lives near to you whose name you do not know. You may ask your friend what the name is of the tall lady who lives in the next street who meets her son off the school bus every afternoon.

> **Example:**
>
> The police have arrested a man whose name and address they don't know; they take his fingerprints and look them up on the police database. If he has been arrested before, his name, address and details of the previous crime could be found.

In many cases a person's name, if used in conjunction with some other information, such as their medical history or the results of a sporting activity, would be enough to identify them. Data can identify an individual, even without their name being associated with it.

QUESTION 8.03

Is a bank statement personal data?

EXTENSION ACTIVITY 8.03

Find out about the issues of plagiarism and of copyright.

Social media and the need to be protected

There are many different **social networking sites** where you can share information with others and make comments; there are also sites specifically for sharing photographs. There is nothing wrong with social networks themselves, but if they are not used carefully, some very serious problems may occur.

KEY TERMS

Social networking sites: types of websites or services that allow you to interact with friends and family online and to find other people online who have similar interests or hobbies.

Problems that may arise

- Cyberbullying could occur when people have access to an individual on a social networking site.

- Because it is easy to contact others using social network sites, some people may try to exploit or abuse others, in particular young people, especially where it is difficult for a young person to know with whom they are interacting.

- There are those who use social networking sites to slander (make a false statement about) other people that could damage their reputation. If someone makes an abusive comment about another person, and it is shared by others, it will not be possible to remove that comment from everywhere that it might be seen.

- When people start using a social networking site, it is usual to create a personal profile. If this can be accessed by the public, rather than being restricted to your friends or associates, your personal details could become the subject of identity theft.

- Users of social networks may not be aware that the sites can be searched. Nowadays employers may look on these sites to assess people applying for a job with them. Sometimes, inappropriate discussions or behaviour can influence employers against employing you, even if these discussions or behaviours are not recent.

It may be helpful to you if you manage your privacy settings on social network sites, most of which also have an option to report abusive users.

First of all, before disclosing your personal data such as name, address, the name of your school and an image of yourself in school uniform:

1   Ask yourself these questions:

- who is collecting this information?

- why is it necessary?

- what will be done with it?

- what will the consequences be for me?

You can change security and privacy settings for your internet browser and for your social media accounts. Below are examples of how this can be done for Microsoft Internet Explorer.

2   Use the built-in tools on your internet browser (the software you use to browse the internet) to help to protect your personal information. These tools deal

with different aspects of your safety, for example: to help you to control the amount of personal information you put online; to clear details of sites you have visited or searches made by you.

This is where to go for *security settings* and for *privacy settings* if you use Internet Explorer:

- Open Internet Explorer by clicking the Start button.

- Look for the search box, and type 'Internet Explorer', then click 'Internet Explorer'.

- Click the Tools button, and then click Internet Options.

- Click the Security tab.

You can change the privacy settings for each of the items in the list below

If you use a different internet browser, the concepts are likely to be the same but the location of the settings may be different.

Cookies

Cookies can be used to track your online browsing. For instance, if you buy something online, you will then have adverts offering you many similar items. Cookies are also used to remember your preferences for a web page and can improve your browsing experience by allowing quicker access to sites. You can read more in Chapter 6.15 Monitoring and tracking.

Do not track

If you choose to turn on the 'Do not track' setting in your browser, it sends a special signal to websites. Turning on Do not track doesn't always have the effect you may think it would as sites do not always change their practice of tracking when they receive this signal. However, some may refrain from personalising adverts that they show you; others might limit the ways they collect information about your browsing activities.

InPrivate browsing

InPrivate browsing prevents data being stored about your browsing session to help to prevent others who might be using your computer from seeing which sites you have visited. However, when you select it, a new Window will open but the setting will only apply to that Window. When you close that browser window, your InPrivate Browsing session will close.

Location

If you have your location settings on, it indicates the country or region where you are at all times so that local information such as news, weather, nearest hotel etc. can be provided to you. If you are on the move and have your smartphone's location settings turned on, in order to know your location, the information about your current location is constantly updated, thus using up your data allowance and possibly causing you to exceed your data limit with your ISP.

Pop-up blocker

A pop-up blocker will disable pop-up advertisements that you see when using your web browsing software.

Tracking protection

Tracking refers to the collection of your browsing data. The tracking protection feature will identify and block trackers. Also see Chapter 6.15 Monitoring and tracking

3 Install antivirus and security software and keep the software updated.

It is a good idea to evaluate your own use of the internet and of email at regular intervals. Start by making a list of all of the social networking sites you use, then list the other websites that you use. Once you have this list, consider for each one if it has the approval of your parents or teacher, whether you have made appropriate choices in security and privacy settings for each one. Next, look through the list again and make a note of all the personal information you have made available on every one of the sites in the list. The final list to make is for all of the actions you need to take, bearing in mind the contents of chapter 8, this section and 8.03.

To evaluate your use of email, you should consider whether you:

- have changed your password recently and is it kept in a safe place

- have shared your password with anyone

- always log out or sign of from you account when you have finished using email

- have ever forwarded chain emails

- have kept your bank or card information private and not shared it via email

- have kept your antivirus software up to date

- have used your email provider's email security and privacy settings appropriately.

Think about the future. What if you didn't get a job you applied for? How would you feel if you found out it was because there are some unfortunate pictures of you on the internet, or opinions you expressed? You may not even know they are there.

Ask your friends to be careful what they post about themselves and you.

- avoiding the misuse of images
- using appropriate language
- respecting confidentiality
- reading the safety guidelines and tips that can be found on many social media sites.

Identity theft and malware

Identity theft is a type of fraud where personal information is stolen and used to impersonate that person. This isn't a new problem because in the past, postal deliveries were intercepted to find out names, addresses and bank account details. The person committing the fraud could then open a credit card account, for instance, or apply for a loan in the victim's name. This is identity theft.

Now, in the online world, we have **malware**, which is what we call software that has been designed to sniff out personal information on a computer, and phishing attacks that can persuade computer users to give personal information. **Botnets** are created using malware for sending spam emails or flooding a website with so many requests for content that the server cannot cope. **Hacking** is also a way of obtaining personal information: large retailers have been hacked and millions of personal records have been stolen. Online identity theft is a growing threat.

KEY TERMS

Hacking: any attempt to gain unauthorised access to data in a computer system.

Botnets: created using malware, a network of computers that allows an attacker to control them and use them to gather personal information or launch attacks against others.

QUESTION 8.04

List some strategies that you could use to minimise any possible dangers that you might encounter when using social media or networking sites, blogging sites, instant messaging or internet chat rooms.

Did you include the following?

- knowing how to block and report unwanted users
- never arranging to meet anyone alone
- always telling an adult first and meeting in a public place

Playing games on the internet

Current technologies and high-speed internet connections have made it possible for online gaming to become a popular way of spending time on the internet. Because of this, large amounts of time and money are being invested in very sophisticated games. This has resulted in some people seeing an opportunity for mischief and ways of making an unlawful profit.

It is therefore important to understand the technological and social risks of online games.

You can play online games with different people from all over the world. When you play these games, you may be playing with people you know and also with people you don't know. When gaming you may also make new friends online who like the same games as you do. You can also chat to the people you meet on gaming sites.

Do you think you know how you can stay safe when you are using the internet? It is best to be able to make the right choices to keep yourself safe.

Tips for playing online games safely:

- Some people can become nasty when they are playing online games because they want to win. Make sure that when you play online games, you don't upset anyone in order to win or get to the next level. Also, remember not to do anything that you know is wrong to get cheats or tips.

- Because some people you could meet online may not be who they say they are, it is always a good idea not to use your real name when you are gaming, just use a nickname.

8.03 Security of data

Security of data is concerned with keeping data safe and uncorrupted by restricting access to the data so that there is less chance of malicious damage to it. Security of data

111

is also concerned with the recovery of data if it has been damaged. In this section we will consider the different ways in which data could be compromised and ways of keeping it as safe as you can.

112

QUESTION 8.05

You probably have your own personal corner of cyberspace. You should be aware of what information you have there that needs protection: your **information assets**.

Compile a list, either in a spreadsheet or using the matrix in Table 8.01, of the different types of information you store on your computer or online. For example, you may have personal correspondence, photographs, work documents, personal details, all of your passwords for online services.

For each type of information, think of its value to you. Label the most valuable types of information as 'High', the least valuable as 'Low' and those that are in between as 'Medium'.

The value could be the cost to replace the information, in time or money, or the impact of its loss on your reputation; for example, any of your emails or photographs could be published online.

KEY TERMS

Information assets: valuable data that you wouldn't want to be stolen or corrupted.

QUESTION 8.06

Do the same exercise for the online activities you engage in. For example, you might use online banking, shopping or social networking services. This time, label each one with a value based on the potential cost of an unauthorised person gaining access to it.

Draw up a table like Table 8.01 in order to assess your own risk. Think of the types of data you have on your computer and what you use your computer for, then write in the shaded boxes below to assess your risk.

You may want to include: study materials, banking details, passwords, downloaded music, photographs, but try to think of more.

High importance	Study materials	Banking details Passwords
Low importance	Photographs	Videos Music
	Low risk	High risk

Table 8.01 Information risk inventory

What is hacking?

Hacking is malicious damage caused by people who get into computer systems when they have no right to access that system. People who do this are called **hackers**.

Hackers have different reasons for doing what they do: some of them gain access just to prove that a system is vulnerable; other hackers may alter or destroy the data just for malicious reasons; still other hackers may try to gain access to a computer system just to see if they can. It is most likely that they are breaking in to steal some of the data so they can make money. For example, if a hacker gets into your computer and steals any financial information you have there, such as your credit card number, or the password to your bank account, they could use that to spend your money.

What effects does hacking have?

You could lose all your data as a result of hacking because hackers will often delete or change files; for businesses, they may find that customer information or order information could be stolen or deleted, or a leak of top secret information could cause huge real-world security problems.

Another effect could be decreased privacy. When hackers gain access to a computer, they can see everything. Since much of the personal, professional and financial areas of people's lives are now kept online, the risk is in losing more than money or information. A hacker with access to your email or your social networking account and personal photos can very quickly destroy your privacy.

> If a lot of information about you is stolen, a hacker could use this to impersonate you online.
>
> They might apply for credit cards, buy a car or apply for a loan in your name!
>
> If they did, this would be called 'identity theft' (see earlier in this chapter).

What can I do to protect my data from hacking?

QUESTION 8.07

First of all, list four things you can do to keep your computer system safe from hackers.

Remember, if you make it difficult enough, a hacker may go away and look for an easier target.

This is what you need to do:

- Try to stop a hacker from getting into the system in the first place by using authentication (the use of user IDs and passwords) to access the system and to access individual files.

- You could make files unreadable for any hacker that does manage to get access to your system by using data encryption on the data. If you encrypt the data, then any hacker who manages to get through the passwords will not be able to understand anything they find, so no damage is done (unless they simply destroy the data).

- Make sure you keep a copy of your files in case hackers do manage to damage any files that they access. This means that keeping backup copies of your files is very important.

The following sections will explain more about these methods.

User ID and password

Poor internet safety habits could put us at risk unnecessarily. Whether we use email, social networks, telephone or electricity online accounts, online auction sites or online banking, we all need to keep track of the increasing number of usernames, passwords and PIN codes that allow us to access these online services securely.

According to research by a leading credit reference agency, on average people each have 26 different online logins, so password management is a very important part of staying safe online. The recommendation never to use the same password more than once is difficult and impractical when we have so many different online accounts. It was also found that even though we might have 26 different accounts, on average we only use five different passwords!

EXTENSION ACTIVITY 8.04

a How often do you use the same username and password?

b Do you use the same password every time you create a new profile?

c If someone hacked your social media account, could they just as easily get into your email account?

Always using the same password, or using a weak password, could make you an easy target for identity theft.

Because of the way passwords are used, they must remain secret. Have you noticed that when you type your password onto the screen, a series of asterisks ******** will fill the space where you type your password so that nobody can see it on the screen? The operating system (OS) keeps the passwords associated with each user in the user ID table.

Passwords are designed to keep our information safe from prying eyes, but passwords can be annoying and remembering them difficult! This is why so many people often use simple passwords that they won't forget. But if they are easy to remember, they will also be easy to guess.

Weak passwords are those that could easily be guessed if it is your birthdate or your house name for instance, or anything that is personal to you or it could be all text which would be easier for someone intent on finding your password if they run through password-breaking programs.

A password should not be a word in the dictionary, and it should have digits as well as letters. Some letters should be lowercase and some uppercase. A password is usually required to be longer than eight characters.

Your password should not be anything that could be linked back to you, so don't use the name of your house, village, dog or similar. Don't use things such as your birth date either.

The best passwords combine letters, numbers and symbols. You can replace letters in your password with a similar looking number. For example, if your password is 'Computing' you could replace the 'o' with a zero '0' and the 'i' with a one '1'. This would change your password to C0mput1ng'. This isn't really enough of a change, though, and a hacker may well try this, so you need to use symbols as well such as + or %, which could give you 'C%mput1ng+'.

On some systems you use, you may be prompted to change your password every month.

This is what happens when you log in with your username and password:

1   The operating system looks up the user ID in the table of user IDs.

2   The operating system is given a list from that table of all of the files and folders on the system which you are allowed to have access to, and the software and hardware you are allowed to use.

3   The operating system then waits for the password to be entered.

4   If the password that you entered matches the one held by the operating system for you, then you will be given access to the things that the table says you are allowed to use. If it doesn't match, then a message is output to the screen warning of an incorrect password.

EXTENSION ACTIVITY 8.05

Find out what a password management tool is, and write a short explanation.

Biometric data

Biometric data refers to records used to identify people, such as fingerprints, which are unique to every person. This section looks at different types of biometric scans that can be used for authentication purposes (Figure 8.04).

KEY TERMS

Biometric data: records that are used to identify people by a physical attribute that doesn't change. An example of this would be a database of fingerprints of known criminals.

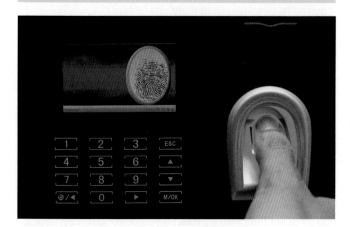

Figure 8.04 Biometrics using fingerprint or hand scan

Biometric data falls into two categories:

•   Physiological biometric data relates to a physical aspect of a person's body (such as a fingerprint or a retina scan).

•   Behavioural biometrics include things like signatures, handwriting analysis and voice pattern recognition.

The data needs to be universal, that is, it should be something that everyone possesses; it should be unique, so that an individual can be definitively recognised; it should also be permanent, meaning that it should not change significantly as a person ages.

Biometric devices tend to work in one of two main ways: verification or identification.

For verification, biometric technologies perform a comparison of the data with a template that has previously been stored, such as a fingerprint scan or other physical tokens such as retina, iris or face scans, on a personal computer or electronic safe. This is authentication, simply finding out if you are who you say you are.

For identification, the next step, once an item of data is captured, such as a fingerprint, the system will try to match that data with any existing item in the database. A good example of identification biometrics is a database of fingerprints of known criminals.

EXTENSION ACTIVITY 8.06

Some people have concerns about biometric technology and the storage of biometric data on a large scale. Do some research and try to find out what these concerns might be.

Security of data online

A **digital certificate** is a pair of files that are kept on your computer. They let you create the digital equivalent of a handwritten signature and sealed envelopes. The files hold a **public key** and a **private key**. The public key is shared, but only you have access to the private key.

KEY TERMS

Digital certificate: is a method of keeping your email message or data private.
Public/private keys: these are held in the two files that allow you to create a digital certificate.

The programs on your computer already understand how to share the public part of your keys so that others can see them, while keeping the private keys secure for you.

When you send an email message, you can sign the message digitally by attaching your digital certificate. When the email is received, the recipient can verify that it came from you by looking at a small attachment that came with the email, which contains your public key information. In other words, it protects you from anyone trying to pretend they are you by sending an email that looks like it came from you but is really sent from a different email account.

Another use for a digital certificate is to electronically sign documents.

When you encrypt a message, you create the equivalent of a sealed envelope so that only you and the person you are sending it to can see the message. It is a bit like when you send a postcard to someone: anyone can read it because it is open, but it would be harder to read a letter because you put it into a sealed envelope.

The encryption offered by digital certificates avoids this problem (Figure 8.05).

What makes up a digital certificate?

A digital certificate consists of:

- the person's name
- an email address
- a serial number
- a public key
- an expiration date (certificates are only valid for a limited time)
- a digital signature.

Secure Sockets Layer (SSL)

Figure 8.06 Secure sockets layer

As can be seen from Figure 8.06, the **Secure Sockets Layer (SSL)** establishes a secure encrypted communication channel between you and another computer on the internet. For web browsing, for example, it allows you to use the secure https protocol rather than the normal http (see Chapter 10 for more details).

115

KEY TERMS

Secure Sockets Layer (SSL): a protocol for managing the security of a message transmission on the internet.

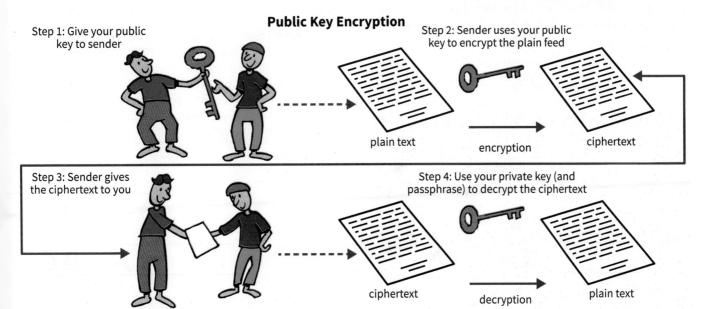

Figure 8.05 Public key encryption

The word 'sockets' refers to how data is passed back and forth between a client (you) and a server program in a network. SSL uses public and private key encryption; this also includes using a digital certificate.

So what is the difference between SSL and a digital certificate?

A digital certificate establishes your credentials (see the six items in the list above) and SSL manages the security of message transmission on the internet.

Encryption

By using encryption, data will be scrambled so that only someone with the secret code or key will be able to read it. This makes it possible to send a secret message from one place to another without anyone else being able to read it.

Encryption scrambles the original message with a very large digital number, called a key. The key that is used is the public key of the intended recipient. The computer that receives the information can then decrypt (unscramble) the message by using its private key.

Encryption is used in e-commerce so that you can send confidential information to any online shops that you might buy from. The payment details that you will need to send in order to make your purchase will therefore be kept confidential.

How do I know if the website I am browsing is secure?

Sometimes you get warning messages when you enter or leave secure sites, but also most browsers display an icon to show that they are secure; it is usually a small locked padlock (Figure 8.07). For Mozilla Firefox, Internet Explorer and Google Chrome, the icon appears in the address bar.

Something else you can check for is whether the start of the URL is https:// instead of http://. If you are sending personal or confidential information, make sure that the URL starts with https://.

The colour of the browser's security status bar can also tell you if the website that you are on is using a secure connection: it displays different colours to indicate whether or not the certificate is valid, as shown in Table 8.02.

Red	The certificate is out of date, not valid, or has an error.
Yellow	The authenticity of the certificate or certification authority that issued it cannot be verified.
White	The certificate has normal validation.
Green	The certificate uses extended validation. This means that communication between your browser and website is encrypted.

Table 8.02 Browser security status colours

Phishing

If any attempt is made to obtain sensitive information fraudulently from you, this is known as **phishing**. The people attempting to get information from you will probably be asking for credit card or bank information, or a social security number or driver's licence number.

You might receive an email that looks authentic but tries to lure you into an email conversation where you end up giving, for instance, your bank details, because you will probably think that the request came from your bank.

KEY TERMS

Phishing: a criminal activity trying to find sensitive information, such as passwords or banking details, by fraudulent means.

Pharming: when a hacker installs a malicious program on a computer or a server. This program code causes any clicks that you make on a website to be redirected to another website without you knowing.

a

b

c

Figure 8.07 Find the security icon in browsers. (a) For Safari, the icon appears in the upper right corner of the browser. (b) The secure site icon for Firefox. (c) The secure site icon for Internet Explorer

What is pharming and how is it different to phishing?

Pharming is similar to phishing, but a phishing attack tries to lure you to visiting a website through a phony email or link, and pharming tries to redirect you to a bogus site even when you have typed the correct web address. This is often applied to the websites of banks or e-commerce sites.

How does it work?

Sites on the internet are really located using a series of numbers, such as 194.144.1.1, and not by the name that you might type in, for instance, www.thenameofthesite.com. This is because there is an internet naming system that allows you to enter a meaningful www address (that is easy to remember). The **DNS server** converts the letter-based website name into the digits that will take you to the website you want.

KEY TERMS

DNS server: Domain name system server. DNS turns the user-friendly version of a domain name, such as www.thisismysite.com, into numbers such as 60.22.161.42. This set of numbers is called an Internet Protocol (IP) address and is used to route you to your requested site. DNS works through a massive distributed database that stores domain names and their IP addresses so that it can find the domain name you want.

Vishing: a combination of 'voice' and phishing, it is when fraudsters obtain personal details of a victim through their landline telephone.

A hacker can install some malicious code on a computer or server that will redirect you to a different, fraudulent site. It is very likely that you will not know that this has happened.

Vishing

Vishing is voice phishing and it uses landline telephone services to steal credit card numbers that can then be associated with the bill payer for the telephone line. Callers try to trick you into giving out your credit card or banking numbers. This information could then be used in identity theft schemes.

Smishing

A bit like phishing, but **smishing** uses text messages to lure consumers in. The text message will probably have a URL or a telephone number. If you dialled the telephone number it would probably go to an automated voice response system. In a lot of cases, the message could have been sent to the telephone by email, and not sent from another cell phone. They may, for instance, tell you that there is a problem with your bank account and that they need to check the information with you.

KEY TERMS

Smishing: uses mobile phone text messages to lure people into returning the call.

How do I guard against phishing, vishing and smishing attacks?

- Do you know the sender of the email? If not, do not open it.

- If there are any attachments in the email, look at the file name of the attachment before opening it as it could be an executable, that is, a file with any of the extensions .exe, .bat, .com, .vbs, .reg, .msi, .pif, .pl, .php. If that is the case, do not click on the attachment. Even if the file does not contain one of these extensions, be cautious about opening it. Contact the sender to verify its contents.

- Does the email ask you for personal information? If it does, do not reply.

- Have you checked the link? Mouse over the link and check the URL that pops up. Does it look legitimate or does it look like it will take you to a different website?

- When receiving landline telephone calls or messages you should be highly suspicious if they ask you to provide credit card or bank numbers.

- Do not respond to smishing messages.

QUESTION 8.08

Find out how to report these attacks and write the information down.

Forums: moderated or unmoderated?

A forum is an online place where you can discuss topics with other people.

In a moderated forum, all posts are approved beforehand by a moderator. Some people prefer this type of forum to an unmoderated forum, as the moderator can keep spam out as well as inappropriate posts that are rude or offensive, or even if they are not about the topic being discussed in the forum. Whichever type of forum you are using, it is often better not to use your real name.

The internet is generally unmoderated because no one owns the internet, but most social forums on the internet have a set of rules (called protocols) that members are asked to follow. This depends on an appeal to responsible people worldwide and has been quite successful.

EXTENSION ACTIVITY 8.07

What are the rules that members of an un-moderated forum should be asked to follow?

Email spam

You may know this as junk email or unsolicited bulk email (UBE), which is a type of electronic spam that involves nearly identical email messages being sent to lots of people.

If you click on a link in a spam email you may be sent to phishing websites or sites that are hosting malware.

EXTENSION ACTIVITY 8.08

Find out how to spot spam emails and how to report them. You could start by finding out how to deal with a spam email received via an outlook.com account.

Computer viruses

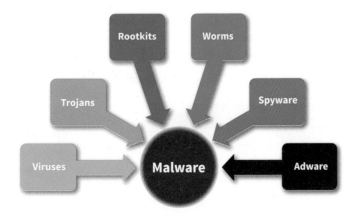

Figure 8.08 Viruses

A computer virus is a piece of software that infects a computer by installing itself and copying itself onto other computers, without you knowing (Figure 8.08).

Most computer viruses come with some kind of malware that does 'something' to your computer. For instance, a virus might install spyware (did you remember that **spyware** is software that watches what you do on your computer?). It might search your computer for credit card information, or it might install software that gives someone else remote control of your computer! A virus can infect your programs and files and alter the way that your computer works, or stop it from working altogether.

KEY TERMS

Spyware: records the activities of the user, such as the passwords they type into the computer, and transmits this information to the person who wrote the malware.

Even if you are very careful, you can pick up computer viruses through ordinary web activities such as sharing music, files or photographs with others. Or you may visit an infected website without realising. Perhaps you open a spam email by mistake. Even when you download free games or install software, you are still at risk.

How can a computer be protected from viruses?

There are some easy ways to help prevent a virus infecting your computer:

- Install anti-virus software and keep it up to date.
- Install anti-malware software to prevent software from installing itself without you knowing.
- Never download and install software from the internet unless you are certain it is from a source you can trust.
- Don't open email attachments unless you have scanned them.
- Don't click on links in websites that seem suspicious.
- If you use a memory stick or CD ROM, run a virus scan on it before opening any files.

EXTENSION ACTIVITY 8.09

Try to find out how many new viruses are written each month. Then find out how often your antivirus software is updated.

Here are some examples of malware:

- spyware (spies on you)
- adware (pops up adverts all the time)
- root kits (allows a hacker full access to your computer).

Risks of fraud when using a payment card online

Credit card fraud is a broad term used to describe theft or fraud that is committed using a payment card, such as a credit card or a debit card, fraudulently. The purpose of credit card fraud will probably be to obtain goods without paying, or to steal funds from an account.

There are different types of payment card fraud:

- If a payment card is lost, someone may find it and use it fraudulently.
- Fake online bank websites can be designed to mimic the official sites of banks.
- Fake emails can be designed to get you to give your card details (phishing).
- Sometimes a card could be counterfeited or cloned.

The golden rules to keep your card details safe are:

- When you make a transaction, never let the card out of your sight.
- Do not write down passwords, login details or PIN numbers.
- Never tell anyone your passwords, login details or PIN numbers.
- Destroy or shred any documents or receipts that you have with personal information on them.
- If you have lost your payment card, report it straight away to your card provider.
- Make sure no one is watching you when you enter your PIN.

EXTENSION ACTIVITY 8.10

What other rules should be followed to keep your payment card details safe online?

The cloud

Cloud computing is when data and programs are stored in a centralised place on the internet and not on the hard drive of your computer.

 KEY TERMS

Cloud: we sometimes refer to something being 'in the cloud'. It refers to software applications and data that are stored online and used through the internet. Cloud computing means that we don't have to think about where our data is, because with cloud computing it will be wherever we are.

The issues relating to security in the cloud are worldwide. These are the main problems for the people who make the laws all over the world:

- Data flows across country borders.
- A lot of data storage servers are in the USA but they are used by people in different countries so it is not clear which laws of which country should be regulating the privacy of the data when it is travelling from the sender to the server.
- People using the cloud for data storage think that their information is confidential to them because it is their property. However, the place where their data is stored (the internet) is not theirs.

With so much legal uncertainty, your only option is to be responsible for your own data. Here are some ideas to help you:

- Don't store sensitive data in the cloud.
- Make sure you read the small print of your cloud provider to find out how their storage works.
- Be very serious about all of your passwords. Don't use your email login and password for any other purpose because all of your login details and forgotten password details come to you via email.
- Use encryption as it is an excellent way for you to protect your data.
- Some cloud services provide local encryption and decryption of your files, so find out about which they are and use that service. It means that the service will encrypt your files on your own computer and store them safely on the cloud.

Did you know? Around 90% of all passwords can be cracked in seconds!

What is a firewall and why is it used?

A **firewall** is protective barrier between you and any other computers that you are connected to. A firewall can be either a software program or a hardware device that intercepts communications between your computer and the outside in order to help block malicious connections.

This is how it works. Whenever you access the internet, you connect to a 'port' on the machine you are communicating with, where different ports are identified by numbers. The internet services you probably use most are the World Wide Web (which normally uses port 80), incoming email (normally port 110) and outgoing email (normally port 25).

There are thousands of these services and each has a port number. A firewall will close off all of the port services that you are not using. If it did not do that, then your computer could be entered through an unused port number.

KEY TERMS

Firewall: a protective barrier between your computer and any other computers that you are connected to.

EXTENSION ACTIVITY 8.11

Discuss in detail the effectiveness of all the different methods of increasing security that you have read about in this section.

QUESTION 8.09

Write a page on the ways that you can increase your online security.

Summary

- Personal data can mean data that is stored on computer, on paper, or elsewhere.
- Think who may be able to see your posting to social networks before going ahead.
- The privacy settings in social networks should be set up.
- Playing games can hold very similar hazards to using social media.
- Use strong passwords to protect your user login account.
- Never reveal your login password to anyone else.
- A firewall is hardware or software placed between your computer and any network to which you are connected.
- Disconnect from networks when you are not using them.
- Encrypt all sensitive information.
- Send signed email messages. This ensures that the recipients know that the message came from you and not someone pretending to be you.
- Encrypt the contents of email messages and attachments, to protect them so that only your intended recipient can decrypt them.
- Encrypt files and/or folders on your computer. This is helpful for lost or stolen mobile devices and laptops because thieves would need to know your password to access any of the encrypted files or folders.
- Do not respond to smishing or vishing messages.
- Data can be protected by passwords, firewalls and encryption techniques.

Exam-style questions

8.01 Describe **three** ways of ensuring your physical safety in a computer room. [3]

a ....

b ....

c ....

8.02 Describe **three** ways of ensuring your e-safety online. [3]

a ....

b ....

c ....

8.03 In the context of ICT, describe what the difference is between physical safety and e-safety. [2]

....

....

....

8.04 Carlos goes to work in a bank. Describe one type of biometric data that the bank may use to let Carlos enter their secure offices. [2]

Method: ....

Description: ....

....

....

....

8.05 A **firewall** is a protective barrier between you and any other computers that you are connected to. Describe how it works. [3]

....

....

....

....

....

8.06 Sasha now has a computer that she will use for working at home via the internet. It will also be for personal use. Describe the different methods that Sasha could use to help prevent getting a virus on her computer and explain what each method would achieve. [8]

....

....

....

....

....

....

....

....

....

....

....

....

....

....

....

....

....

....

....

....

....

....

8.07 Explain the difference between SSL and a digital certificate. [2]

....

....

....

....

Chapter 9:
Audience

Learning objectives

When you have finished this chapter, you will be able to:

- create ICT solutions that are responsive to and respectful of the needs of the audience
- discuss the legal, moral, ethical and cultural implications of creating an ICT solution
- target ICT solutions to respect the legal, moral, ethical and cultural needs of an audience
- explain the need for copyright legislation and principles of copyright
- describe methods to prevent software copyright being broken
- discuss why the internet is not policed.

Overview

You will have discovered, in Chapter 7, the importance of meeting your customers' or client's needs when designing an IT system. In this chapter we will consider audience appreciation and why the starting point of whatever you do is to determine the needs of the audience. This will entail finding out about your target audience before you start writing or creating a solution for them, whether it be a multimedia presentation, a scientific article, instructions for installing software, a relational database, a website, a report, a speech, a spreadsheet for keeping track of results from sports day or a customer database. In every case, to make any type of writing or presentation as effective or successful as possible, you will need to understand your audience.

What your audience wants, needs and already knows about a topic are important factors that may affect how your work will be received.

For the purpose of this section, the word 'presentation' will be used to cover all of the types of document or presentation mentioned in the first paragraph of this overview.

9.01 Audience appreciation

Analyse the needs of an audience

Once you have analysed the expectations of your audience, you will be well placed to carry out the work of creating a presentation that will be as close as possible to what they require.

You may find that you already know quite a few facts about your audience, such as age range and background (Figure 9.01), but take it step by step:

a **Define who your audience is**. In other words, who will be receiving the presentation? You probably won't know that in detail to start with and that is why you need to carry out an audience analysis.

b **Define what you need to know about your audience**. You will nearly always need to know your audience's existing knowledge about the topic as well as their demographic factors: age, gender, cultural background and so on.

c **Decide how to conduct your analysis and then create the means of carrying it out**. You may decide to collect the information by using a questionnaire or a list of interview questions, the content of which should be a result of what you decided in step b) above.

d Once you have your questions ready, it's time to **select a representative group from your intended audience**. You don't need to include everyone in your analysis, but make sure that you choose a representative sample.

e **It is now time to analyse your findings**. To do this, you may decide to use a spreadsheet to help you summarise your findings quickly.

f Now you have a good sense of your audience and can address their needs and objectives.

Figure 9.01 Who is your audience?

Why is it necessary for solutions to meet the needs of the audience?

QUESTION 9.01

As a class, or in small groups, have a brainstorming session to provide as many answers as you can to the above question, then write down your answers.

The reasons for considering the needs of the audience relate to the type of solution being created for them:

- If it was an instruction booklet for a new router, your audience may comprise those who have never bought a router before, as well as IT professionals. The language has to be clearly written with each end of the spectrum in mind or the instruction booklet will be of no use.

- If you were asked to design a house style for all of the documents used within an organisation, you'd need to consider all the types of information that would need to be covered, as well as all the people in the organisation who would have to use it.

- If you didn't meet the needs of your customer (Figure 9.02), you may not be paid in full, or at all.

Figure 9.02 It is important to ensure that you know what your audience requires

It is often the case that when there is a new project to work on, we just want to get on with it; it is tempting to start straight away without the benefit of detailed planning to ensure that the required outcome is achieved.

9.02 Legal, moral, ethical and cultural appreciation

There are many legal constraints that apply to the design of ICT. You have already carried out some work on the principles of data protection legislation in Chapter 4, and know that it is there to protect personal information about individuals and private information about organisations. We are now going to consider the necessity for copyright legislation.

Copyright

If a person or a firm spends a lot of time producing something then they expect to benefit from their efforts. This is easy to do if the thing that is being produced is something solid.

Imagine that a company produces a new 3D printer and then puts the printers on sale. If you want to use one, you have to buy it. The price that you will have paid is probably far more than it took to make the printer. That is because you are also paying a share of what it cost the company to develop the idea of the product. Also, some money must go to the people who first thought up the idea of 3D printers and how they could work. You have paid some money for the actual printer, some for the development and some for the initial idea. The solid bit is easy to understand but it is less obvious that you are paying for the other two parts.

The research and development work is probably done in the company's laboratories; the scientists there must be paid and the equipment that they use must be bought. The original ideas behind the 3D printing technology are less easy to pin down. Someone, it could even have been you, had the original idea and registered that idea. If the company wants to use the idea and develop it then they need permission and will have to pay to use the idea. Ideas are difficult things to charge for because you cannot actually see them.

A film released on DVD is another example. The DVD is the 'solid' bit and probably costs very little, but a company has had to put the film onto the DVD and then distribute it, which can be expensive, and so the price of the DVD goes up. But somebody else had to write the story, people had to act in it, someone had to compose the music for the film and so on. These extra bits that are not so obvious are what you are really paying for when you buy the DVD. You are paying for the ideas and skills of other people. This is known as their **intellectual property**.

KEY TERMS

Copyright: the exclusive and assignable protection of intellectual property by law.

Intellectual property: the ideas and skills of other people that belong to them.

EXTENSION ACTIVITY 9.01

Why would one internet browser be more successful than others? They are a free service on the internet, so where do they get their money from?

Where do all the adverts come from? Are the adverts the same for all users?

What is Ubuntu? Does it earn money? Where does it get its money from? What are the copyright issues here?

There is a law that protects books, music, art and other things that are written or recorded in some way; it is called **copyright** law. Copyright is an automatic right, it does not need applying for. If something is copyrighted, it means that the person who owns the copyright must be asked for permission to copy it, and will often expect to be paid for its use.

Software is specifically created and written on a computer just like a book or magazine article. Therefore it needs to be protected because it is so easy for people to copy it without paying for it.

Software copyright is a way of protecting software from being used by a person that does not have permission. It applies to applications, websites, games and databases. Usually, with software, if the owner wants to be paid for its use then they will create a licence that defines the terms and conditions of its use, including the price.

EXTENSION ACTIVITY 9.02

Go to a website either for your favourite football team or for your favourite film, or you could try, for example, http://www.leviaducdemillau.com. Now, in pairs, work out the different parts of the content that the site's creators might have needed copyright permission to use.

Most software requires a unique licence key to be entered when you are installing the software on your computer. Remember that in fact, when you buy software, it is not actually the software you are buying, but a licence to use

QUESTION 9.02

a Try to decide what the different types of costs are in producing a textbook like this one and who needs to be paid. If someone copied the text and sold it themselves, would they be doing anything wrong?

b What if you had a school website and music is playing in the background? If you used some pictures in a project, would it make a difference where they came from or whether the project was for use in school or for your IGCSE assessment?

c When someone buys a piece of software they buy the right to use it. Does this mean it can be used on a lot of machines or just one?

d Can one person use the software or lots of people? Can copies of it be made?

e Find out about the different types of licence available when software is bought. What sort of licences does the school have for its software?

f Can you find any examples of free software? What about free versions of games that can be downloaded from the internet?

it; at the time of purchase you can specify whether to buy the licence for one PC, for five or for more; the amount you pay will vary accordingly.

The Federation Against Software Theft (FAST) is an organisation that has been set up by the software industry in the UK to try to prevent users from breaking copyright law; offenders can be prosecuted, or even sent to prison if they are caught. FAST also provide advice and guidance.

QUESTION 9.03

Look at http://www.fast.org.uk, and then carry out some research for the country where you live to see if there is a similar organisation.

Moral, ethical, cultural and environmental issues

Seeking to minimise negative effects on the environment is called a **sustainable** approach, because it does not damage the livelihood of future generations.

In order for you to be able to discuss that and other values associated with ICT products and technologies you need to consider some key questions to determine whether ethical issues may arise:

- Does the product reflect or offend the conventions of society?

- Does a product designed for western society have appeal in African or Middle Eastern cultures, or elsewhere in the global market, and does it affect moral values? In other words, what impact might their products have on people's cultural sensibilities? Some images and slogans have the power to deeply upset or offend people.

- What the implications are for the future and making sure that products don't have too damaging an impact on the environment by seeking to minimise negative effects is called a **sustainable** approach, because it does not damage the livelihood of future generations.

- What about sustainability, recycling and conservation?

Organisations will also need to manage the integrity of data and the creation and retention of documentation, the preservation of privacy and prevention of fraud and computer misuse. They should also consider the effect of global ICT on change for their employees and for other people.

Environmental issues

The type of issues that designers may feel they have a responsibility to take into consideration include:

- The use of technology materials that limit the damage to the world's environment caused by pollution from industry, transport, and so forth.

- The use of renewable energy that is replaceable or cannot be used up. Replaceable energy sources could include natural renewable sources such as solar, wind, hydroelectric and tidal energy.

- Materials that are renewable are ones that can be replaced at least as fast as they are used, for instance paper from managed forests.

- Reusable products are those that can be reused without the need for processing; for example, chips taken from an old circuit and reused in a new one.

- Recycling and reusing. This is when materials such as aluminium cans and paper are processed and then used to produce new products.

QUESTION 9.04

Products that are made using recycled materials are usually clearly marked (Figure 9.03).

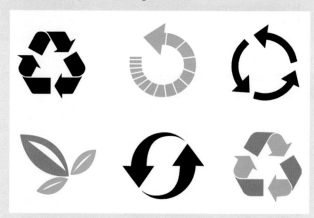

Figure 9.03   Examples of recycling icons to be found on some packaging

a Look at the packaging on the printer paper you are using. Can you see a recycling icon?

b What other products have you seen that have been made from recycled materials?

Policing the internet

Should the internet be policed? If so, who will regulate it and how can this be achieved?

Never before have mass communication and social interaction had the opportunities and impact now offered by the internet. At the same time, unprecedented opportunities exist for governments to monitor and control how we use the internet to communicate. This leads to a conundrum (Figure 9.04): should the internet be regulated, and if so, by whom?

Figure 9.04   Policing the internet

Different levels of control are imposed around the world. The most basic way to control what sites are used is to block those that, for a wide variety of reasons, a government does not want us to use. The blocking of sites is fairly widespread.

Sites will often be blocked to help to stop what is seen as inappropriate material: huge social media sites have been blocked by some countries to combat this.

Sometimes search terms may be blocked if it is thought that they could lead you to information thought to be unsuitable. Such actions are, in effect, internet policing. Many thousands of people may be employed to monitor social media to find terms and information deemed to be sensitive. More may be employed to intervene in discussion groups, for instance to look at all the discussion threads for signs of content thought to be inappropriate.

Figure 9.05 Depending on where you live, you may find that you are denied access to a variety of different types of sites

---

EXTENSION ACTIVITY 9.03

There are many questions that offer themselves for discussion and debate as a class. Your teacher will probably split you into groups and allocate one or two questions to each group for discussion. Each group could then offer their conclusions to the rest of the class.

a   Has the growth of the internet gone too far now to be regulated? If so, should we just take the bad with the good?

b   Is the larger issue to decide who should be assigned to regulate content bearing in mind that content is generated by billions of people across the world and that it can be interpreted in different ways by different people?

c   Some content that violates a local law can be taken down immediately, but what about the global issue?

d   You have read about the current intellectual property laws that exist because of piracy or infringement going back to the invention of the printing press.

   Does intellectual property only exist when it is defended or acted upon? If we stop trying to enforce intellectual property, will it no longer exist?

e   Is copyright law only reactive? In other words, does it only come into being when someone reacts to it? Although current intellectual property laws exist, is it their enforcement that is the problem? If an author, for instance, thinks that his intellectual copyright has been infringed, he can do something about it, but if he doesn't then the transgressors will get away with it. Nothing has happened if no one reacts.

f   Attempts to get the middlemen, such as internet service providers, to take legal responsibility have failed. Probably because of this, different strategies are emerging: should a film-maker be able to force an ISP to hand over the IP addresses of those who have illegally downloaded a film? (Bear in mind that this would involve loss of privacy to the customers of the ISP.)

127

EXTENSION ACTIVITY 9.04

There are ethical issues at a personal level and at a wider level. In pairs or small groups, discuss one from each of the two lists below.

Personal ethical issues

a   If you use copy and paste to copy material from the internet to use in your own work, what should you do to ensure that you are using that content correctly?

b   What do you think about downloading films or music without thoroughly checking the copyright terms?

c   What would you do if you encountered cyber-bullying (if you use social networks)?

Figure 9.06 How would you react if an uncomplimentary picture of you appeared on the internet?

d Why is it wrong to use someone else's password? What could the consequences be?

e What is wrong with using social media to pass on gossip you have heard about someone?

f When would it be wrong to take pictures of your friends and put them on the internet (Figure 9.06)?

Wider ethical issues

Decide whether each of the following issues is ethical, not ethical, infringes freedom of speech, doesn't have a clear black or white answer. More than one of these options might apply to each. Make sure that you can justify your choices.

a Reporting suspected wrongdoing within your organisation (whistle-blowing).

b Governments blocking search engines or search terms.

c Using social media to organise a demonstration.

d A government blocking or shutting down the internet.

e Using the internet to leak sensitive information.

f The use of the tracking device on smartphones.

Summary

- You should always research your customer(s) before starting to create a presentation for them.

- Ensure that you produce work in accordance with your customer's needs.

- Consider legal, moral, ethical and cultural aspects of any work you produce.

- Do not infringe copyright law.

Exam-style questions

9.01 Define what intellectual property is. [2]

....

....

9.02 Apart from authors and songwriters, list four types of workers who would be protected by copyright law. [4]

....

....

....

9.03 Explain what the term 'renewable materials' means. [3]

....

....

....

9.04 Discuss the advantages and disadvantages of policing the internet. [8]

....

....

....

....

....

....

....

....

9.05 Describe the ethical issues associated with the use of 3D printers. [4]

....

....

....

....

....

....

9.06 You have been asked to give a short presentation to a live audience about the ethical issues involved in disposing of computer equipment. Explain what you need to know about your audience before creating your presentation. [4]

....

....

....

....

....

....

Chapter 10
Communication

Learning objectives

When you have finished this chapter you will be able to:

- describe the constraints that affect the use of email
- define the term spam
- explain why spam needs to be prevented
- describe the methods which can be used to help prevent spam
- explain why email groups are used
- understand fundamentals of the internet
- explain the advantages and disadvantages of using the internet.

10.01 Communicate with other ICT users using email

To communicate with a specific person there are several applications that can be used, the most common being **email**, electronic mail. The communicating computers must both have an email application on them, but the applications don't have to be of the same kind. Messages can be composed, files attached, recipients chosen and the message sent from the email application. And of course the recipient can do the reverse: read the message, extract the attached file and see who sent the email.

The internet can also be used for personal and group communication. An email arrives in the recipient's mailbox almost instantly, but don't forget that the actual speed of the communication depends on how often they check for emails and read them.

An advantage of email communication is that communications are addressed to the person rather than a physical place. A letter will be delivered to a place, whether or not the person is actually there, whereas, an email is delivered to the person. They can then collect it using any computer wherever in the world they happen to be. This ability to stay in touch is important to anyone who travels a lot, especially to business people who need to be mobile.

Constraints
Laws of the country

> **QUESTION 10.01**
>
> Carry out some research by entering the keywords 'email laws in other countries' into an internet search engine. You should see a list of countries and some of them will show the laws that are applied there.
>
> You should make a note of the laws or rules applying in the country where you live, and then investigate them further, making some brief notes so that you remember what they are and what they do.
>
> If you can't find an entry against the name of your own country, you should make a few brief notes outlining the type of laws that you think may be appropriate.

Acceptable language

Depending on the purpose of your email and your intended audience, the way you word your messages might be formal, or casual, or brief. You read about the importance of considering your audience in Chapter 9. Remember that you need to consider:

- who your audience is
- what their relationship to you is
- what sort of impression your message will give about you.

Some tips for emailing:

- Decide, before sending your message, if it is alright to be brief or whether it would be more appropriate to send a more professional sounding message.
- If you would hesitate to say something to someone's face, then don't write it in an email.
- Subject lines are important. You should always use a subject line that indicates what the email is about. Also, some people will not open an email that does not have anything in the subject line.

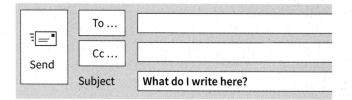

Figure 10.01 Make sure you use a strong subject line to indicate what your email is about

- Greetings and signing. Don't just start your email with text, always use an appropriate greeting; it is also important to put your name at the end of an email.
- Including others in the conversation. Use the cc box if you want to send a copy of the email to someone. The bcc box is for when you want to send a copy of the email to someone without the recipient knowing that you have done so.
- Be brief and clear in your writing.
- If your message is work related or formal, you need to proofread it to check for proper use of grammar, spelling and punctuation, as well as appropriate use of capitalisation.

Netiquette and copyright

The term 'netiquette' is a corruption of 'net' from the word internet and 'etiquette'. From that you will get the idea that it means being courteous when you are posting online and respecting the views of others.

If you use online discussion groups, you may have noticed that most groups have their own expected rules of behaviour.

Some general 'rules' to observe are:

- No personal abuse.

- You can strongly disagree with the point of view of others while still being polite.

- Don't spam.

- Write clearly and remember that whatever you post is public and there forever; it could be read by possible future employers (see Chapter 8), your parents, partner, children, etc.

- Don't post any material that is copyrighted if you don't own the rights or you could be prosecuted by the person who owns the copyright.

It may seem surprising that emails can infringe copyright laws, but remember that photographs, videos, text and music are all copyrighted the moment that they are created. Theoretically, if an email has been sent to you and you forward it to others, it is possible that you could be breaking a copyright law!

According to the World Intellectual Property Organization (WIPO), 'The laws of almost all countries provide that copyright protection starts as soon as the work is created.' Therefore, the works mentioned in the previous paragraph do not need any copyright symbol © or the words 'All rights reserved' to be protected.

Because copyright law has not kept totally up to date with advancing technology, the forwarding of emails has not come under much scrutiny, and the forwarding of emails is commonplace. However, just as copying and distributing a handwritten letter would violate the writer's copyright, an email that you either forward or copy onto a web page could become a copyright infringement.

Note that emails can be used as evidence in a court of law in some countries if they constitute harassment.

QUESTION 10.02

a Research the local guidelines, i.e. whether the laws relating to written communications automatically apply to emails.

b Find out if your school or your workplace has guidelines for forwarding or copying all or part of an email.

Need for security

Email security should be a priority for businesses because of the growing threats from hackers, viruses, spam, phishing and identity theft (see Chapter 8).

Why is email security necessary? Failure to have security could result in a virus infection that could destroy your system. From a commercial aspect, loss of systems could severely damage a business if they lost data and records. There is also a possible legal aspect, that you may be held liable for the losses suffered through an infection that you may have unknowingly passed on to others, some of whom could even be business competitors.

In Chapter 4 you read about how data packets travel through a network, and that the computers and other hardware on the network determine the best delivery route for data, including your emails, as they pass through the network.

Have you heard of a packet sniffer?

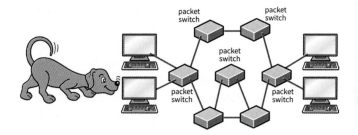

Figure 10.02 A packet sniffer is a program that can sniff out and decode each packet flowing over a digital network

A packet sniffer (Figure 10.02) is also known as a network analyser, wireless sniffer and other names. It is a computer program or a piece of hardware capable of intercepting packets as they flow across a network. It can decode the data to find the values of fields in the packet and analyse the contents.

What the sniffer sees may only be fragments, but it is relatively simple for it to spot an email because it may see a 'Subject' line or part of an SMTP command (see Section 10.02) such as 'Mail From: <sender>'. On its route to the recipient, your email passes through hardware, cables and airspace that may be operated by different countries or organisations. Anywhere during this journey it could be scanned to find out if it resembles spam or to see if it contains malware; the contents are able to be read to find out what kinds of advertising the person receiving the email may respond to.

These are some of the reasons that emails need to be encrypted. When the internet and such protocols as SMTP, Telnet, FTP and DNS (see Section 10.02) were new technologies transforming computing, the necessity for security was not the issue that it has become these days. To now add security layers to such a deeply rooted system is not simple.

Transport Layer Security (TLS; an evolution of SSL) is one method that can be used to ensure that your emails cannot be intercepted when en route between servers, but not when they are actually in the servers along the route. In other words, they are not encrypted before they leave your own computer, nor during the short time that they are in servers along the route, nor after they arrive at their final server.

In Chapter 8 you looked at the importance of keeping your password safe, not using the same password for more than one account and not using a password that could easily be guessed by someone else.

Make sure that you keep your password private, including for your email account.

Spam

What is spam? It is junk mail that you haven't asked for; you probably get some in paper form through the letter box as well. Most email providers can filter out much of the spam sent to you, but still some of it gets through and it can be a nuisance as well as posing threats (Figure 10.03).

Figure 10.03 Manage your emails!

KEY TERMS

Spam mail: junk email. Often the same message is sent to many people by email.

People sending spam build mailing lists from email addresses that they collect. When you use the internet to sign up to any website or to register software, or buy something, you may be asked either to tick or to untick a box if you agree to be sent correspondence from other similar sources. If you are aware of this and read it carefully, you will avoid some spam. However, most spam will be emails that you have not agreed to receive.

Even if you are careful where you leave your email address, spammers will get your email by buying lists of email addresses from people who will have legally collected them.

How to deal with spam
Some tips to help to counter spam mail are:

- When you register with a site, read the terms to see whether you are agreeing to being sent emails and look for any check boxes that you may be opting into or opting out of.

- Use the 'unsubscribe' option at the bottom of any marketing emails that you receive. Your details should then be removed from their distribution list.

- Use the 'Mark as Spam' option as well as the 'Block Senders' feature on your email account.

- Make sure that your password is secure (see Chapter 8).

- Keep your antivirus program up to date.

Email groups
An email group is also known as a contact group or a mailing list, and they help you to simplify the process of sending the same email to a group of people. If you address a message to a contact group, it saves you a lot of time as you don't need to key in every recipient's address; it will go to everyone in that group at the same time.

Creating a contact group is an option that will be available in your email account.

10.02 Effective use of the internet

As you saw in Chapter 4, the **internet** is a global network of interconnected computer networks that is used to connect people, communities and countries worldwide.

And an **intranet** is a private computer network within an organisation. Even though an intranet uses internet technologies, it is safeguarded from the global internet. But what then is the **World Wide Web** (www or web), and how does it differ from the internet?

The terms 'internet' and 'World Wide Web' are quite often used interchangeably, but as you will see, they are not the same, even though they are related.

While the internet is a massive network of networks forming an infrastructure to connect millions of computers together globally, the web is a way of accessing information using the internet; it uses the **HyperText Transfer Protocol** (HTTP) to transmit data. This allows applications to communicate and share information.

KEY TERMS

Internet Service Provider (ISP): ISPs allow a connection to the internet (usually with a price attached to different levels of service).

HyperText Transfer Protocol (HTTP): Used by the World Wide Web to define how a web page is formatted and transferred.

HyperText Transfer Protocol secure variant (HTTPS): HTTP using a secure encrypted link.

It is the web that uses browsers such as Internet Explorer, Safari, Firefox and Chrome to access web pages that are linked via **hyperlinks**. Therefore, the web is just a method of disseminating information using the internet.

However, it is the internet, rather than the web, that is used for email. Email uses the **Simple Mail Transfer Protocol** (SMTP), which is a communication protocol for mail servers for transmitting data.

The structure of a URL

There are other terms that you need to understand. In Chapter 4 you learned about the different parts of a **Uniform Resource Locator** (URL), which is the unique address of any particular web page. It works in a similar way to writing an address on the outside of an envelope to show where you want the letter to go to.

KEY TERMS

Hyperlink: a clickable area or word on a web page that lets you jump to a different page.

Uniform Resource Locator (URL): the unique web address of every page on the World Wide Web.

QUESTION 10.03

Look back at Chapter 4 to remind yourself of the structure of a URL, then do the following exercise:

Name the different sections of the following URL indicated by different colours. The first one has been done for you:

Protocol

http://www.bbc.co.uk/education

An URL is therefore the complete instruction of where a resource is on the internet, and is made up of several parts. The first part, which is not technically part of the URL but which identifies the protocol to be used (usually http), can also specify other protocols such as https (secure hypertext transfer protocol) or ftp (file transfer protocol).

Table 10.01 sets out the different protocols that have been discussed in this chapter (and a few more).

Acronym	Protocol	When it is used
FTP	File Transfer Protocol	Transfers files from one host to another. Used when downloading or uploading a file.
HTTP	Hypertext Transfer Protocol	Used by the World Wide Web to define how a web page is formatted and transferred.
SSL	Secure Socket Layer	A standard form of security to enable an encrypted link between a server and a browser. All of the data passing between them remains private.
HTTPS	Hypertext Transfer Protocol Secure	This means that HTTP is using SSL to protect against eavesdropping.

Table 10.01 Internet protocols

134

Web browsers and search engines

What is a web browser used for? A web browser is a software application used to retrieve web pages from servers on the internet and to display them to the user.

What is a search engine used for? A search engine is a website that has indexed billions of web pages; it is used to enable you to search the internet to find information. If you go to any search engine's home page you will see a box for you to type in the key words to be searched for. You will get a long list of pages that best match your key words.

What is the difference? You use a browser to access information over the internet and the search engine will find it for you. You need a browser to be able to get to and use a search engine.

QUESTION 10.04

Look at Table 10.02 and decide which are search engines and which are web browsers.

Put an 'S' in the box if you think it is a search engine and put a 'B' in the box if you think it is a web browser.

If you are unsure of any, you could use a browser and a search engine to find out!

Altavista		AOL	
Bing		Chrome	
Deepnet Explorer		DuckDuckGo	
Excite		Firefox	
Google		Google Chrome	
Internet Explorer		Lycos	
Maxthon		Opera	
Rockmelt		Safari	
Yahoo			

Table 10.02 Browser or search engine?

Blog as a means of communication

The word **blog** is a corruption of the term 'web log'. It is a website that you can use either as a diary of thoughts (a reflection), or to share ideas and opinions and links (Figure 10.04). People reading your blog have the facility to comment directly on any of your entries. Blogs are really useful for sharing knowledge, and some attract a large following.

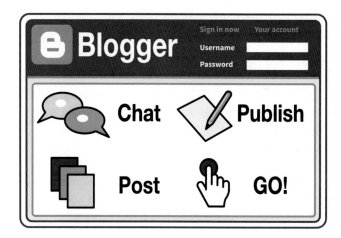

Figure 10.04 Front page of a typical blog site

Wiki as a means of communication

A wiki is a website that allows you to become a participant in its creation (Figure 10.05). In fact, you can either create or edit the site contents. It is, therefore, a collaborative site that is always being revised. A famous example is Wikipedia.

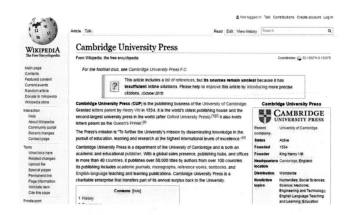

Figure 10.05 A Wikipedia page

QUESTION 10.05

Find out what the term 'wiki' means and where the word comes from.

Although a blog allows the general public to post and to comment on the posts of others, no one is able to change a post or a comment. A wiki does allow other people to change what has been written. That is why a blog is more about individual opinion and a wiki about group consensus.

135

Social networking websites as a means of communication

Social media can form a central part of how we communicate, and online communities can be very influential. This isn't limited to individuals; companies of all sizes are using it as a marketing and branding tool. Large organisations monitor discussions about their company or products because the collective voice of a discussion on social media can alert them to problems and also to what holds appeal, enabling them to focus their marketing accordingly. They can communicate messages about what they offer and blog posts and tweets also help organisations to create communities, all of which help towards the promotion of their products or service, making social media much more cost-effective than traditional approaches to marketing.

Social media has different levels of communication. There is also something called 'direct messaging' that allows you to send a direct message inside a social network to someone with whom you have established a relationship. It is, as it says, a direct message from one person to another, without having to use email which may bring with it lots of junk mail and messages from people you have never heard of. For much of social media, such direct messages have a limit on the number of characters allowed.

This leads on to considering traditional email. Emails still have a place in communication, but because they can often be lengthy, they are causing a lot of time loss in the workplace as people can spend much of their day managing their emails (Figure 10.06). This means that for email to maintain its place, the messages need to be kept succinct and focused.

Figure 10.06 People in the workplace can struggle to find time to manage their email effectively

Advantages and disadvantages of using the internet

The internet is one of the main reasons that we spend a lot of time on laptops, tablets and smartphones. It is such an interesting and useful tool, but you need to be very alert when using the internet. Have a look at the list of advantages and disadvantages of using the internet in Table 10.03.

Advantages	Disadvantages
Limitless amount of available information	Searches for *relevant* information are not always as fast as you would like
Speed of accessing information	Not always easy to find *reliable* information on the internet
Carry out research from home instead of visiting libraries	Possibility of theft of personal information
Provides a platform for other products such as VOIP applications	Viruses
Entertainment	Extreme images, opinions, violence and dangerous sites available to all
Online services, e.g. make purchases and pay bills online	Spamming
Download software and music	
Storage in the cloud	

Table 10.03 Advantages and disadvantages of internet use

QUESTION 10.06

a Look at the first two disadvantages in Table 10.03 and list some reasons

   i why searches do not always find relevant information, and

   ii why the information found is not always *reliable*.

b Discuss the advantages and disadvantages of using the internet and try to fill in some more boxes.

How to evaluate the reliability of information found on the internet

Here are several considerations to help you to decide on the reliability of information:

- **Authorship:** who wrote it?

- **Accuracy:** is the information consistent with other information on this same topic either published on the internet or in books or magazines? Is it free from spelling and grammatical errors?

- **Currency:** does the document show a publication date, and is it reasonably up to date or still relevant? Are the links up to date and do they all work?

- **Bias:** is the document on the web server of an organisation associated with politics or particular philosophical beliefs? Does the site reflect just one individual view (is it their personal home page)?

- **Country and domain:** is it a government site (.gov), an educational site (.edu, .ac)? Is it a not-for-profit organization (.org)? Although many country codes are not strictly controlled, it is worth looking to see what the country code is.

EXTENSION ACTIVITY 10.01

Evaluate two different internet resources and write a short report on each of them. You should use the following criteria as headings in your report. At the end, add a conclusion about whether the website meets your own needs and quality standards:

- Author
- Bias
- Currency
- Audience
- Accuracy
- Links

QUESTION 10.07

Name the country! Copy Table 10.04 on a separate sheet. To complete it use the second column to write in the name of the country that uses the country code in the first column. Then use the fourth column to fill in the type of organisation that might use the endings shown in the third column.

Country		Main use	
.uk		.com	
.de		.org	
.fr		.ac	
.au		.net	
.lt		.co	
.kz		.eu	
.ca		.biz	
.cn		.info	
.my			
.mg			

Table 10.04 Internet country and organisation designations

If your country is not represented here, add it to the table. You may also add to the other gaps if you can.

137

Summary

- A web browser is an application that lets you view World Wide Web pages.
- A search engine performs searches for your key words in its index.
- Photographs, videos, text and music are all copyrighted to the author the moment they are written without the need for any other action.
- Spam is unsolicited junk mail.
- It is important to evaluate the contents of a website before trusting it.
- Netiquette is the importance of being courteous to other internet users.

Exam-style questions

10.01 Describe what an email group is. [1]

....

....

10.02 Name **four** things that you should check for when evaluating a website. [4]

a ....

b ....

c ....

d ....

10.03 Discuss the differences between a blog and a wiki. [3]

....

....

....

....

....

....

10.04 Explain the difference between a web browser and a search engine. [3]

....

....

....

....

....

....

....

10.05 Describe the difference between HTTP and HTTPS. [2]

....

....

10.06 Explain the differences between the internet and the World Wide Web. [4]

....

....

....

....

Chapter 11
File management

Learning objectives

When you have finished this chapter you will be able to:

- identify different file types that are used for different purposes, such as css, csv, gif, htm, jpg, pdf, png, rtf, txt, zip
- quickly locate files you have stored
- open and import different types of files
- save files in a hierarchical directory/folder structure that you plan and create
- save files using appropriate file names that enable you to identify content
- save and print files in a variety of formats
- save and export data into file formats for your application packages, such as .doc, .docx, .xls, .sdb, .sdc, .rtf, .ppt
- explain why generic file formats are needed
- save and export data into generic file formats, including .csv, .txt, .rtf, .pdf, .css, .htm
- explain the need to reduce file sizes for storage or transmission and identify where this will be necessary
- reduce file sizes using file compression techniques.

Overview

Depending on the application you use to create a file, it will have specific characteristics. For example, a file created using a word processor will have different characteristics to a file created using a spreadsheet. Files associated with different applications or purposes have to be labelled so that you know which file type they are and, more importantly, so that the computer will know which file type they are (Figure 11.01). The way that files are labelled is called a **file extension**.

140

> **KEY TERMS**
>
> **File name:** a way to identify a file.
> **File extension:** a way to identify the type of file.

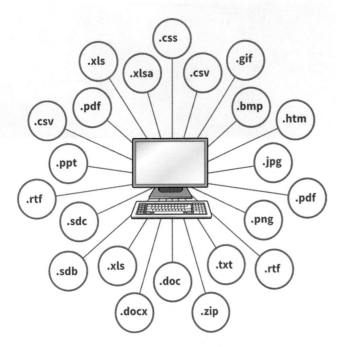

Figure 11.01 There are many different file types

As you would think, a file extension goes at the end of a filename, separated from the filename by a full stop which, in computer terms, is referred to as a 'dot'.

Simply put, a word-processed file might be named agenda.doc or agenda.docx, depending on which version of the word processor you are using; an audio file may end in .wav and a spreadsheet file in .xls.

If you open a file by double-clicking on it, the extension tells the computer which program to run to open that file.

The default setting in Windows is to hide the file extensions from the user, so unless you change the setting, you will not see them. You can turn on the display in the Folder Options menu: select View and click the box labelled 'Hide extensions for known file types' to untick it.

11.01 Managing files effectively

It is important to keep your files organised so that you know where to look for them when you next want to open them (Figure 11.02). The goal of file management is to make sure you can quickly and easily find what you are looking for.

Figure 11.02 I'm sure my files are in there somewhere!

Identify different file types and their uses

It is important to be able to recognise the different file types that you use. If you had an application open and then tried to open a file that wasn't of the expected type for that application, the file may become corrupted. To recover from this, you might have to perform a complete system restore, back to the time before you made the error.

However, most applications can import and export data as long as you save the data file in a format that is able to be read by other applications. You can then open a file created in another application, view it and edit it.

First, you need to be able to identify common file types.

Copy Table 11.01 on a separate sheet. First fill in the name of any extensions that you might already know, then do some research to complete the others. The first one has been done for you.

Extension	Identification and use
.bmp	Bitmap file
.css	
.csv	
.db	
.gif	
.htm	
.jpg	
.mdb	
.pdf	
.png	
.ppt	
.psd	
.rtf	
.tif	
.txt	
.zip	

Table 11.01 File types

Export and import files of different types

Despite what you have learned above, there are still many occasions when importing data files is required. Because of this requirement, standard file types have been developed that can be understood by a variety of applications.

Examples of these sorts of file are: .mp3 files for sound, .gif and .jpg for images, together with standard file types for text and spreadsheet data for example, and many more.

If you save a spreadsheet in a **comma separated values** (.csv) format it can be used with any spreadsheet program.

However, they are different to other spreadsheet file types because you can only have a single sheet in any one csv file and it will not save details of cells, columns or formatting; neither can it save formulas. It saves in the form of a text file with the information separated by commas.

KEY TERMS

Comma separated values (CSV): data saved in a table structured format.

To understand how a file is imported, first look at how it is exported. This example uses Microsoft Excel, but any spreadsheet software will follow a similar process.

To save a spreadsheet as a .csv file, have your spreadsheet file open and click on File > Save As >.

Under **Save as type**, choose CSV. Click Save (see Figure 11.03).

File name:	Book1
Save as type:	**Excel Workbook**

Excel Workbook
Excel Macro-Enabled Workbook
Excel Binary Workbook
Excel 97-2003 Workbook
XML Data
Single File Web Page
Web Page
Excel Template
Excel Macro-Enabled Template
Excel 97–2003 Template
Text (Tab delimited)
Unicode Text
XML Spreadsheet 2003
Microsoft Excel 5.0/95 Workbook
CSV (Comma delimited)
Formatted Text (Space delimited)
Text (Macintosh)
Text (MS-DOS)
CSV (Macintosh)
CSV (MS-DOS)
DIF (Data Interchange Format)
SYLK (Symbolic Link)
Excel Add-In
Excel 97-2003 Add-In
PDF
XPS Document
OpenDocument Spreadsheet

Figure 11.03 Saving a spreadsheet file as .csv file type

If a message appears saying that your file 'may contain features that are not compatible with CSV', click 'Yes' to continue; it is only reminding you that any formatting (colours or bold text, for example) or formulas you have used will not be saved.

One advantage is that it can be much faster to import spreadsheet data in this way rather than entering the data, especially when you can import more than a million rows and around 16 000 columns! Another advantage is that they can be imported to a different spreadsheet program.

When you want to import a .csv file, the easiest way is simply to open it in your spreadsheet and then save it as file type .xls.

Here is just a sample of other file types that can be imported and opened:

- .xml: because computer systems and databases contain data in incompatible formats, XML provides a software and hardware independent way of storing data; it is stored in a plain text format to make it easier to be shared between different applications. The easiest way to open an XML file is to double-click on it and let your PC decide which default application should open the file.

- .zip: uses compression technology as an efficient way of distributing data.

- .pdf: allows you to open and read files using a free downloadable reader application.

- .txt: plain text file with no formatting.

KEY TERMS

Extensible Markup Language (XML): a markup language that sets rules for coding documents so that they are readable by both humans and computers.

QUESTION 11.02

Another way of translating between file types, that you will have used already, is by storing data temporarily in the RAM of your computer to transfer something from one application to another. For example, if you create a graph using a spreadsheet application and want to use the graph in a desktop publishing application.

Can you think what this method is called?

Storing and locating files

A few tips for managing your files:

- Give every file a name that immediately tells you what is in it.

- Make folders to hold files of a similar nature.

- Keep your folders in a hierarchical structure.

A hierarchical filing system might be structured like Figure 11.04.

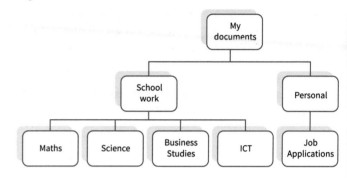

Figure 11.04   Typical hierarchical file management structure

File names

There are many methods of naming files that work well. The important thing is to decide on a method that suits you and keep to it consistently.

- Include the date the document was composed in your file name; this can be in the form of, for example, 18-04-15.

- Indicate what is in the document in the filename; for example, it may be 'Notes for English essay'.

- This would result in a filename such as '18-04-15 Notes for English essay.doc' (you don't have to type in the dot or the extension after the filename; the software application you are using will automatically do that for you).

- Before you finalise the save, you need to specify which folder the file should be stored in; in this case it would belong in 'My documents/School Work/English'.

Printing files in different formats

In Chapter 19, you will read about printing different presentation formats, specifically printouts in the form of speaker's notes, outline slides and notes; in Chapter 20, you will also read about printing to fit to one page. There are many other, different formats in which you can print.

Draft documents

Instead of printing a **final copy** of your document you can print a **draft document**. Most applications will give you the option to print a draft version of your documents; this speeds up printing, in particular when your document has several different fonts or graphics, because when printing drafts, the different fonts are not used and the graphics will not be in place.

Screenshots

If you want to capture an image of whatever is on your screen, you can do this with the print screen button on your keyboard if you are using Windows. The button may be labelled 'PrnScr', 'PrtScn' or similar. On a laptop, you may have to hold down the 'Fn' or function key when you tap Print Screen. Once you tap it, the image of your screen is stored on the pasteboard. You can then paste the image into a suitable program in order to print it. If you want to save it as an image file, you should paste it into an imaging application and it will save as an image file that you can use wherever you want.

Database reports

You will learn how to create a report from your database in Chapter 18, Section 18.03. Once you have created a report and formatted it to your requirements, you can click on 'Reports' from any view page and then click the printer icon to see a preview page. Once you are satisfied, click 'Print Report'.

Data table

Once you have entered data into your database table, you can print a copy of the table. From the Database window, select 'Tables' and click the name of the table you want to print. Then simply select to print, either from the file menu or by clicking the print icon.

Graph/chart

Once you have created a chart in your spreadsheet application (see Chapter 16), you will probably want to print it. You can do this either with or without the worksheet data. You can drag the chart to the position on the worksheet where you want it and resize it to suit the data, then print. You can also print a chart on its own; the simplest way to do this is to copy and paste it into a worksheet on its own, then resize it to fit one page, then print.

Web page in browser and HTML view

Before printing a web page in HTML, you need to first view it in that format: select the View menu, then click on Source or Source Code. Many web pages use frames; this means that they can display several web pages on the same screen. When you want to view the source code of such a screen, you need to do it one frame at a time by right-clicking the web page in a frame, then click on View Source.

Once you have the source view displayed, you can print.

11.2 Reducing file sizes for storage or for transmission

In order to achieve faster transmission times for electronic files you can compress the files, which will result in a lower number of bytes used to store and then transmit (or download) the file. This is achieved through the process of compression to encode a file's data information more efficiently by altering the structure of the data temporarily.

There are two types of compression to consider: **lossy** compression and **lossless** compression (Figure 11.05).

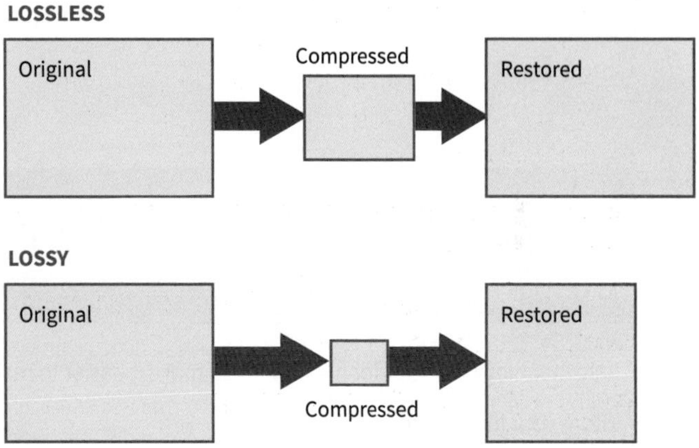

Figure 11.05 Compression types

Lossless compression

Lossless compression, as its name implies, reduces files with no loss of information during the process. Therefore this enables the original file to be recreated exactly when uncompressed. Algorithms are used to create reference points for recurring textual patterns; these are stored and sent with the (now smaller) encoded file. When the file is uncompressed, it is reconstructed by using the reference points to put back the original information.

Lossless compression is mainly used for documents, text and numerical data where it is essential not to lose any information. Zip compression, mentioned earlier in this chapter, is a lossless compression type that detects patterns and replaces them with a single character.

Lossy compression

Lossy compression works by eliminating some bits of information to reduce the file size; in fact, it permanently deletes unnecessary data. Lossy compression is often used with images, audio and graphics because a loss of quality is usually a reasonable option. However, with lossy compression, the original file is not retained.

For example, an image may contain a blue sky, with differences in shades of blue so minuscule that the human eye cannot detect them, so some of the shades are lost. The data is still viable because the essential colours are still there. Joint Photographic Experts Group (JPEG) is an example of a file type that uses lossy compression.

Text encoding

Using the file type .txt means that you can share text files without needing to know how the text is stored. Even if you need to share a text file with people who use other languages, or share them with other computer systems, it is best to use an encoding standard to open or save the file(s).

The text you see on your screen is stored as numeric values in the text file and your computer translates those values into characters that you can read. It does this by using an encoding standard.

An encoding standard is a numbering scheme that assigns each text character in a character set to a numeric value. A character set can include alphabetical characters, numbers and other symbols. Different languages commonly consist of different sets of characters.

EXTENSION ACTIVITY 11.01

Research ASCII and Unicode and make some notes on what they are and how they work with .txt files.

Summary

- Use meaningful names for file naming to make it easier to recognise what they contain.

- Store your files in a hierarchical structure.

- Lossless compression will mainly be used for documents, text and numerical data where it is essential not to lose any information.

- Lossy compression reduces the file size by eliminating some bits of information, permanently deleting unnecessary data.

- Zip compression is a lossless compression type that works by detecting and replacing patterns with a single character.

- There are many different formats in which you can print documents, so it is important to think about and to select exactly the format or view that you wish to print beforehand.

Exam-style questions

11.01 Explain what types of file you would use lossy compression for and why. [3]

....

....

....

....

....

11.02 Explain when you would use lossless compression and why. [3]

....

....

....

....

....

....

11.03 List four ways you can help to ensure you will be able to find your file quickly. [4]

a ....

b ....

c ....

d ....

11.04 Complete the second column of Table 11.02 with the type of file that would be best for each circumstance described in the first column.

File content	File type
A high resolution picture of the members of a football team	
A short video to be uploaded to the internet describing how to use a spreadsheet	
A text document giving information about how to use a software application	
An image showing a map of a campus	

Table 11.02 File types

11.05 Give a definition of .csv and discuss the advantages and disadvantages that this file type offers. [4]

....

....

....

....

11.06 Raoul wants to send several files as email attachments but he is limited by the size of files that his provider allows. He is thinking of using zip technology. Explain how it works, both for sending and receiving. [4]

....

....

....

....

11.07 A computer shop is setting up a file storage system to hold data in different locations on their shop computer. It will need to store information on the following:

- Laser printers
- Ink jet printers
- Portable printers
- Desktop computers
- Laptop computers
- Antivirus software
- Applications software
- Utility software
- Cases for laptops, tablets, mobile phones, external hard drives.

Set out a hierarchical folder structure in three levels that would best suit their needs. Give the name of each folder. [6]

11.08 You have just clicked on a filename to open it. Explain how the computer knows which program to use to run that file. [2]

....

....

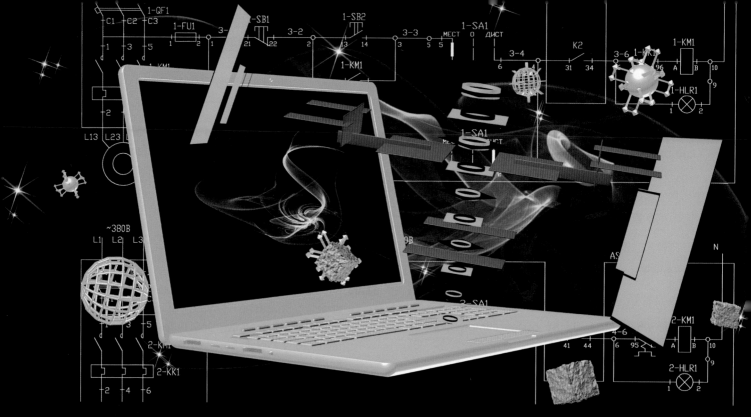

Chapter 12:
Images

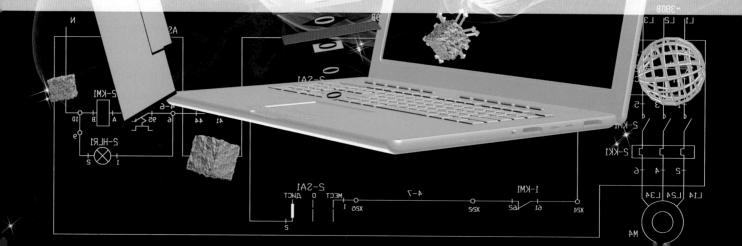

Learning objectives

When you have completed this section, you should be able to:

- use software tools to place and edit an image to meet the requirements of its intended application and audience
- know when it is necessary to edit an image
- place an image with precision
- resize an image
- maintain or adjust the aspect ratio of an image, or distort an image where appropriate
- crop, rotate and reflect an image
- adjust the colour depth, brightness and contrast of an image
- understand the need to reduce image resolution to increase speed
- reduce the resolution of an image to reduce file size.

Overview

The skills you need to use software tools to edit and manipulate images are very useful because you can use them in other applications as well. When you create a document in a word processor you will most likely need to place images at appropriate places in the document. You will also most likely need to edit the image to make it fit in with the needs of your intended audience.

At times images might need to be resized or you might wish to cut a part of the image out (crop an image). At other times you might place one image on top or partially on top of other images (layering of images) or need to turn an image around from the way it was originally facing (reflect or rotate an image). For example, many adverts showing people's ages use photo editing skills to change the colour of some parts of the image, e.g. a person with grey hair in the original image can have the grey changed to brown by using image editing techniques. The 'red eye' problem in some images can also be edited out, and image processing techniques are used in blue-screen and green-screen technology which makes video clips appear as if they were filmed on location.

Most websites use images, but if they are too large in terms of the storage space, and not stored in compressible file formats, they will cause the web pages to take too long to download. This can cause problems for businesses that rely on customer satisfaction when visiting a web page. Generally, users tend to skip websites whose pages take too long to download.

However, there are many instances when images are used other than on websites, such as those used in advertisements for other media and for those used in movies, videos, posters, brochures and so on.

EXTENSION ACTIVITY 12.01

Think of different times when you might be required to edit images. Discuss the reasons why you think they might need to be edited.

12.01 Using software tools to place and edit images

After copying an image and pasting it on the page where you want it to go, it might still need to be positioned or aligned to exactly where you want it be.

You can align your image in several different ways:

- use your cursor to move it to the left or right
- **resize** it to make it smaller or bigger so that it fits into the space you have available for it
- use margins to align the image horizontally or vertically
- use text wrapping to align it according to your requirements, as demonstrated in Figure 12.01.

KEY TERMS

Resize: change the width and/or height of an image to fit its intended purpose.

Aligning an image with text

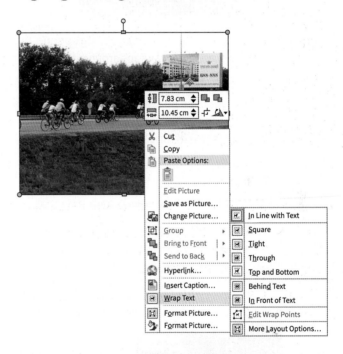

Figure 12.01 Using the 'Wrap Text' tool to align images with your cursor

The 'Wrap Text' tool (Figure 12.01) has a number of different options to control how text and images interact.

When you choose to use the 'In Line with Text' option, you can move your images left or right with your cursor. This can be a tiresome way to align your images and you might also wish to move an image vertically, not just horizontally, according to your requirements. This can be achieved by resizing the image on the same horizontal line.

147

a

In this across the cycling all ages about on

scene cyclists from country participate in a competition. People of and sizes were out and their bicycles.

POSITION A

b

In this scene cyclists the country a cycling competition. ages and sizes were on their bicycles.

from across participate in People of all out and about

POSITION B

Figure 12.02 (a) Using the 'Square' text wrapping option. (b) As the image is moved, the text wraps around it

The 'Square' text wrapping option allows you to wrap the text around the border of an image; see Figure 12.02(a). In this document, the text wraps around the image. If the image is moved, the text also moves; see Figure 12.02(b).

Using the 'Tight' option is more useful for wrapping text around an irregular image.

Figure 12.03 Using 'Edit Wrap Points' to wrap text closer to the image

The 'Through' option allows you to use the 'Edit Wrap Points' tool (see Figure 12.03). This enables you to drag the text even closer onto the image, as Figure 12.04 shows.

a

This is an travelling

image of cyclists through the city.

b

This is an image of

cyclists travelling through the city.

Figure 12.04 (a) The position of the text before using 'Edit Wrap Points'. (b) The position of the text after using 'Edit Wrap Points'

In order to align text and images more precisely, the 'Through' tool can be very useful. However, it shouldn't be confused with the '**Crop**' tool which allows you to cut parts of an image out leaving only the parts you wish to be visible; the 'Through' tool only helps you to align your text closer to different parts of your image.

PRACTICAL TASK 12.01

a Open the file 'Asset 12.01.docx' from the CD.

b Place the image 'Asset 12.02.jpg' from the CD in the centre of the page of text.

c Ensure that the text flows as closely around the image as possible.

d Use the 'Edit Wrap Points' tool to ensure that some of the text covers the bottom part of your image.

KEY TERMS

Crop: cut out a part of an image that is not required for the intended purpose.

148

The 'Top and Bottom' option allows you to place your image on its own line. When you have two or more images all positioned on the same line, you can ensure that they each remain on their own line horizontally by using 'Top and Bottom' (see Figure 12.05).

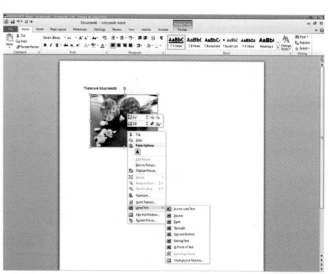

a

a

b

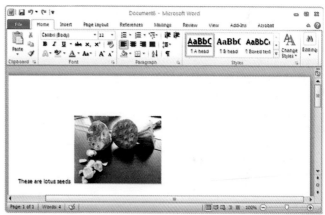

b

Figure 12.05 (a) Before using the 'Top and Bottom' option. (b) After using the 'Top and Bottom' option

If you try to align the two images onto the same line, you will not be able to do so after using the 'Top and Bottom' option.

If you have text next to an image but would prefer to include it on the image, as illustrated in Figure 12.06, you should use the 'Behind Text' option.

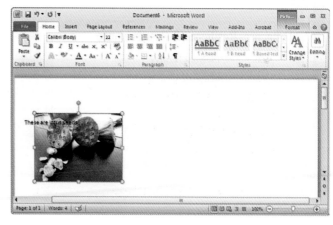

c

Figure 12.06 (a) Using the 'Behind Text' option. (b) Before using 'Behind Text'. (c) After using 'Behind Text'

There is yet another option, called 'In Front of Text' (Figure 12.07). This allows you to display the image over the text and is usually used when you need to use a watermark on a document, such as for certificates and important legal documents.

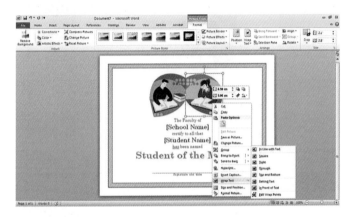

Figure 12.07 Using the 'In Front of Text' option

If you try to add some text over the image, your existing image will disappear; see Figure 12.08(a).

In order to retain your text and make it appear over your image, you should use 'In Front of Text'; see Figure 12.08(b).

PRACTICAL TASK 12.02

Create a watermark for a certificate document.

a Open the file 'Asset 12.03.pub' from the CD.

b Place a watermark on this document.

c Use screenshots to demonstrate how you accomplished this task. Annotate your screenshots by labelling them clearly.

In addition to the software tools mentioned above that can be used for aligning images in order to meet the requirements of the intended audience, there are a host of others to be found in the various application software packages used for editing images.

a

b

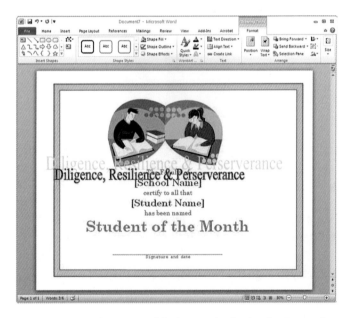

Figure 12.08 (a) Inserting text over the existing image causes the existing image to disappear. (b) The result of using 'In Front of Text' to place text over an image

150

Place an image with precision

When you are required to select an image of specific size, you can use the 'Size' and 'Position' menu options. You can select how wide and long you would like your image to be. Notice that the aspect ratio of the image is maintained throughout the re-sizing process.

Figure 12.09   After changing the size of the image

Positioning an image

You can also change the position of an image on the page relative to the corners of the page.

Figure 12.10   Before changing the position of an image on a page

If you adjust the numbers of the 'Horizontal' option to become more negative, the image will move towards the left-hand side of the page or if you increase the numbers to become positive numbers on the 'Horizontal' option, the image will move towards the right-hand side of the page. Likewise, if you increase the 'Vertical' option, the image will move downwards relative to the page (see Figure 12.11).

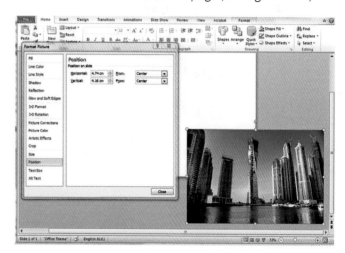

Figure 12.11   After changing the position of an image on a page

151

Resizing images

If you are using Publisher from Microsoft's Office suite, then you can also align your image by shifting the margins on both the vertical and horizontal axes (see Figure 12.12).

Figure 12.12   Using margins to align an image to the left or right horizontally

If you resize your image the position will change to reflect the new horizontal position at the bottom left-hand corner of your page (see Figure 12.13).

Figure 12.13 Resizing an image shifts the margins accordingly

PRACTICAL TASK 12.03

Using an appropriate software package, illustrate how you would resize an image by adjusting the margins accordingly.

Adjusting the aspect ratio of images

Sometimes you might wish to maintain, distort or adjust the **aspect ratio** of an image when you resize it. The reasons for doing so might be to emphasise for effect, as is often required in advertisements or for creating a humorous picture.

Images that you copy and paste sometimes appear quite large on your page, as demonstrated in Figure 12.14. When resizing such an image it is important to ensure that the aspect ratio is maintained so that the image does not appear out of proportion when compared with the original image.

KEY TERMS

Aspect ratio: the ratio of the width of an image to its height.

Figure 12.14 The original size of this image after it was copied and pasted into this page

If you resize the image from one side only, e.g. from the right side only, it will look like Figure 12.15.

Figure 12.15 The image is distorted after being resized from the right side only

However, you can correct this distortion by resizing the same image from either the top or the bottom (see Figure 12.16).

Figure 12.16 The image resized from the bottom to correct the distortion

EXTENSION ACTIVITY 12.02

Evaluate the issues involving editing other people's images and compare this with the issues involved with editing images for the purposes of false advertising.

Although the image in Figure 12.16 appears less distorted than the previous one, the aspect ratio might still not have been maintained accurately. An alternative method to maintain the aspect ratio of an image when resizing it is by clicking on one of the corner resizing handles at the same time as holding down the 'Ctrl' key on your keyboard, before moving the handle in the direction in which you wish to resize (Figure 12.17).

Figure 12.17 Resizing an image from one of the corner resizing handles

The inner image in Figure 12.17 is the original, and the outer shaded part shows how far you have resized the image. In this way, the aspect ratio of your image is maintained because both the height and width are being resized simultaneously.

Alternative methods to maintain the aspect ratio or to distort an image can be found by using the software tools within the 'Crop' tool.

Cropping an image

There are times when you might not require a whole image, but just a part of it. This can be done by 'cropping' a part of it away so that only the part you require remains visible. Some software packages allow you to crop an image only in a regular (rectangular) shape, while others allow you to cut out any irregular shape from the image in the same way that you would manually use a pair of scissors to cut out shapes from a picture. This process is referred to as 'cut-out' and is different from the 'cropping' process.

Figure 12.18 shows an image of an electronic unmanned library dispenser; there are areas around the actual machine that makes it look 'untidy'. It could be 'tidied' by cropping away those areas around the machine.

Figure 12.18 The original image of the library dispenser machine before cropping

This image can be cropped while at the same time maintaining or distorting the aspect ratio, as demonstrated in Figure 12.19. If you use only one of the resizing handles to resize an image it will become distorted because only one side is being resized. In order to maintain the aspect ratio of an image, all four resizing handles need to be moved simultaneously.

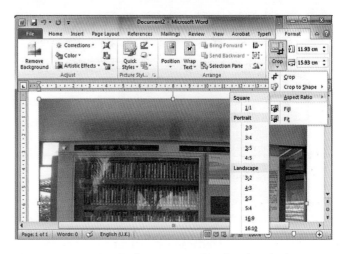

Figure 12.19 Using the 'Aspect Ratio' tool within the ' Crop' tool

Changing the aspect ratio allows you to cater for different orientations and sizes of screen or page. See Figure 12.20 for the effect of changing the aspect ratio.

153

Figure 12.20 Using an 'Aspect Ratio' of 3 : 5 for cropping the image

It is well worth noting that cropping an image in this way is quite different from resizing an image.

If you chose to crop the image in Figure 12.18 with an 'Aspect Ratio' of 3 : 5 again but placed it in a 'landscape' orientation on the page, it would look very different, as can be seen in Figure 12.21.

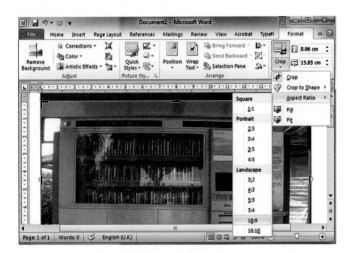

Figure 12.21 Using a landscape aspect ratio more suitable for a wide screen

Images can also be cropped by shape, as shown in Figure 12.22.

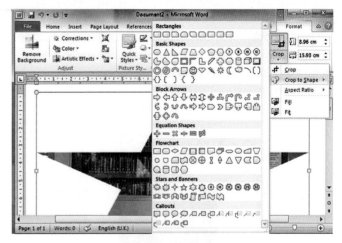

Figure 12.22 Using the 'Crop to Shape' tool

In Figure 12.23, the 'Explosion 2' shape was chosen to achieve the cropped image.

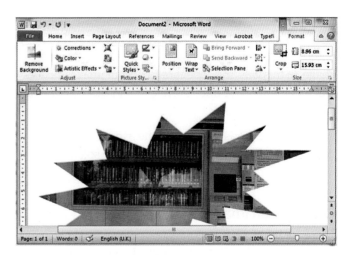

Figure 12.23 Using the 'Explosion 2' shape to crop the image

Rotating an image

Rotating an image refers to turning it through an angle. It can be turned upside down or, if it is already upside down, it can be turned the right way up by using the rotation handle which becomes visible once you have selected an image (see Figure 12.24).

154

Figure 12.24 (a) Before rotating the image. (b) While rotating the image

Reflecting an image

Reflecting or flipping an image means producing a mirror image of the original image. The software tools vary between the different software packages, but if you are using Microsoft Word, you can achieve reflection by following the instructions in Figure 12.25.

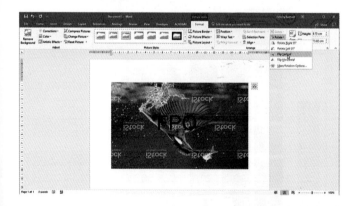

Figure 12.25 Using the 'Flip' tool under the 'Rotate' menu

In Figure 12.26a the original image is reflected (flipped) vertically, so the bird now appears upside down.

In Figure 12.26b you can see that if you reflect the image horizontally, the bird's beak, which is facing left in the original image, will face right instead.

Figure 12.26a Original image and image reflected vertically

Figure 12.26b Original image and image reflected horizontally

KEY TERMS

Reflect horizontally (flip): if an original image faces the left-hand side, it will face the right-hand side after it has been flipped. It will still be upright.

Reflect vertically (flip): if an original image is upright, it will appear upside-down after it has been vertically flipped. It will still face in the same direction (right or left).

Rotate: turning an image around from its original position.

Reflect: producing a mirror image of the original image.

Changing colour in an image

You can adjust the colour depth of an image by adjusting the colour saturation, which refers to how an image's colour can range from faded and dull to vibrant and bright (see Figure 21.27).

Figure 12.27 Using the 'Colour Saturation' tool to select from the range of luminosities available from a range of colours for an image

The image choice on the extreme left-hand side is quite dull and of low colour saturation compared to the very brightly coloured one (high colour saturation) on the extreme right-hand side of the available choices for the 'Colour Saturation' tool. Colour saturation refers to how dull or bright the colour in an image is.

Colour tone of an image

The colour tone of an image affects the image in such a way that if it is low, the image appears as if there was less light shining in the room where the image is being photographed; if the colour tone is high, then it appears as if the image is being photographed in a room where there is more light shining (see Figure 12.28).

Figure 12.28 Applying a low colour tone to an image makes the colours appear darker

In contrast to an image with a low colour tone, images can also achieve a high colour tone by increasing the 'temperature' of the colour depth (see Figure 12.29).

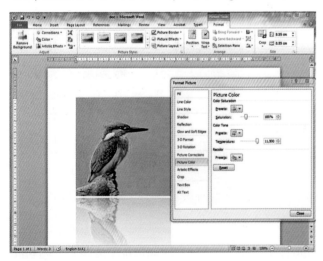

Figure 12.29 Applying a high colour tone to an image makes the image appear to be taken with a lot of light around it

Recolouring an image

An image could also be recoloured to any colour you wish by using the 'Recolour' tool (see Figure 12.30).

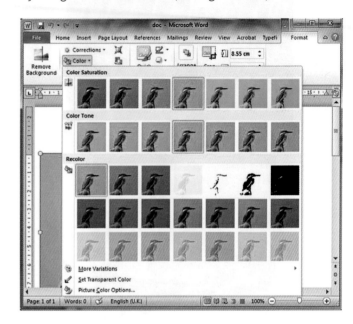

Figure 12.30 Recolouring an image

Adjusting the brightness and contrast of an image

The brightness of an image refers to how much light the image is emitting. It can be changed using the 'Brightness' tool found in the 'Colour' tab (see Figure 12.31).

Figure 12.31 Changing the brightness of an image

You can also adjust the contrast of an image in the same way.

Original

This is the image you uploaded.

Simulation

This is how your image might appear to a person with protanopia.

Figure 12.32 The effects of protanopia

When one colour is surrounded by another colour it appears to be a slightly different colour from the colour that it actually is. An example of colour **contrast** can be tested by surrounding a grey colour by a yellow colour. It should appear to be more bluish in colour but is in actual fact still the colour, grey. Changing the colour contrast of an image can help sufferers of protanopia, a form of colour blindness where someone might be insensitive to the colour red and this results in confusion of the greens, reds and yellows in an image (see Figure 12.32).

Image resolution

When images are used on websites and transmitted over the internet, it is important that they can be downloaded in the quickest time possible. There are several reasons why the transmission speed might be important.

Businesses depend on customers experiencing a satisfactory web surfing experience, not getting frustrated by having to wait for long periods while images are downloading, for example. Many disgruntled customers will quickly move on to other similar websites, thereby causing some financial loss for companies with websites with slow-loading web pages.

Some booking websites need to process customer requests quickly in order to offer the next available seat or ticket to other website users competing for the same seats or tickets at the same time. It is unpredictable how many users may be online and trying to access the same service at precisely the same time. It is therefore extremely important that such businesses have web pages with images that can download very quickly so that the business can book as many seats or tickets at any given moment and not cause customers to go to other, faster websites.

Some online services may be critical for life and death situations, and as such must be able to upload or download images as quickly as possible. In the case of citizen journalism, members of the public can act like journalists to record and upload information about current events as they occur and upload images to social media portals without delays. In many cases they can save lives by their ability to alert emergency authorities about human tragedies and natural disasters.

Reducing image resolution

Image resolution refers to the number of pixels per inch for an image. The higher the number of pixels per inch in an image, the higher will be the image resolution and vice versa. In order to reduce the resolution, you would reduce the number of pixels per inch. If such an image is then used on a website, providing its resolution is optimised for that website, it will download quickly enough to make surfing the website a tolerable or pleasurable experience for its users.

Image resolution can be changed in image editing software, as shown in Figure 12.33 on the next page. When you reduce the **resolution** of an image, you also reduce the size of the image.

KEY TERMS

Contrast: the difference between how dull or bright an image is and how it appears in reality or as can be seen by the human eye.

Resolution: the number of pixels per inch in an image.

a

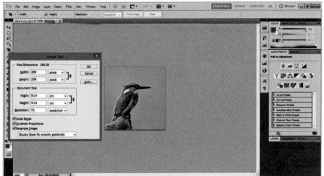

b

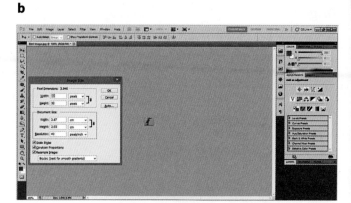

Figure 12.33 (a) Reducing the resolution of an image. (b) Reducing the resolution also reduces the size of the image

QUESTION 12.01

a Your school newsletter needs an image to be placed in the centre of a page so that text flows around it. Which tool would you use? Explain how you would use this editing tool.

b For the special newsletter issue for Nature's Day, the editor wants each article to be enclosed in leaf shapes. Which tool would you use? Explain how you would use this editing tool.

c In addition, the theme colours for the Nature's Day page should be different shades of green and white. Which tool would you use? Explain how you would use this editing tool.

d There needs to be an appropriate image placed and aligned with the top line of the first paragraph and the left margin on the fourth page of the newsletter. Which tool would you use? Explain how you would use this editing tool.

PRACTICAL TASK 12.04

Complete the task described in the file 'Asset 12.08.docx' on the CD.

Summary

- Images are used in a wide variety of situations and by an ever-increasing number of individuals, ranging from private use on social media to business and corporate use with both hard copy and soft copy options.

- Images can be enhanced, edited or manipulated to suit a variety of different purposes such as to emphasise points or issues, to clarify and simplify complex situations, to represent data graphically and more visually for improved understanding, for humour and ridicule, and sometimes to raise awareness of human tragedy or natural disasters (and many other things; this list of image uses is not exhaustive).

- Placing an image with precision within a document can be accomplished by using these tools:

  - text wrapping

  - margins

  - resizing.

- Maintaining or adjusting the aspect ratio of an image controls the amount of distortion of that image when adjusting it to fit onto a different-sized screen or frame.

- Cropping is a useful way to remove parts of an image but is different from using the more sophisticated 'cut-out' tools available in some software packages.

- Rotating an image is useful to change its display angle.

- Reflecting an image is simply creating its mirror image.

- Images can be enhanced by adjusting their colour depth, brightness or contrast to suit the needs of the intended audience.

- Images sometimes need to have their resolution reduced in order to reduce their file sizes, especially when being used on the internet to ensure website users experience quick download times in most web browsers.

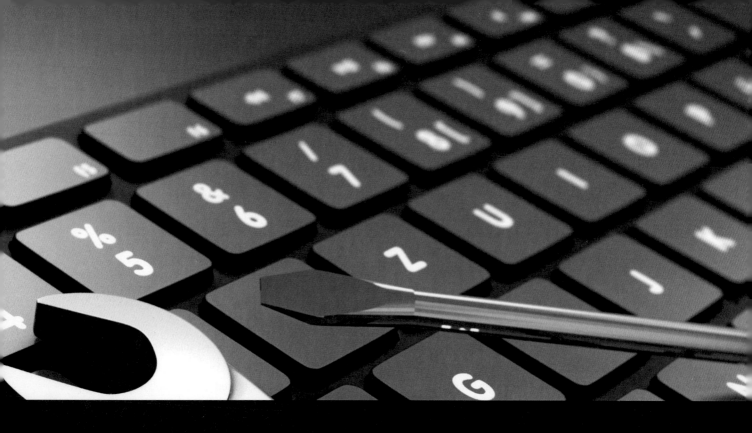

Chapter 13:
Layout

Learning objectives

When you have completed this chapter, you should be able to:

- use software tools to prepare a basic document to match the purpose and target audience
- use software tools to use headers and footers appropriately within a range of software packages.

Overview

Every document is laid out in a different way. **Layout** refers to the way that the different items are spread out on the page. Typical questions that would arise when deciding on the layout of a page might be:

- What orientation is best for this document, **Landscape** or **portrait**?

- Where should the heading and the subheadings be situated?

- Should they be left or right aligned, or is it better to be placed in the centre?

- How much 'white space' would be appropriate to match the needs of the user?

- Should there be columns or not?

- Where is the best position for the image(s)?

- What font type, size and colours should be used?

In order to answer these questions, you must have a clear idea of the type of document you are working with because the layout styles differ significantly for each different type of document. A word-processed letter has a different layout from an advertisement poster or a brochure. The word 'document' in this chapter relates to any of the applications used within Chapters 16 to 21.

QUESTION 13.01

Copy and complete Table 13.01 by suggesting the best layout choice for each specific type of document.

Type of document	Number of images and size of image in relation to the page	Title, subtitle, headings and subheadings: aligned left, right or centre?	Font type, size and colour	Other layout considerations
Advertisement				
Award certificate	Example: One image – logo, 1/20th the size of the page	Titles and subtitles all centre aligned	Freestyle Script, size 14 mostly; colour to match the document's house style	There should be approximately 50%–60% white space over the whole document
Banner				
Brochure				
Business card				
Email				
Flyer				
Greeting card				
Invitation				
Label				
Letterhead				
Website				

Table 13.01 Document layouts

KEY TERMS

Layout: the way objects are arranged in the space provided on the page of a document.

Landscape: the wider, shorter orientation of a page compared to the narrower, taller version of a page with a portrait orientation.

Portrait: the narrower, taller orientation of a page compared to the wider, shorter orientation of a landscaped page.

as labels, receipts, memos, account ledgers, and so forth (Figure 13.02).

KEY TERMS

Template: a frame upon which to build a document by simply copying the same style or filling in your own relevant information in the spaces provided.

13.01 Using software tools to match purpose and target audience

Most software applications have tools that will carry out the more common tasks in a similar way. These include creating a new document, opening an existing document, entering text and numbers, and so on. For more on this see Chapter 9, Section 9.01.

Opening a new document

If you would like to open a new document, most application software packages follow a similar method (see Figure 13.01).

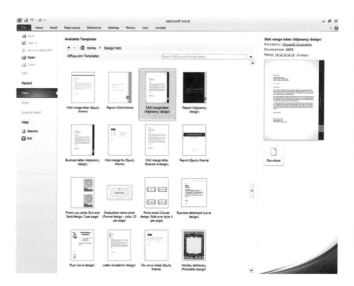

Figure 13.02 Selecting from a wide range of different business-related document types with different layouts

If you select the 'Mail Merge Letter' option, a **preview** of the document can be seen on the right-hand side of the screen (see Figure 13.02). A clear layout is there for you to use as a guide by deleting the text in place and replacing it with your own relevant information.

KEY TERMS

Preview: a tool that allows you to see what your document will look like before you either print it out, save it or send it somewhere else.

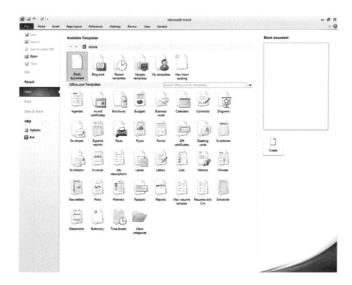

Figure 13.01 How to open a new document in a word processor

There are many different types of document you could choose from and there are also many different **templates** to help you with ideas on the layout of the document. If you select the 'Business' type of document you will have a further selection of document types, such

If you select a different 'Business' document such as a 'Sales Order', it is clear that the layout is very different from the 'Mail Merge Letter' document. You can see that you have a lot of options to choose from.

If you use a different software package, such as a desktop publishing package, the choices of available document types will be different.

When you need to open a new document in a desktop publishing package you could select from the wide range of different types of document available within the software's downloaded files, or if you cannot find what you are looking for you could also access the online resources.

However, if you choose a similar type of document, such as a 'Mail Merge Letter' type, the layout will be very similar to that found in the previous software package (see Figure 13.03).

Besides the templates available to guide you with the layout of your chosen document, you can also find templates with different styles to suit your particular requirements.

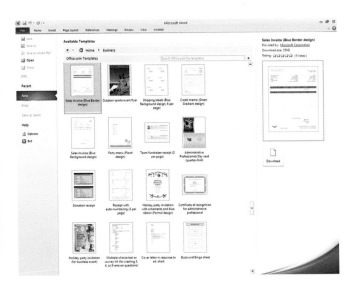

Figure 13.03 Using the 'Sales Receipt' template is the same in a different software program

Before computers became generally available for doing most clerical tasks, preprinted stationery for these types of business documents could be purchased in book stores. Nowadays, there are many more options, styles and types of document freely available within the various software packages, and also on the internet. You do not necessarily have to design one from scratch because many types of documents are templates.

Entering text and numbers

Text can be entered in different ways in different types of documents. If you want to add a funky heading or title on a poster or advertisement, you may wish to use the 'WordArt' tool which offers a range of colourful options; other ways of entering text are also available (see Figure 13.04).

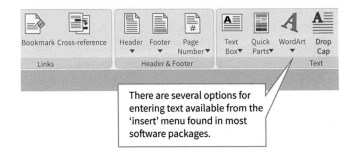

There are several options for entering text available from the 'insert' menu found in most software packages.

Figure 13.04 Using different options to enter text

Using the 'Text Box' option

A text box can be treated like an image. You can position it anywhere on your page, thereby giving you the opportunity to change the layout on your page quickly. The text in the text box can be **formatted** in the same way as if it was being formatted in any **applications program**.

> **KEY TERMS**
>
> **Formatting text:** using the font type, font size, font colours, etc. that you prefer for your text.
>
> **Applications program:** a type of software that allows you to create many different types of documents, such as letters, invoices, presentations, web pages and so on.

Using the 'Quick Parts' tool

The 'Quick Parts' tool has mini-templates of the various parts that you might wish to insert in a particular type of document. There are four different options to choose from: Auto Text, Document Property, Field and Building Blocks Organise.

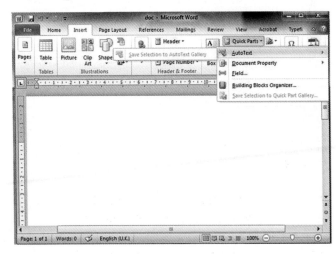

Figure 13.05 Using the 'Quick Parts' tool

163

'Auto Text' refers to text that you would use repetitively. The advantage of using the 'Auto Text' tool is that it can save you the time you would normally take to retype the same text over and over again by simply allowing you to use this feature. If, for example, you were writing a poem with a line that is repeated several times throughout the poem, you could use this feature to save time and to reduce the possibility of making spelling errors or other data input errors.

The 'Document Property' tool includes several options for you to improve the layout of your particular document.

This tool can be useful if you are creating a form for others to fill in, because you can determine the layout of each element on your form. The places where the user has to fill in the data will be clearly marked on the page (see Figure 13.06).

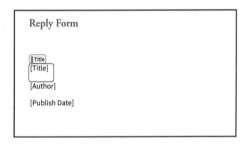

Figure 13.06 User-friendly layout for filling in forms

EXTENSION ACTIVITY 13.01

What other documents can you create using some of the other tools of the 'Document Property' tool? What are the advantages and disadvantages of using this tool?

If you choose to use the 'Insert Field' tool, you can affect the layout of your document in many different ways (see Figure 13.07).

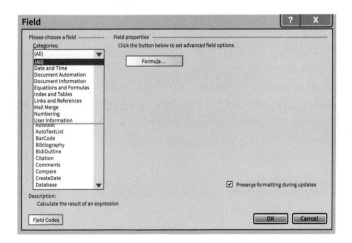

Figure 13.07 Using the 'Insert Field' tool

Should you want to add some information about your document in the document itself, such as how many words it contains, you can use this feature of the 'Insert Field' tool (see Figure 13.08).

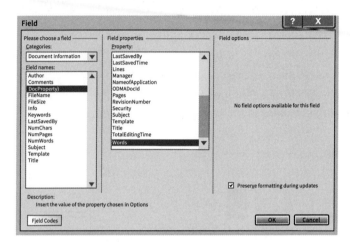

Figure 13.08 Adding a word count to a document

After clicking on the 'OK' button, the answer will appear in your text, for example '4678'.

The 'Building Blocks Organiser' can be useful to have more control over the layout of a multi-page document because it has options for each part, such as the cover page, headers and footers, text boxes, page numbers, bibliographies, and so on.

Figure 13.09 shows one way to select a template for a cover page which allows you spaces to fill in your relevant information.

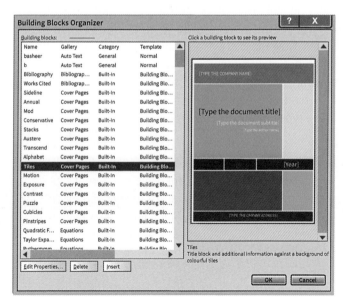

Figure 13.09 Choosing a cover page from the 'Building Blocks Organiser' tool

If you prefer a different layout for your cover page, you can select from any of the other available options (see Figure 13.10).

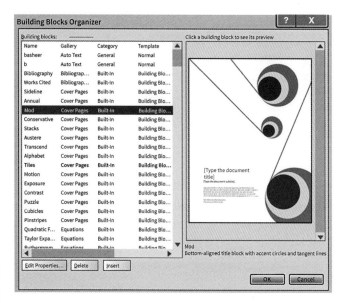

Figure 13.10 A different cover page option chosen from the 'Building Blocks Organiser' tool

PRACTICAL TASK 13.01

Create a multi-page document using the 'Building Blocks Organiser' tool. Make sure that your document has all the following features:

- a cover page
- headers with your name right aligned
- footers with the page numbers centre aligned
- vertical text boxes on one of the middle pages
- titles on each page, all in the same house style
- a table on one of the pages
- **watermarks** across all the middle pages, stating 'DRAFT'.

KEY TERMS

Watermark: faded out (close to being transparent) image or text that can be used like a background image in a document.

Using the 'WordArt' tool to place text on a page-Extension

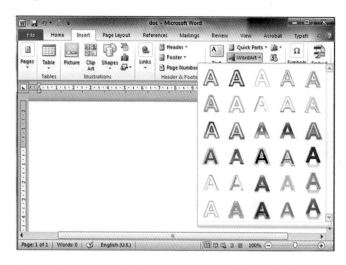

Figure 13.11 Using the 'WordArt' tool to improve the layout on your page

WordArt (see Figure 13.11) can be moved around and manipulated in the same way that images can be manipulated on a page. You can rotate or reflect it, and align it wherever is suitable for your requirements.

Inserting a signature line in a document-Extension

Signing documents digitally is becoming a common request, especially as the idea of saving trees by reducing the need to print out documents becomes more acceptable. There are two ways you can do this:

- insert a pre-signed image of a signature
- use an online signature verification facility (see Figure 13.12).

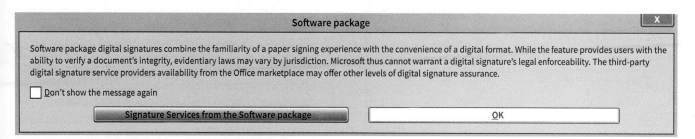

Figure 13.12 Using Software package facility to insert a signature line in a document

PRACTICAL TASK 13.02

Sign up to have your signature digitally verifiable by using an online service. You can select from those available from the 'Add Signature Services' tool (see Figure 13.13).

Figure 13.13 Using the 'Add Signature Services' tool

EXTENSION ACTIVITY 13.02

Why can Microsoft not guarantee the authenticity of an individual's signature by using their digital signatures tool? What are the issues involved with digital signatures?

EXTENSION ACTIVITY 13.03

Conduct a short survey to find out how secure others feel about using digital signatures. Discuss the findings of your survey.

Inserting objects into a document

Objects refer to files you may already have stored elsewhere, such as graphs and charts, images, presentations, and so forth (see Figure 13.14). This is a time saver because copying and pasting can take longer to achieve the same result.

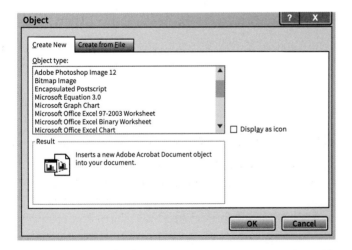

Figure 13.14 Different types of objects that can be inserted into a document

If you wish to insert some text you have previously saved in another document, you can insert it by choosing the 'Text from File' option (see Figure 13.15).

Figure 13.15 Inserting text from another document into your current document

PRACTICAL TASK 13.03

a Create a report that shows the results of the survey you did about signatures as a graph or chart.

b Include a presentation that you would use to explain your findings to a group of people.

c Include a bitmap image in an appropriate place in your document.

Entering numbers

Numbers can be represented in a document in various formats depending on the context of the information, especially in spreadsheets and databases. Some numbers should be in the right format for currency, date and time, integers, real numbers, percentages, temperature degrees or mathematical degrees, and so on. You can use your keyboard to enter the symbols associated with these types of numbers, but that can be cumbersome. If a number is formatted to be entered as a particular type of number then it can save you some time by using some of the built-in automated features found in most applications.

Figure 13.16 shows the range of number formats.

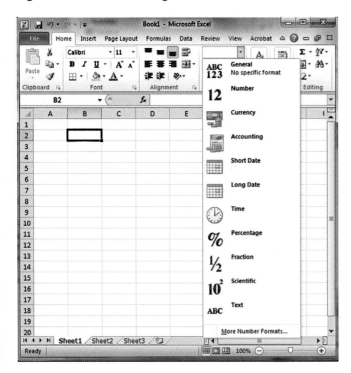

Figure 13.16 Number formats found in a spreadsheet application

'General' refers to numbers that do not require any symbols attached to them to add contextual meaning. Zeros in front of these numbers will not be made visible.

'Number' refers to any number with or without decimal places. Zeros in front of these numbers will not be made visible.

If you wish to have a zero in front of a number, as you do when you use telephone numbers, for example, you should format the number as 'Text'.

Currency formats include the currency symbols from most countries and usually have two decimal places to accommodate the smaller amounts of money like pence or cents.

The short and long date formats can be used depending on the requirements of your particular document. Time also allows different formats for hours, minutes and seconds, depending on which ones you require.

The percent symbol (%) will appear after each number that has been formatted as a percentage.

Fractions will appear as fractions when you enter two numbers separated by a 'slash' (/) character, because most fractions can't be entered directly.

'Scientific' format allows numbers to be shown in 'standard form' (as multiples of powers of ten).

PRACTICAL TASK 13.04

a   In a spreadsheet application, open the 'Template' worksheet in the file 'Asset 13.01.xlsx' on the CD.

b   Suggest number formats for the cells in the columns under each of the following headings: Hours, Pay Rate, Total Weekly Pay, Tax, Net Pay.

c   Suggest number formats for the values associated with each of these labels: Totals, Average, Tax Rate.

Editing techniques to manipulate text and numbers

The techniques you can use for both text and numbers include highlighting, delete, move, cut, copy and paste, drag and drop. Before you can manipulate any part of a document, you must always first select it. This can be done by placing your cursor at the beginning of the text, holding down the left-click on your mouse or touchpad and dragging the cursor to the end of the text to be modified. Its background will change to show that it is selected, and you can then either delete, move, cut, copy and paste or drag and drop it accordingly.

If you just want to highlight some text in a different colour, you can use the highlighting tool (see Figure 13.17).

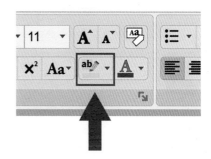

Figure 13.17 Using the highlighting tool

Deleting text means the text will disappear from your screen (and your document). It usually goes onto the 'Clipboard' and can be retrieved (pasted) if necessary, though only until the next bit of text is deleted. It can also be retrievable by using the 'Undo' or 'Redo' buttons, depending on which text you are trying to retrieve (see Figure 13.18).

Figure 13.18 Using the 'Undo' and 'Redo' buttons

When you wish to move text or numbers from one part of a document to another or to another document, you have to first cut it to remove it from the original document and then paste it in the new place where you want to put it. It will not be in the previous place where you moved it from. Moving text is a different technique from the technique of copying and pasting because in the latter the original copy will remain where it was and there will be a copy in the new place it was pasted to. A similar technique to moving text or numbers is the 'drag and drop' technique where the text or numbers is selected and then 'dragged' from one place to another place. This means it will no longer be visible in its previous position.

Placing objects into a document from a variety of sources

When you choose to insert a picture or some text from a different file, you will get to choose where you want to get the picture or text from (see Figure 13.19).

A screenshot is an image of everything that is on your computer screen at the time you press the 'PrtScr' button on your keyboard. Often it is necessary to crop

Figure 13.19 Placing an image in a document from a source where it has been stored previously, such as the 'Pictures' folder

a

b

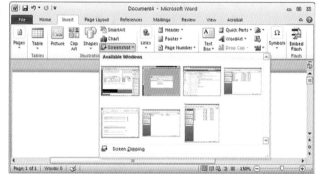

Figure 13.20 (a) Using the 'Screenshot Clipping' tool. (b) The resulting image

the screenshot down to highlight only the parts that you require. In Figure 13.20a you will notice that even the horizontal taskbar at the bottom of the screen is included in the screenshot. The grey sections on either side of the screenshot are not needed, and the blank page on the right-hand side is also unnecessary. In addition, the text on the left-hand side of the screenshot is too small to be seen clearly enough, so it may be necessary to resize the cropped image to make it clearer (see Figure 13.20b).

There is a 'Screenshot Clipping' tool which will allow you to insert only the part of the screenshot that you need.

Spreadsheet extract

A spreadsheet extract is the result of copying, for example, one column of data from one worksheet and transferring it to another worksheet or workbook. In spreadsheets you can usually use the VLOOKUP function to carry out this way to place (lay out) parts of a spreadsheet in other documents. However, the practical task below will use a different way to transfer data from one part of a spreadsheet to another worksheet or spreadsheet.

PRACTICAL TASK 13.05

a Open the spreadsheet 'Asset 13.01.xlsx' on the CD, and follow the instructions below to extract the data for all those who had worked 45 hours and place that data into a new workbook:

- Copy and paste the fields 'Hours', 'Pay Rate', 'Total Weekly Pay', 'Tax' and 'Net Pay' from the top row of the 'Wages 1' worksheet over to a new worksheet, where we're going to extract the data to.

- In the new worksheet, type in 45 in the 'Hours' column.

- Select the 'Data' then 'Filter' options from the toolbar.

- Choose 'Advanced Filter' and then 'Copy to another location' (see Figure 13.21).

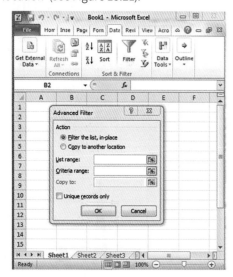

Figure 13.21 Using the 'Copy to another location' tool to place data from one worksheet in a spreadsheet to another worksheet

- Select your 'List range' by going back to the 'Wages 1' worksheet and highlighting the range of data that has to be extracted from.

- In the 'Criteria Range', select A1:H2 (see Figure 13.22).

Figure 13.22 Selecting the criteria range in the new worksheet

- In the 'Copy To' box, type in where you wish to show the results of the spreadsheet extract.

- Click 'OK' to see the results of placing the spreadsheet extract in a new worksheet (see Figure 13.23).

Figure 13.23 The results of extracting the data from one worksheet to another using the 'Advanced Filter' tool

EXTENSION ACTIVITY 13.04

Discuss alternative methods to achieve the same result of placing data from one part of a spreadsheet into another worksheet.

An important point to remember is that extracting data in a spreadsheet is not the same as copying and pasting data from one part to another within a spreadsheet. It is a combined action of filtering for particular data and then copying and pasting the result of such a filter to another part of the spreadsheet or another workbook. Auditors often use this technique to compare data for checking purposes when they are faced with very large data sets. This technique enables you to narrow down your filtering and see only the results of such a filter on all the data.

Database extract

Database extraction refers to searching through data for the purposes of further processing and placing it in another place for layout purposes.

Placing clip art into a document

The Clip Art tool allows you to access a large collection of images which are quickly available. To access the wide range of illustrations and photographs, you have to use keywords that describe the type of image you hope to find in this collection. If, for example, you type in the keyword 'people', you should get the results shown in Figure 13.24.

Figure 13.24 The result of using the keyword 'people' in the Clip Art search box

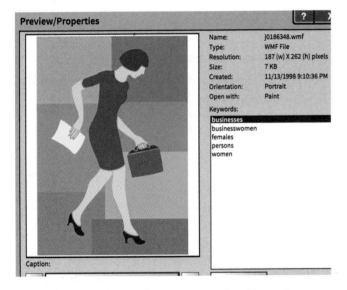

Figure 13.25 Displaying the properties of an illustration

Information about the properties of an illustration is useful when you need to know its size, type of file, location and even who created the first copy of it and when it was edited (see Figure 13.25).

It can be useful and save you some time in cropping off the edges of a normal 'prt sc' by simply using the 'alt + prt sc' buttons simultaneously. The difference between using these two options is that a normal 'prt sc' captures the whole screen including all you windows that may be open

but not working at that moment, whereas the 'alt + prt sc' buttons used together will only capture the screen you have opened at that time.

Placing a chart in a document

Charts or graphs are usually created in spreadsheets. However, charts and graphs can be helpful if they are placed in reports, presentations and some promotional material. This can be achieved in more than one way:

- copy and paste
- insert as an object
- insert a chart directly from a previously created spreadsheet.

The results of this last option can be seen in Figure 13.26, where the embedded chart was created from the data in a spreadsheet (see Figure 13.27).

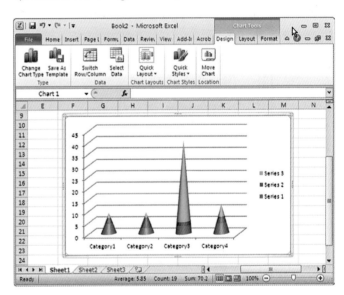

Figure 13.26 The chart after being inserted

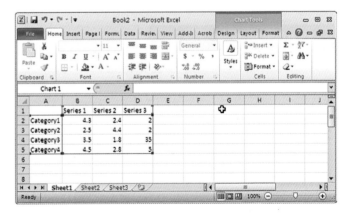

Figure 13.27 The spreadsheet from which the chart was generated

Creating a table with a specified number of rows and columns

If you need to insert a table into a document, and you know how many rows and columns you require, you can insert them directly using the 'Insert Table' tool (Figure 13.28). You can then examine the properties of the table to modify its content and its formatting (see Figure 13.29).

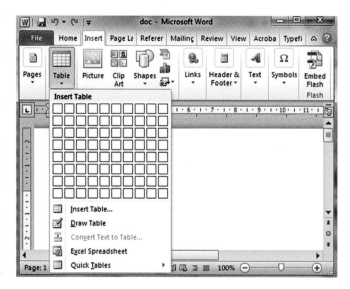

Figure 13.28 Using the 'Insert Table' tool

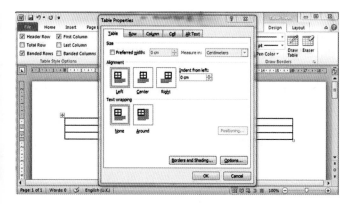

Figure 13.29 Using the properties to format the table and its contents

Essentially, spreadsheet are tables in which you can use formulas and functions. The cells of a spreadsheet can also be formatted to have different-coloured backgrounds, font types and sizes, colours, bold, italics, and so on. However, using tables in other applications is different in that you cannot use the formulas and functions, but you can include screenshots or images of parts of your spreadsheet in other documents. If you have created a table in an application program other than a spreadsheet,

then you are also able to format it. For example, if you want to change the borders you can do so by right-clicking on the handle for the whole table found in the top left-hand corner and selecting your choice from the range of options available (see Figure 13.30).

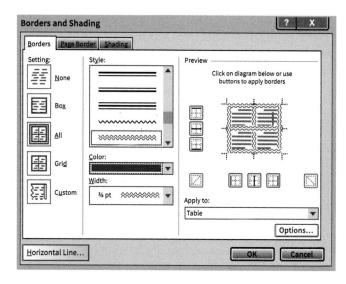

Figure 13.30 Formatting the borders of a table

In order to format the contents of a table you should simply highlight the contents first and then format the text and numbers in the same fashion as you would any other text or numbers in any other application.

Placing objects in a table

You can place objects in a table in the same manner as you would place objects anywhere else. The only difference is that you may have to do a lot of resizing of the object or resort to widening the columns and rows to fit the size of the object you wish to place in a cell of your table. In some instances you may wish to join two or more cells in a table together. This is called merging. If you wish to merge two or more cells together, you should first select the cells and then right-click and choose the 'Merge' option.

Wrap text around a table, chart or image

When you wrap text around a table, chart or image, the table is being treated like an image by the program. You would wrap text around it in the same fashion as you would wrap text around any other image. This procedure is explained in depth in Chapter 12.

Placing database extracts into a document

There are different ways that you can place objects into documents (see Chapter 11.01).

171

Two examples are shown below: how to import an extract from a Microsoft Office database into a spreadsheet and how to export to Microsoft Word.

Import to a spreadsheet

- Open the worksheet where you want to enter the imported data and select the cell where you wish the import to start.

- Select the Data tab and click 'from text' to allow text file types, such as .prn, .txt and .csv to be imported; browse to find the file that you want to import, select it, then click Import. The Text Import Wizard will appear to guide you through importing your data.

- Select 'Delimited', then select the type of character you want to use to separate each field (a comma is most commonly used).

- You now choose the format for each of the columns. Select the column heading in the Data preview and then select a data type from the Column data format options.

- When you have selected the data type for each column, click Finish.

Export to Word

- In the Navigation Pane, select the object that contains the data you want to export. You can export a table, query, form, or report.

- In the database, if you want to export only a portion of a table, query, or form, open the object and select just the records you want.

- Select the External Data tab, in the Export group, click Word (he database has to remain open).

- In Export Wizard, give the name of the destination (Word) file.

- If you had selected the records to export before you started the export operation, select the **Export only the selected records** check box. But if you want to export all the records then leave the check box cleared

- Click **OK**.

How to add automated information into your headers and footers

Some information that you could add into a header or footer can be classified as automated information because once added, the rest of it will be added in

automatically, i.e. after you have added the first page number, the rest of the page numbers can be added in automatically on subsequent pages. In addition, if you add your name on the first page it can appear on all your pages automatically. The steps to follow are as follows:

1 Open your document.

2 Go to 'Insert' and select 'Page Number'.

3 Select 'Bottom of Page' or whichever one is required according to your user's needs.

4 You will notice that the first number is already filled in for you – move the cursor to where you would like to write your name or the particular name you wish to write down and then write your name there.

5 Close the window by selecting the 'Close the Header and Footer' Tab at the top right-hand corner of your page.

Using the same method you should be able to add other automated information such as 'date and time' into a header or footer

13.02 Creating headers and footers

Headers and footers are useful to show information that may not be directly related to the content of your document but that is still important, such as the name of the author, the publication date, page numbers, titles, and so forth. Headers and footers appear on the page as faded out text and are usually positioned at the top (header) or at the bottom (footer) of a page. Headers and footers can include **automated** file information. This means you only have to specify what information you want once, and not on each page; for example, page numbers are updated and entered automatically whenever you begin a new page. Other benefits include the fact that you do not have to enter your name and title on every page but just on one page and your name and title will be filled in on all the pages of your document.

Using headers and footers in a spreadsheet application

The **interface** for inserting headers and footers in a spreadsheet is slightly different than in the other standard Office suite programs (see Figure 13.31).

KEY TERMS

Automated objects: objects that update automatically every time your page is updated, for example date and time, page numbering, and so on.

Interface: the view an application presents to you when working on a document, with all its icons and clickable links; also, the front panel of a device that has buttons to press to facilitate its use.

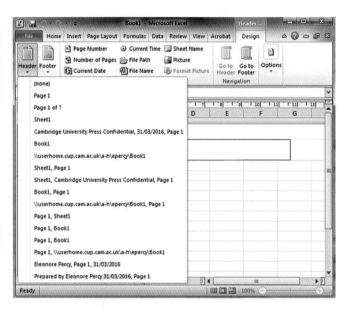

Figure 13.31   Header interface in a spreadsheet program

In this case, you can select from different options for your header. Some options include just page numbers, others include both page numbers and a title; because this is a spreadsheet, it can also include the worksheet number or name.

PRACTICAL TASK 13.06

a   Open a new spreadsheet and rename the first three worksheets: Income, Expenses, Profit.

b   Create headers for each of these worksheets that include the corresponding title.

c   Format the contents of the headers to be bold, Comic Sans, size 14, red in colour and centre aligned.

d   Create footers that include your first name and surname. Format this to be black, Arial, size 12 and right-aligned.

EXTENSION ACTIVITY 13.05

What are the possible problems when using some of the features of headers and footers? What kind of information is not appropriate for inclusion in them? Could there be another similar feature to accommodate these? Discuss.

PRACTICAL TASK 13.07

You are now going to edit a document about to be presented to the school board of an international school. Open the file 'Asset 13.03.docx' on the CD and follow the instructions there.

KEY TERMS

Sans-serif font: font types that do not have any serifs or 'tails' at the ends of characters.

Alignment of the contents within headers and footers

Once you have opened the 'Header and Footer' tool, you can treat the content the same as you would treat it in any other application.

173

Summary

- Creating a good document layout is an important part of producing a document that conforms to accepted professional standards.

- Different applications have slightly different techniques for entering text and numbers.

- The difference between copy and pasting text and moving it is that the text is still in its original place after copying and pasting, whereas moving text means that the text is no longer in its original place after you have moved it.

- Placing objects in documents can enhance the layout of a document substantially, provided you use the correct object and use the appropriate techniques to place the object exactly where it would make the best impact on its target audience.

- Formatting techniques are very similar in most applications.

- The use of headers and footers enables you to include information in a document that is not related to the content of the document but that is still important to show.

Chapter 14:
Styles

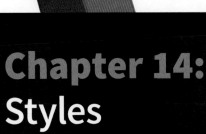

Learning objectives

When you have completed this chapter, you should be able to understand:

- the purpose of a corporate house style and ensure that all work produced matches this
- apply styles to ensure consistency of presentation.

Overview

Style is visible in every facet of life, such as in fashionable clothing, stylish cars, modern houses, and so on. The question is, 'How do you know that something is stylish?' Usually the colours, shapes or some element of sameness across the whole of something qualifies it as being 'stylish'. If you consider your school as an example, you will notice that your school has its own colours which distinguish it from other schools. It should also have a logo, a slogan and all its stationery and online communications will have a look of 'sameness' about them because of the positioning of these items on them. The font types, colours and backgrounds should be the same on all a company's electronic communications, such as emails, website, blogs, and so forth, and also on all hardcopy stationery such as letters, invoices, flyers or brochures.

14.01 Corporate branding and house styles

Corporate branding refers to promoting a company or organisation through making it visible to as wide an audience as possible, and in particular to its target audience. This visibility is created by using a particular **house style** on all the company's documentation and online materials. The house style is a **consistent style** that helps to distinguish one company from another by its choice of colours, images (logo), shapes and other items used in producing its chosen house style.

Typical hardcopy corporate documentation includes letterheads, fax sheet templates, various types of forms, invoices, receipts and sales slips, and so on. There are others which pertain to the particular type of organisation or business. Typical online documentation includes web pages, email page templates, forms, and so forth. Depending on the type of organisation, you could expect a range of different types of web applications; for example, an educational institution may have online tests or quizzes, surveys, registration forms, forums and blogs. Some of the hardcopy documentation, such as fax documentation, may soon become redundant as more online substitutes become available that can carry out the same tasks more efficiently.

The reasons for using specific house styles are linked to the idea of **corporate branding**. If the documents of one particular company had no particular logo or house style to it, you may not notice them even if they did something that you really liked, and you wouldn't be likely to pass on information about them to your friends. Being able to recognise a company in some way helps you to form an opinion about them. The more you see the same company's house style in advertisements the more you will remember what the company is able to do for you, making it more likely that you will use this company compared to others (who may be just as good if not better) that you may not have seen or heard that much about.

KEY TERMS

House style: the elements in corporate documents that create a 'sameness' in the documents of the company.

Corporate branding: the promotion of a particular company or organisation through the advertising style it uses. The more people see the style the more they associate it with that particular company or organisation.

Consistent style: the style on all of a company's promotional materials, with the same colours and logo position on all documents, using the same images and there being a 'sameness' in the look of all their materials.

QUESTION 14.01

a Explain what is meant by using a consistent style in your documents.

b What do paragraph marks signify?

c Why is corporate branding important?

14.02 Producing documents that conform to a corporate house style

In order to understand this section you will be asked to carry out some practical tasks.

PRACTICAL TASK 14.01

Imagine you are a marketing manager for a new fast food outlet and have to create a training presentation for the new staff. Before you begin to create your presentation, you need to create a **master slide** for this presentation.

In a presentation software package set up a new presentation consisting of four slides. You will find many sub-master slides beneath the main master slide. These master slides are templates showing different layouts for different types of slides you may wish to use in your presentation.

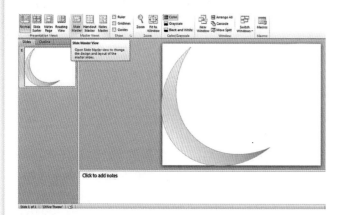

Figure 14.01   Designing a master slide

First, you should select the templates you wish to use for the sub-master slides. Secondly, you should design the style you wish to see on all your slides by using your prepared logo, **slogan**, images and any other item you wish to see on all the slides (Figure 14.01).

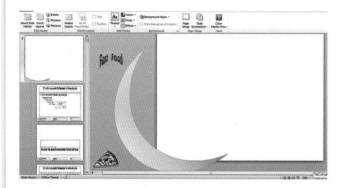

Figure 14.02   The master slide and the sub-master slides

The main master slide has to be designed by using your prepared items, such as the logo, image and other design items (Figure 14.02).

Rearrange these items so that the style will be set on the master slide. When you wish to cascade your style from your master slide onto all your other slides you must select all your slides, then go to 'View' and select 'Slide Master'. Choose the font types you wish to use for each part of your slides, such as the headings, sub-headings, where you want to place the logo, etc. and then select the 'Close Master View'. This will save your style and cascade your style across all your slides as can be seen in figure 14.03.

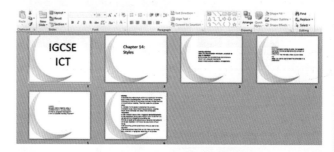

Figure 14.03   The design on the master slide has cascaded onto all the sub-master slides automatically

Apply a background colour to the master slide to match the house style for the organisation (Figure 14.04).

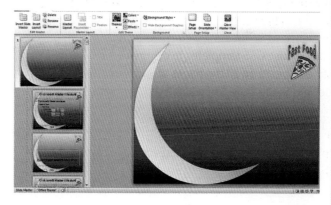

Figure 14.04   Background colours on the master slides

Close the Master View to return to the view where you can edit your slides.

177

PRACTICAL TASK 14.02

When you select your new slides to make up your presentation, you will find that your master slide's designs will appear on all the slide layout options (Figure 14.05).

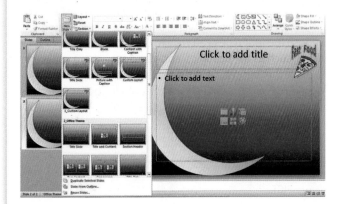

Figure 14.05 Inserting new slides

The top section of the slide layout contains the sub-master slides that you selected when you were designing the master slide. The templates that you selected from the list of templates will also have the same style as the main master slide you designed.

The bottom section of the slide layout section contains all the design templates without the designs you created on your master slide. Notice that these slides will also have the background colour you had set up on the master slide. If you do not wish to have the same background colour you can change it by altering the background.

KEY TERMS

Master slide: the main slide where you can create the design you want to use across all the other slides in a presentation.

Slogan: a phrase or a string of words (not necessarily a sentence) that are representative of a company or organisation.

Similarly, when creating a consistent style for web pages, you can use CSS templates to ensure that the same style appears on all the pages of your website simply by designing the style you want in the template. Using CSS to create a particular style on web pages is covered in Chapter 21 on website authoring.

In a DTP program, you could create a double master page if you need to do so (see Figure 14.06).

Figure 14.06 Creating a double master page in a DTP package

Refer to the file 'Asset 14.01.pub' on the CD to see how this style can be applied to all pages, the current page only or to the master page. Other options include adding headers and footers; inside these you can also add date and time, page numbers or just the time (Figure 14.07).

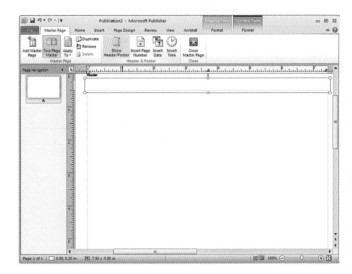

Figure 14.07 Inserting other items in the header and footer on the DTP master page

14.03 Ensuring consistent page/slide layout

The use of master pages and templates ensures that the layout on all the pages of a multi-page document is consistent. This means the font styles, text alignment, spacing between lines, spacing between paragraphs and spacing before and after headings are the same on each page of your document. The same result could be achieved if you adjusted the layout and style on each page as you began to work on each new page of the document, but then you could find it difficult to align the text to the exact same place as you did on a previous page.

Font styles

There are several font styles to choose from within each of the various applications software packages. Usually you would have a different size for each level of text in a document and sometimes you might prefer to have a different colour, font type or size as well. In a word processor, you could use the 'Outline' view option to set the text alignment.

You would have to use templates to set the spacing between lines, spacing between paragraphs and spacing before and after headings to ensure a consistent style, or use placeholders to ensure the formatting styles are fixed.

Appropriate font styles for different audiences

Different fonts appeal to different people, because they affect how people interpret what they read and whether they want to continue reading or stop and try something else. The only problem with fonts and choosing the right one is that one person's font choice can never appeal to everyone. However, there are some general practices that most people follow and that seem to work well. Serif fonts appear to create a more cosy and warm feeling on the pages of a book compared to sans-serif fonts, whereas the sans-serif fonts have more onscreen

appeal with their neat, clean-cut and clinical look (see Figure 14.08).

Cursive and script fonts have a more old-fashioned and fancy look about them and are usually used on invitations, greeting cards and for some parts in a website. Onscreen they are more difficult to read.

The different types of computers, such as Macs and PCs, have different default fonts. Macs typically have Helvetica or Geneva, while Arial looks best on PCs. The more neutral fonts, such as Verdana, are suitable for both Macs and PCs.

Overall, choosing a font type can be very personal because different fonts serve as positive or negative reminders; if you choose a font that most of your customers do not like then it may quite easily affect your business negatively. Font choices are important when creating advertising materials, whether they are destined for print or screen, because of the emotions they can evoke in the audience. Creating visually appealing documents can contribute to success or failure for an organisation, therefore choosing fonts with wide appeal is very important.

179

QUESTION 14.02

What is the difference between a serif and a sans-serif font?

PRACTICAL TASK 14.03

a Open the Word document 'Asset 14.06.docx' from the CD.

b Open the 'View' tab then select 'Outline' from the top toolbar, as shown in Figure 14.09.

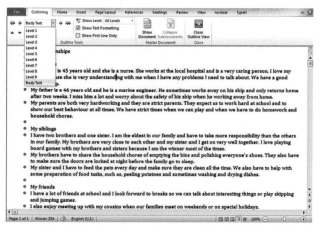

Figure 14.09 Using the 'Outline' tool in the 'View' toolbar

The 'Outline' tool allows you to set the alignment for the text for each level of heading and paragraph. The main heading, 'My Relationships', should have a Level 1 status. Each subheading, 'My parents', 'My siblings' and 'My friends', should have the next level status, Level 2, and so on. When you start each paragraph, you can designate it as 'Body Text'.

c Place your cursor at the beginning of the text to start creating the outline. Select the level for that section of text and go through each bullet point until your whole document is completed (Figure 14.10). You could set the style before you create the whole document, or you could set the style after you have created the document.

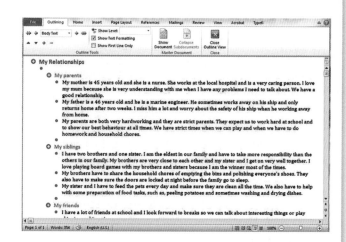

Figure 14.10 Setting the levels for headings, sub-headings and body text

This is a useful feature but it doesn't fix the space between paragraphs, or the line spacing.

Paragraph marks

When you begin a new paragraph you would usually leave some space between your last sentence and the beginning of your new paragraph by pressing the 'Return' key on your keyboard. You'd probably press it twice in order to also create a line break before starting the new paragraph. If you use the paragraph marks, the characters appearing in your text will indicate where the writer last used the 'Return' key on the keyboard (see Figure 14.11). This would indicate where the intention to begin a new paragraph would be.

The headings also have the paragraph marks after them indicating a space after the text in the last heading and the space before the next heading's text.

Line spacing

Some academic writing requires you to format your text with double-spaces between the lines of text. This can be fixed by highlighting all of the text and choosing the number relating to how much spacing you need between the text lines (Figure 14.12).

Figure 14.11 Using paragraph marks to ensure spacing between paragraphs and before and after headings

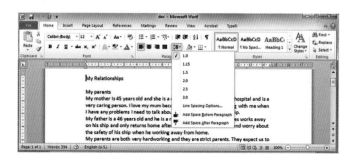

Figure 14.12 Using the line spacing tool

Another method of setting the formatting styles for line spacing can be achieved by following the method shown in Figure 14.13.

Figure 14.13 Using the 'Styles' tool for 'Paragraph Spacing'

The paragraph spacing could be compact, tight, open, relaxed or double. If you wish to customise your paragraph settings even further you could also choose the option shown in Figure 14.14.

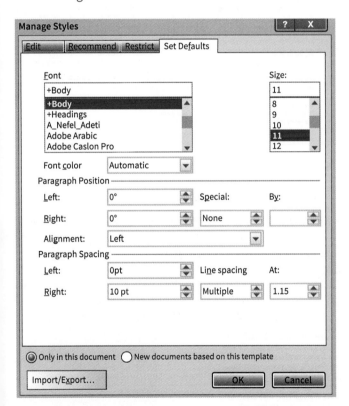

Figure 14.14 Setting and fixing the paragraph margins to be used in your current document and to set the paragraph spacing

Applying paragraph styles

Once you have chosen your formatting, paragraph spacing and heading spacing, you can set the style as the 'Default Style'; if you choose the 'Template' version, it will achieve the same result. In other words, your chosen style will be fixed or set and can be used every time you open a new document.

If you choose one of the 'Quick Styles', it will cascade throughout your document. If you already have a style that you are comfortable using, you could add it to the other 'Quick Style' choices and be able to refer to it readily for future documents (Figure 14.15).

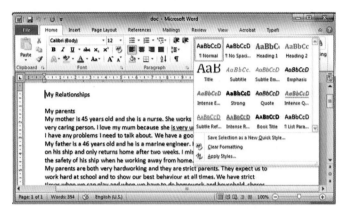

Figure 14.15 Saving your own formatting style as a 'Quick Styles' choice

You can also clear all the formatting from existing documents and apply new styles to it by using the relevant options.

Creating a 'New Style'

You know how to adapt existing styles and how to apply paragraph styles with a new name to match the corporate style, but the next section will show you how to create a completely new style with new style names that will include the styles for the body, sub-headings, titles, etc.

After you have created your document, you can apply a new style to it because each document will already have its own default style that may or may not match your user's required style or the corporate style you may be trying to create. If you use the scenario that you are trying to create a new style that you can use to complete your homework, you can apply this style to all your homework documents. Follow the steps indicated in the following screenshots:

1 Open the file, 'Asset 14.06.docx' found on the CD. Notice that it already has a default style of its own but this style is not the same style I wish to use because it doesn't match the style required by my users.

2 Click on 'Styles' tab found in the 'Home' toolbar and select the 'Save selection as a New Quick Style …'.

3 Fill in a relevant name for your new style, such as, 'Homework Style' in this case and then click on 'MODIFY'.

4 You should have this screen:

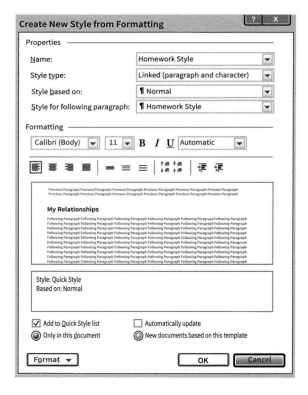

Figure 14.16 Creating a New Style

In this window you can choose your new font style, font size, colour, etc. At the bottom of the screen, you can choose to 'Add to Quick Style list' and to 'Automatically Update' as well. In addition, you have the choice as to whether you only want to use your new style in the document you are currently working in or on other documents you create in the future as a template. When you are completed, click 'OK'. This will add your new style to the list of styles already stored in the program and you can use it whenever you wish to apply your new style to documents in the future. In order to test your new style, you can start another new document and type something into your new document. Highlight it and go to your 'Styles' tab and you should see your saved new style there for you to apply to your new document.

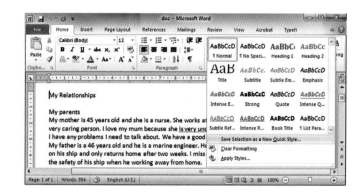

Figure 14.17 The saved new style

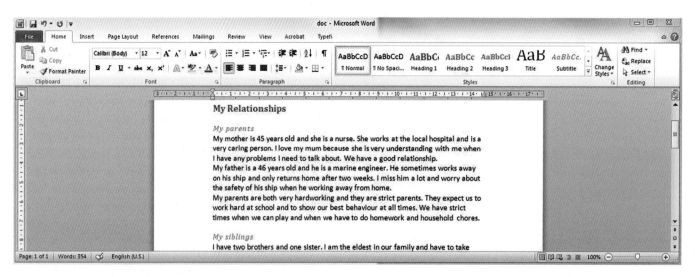

Figure 14.18 The new style applied to the new document

182

In the same way, you can create a new style that can be applied to the body of your document or to any other part of any new document that you may be creating. It will have to be saved to the list of 'Quick Styles' and then you can apply the new style to that part of any document, such as sub-headings, titles, etc. you create in the future.

Keeping control of widows and orphans in the development of new styles could be particularly useful and be an excellent way to save you the extra time you would need to correct issues relating to widows and orphans later.

How to include 'widow and orphan' control in a new style template

Refer to chapter 17 on the section on 'Widows and Orphans'. A widow refers to the last line of a paragraph that spills over onto the top of next page where it is left on its own and an orphan refers to the first line of a paragraph that is left on the bottom of a page by itself. In order to avoid these situations, you could ensure that these are controlled from within your new style template, as follows:

In the window, 'Create New Styles from Formatting', select the option, 'Paragraph' and then select the option, 'Line and Page Breaks'. Tick the box for 'Widow and Orphan Control'.

PRACTICAL TASK 14.04

Open the spreadsheet template for a family budget found on the CD in a file called 'Asset 14.02.xlsx'. It should look like Figure 14.19.

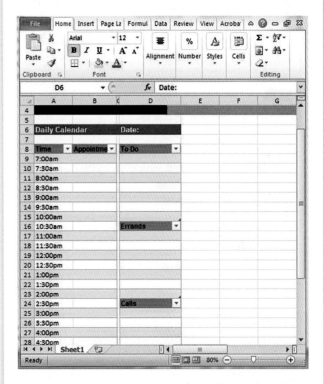

Figure 14.19 Using templates to ensure consistency of style

Fill in some information about your plan for the day's activities. Usually this type of daily plan is used by someone who is trying to manage their time more effectively in order to analyse exactly how much time they are actually spending on the different activities they are doing each day. You would need to create one for every day, and if you started from scratch to design the style of this daily time sheet, it would take a much longer time compared to if you simply used this template and copied and pasted the template for each day.

You could copy and paste each day's schedule next to each other on the same worksheet or you could use a different worksheet for each day and then use formulas and functions to analyse your trends according to your needs.

However, the main idea is to repeat the same style and formatting from the template and apply the same style to all the other day's sheets more effectively.

QUESTION 14.03

a What is the alignment of the 'Time' column?

b Describe the formatting in cells A1 to D1.

c Look at the screenshot in Figure 14.20 and describe what the problem with the style in this cell is. How can it be corrected so that there can be more space available to write down more details in the 'Appointment' column? Justify your choice.

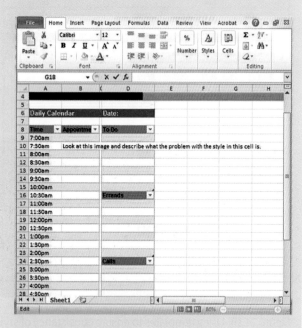

Figure 14.20 Formatting each cell

PRACTICAL TASK 14.05

A new restaurant, Artista, is opening in Buxtom in Khartoum and a new style has to be created for their documentation, presentations and online articles. You are going to produce a sample master slide for their presentations. Follow the instructions in the file 'Asset 14.07.docx' on the CD for this task.

Summary

- Corporate documents should conform to a particular formatting style in order to be distinguished from other similar companies.

- Branding is a method of promoting a company through the style on its promotional materials. The more visible the corporate brand is, the easier it is for people to remember the company.

- Consistent styles means that all the promotional materials should have a 'sameness' look about them and be easily recognisable by their choice of colours, fonts, images and **text enhancements**.

- Most applications have a wide choice of built-in styles that you can use, add to or change from an existing one.

- Styles can be set as the default style or saved as a template and can be used repeatedly in all future new documents without having to set everything up from scratch every time you open a new document.

- Text enhancement means that you can make your text bold, italic, underlined or highlighted depending on its purpose.

Chapter 15:
Proofing

Learning objectives

When you have completed this chapter, you should be able to understand:

- how to use software tools to ensure that all work produced contains as few errors as possible
- how to use proofing techniques to ensure accuracy of data entry
- what verification is.

Overview

Proofing is the term referring to checking all your computer-produced work to ensure it contains as few errors as possible. It is different from testing your computer-produced work in that it only checks on a more superficial level. It is similar to proofreading a manuscript for spelling, punctuation and grammatical errors and that data has been entered is valid.

KEY TERMS

Proofing: the general term for checking documents for accuracy and correctness using various techniques.

15.01 Using software tools for proofing

Spell check software

Spell check software checks a word against all the listed words in its dictionary and will flag a word up that doesn't match any of its known words by underlining it with a red wavy line. When right-clicked on, a list of possible alternative words appears for you to choose from. You can add a word to the dictionary if you think that it is spelt correctly.

There are many aspects to consider when using spell check software. First, you should set your language preferences for editing and note that the English language has several versions, such as UK or USA English; there are a few different spellings of the same words in these two countries, and in many others as well. There are also extra words in some countries' English dictionaries that are not included in others', hence the different dictionaries for the same language, English (see Figure 15.01).

PRACTICAL TASK 15.01

Find some words that end in '...ise' and '...ize' and carry out a spell check on them. Which country's dictionary accepts these words?

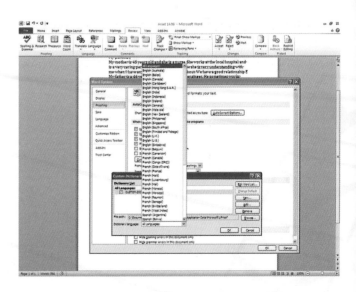

Figure 15.01 Different 'English' dictionaries for different countries in a word processor

If you try to write the word 'excell' you will notice that the spelling is automatically corrected to 'excel'. This feature is called 'autocorrect' and it suggests a 'correct' version of the word it believes you are trying to spell. Some mobile devices use a similar feature called predictive text: as you type the letters in, it suggests possible words you may be trying to type before you have actually completed the whole word. You can then choose the word you wish to include without having to spell it out.

EXTENSION ACTIVITY 15.01

Discuss the pros and cons of these autocorrect features that suggest words for you.

You should be aware that you should not rely entirely on spell check software because it does not understand the context of your sentences in the same way that humans understand their own language. Spell check software can only match words against the words stored in their dictionary and alert you to the possibility that you may have made a spelling mistake. You still need to check that you have used the correct word for your sentence to make sense.

Humans are prone to making data input errors and spell check software helps you to notice your spelling mistakes and correct them quicker as you type, rather than waiting until you get to the end of your typing and then have to retype it all over again. It saves you some time. Everybody works in different ways and some people do actually type in everything quickly and then run a spell check through the whole document afterwards in order to save time.

Spell check software can also be useful for people who are dyslexic, and it can help some people to learn how to spell correctly by constantly flagging up incorrectly spelt words and suggesting the correctly spelt versions. This repetitive action helps you to remember how to spell a word correctly the next time you need to use it.

On the other hand, some people have become too reliant on spell check software and have lost the motivation to learn how to spell correctly on their own. If they had to handwrite a document, they would be prone to making more spelling mistakes than they would if they used a computer to do the same task. In addition, it would take them longer to correct all their spelling mistakes, especially as they would have to rewrite the handwritten document (probably several times) until all the errors have been eliminated. However, does it matter that some people end up not being able to spell when they use handwriting?

Generally, the answer would be 'yes, it does matter', depending on the target audience. The target audience doesn't seem to mind what appears in sms texts, for example, though that applies to an electronic device rather than paper, while most other target audiences would take incorrect spelling into account in some way or other. Often it would be the same individuals, such as in an informal setting people use a more informal tone and type of language than they would in formal situations and let their guard down by not correcting their misspelt words.

Typographical errors

Typographical errors are errors made when you do know how to spell a word correctly but accidentally type it in incorrectly, either because of problems with the keyboard or because you may simply have been typing too fast and left a few characters out (or added a few extra characters in). Common mistakes are not leaving a space between words, or typing letters in a different order in a word on a regular basis. A common example of this is typing the word 'the' as 'teh'. The way to help you with such a problem is to reset your spell checker, as seen in Figure 15.02.

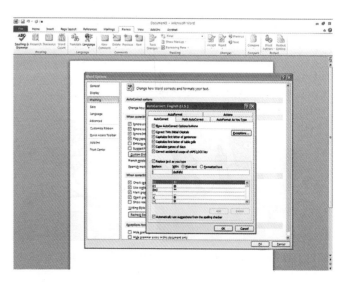

Figure 15.02 Using AutoCorrect options in the spell checker

PRACTICAL TASK 15.02

Think of all the words you frequently spell incorrectly, possibly because of the order you may be typing in the letters (even though you certainly know how to spell these words correctly). Configure your spelling and grammar checker by following the four steps in Figure 15.02. Test it out with some example text to see if it works better for you.

The 'Replace' tool

There is another way you can replace all your commonly misspelt words or incorrectly used words, and that is by using the 'Replace' tool. Although it can be used to correct words that you may have spelt incorrectly throughout a long document and can save you time in place of using the usual spell check procedure, the 'Replace' tool can also do other things compared to spell check software. If, for example, you have used a word incorrectly throughout a document, you could replace the incorrect word with the correct word and all instances of that word will be changed by one action.

EXTENSION ACTIVITY 15.02

Discuss the differences between using spell check software and the 'Replace' tool. Give examples to explain your answers.

Words that sound the same (homophones) are sometimes problematic (see Figure 15.03), and spell check software cannot be of any help in this regard because if you spell both words correctly but use them in the wrong context then your sentence may not make proper sense. If you use spell check software on such a sentence it will not flag the incorrect word as being a spelling mistake, because technically speaking it won't be a spelling mistake.

BOARD OF EDUCATION   **BORED** OF EDUCATION

Figure 15.03 An example of a homophone

In addition to those mentioned above, spell check software can have other features built into it that give users more options when they have spelt a word incorrectly. You can **change** the word and accept one of their suggested words to replace your incorrectly spelt word. If you have made this same spelling mistake with more than one word, you can **change all**, or you can **ignore** the incorrectly spelt word or **ignore all** of them if appropriate. If you know that your word is spelt correctly, you can choose **add to dictionary**.

Checking grammar

Which of these sentences makes proper sense? 'I have seen them movie' or 'I have seen the movie'? Both of these sentences have passed the spell check without any words being flagged up as a problem because the spelling for the words 'them' and 'the' are both correct. However, the first sentence is grammatically incorrect. You might think that your work is fine because no problems are flagged up, but there can still be problems with other aspects in your text that a grammar checker cannot detect. You should not rely entirely on a grammar checker for checking all your grammar.

Using validation routines to minimise errors

When you input data into a spreadsheet or database program or fill in forms online, you can minimise inputting the incorrect type of data by using validation techniques. **Validation** is a method that helps to prevent incorrect data from being entered. When you set up your database or spreadsheet, you can set up the validation rules about which type of data you want to allow to be entered into

a particular cell. Data entered into a computer system can be valid but still incorrect. An example of this can be if someone's age is filled in as 16 instead of as 11. Both of these could be valid if the validation rule includes all ages ranging from 1 to 50, but the data would still be incorrect. To ensure a higher degree of accuracy when entering data into a computer system, another proofing technique is usually also carried out, called verification. During verification, data could be entered by a second person and when the two sets of data are compared with each other, any differences are then checked against the original place where the data was being entered from to verify the accuracy of the entered data. There are a number of different types of validation check that you can use to reduce the possibility of inputting errors.

KEY TERMS

Validation: a proofing technique whereby rules can be set up that prevent you from entering incorrect types of data.

Range check

This checks that any data you enter falls within a specific range; for example, you may wish to enter numbers between 10 and 30 only. If you accidentally enter a number outside of this range, the system will not allow you to do so, thereby reducing the possibility of you inputting any errors. If you were required to input exact numbers, for example a student's test marks for a test with a maximum mark out of 30, then you could use this validation technique to prevent you from entering a mark more than 30. However, if you enter Joe Blogg's test mark as 21 but it was meant to be 12, then your validation routine will still accept the mark as 21 even though Joe Blogg's test mark has been entered incorrectly. Validation techniques can only help to reduce the possibility of entering inaccurate data into a system. It cannot guarantee the accuracy of the data that can be input.

Presence check

This ensures that you cannot omit any data, and will usually not allow you to proceed any further until you have entered the required data. It checks that data has been entered irrespective of whether the data is the correct value or of the correct type. This type of validation check is useful for obtaining your permission, such as before submitting a form electronically.

Type check

There are many different types of data, such as numerical data, text data, currency, date and time data, and so on. A type check will prevent you from entering a date like 31/02/15 because the month February has only 28 days except in a leap year when it has 29 days, not 31 days as implied here.

EXTENSION ACTIVITY 15.03

Think of examples where applying a type validation check will not prevent you from entering incorrect data into a system.

Length check

This checks that the length of the data you entered is not too short or too long. Mobile phone numbers usually contain 11 digits, and if you try to enter fewer than 11 digits your validation system will usually inform you of your error or prevent your incorrect data from being accepted by your system.

QUESTION 15.01

What are the advantages and disadvantages of using a validation 'length check'?

Give some examples of where these can be used successfully and where it would be inappropriate to use this type of validation technique.

Check digit

This is a number that is generated by applying an algorithm to some data. It is checked against another number and if the two numbers match then that is an indication that your digits have been entered correctly. An example of when it would be appropriate to use the 'check digit' type of validation technique is when you try to enter the ISBN numbers of books into a system. You can apply the 'modulo 11' system to it. This will generate a remainder after dividing the number you wish to input by 11. You can also try other modulo systems, such as 7 mod 4 = 3.

If you wish to input a series of ISBN numbers into a system and you apply the modulo 11 technique, then this is how it would work for the ISBN (13) number 978-1-1075-4673-8.

The last digit in each of these ISBN 1 3 numbers is called the 'check digit'. In the first case it is the digit 8. The check digit is the number you will match against the number you get after you have applied the algorithm to the ISBN. If these two numbers match, then it means you have entered your ISBN number correctly into the system.

Beneath each digit write a 3 and alternate it with a 1, starting at the extreme right-hand side, as shown in Table 15.01.

Multiply each digit with the 1 or the 3 as shown in Table 15.01, and then add all the products together to give you the answer 102. Next you should work out what you need to add to your number (102) to round it up to the nearest 10. In this case, 102 + ? = 110. The answer is 8. This is the digit you have calculated after applying the algorithm to the original number, and you can see that it matches the check digit which is the last digit in the ISBN number. This means that you have entered your ISBN number correctly into your system. This particular algorithm applies only to the ISBN (13) numbers and not for the ISBN (10) numbers; they use a different algorithm.

Two types of ISBN numbers exist because the 10-digit ISBN numbers are the older type and the 13-digit ISBN numbers are the newer version. The two are coexisting while the older one is being phased out and the newer version is being phased in.

9	7	8	1	1	0	7	5	4	6	7	3	?
1	3	1	3	1	3	1	3	1	3	1	3	
9×1	7×3	8×1	1×3	1×1	0×3	7×1	5×3	4×1	6×3	7×1	3×3	
9	21	8	3	1	0	7	15	4	18	7	9	$= 102$

Table 15.01 Calculating the check digit for 978-1-107

EXTENSION ACTIVITY 15.04

Apply the same algorithm to the two ISBN numbers 978-1-131-650074-3 and 978-1-3166-2741-9 by following the same procedure.

Find two or more ISBN (10) numbers from books and research the algorithm that you could apply to it. Apply this different algorithm to it and explain your understanding of the advantages and disadvantages of using check digit validation as a means to reducing input errors into computer systems.

💿 Lookup

In a spreadsheet or database application you can use a lookup table that will allow you to select from a predetermined list of items. In this way you will not make a mistake when entering data because your choices are limited to the acceptable items in the lookup table. You can see how this works in a spreadsheet by looking at the file 'Asset 15.01.xlsx' on the CD.

Picture/format check

The format of a UK car registration number is LLNN LLL, where 'L' represents a letter from the alphabet and 'N' represents a number from 0 to 9. Knowing the format of a number or code means that you can check the validity of such data quickly.

PRACTICAL TASK 15.03

Think of similar types of nationally used codes, for example identification numbers, registration numbers and so on where you live and write the format in the same style as above.

15.02 Proofing techniques

The importance of accuracy when entering data can have far-reaching consequences because accurate data yields reliable results after the data has been manipulated. If the data is inaccurate then the results will also be inaccurate and therefore cannot be used despite a lot of work having been done on it. A simple example could be data for weather entered into a system for pilots to use to plan their flight paths; if the wind direction is erroneously recorded as being north-easterly instead of south-easterly, the pilot may take a very different flight path which may be longer and this could result in more fuel being used or flying a more dangerous route, which could have been avoided if the data was accurate in the first instance

Transposition errors

Transposing numbers happens when you change the order of the digits in a number when rewriting it or keying it in. This is referred to as a transposition error. An example of transposing a number could be writing 1325677 instead of 1235677. In this case, the second and third digits have changed position. Although this appears to be a small error, it can have catastrophic consequences if it results in a financial loss. In order to detect such an error, you can check if any two adjacent numbers are divisible by 9. In the example above, you could check if the first two numbers can be subtracted from each other and be divisible by 9, and it would then indicate that a transposition error may have occurred. Each pair of adjacent numbers can be checked using this method until the error can be detected. The first two adjacent numbers are 12 and 13. If you subtract 12 from 13, the answer is not divisible by 9. Again you could check the next two numbers in the sequence: 23 and 32. If 23 is subtracted from 32, the answer is 9, which is divisible by 9, so then you can see where the transposition error has occurred. The next two adjacent numbers would be 56 and 56, and you can see that all the rest of the numbers in the sequence match each other perfectly. Bank tellers usually use this method to detect where an error might have occurred when rewriting numbers.

Proofreading by a third party

Proofreading is the technique whereby a third party checks your work for errors. You can proofread a document against an original, by comparing the two, or simply check a document on its own. Proofreading is different from reading for pleasure where you would focus on the content for facts and information. You should only be checking that every single word is spelt correctly and the grammar is mostly correct. Since you may have to change the structure of some sentences, you should use the change tracking tool to indicate any changes you suggest to the original document.

If you are proofreading one document against another copy, you should be looking at both documents in the same window and go through each sentence line by line and word by word to ensure that both documents are exactly the same.

Consistent character spacing

This is required for some words or items such as units of measurement, people's initials or page numbers. In these examples you will notice that there can be different spacing between characters. Usually the copy-editor decides on whether the spacing should be **variable**, **fixed** or **no spacing at all**. Once the decision has been taken, the proofreader has to apply that character spacing consistently throughout the document. Here are some examples of different character spacing options:

- 65 kg or 65kg

- Mrs. D P Mipet or Mrs DP Mipet or Mrs D. P. Mipet or Mrs. D.P. Mipet

- p.398 or pg.398 or p. 398 or pg. 398.

In order to check that there is consistent character spacing throughout the document, you should avoid justifying the text because that would add extra space between the words in order to fill the line so that the end of a sentence doesn't leave a dent in the shape of a block of text.

Consistent case

This refers to using upper case or lower case for certain parts of your document, and using them in the same way throughout. Sometimes upper case is used in headings, and perhaps the first letter of a subheading will only be required to be in upper case. The 'AutoCorrect' tool in the 'Proofing' option in a word processor allows you to ensure the case options you set are applied consistently in your documents (see Figure 15.04).

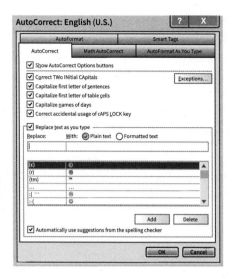

Figure 15.04 Using the Proofing AutoCorrect tool to ensure consistent case

Factual errors

There could be errors in the factual content of a document. Checking for them requires the expertise of subject specialist to review the content of a document for correctness. However, if you are looking for a particular word to express an idea or have forgotten the word, you could make use of the 'Research' tool which includes a thesaurus, dictionaries and access to research articles and definitions. These research options are found in most Office documents under the 'Proofing' tab (see Figure 15.05).

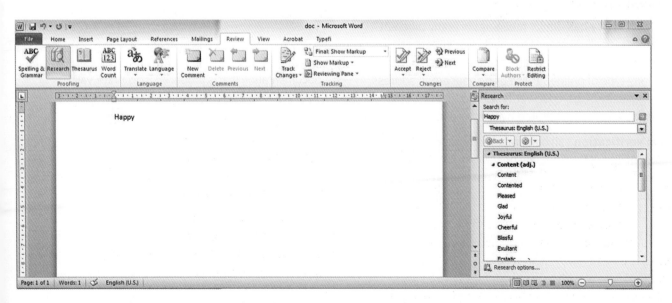

Figure 15.05 Using a thesaurus to improve factual errors

EXTENSION ACTIVITY 15.05

Discuss the limitations of using a thesaurus to correct the factual errors in a document.

Consistent line spacing

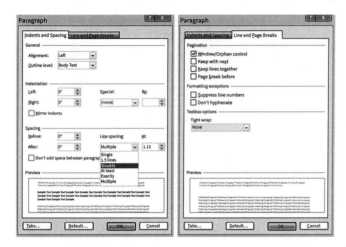

Figure 15.06 Using advanced options to set the spacing between characters, lines and paragraphs to be consistent

'Widows' are when the last line of a paragraph appears as the first line of a new page or column; 'orphans' are when the first line of a paragraph appears as the last line of a page or column. These can be controlled by choosing an option to accept or reject them (see Figure 15.06). They don't look very professional and are confusing to read. The same applies to lists, columns and slides.

Verification

The word, **verify** has similar meanings in many different contexts. Basically, it means to check, test or agree that something is true or correct and accurate. When you sign up for any type of online service using your email address, you will usually be asked to verify your authenticity by replying to an email generated by the system.

Visual verification can be compared to proofreading a document against the original document, where a visual comparison can be made between data entered and a data source. Refer to the section on 'Proofreading' earlier in this chapter.

KEY TERMS

Verification: a proofing technique that allows you to correct or suggest alternatives to data being input into a system.

Visual verification: a proofing technique whereby you visually check a document for accuracy and correctness.

Double data entry: a proofing technique that uses the COUNTIF spreadsheet function together with conditional formatting to highlight the differences in two lists of items.

Double data entry is another verification technique whereby data is entered twice and then the computer compares the two sets of data. This can be done after the two sets of data have been entered or by comparing them during data entry. In a spreadsheet you can use the 'COUNTIF' function and conditional formatting to highlight any data entries that are different in your two lists.

The need for validation as well as verification

Each of these proofing techniques offers different aspect of checking the accuracy or correctness of data that is entered into your documents. Validation ensures that the format of the data being entered is correct according to the validation rules you have set up prior to your data entry process. Verification ensures that the data entered makes sense and is more accurate than if only validation was applied to it. Proofreading, which is a verification technique, ensures that a document can be as accurate and correct as it can be, and this technique is the most time-consuming of all because it requires a human to carry out this check for accuracy and correctness.

PRACTICAL TASK 15.04

As the Personal Assistant to the Director of Busy Bees Stationery Company, you have to ensure that all the documentation that is produced is accurate, valid, correct and as free from errors as possible. Refer to the file 'Asset 15.02.docx' on the CD and answer the questions there.

Summary

- Proofing can never really eliminate all the errors that could possibly occur in a document.

- Spell check software is a useful tool and can be used to correct incorrectly spelt words, provided the correct dictionary is used and the context of the word has been considered. Spell check software should not be relied upon as the only solution for checking all the spelling in a document.

- The different types of proofing can achieve different levels of accuracy and correctness in documents.

- Validation helps to reduce the possibility of errors being made at the data input stage.

- Verification helps to correct or suggest changes to data that has already been input into a system.

- Both validation and verification are necessary to achieve the highest possible levels of accuracy and correctness in documents because each type of proofing covers different aspects of reducing errors in documents.

Chapter 16:
Graphs and charts

Learning objectives

When you have completed this chapter, you should be able to understand:

- how to produce a graph or chart from the given data
- selecting data
- selecting the graph or chart type
- labelling
- adding a second data series
- adding a second axis
- changing values of axes
- enhancing the appearance of a graph or chart.

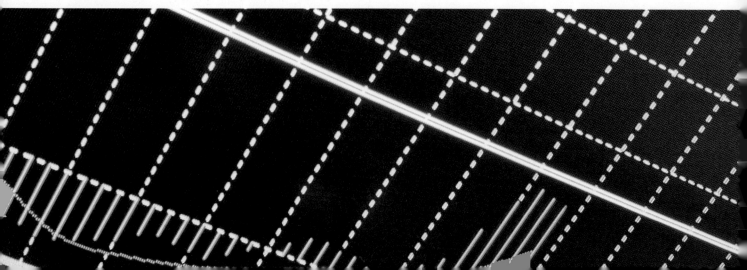

Overview

Graphs and charts present numerical data in a visual format that makes it easier for the human brain to understand the relationships between different data series and their categories. Presenting numerical data in the form of charts and graphs allows you to compare data, to predict possible future trends and to observe the historical trend of the data series. Schools can compare students' grades for different subjects, terms, tests, between students, and so on. You can see the trend of your data series in a chart or graph as going upwards, downwards or staying the same. You can also observe a change in a trend; for example, when a student begins to under-perform, the chart's trend will point in a downward direction. Another example can relate to predicting what might occur during the next period, such as, will the student be able to improve on the existing grade? Many educational institutions predict the grades they expect their students to achieve in their examinations by using the students' previous grades and other student data at their disposal.

16.01 Producing a graph or chart

When you decide to create a chart, you should first have a reason for doing so. You should understand what message you wish to convey to your audience. However, before you begin to create your chart or graph you should also understand the terms associated with a chart or graph and what the different types of charts and graphs are. In addition, you should also know which type of chart or graph would be the most appropriate type for the message you wish to convey to your audience.

The different types of charts available can seen in Figure 16.01.

Figure 16.01 Different types of charts and graphs

A column chart is the most appropriate chart for comparing values across categories; for example, you can compare the grades for different students to each other.

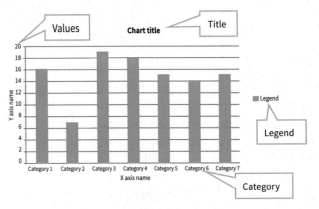

Figure 16.02 Using a column chart to compare values across different categories (different students in this case)

Elements of charts and graphs

A chart or graph has different parts to it. The title should indicate the message you wish to convey to your audience by using the chart or graph. In Figure 16.02, the chart is showing the 'Marks' of different students compared to each other. The different categories are the students in this case, but it could be any other category depending on what your topic is. Another example could be comparing the prices of the same product in different stores. Categories in a column chart are represented along the horizontal (X) axis.

The values represent the marks each student (category) achieves and these are represented along the vertical (Y) axis.

A bar chart is more appropriate for comparing multiple values (see Figure 16.03).

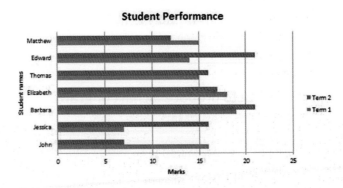

Figure 16.03 Using a bar chart to compare multiple values ('Term 1' and 'Term 2') across categories (different students)

To follow the discussion in the rest of this chapter, refer to the spreadsheet in the file 'Asset 16.01.xlsx' on the CD.

195

Line graphs can indicate how a category performs over time by showing trends. In Figure 16.04, one category is shown: how John has performed over time in completing four different tasks. He has a downward trend, which means he is performing less well with each successive task. In Figure 16.05, trends for two categories are shown and Jessica has an upward trend compared to John's downward trend. Figure 16.05 can be used both to show the trends and compare the trends in more than one category.

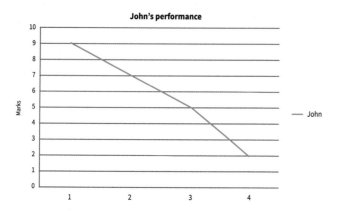

Figure 16.04 Using a line graph to indicate John's performance (trend) over the different tasks (over time)

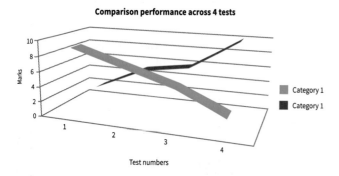

Figure 16.05 Using a line graph to show the trend for more than one category

Selecting data to produce a chart or graph

Using non-contiguous data

A	B	C	D	E	F	G
	Horizontal axis values	Series name	Series name			
	John	16	7			
	Jessica	7	16			
	Barbara	19	21		Series values	
	Elizabeth	18	17			
	Thomas	15	6			
	Edward	14	21			
	Matthew	15	12			

Figure 16.06 The terms associated with creating a chart or graph

Using the data from the spreadsheet in the file 'Asset 16.01.xlsx' on the CD, in order to display a chart of student grades for Terms 1 and 2, you should choose a column chart and select data. This will open the window for you to add a series name, such as 'Term 1', followed by selecting the series values. This will insert the data for only one set of your **non-contiguous data** (Term 1). In order to insert your second set of non-contiguous data (Term 2), you should click 'OK' and repeat the process until you have completed inserting all your sets of non-contiguous data (see Figure 16.07).

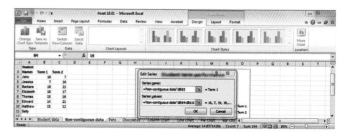

Figure 16.07 Selecting non-contiguous data ranges

The last stage would be for you to insert your horizontal axis label range (see Figure 16.08).

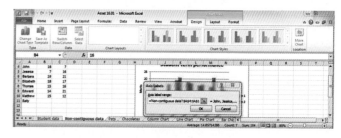

Figure 16.08 Adding the axis label range

Using contiguous data to create a chart or graph

Contiguous data is data ranges or series which are adjacent to each other and is easily highlighted and inserted to create charts and graphs.

KEY TERMS

Contiguous data: data in columns and rows that are next to each other and easy for highlighting together to make charts with.

Non-contiguous data: data where the columns and rows are not adjacent to each other and which is not that easy to use together.

EXTENSION ACTIVITY 16.01

Research online tutorials that demonstrate how to create charts and graphs and discuss the different ways of creating charts if you had both contiguous and non-contiguous data ranges.

How to select a specified data range to make a graph/chart

You can use various keyboard shortcuts to select specified ranges of data to make a graph or chart. An example of such a shortcut is if you needed to select a very large data range that spans several screens, it might be useful to use the shortcut 'Ctrl + Shift + 8'. In the following practical task, you can practise with the various shortcuts to discover how they can be used in different scenarios.

Types of charts and graphs
Column charts and graphs

When you create a chart or graph you must match the type of chart or graph to the required purpose in order to meet the needs of your audience. In the examples above, you have explored how a column chart or graph is most suitable for displaying data where you are comparing values across categories. In the example of student data, the values are represented by the students' marks and the categories are represented by the different students' names.

PRACTICAL TASK 16.01

Refer to the 'Student data' worksheet in the spreadsheet from 'Asset 16.01.xlsx' on the CD. Use the shortcuts in Table 16.01 to carry out the following short tasks. Each of these will enable you to select specified ranges of data according to your needs.

You can also use the number pad on your keyboard with 'Num Lock', although in some versions of the software it may not work.

Produce a word-processed table such as the one shown in Table 16.01. Place your cursor in any cell where you have student data displayed and use the shortcuts in the left-hand column. The middle column explains what the shortcut will do and you should take a screenshot of your result and paste it in the right-hand column.

Shortcut	What it does	Your task: insert a screenshot here
Ctrl + Shift + 1	This shortcut selects a range of data downward and across to the right from your active cell. This is limited to all the data in that worksheet.	
Ctrl + Shift + 2	This shortcut selects a range of data which spans down the column where your active cell begins as far as the end of the data in this worksheet.	
Ctrl + Shift + 3	This shortcut takes you to the next worksheet in your spreadsheet.	
Ctrl + Shift + 4	This shortcut selects all the data in the row where your active cell begins and proceeds to the left of that position.	
Ctrl + Shift + 6	This shortcut selects all the data in the row where your active cell begins and proceeds to the right of that position, but only as far as the end of your data range in that worksheet.	
Ctrl + Shift + 7	This shortcut selects all the data upward from the starting point of your active cell and across until the end of your data range.	
Ctrl + Shift + 8	This shortcut selects two columns upward from the active cell and to the left until the end of your data range.	

Table 16.01 Range selection shortcuts

Bar charts and graphs

Although column charts and bar charts look similar, they can be used to display data differently. Bar charts are most suitable for displaying multiple values. This could be useful for showing how these values change over time or can be used in 'what if?' scenarios. In the same example of student data explained earlier, students' marks for more than one test could be displayed in a graph. This would display their marks over time, such as term 1, term 2 and so on. Alternatively, you could see how the students performed in different papers in an examination, such as paper 1, paper 2 and so on. A comparison such as this allows you to ask questions, such as what would happen if a student got a lower mark or a higher mark. Similarly, you could see, at a glance, how far off a target grade a student is much more easily than if you were simply looking at a table with the same multiple values.

Line graphs

Line graphs are the most suitable type of graph to display time trends. The example explored earlier depicts one student's test performance over time; you could easily compare the test performance of multiple students over time in this way.

Pie charts

Pie charts are the most suitable type of chart to use to display the contribution each value makes to a whole item or entity. An example could be how much each person has contributed to the total amount of money raised in a certain fundraising effort. It shows each person's percentage compared to the total. Even if the values do not all add up to 100, the spreadsheet will convert the values to a percentage when it is displayed as a pie chart.

Area charts and graphs

An area chart (Figure 16.09a) is the most useful type of chart to use to emphasise differences between several sets of data over time. They are similar to line graphs but have the area beneath the lines coloured in. The problem with area graphs is that any data series with smaller values are blocked from view by those with larger values. This problem can be overcome by using the transparency tool to show the outlines of all the graphs, both with larger and smaller values.

Scatter charts and graphs

You can use a scatter graph (Figure 16.09b) to represent the relationship between two sets of numbers, such as when you have x-axis and y-axis data and need to show the relationship between the x and y values. You should always put your x values to the left so that the chart is interpreted correctly and the label should be at the top of your columns of numbers for both the x-axis and y-axis numbers.

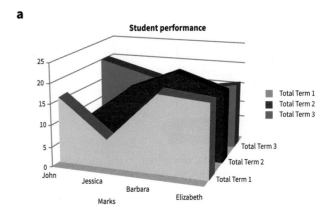

a

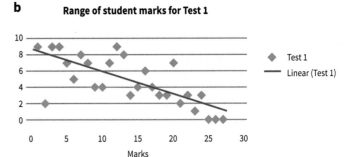

b

Figure 16.09 Examples of (a) an area graph, (b) a scatter chart

Other types of charts and graphs

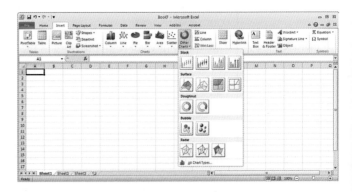

Figure 16.10 Other types of charts and graphs

Figure 16.10 shows examples of many other types of charts and graphs. Some of these are combinations of some of the earlier types discussed above.

Refer to the graphs that are similar to those in Figure 16.10 in the spreadsheet in 'Asset 16.01.xlsx' and distinguish between each of these different types of charts and graphs. Give examples that demonstrate your understanding of the differences between them.

Labelling charts and graphs

There are many new terms to understand regarding labelling a chart or graph. You should know what each of the following means or refers to before you attempt the practical task of labelling a chart or graph.

A **chart title** is usually displayed at the top of a chart and should ideally inform the audience about what the chart is depicting. A chart title is not the same as the headings or labels appearing on any of the axes of some types of charts or graphs.

A sector label is a label for a smaller part of your chart, as shown in Figure 16.09a. In order to label a sector, you should click on the chart and format it by clicking on 'Alt Text', as depicted in Figure 16.11.

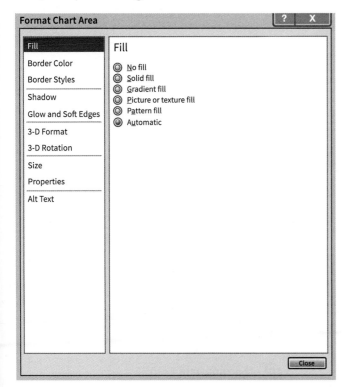

Figure 16.11 Inserting titles on graphs and charts

You can use a similar procedure to insert a legend, sector values, segment labels and values, category axis titles, category axis labels, value axis labels and labels and scales (Figure 16.12).

Figure 16.12 Editing the label names

However, you should know what each of these means. A sector refers to a slice out of a pie chart. A segment refers to a slice out of a radar chart. A **legend** is a key or codes to understand what the colours represent in the graph or chart. Scales refer to the dimensions you wish to use for both the *x* axis and the *y* axis, and they can be altered to suit your requirements accordingly.

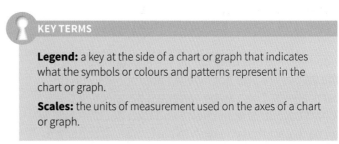

KEY TERMS

Legend: a key at the side of a chart or graph that indicates what the symbols or colours and patterns represent in the chart or graph.

Scales: the units of measurement used on the axes of a chart or graph.

In order to insert a title on a chart or graph, you should complete creating your chart by highlighting the data you want to display in your chart and graph, Go to 'Insert', select the type of chart or graph you wish to create and click OK. This should create a chart that is similar to the one shown in Figure 16.13.

199

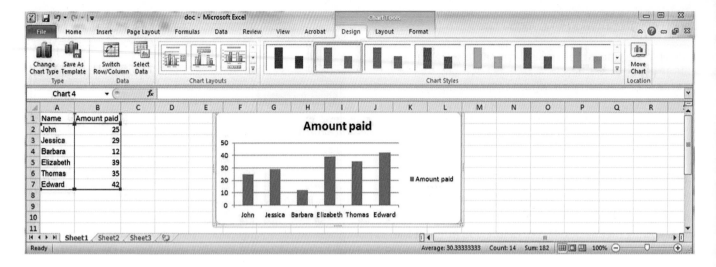

Figure 16.13 Inserting titles in charts and graphs

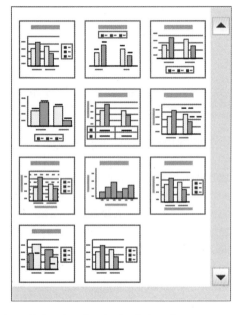

Figure 16.14 Selecting the desired chart layout

However, the title may not be the appropriate one and the values are also not labelled appropriately on the vertical axis. This can be corrected by selecting the 'Chart Layout' of your choice and then double-clicking on each part that you wish to customise, according to the user's requirements.

You can change the label names by double-clicking on a segment of a radar chart or a slice out of a pie chart and select the 'Chart Layout' of your choice. Customise each part according to your user's needs.

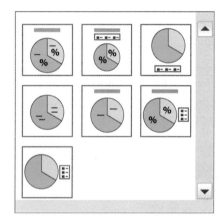

Figure 16.15 Selecting the chart layout to edit the labels of only the slice.

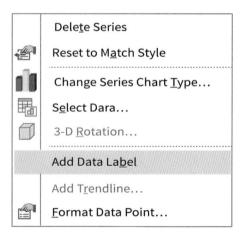

Figure 16.16 Editing the data label of only the slice

Right-click and select 'Add Data Label'. This is what it should look like if you have chosen to use a pie chart.

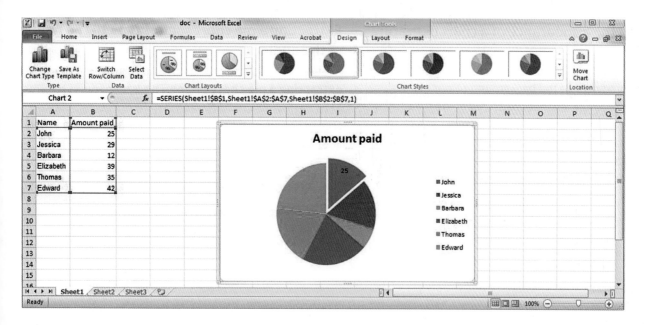

Figure 16.17 Labelling the slice of the pie chart

How to add a second data series to a chart

In the 'Student data' worksheet of the spreadsheet in 'Asset 16.01.xlsx', each test represents a separate data series, such as Test 1, Test 2 and so on. If you wish to add more data series to a chart, you highlight the specified column or row in addition to those you had already highlighted to include more data series in a chart or graph.

How to add a secondary data series to a chart

Occasionally you might wish to display two or more different types of data or mixed data; you can plot one or more of them on a secondary data axis. The first step would be to create your chart as usual and then change the chart type of one or more of the other data series (see Figure 16.18).

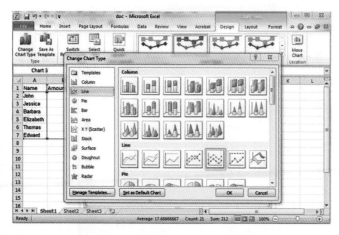

Figure 16.18 Adding a secondary data series by using different chart types for each data series

In the example shown in Figure 16.18, there are two data series being depicted graphically: the number of feeding

times per day and the average cost of food per week for each type of pet. The first data series, the number of feeding times per day, is depicted as a column chart; the second data series, the average cost of food per week, is depicted as a line graph. The two different pieces of information can be compared more easily than if they were represented by the same types of data series charts.

Changing the axis scale values

Most charts or graphs begin at zero as the default starting point. However, you may find that an axis could display your data more clearly if it began at a different starting point from zero. Your scale could display units of measurement starting from 20, at intervals of 5, up to 90. This scale can be adjusted by following these steps:

1 Create the chart.

2 Right-click on the y axis to format it.

3 Select 'Format Options' in order to set the minimum and maximum levels you want on the y axis.

In the 'Asset 16.01.xlsx' spreadsheet, refer to the worksheet 'Chocolates'. Note that the y axis has been set to begin at 20, not zero, and to increase by intervals of 5 until it reaches a maximum level of 90. You can change these to the required levels, as necessary. Similarly, you can change the scale on the x axis accordingly.

PRACTICAL TASK 16.02

Refer to the spreadsheet in the file 'Asset 16.01.xlsx' on the CD and change the scale of the y axis in the worksheet 'Chocolates' to intervals of 10.

201

Enhancing the appearance of a chart or graph

At times it may be necessary to format a chart differently in order to persuade your audience or to emphasise a point. You could change the background colour of the whole chart, or simply change the colour of the data series. There are several options to add colour to a chart. You could choose to have a picture, a gradient, a pattern, a solid colour, a mixture of different colours or choose from a bank of preset colours (see Figure 16.19).

You can also remove or highlight the gridlines in the background, depending on your requirements.

Extracting a pie chart sector to meet the needs of the audience

At times you could further emphasise a point by **extracting a pie chart sector**. This is sometimes referred to as exploding a sector from your chart. You can pull the slice of the pie chart as far away from the whole pie as you like (see Figure 16.20).

KEY TERMS

Extracting a pie chart sector: when a section of a pie chart is extracted out of the pie chart in order to highlight or emphasise a point.

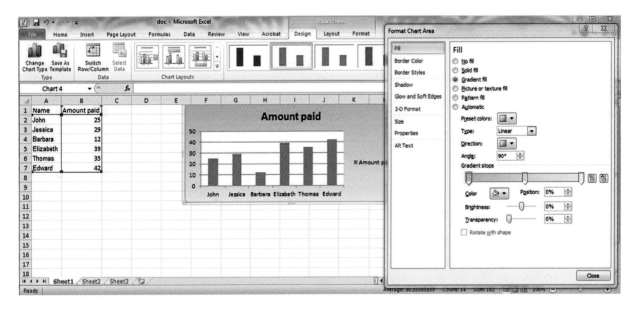

Figure 16.19 Enhancing the appearance of charts or graphs

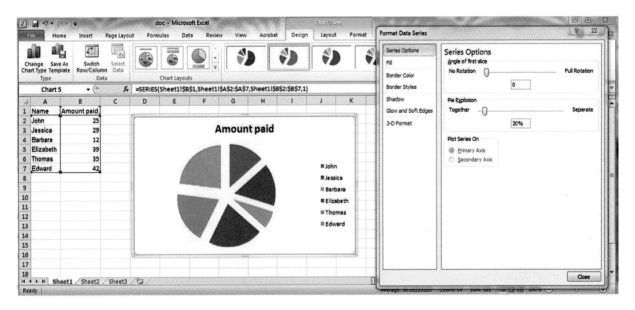

Figure 16.20 Exploding a chart sector

Summary

- All types of data (contiguous, non-contiguous and specified data) can be depicted in a chart or graph.

- You can format the different parts of a chart or graph, so the background, the data series, the axes, the legend and title can be edited to suit the needs of your audience.

- The same chart area can depict two or more different types of charts and graphs by changing one or more of the data series chart types.

- The scale can be adjusted to start with any number and does not always have to begin with a zero.

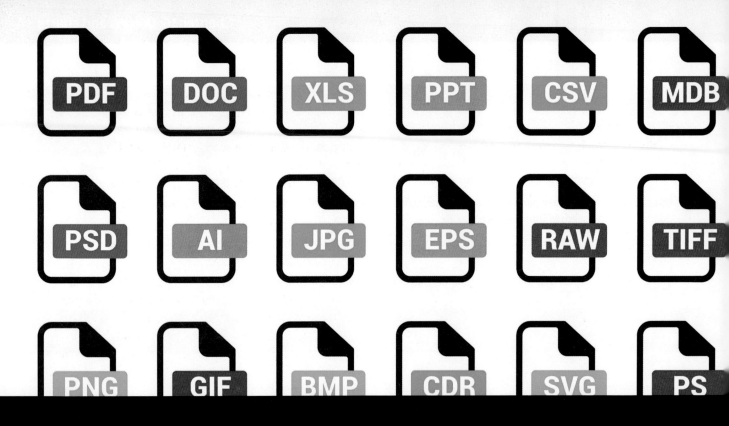

Chapter 17:
Document production

Learning objectives

When you have completed this chapter, you should be able to understand:

- how to format text and organise page layout
- how to use software tools to edit tables
- how to mail merge a document with a data source.

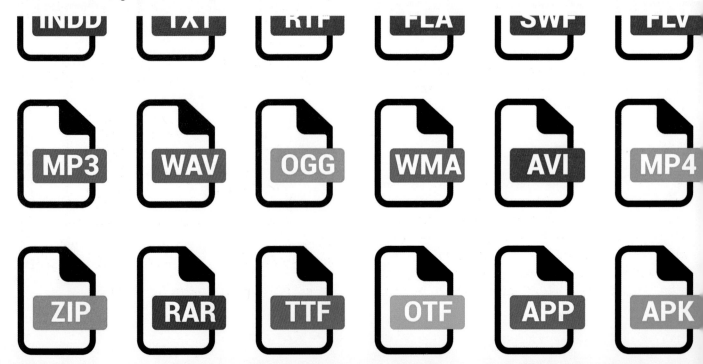

Overview

Every time you use an 'office suite' application program on your computer to write up an assignment, do your homework, answer test questions, create posters, send an email and so on, you are producing a document. Each of these types of documents vary in their style considerably. If you were not using your computer to produce these documents you would have to consider the size of the page and how far away from the edges of the paper you wanted to start your writing. Some documentation already has a predesigned layout, such as the lines and margins in your exercise books. They serve to determine where you will write your answers: usually between the lines and margins. Some more specialised documentation, such as invoices, are usually on preprinted paper.

When you use your computer to produce documents, you have to make similar considerations. You have to think about the size of the page and what **page orientation** is the most appropriate one for the type of document you are producing.

KEY TERMS

Page orientation: the way you position your page: having the narrower width across the top of the page is called 'portrait' orientation; having the wider width across the top of the page is called 'landscape' orientation.

17.01 Formatting text and page layout

Page size

The size of the page becomes important if you will need to print it out after you have produced the document because the program that you are working in determines the onscreen page size.

Page orientation

If you select a blank document, you will usually have to select the page orientation that will determine how wide a page is from left to right. There are two page orientations you can choose from: landscape and portrait. Portrait is narrower across its width and longer down its length, whilst landscape is wider across its breadth but shorter down its length. The page orientation affects the layout of the items you place on your page. At times, it becomes necessary to change from the default page orientation, which is usually set as portrait, in order to accommodate items that may have been copied or cut from another program but don't fit very well in the small space of a portrait orientation. Changing the orientation of a page can sometimes be necessary if you wish to show all the information on a page after resizing or changing font sizes accordingly.

Page and gutter margins

The space around the edges of a page is referred to as a margin. Usually you would write all your text inside the margins, except for the page numbers which could be included in headers or footers. A **gutter margin** is an extra margin that allows extra space in documents that will be bound into book format so that all the text on each page is clearly visible close to the binding area.

KEY TERMS

Gutter margins: the extra margins created for documents that need to be bound into a book format, so that the binding doesn't obscure the text.

Columns

When you need to create columns for your text, you should first highlight your text and then use the 'Columns' option from the 'Page Layout' toolbar (Figure 17.01).

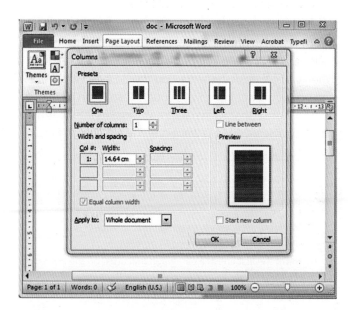

Figure 17.01 Setting columns in a document

If you select two columns and tick the box to insert a line between the two columns, the result will look like the text in Figure 17.02.

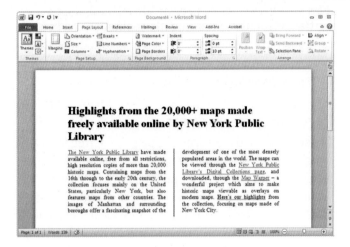

Figure 17.02 The result of setting two columns with a line in between

You can increase the number of columns to suit your requirements, and you can select the layout of the columns from the 'Preset' group of options available. These options allow you to select between left- and right-aligned columns. In addition, you can adjust the width of each column and the spacing between each column. Alternatively, you can set the columns so that they have equal spacing between them and so that each column is the same width. Columns are usually used in documents such as newsletters, newspapers and magazines.

Widows and orphans

Widows and **orphans** are separated from the rest of their paragraphs and can be distracting for their readers. When you create documents, you should avoid widows and orphans by either editing your text so it can all fit onto one page or so that each paragraph remains intact as a block, or at least doesn't leave one line either at the top or bottom of a page.

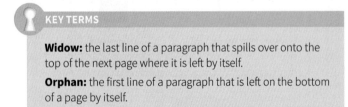

KEY TERMS

Widow: the last line of a paragraph that spills over onto the top of the next page where it is left by itself.

Orphan: the first line of a paragraph that is left on the bottom of a page by itself.

Page, section and column breaks

A page break shows where one page ends and another page begins. It could be used when you have the last bit of text or a short paragraph of text left on a page before you begin a new chapter or section of text. It is important to use page breaks because they give readers the idea that they have come to the end of one part of a document. It is better to leave the rest of the page blank after the last section of a document, rather than begin a new section straight away because each new paragraph or section usually begins a new scene or idea, and the blank space at the end of that section signifies the end of one idea or scene. When you insert the marker for a page break, it will arrange the text in such a way that the new section will begin on a new page.

When you have text in columns, the text will automatically flow from the bottom of one column into the next column as you type more text into the document. If you prefer the text to stop at a certain point in any particular column, you can insert a column break at the exact point where you want to stop the text from spilling over into the next column. The next bit of text will then begin at the top of the next column. This can be helpful when you are writing newsletters, magazines or newspaper columns.

Setting the line spacing

Line spacing refers to the spaces between the lines in a block of text. The default line spacing is usually single line spacing. Alternative options of line spacing are 1.5 times, double or multiple. In order to change the line spacing, you should highlight the text you want; go to 'Paragraph' and choose the line spacing option, as shown in Figure 17.03.

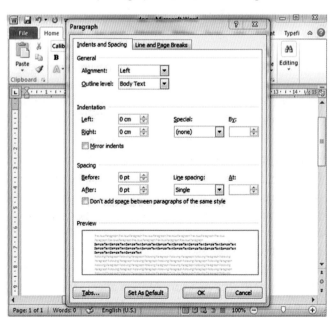

Figure 17.03 Line spacing options

Word processors usually have a default of single line spacing for text with no blank line between paragraphs. However, some more recent versions of word processors default to 1.5 line spacing with ten points spacing between paragraphs. You can change the line spacing by choosing one of the preset styles that already have the line spacing you want, or you can change it manually by selecting from the options available in the 'Paragraph' section of the 'Home' toolbar. When you are creating a manuscript for an assignment or an academic piece of work, such as a dissertation or thesis, you are mostly likely expected to submit it using double line spacing. In such a case, you should use a Quick Style to change the line spacing of the entire document. However, if you wish to change the line spacing of only a part of your document, you can simply highlight the specified section of text and apply the line spacing of your choice to it.

In addition, you can add or remove space before or after a paragraph by using the options shown in Figure 17.04.

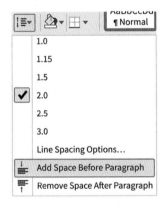

Figure 17.04 Adding or removing space before or after a paragraph

The 'At least' option allows the minimum amount of line spacing to fit any text or images on a line. This can be useful because it will not obscure any text or image even when you have not specifically set the line spacing to be enough to make all your text or images visible.

The 'Exactly' option sets a fixed number of points for the line spacing, such as 10, 12 and so on. If your font size is 8 you should select 'Exactly' 10 in order to ensure that all your text is visible and not cut off at the top and bottom edges of a line.

 KEY TERMS

Pagination: the numbering of pages in a document.

Tabulation: refers to how far to the left or right text is indented.

Setting tabulation settings

Tabulation refers to leaving spaces before you start your text in a paragraph so that it marks the beginning of a new paragraph. Historically, when typewriters were used to type text onto a blank piece of paper, you would have had to use the space bar to create the same number of spaces before starting each new paragraph. However, word processed documents or documents created using application software operate in a different way. These spaces can be created by setting the tabulation measurements by using a tabulation ruler (Figure 17.05) before you begin to enter your text into the document. You can access the tabulation ruler from the 'View' toolbar and placing a tick in the 'Ruler' box, or toggling the 'View Ruler' icon in the top right-hand corner of your document.

Figure 17.05 Tabulation rulers

KEY TERMS

Indented paragraph: a paragraph that begins its first line of text a few spaces away from the left-hand margin.

Hanging paragraph: indentation of the second and subsequent lines of a paragraph that is different from the first indentation of the paragraph.

The top section of the ruler button will allow you to **indent** the start of a new paragraph so you can set the amount of space you want to leave before you have begun writing a new paragraph. The bottom button will mark the position where the rest of the text in that paragraph will begin. The last button on the ruler shows the position up to where any extra text can be entered on that line. Text will begin to flow onto the next line after reaching this

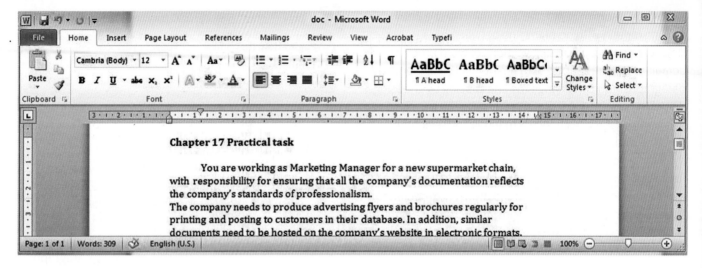

Figure 17.06 Indentation to mark the beginning of a new paragraph

position. In Figure 17.06 you will notice that if you shift the top button, it will move the starting position of the top line of text to mark the beginning of a new paragraph.

Hanging indentation

The other type of indentation in a paragraph refers to a **hanging** indentation. This is when the second line and the rest of the paragraph are more indented than the first line in the paragraph (Figure 17.07).

Bullets and numbers

At times it might be more effective to format your text as bulleted or numbered lists rather than using hanging indentation in a paragraph. This can be achieved by highlighting your text and applying the type of bullet or numbering style that you wish to use to suit the needs of your audience.

Bullets and numbering are useful when you need to create lists. Bullets can be used for non-specific types of lists, such as a shopping list or a list of your favourite pastimes.

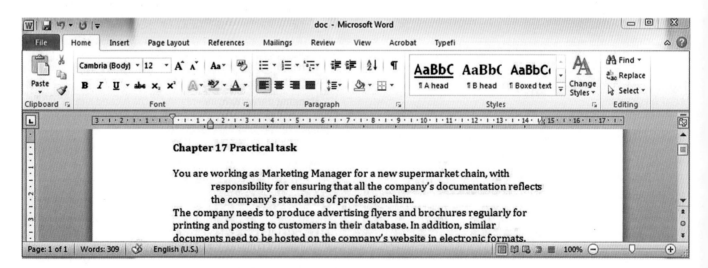

Figure 17.07 Hanging indentation in a paragraph

208

However, should you require a list that follows a certain sequence or order of events, then a numbered list would be more appropriate.

Most application programs have a variety of different shapes for bullets, as shown in Figure 17.08.

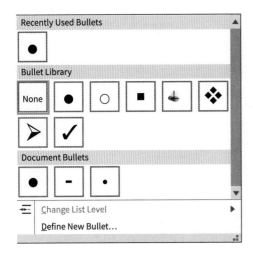

Figure 17.08 Variety of bullet shapes

Interestingly, you are not restricted to the few shapes available in the application program because you can draw your own shapes to use as bullets as well.

Similarly, numbered lists also include a variety of different numbering formats, such as ordinary numerals, Roman numerals and letters from the alphabet, with or without brackets on one or both sides of the numeral (see Figure 17.09).

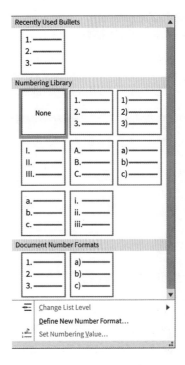

Figure 17.09 Varieties of list numbering formats

17.02 Using software tools to edit tables

Tables are found within most application software programs, and they can all be edited in similar ways. However, there are slight differences in the ways you edit the tables in the spreadsheet and database programs compared to the tables in word processors, desktop publishers and drawing packages. Editing tables involves inserting and deleting rows and columns, and merging cells together. Merging cells together means creating one big cell out of two or more cells.

In Table 17.01 you will find screenshots in Figures 17.10–17.13 depicting how you could edit the tables within each of these programs. They are all slightly different in the ways that you can add or delete a row or column in or from an existing table. Describe the steps you would need to take to add or delete a row and also a column for each program.

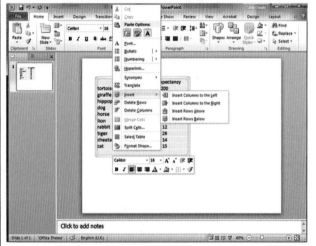

Figure 17.10 Presentation software

Figure 17.11 Desktop publishing software

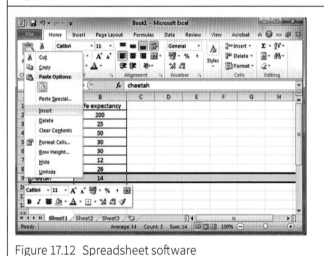

Figure 17.12 Spreadsheet software

Figure 17.13 Spreadsheet software with text wrapped in a cell

Table 17.01 Inserting and deleting rows and columns

In order to merge two or more cells together, you should highlight the cells, right-click on them, and then select the option to merge them together. Use the spreadsheet found in the file 'Asset 17.01.xlsx' on the CD to practise merging two or more cells together. If you have data in each of the cells that you want to merge, you should be aware that only the data in the first cell will be retained; the rest will not be visible at all. You should move any data first to a safe place or delete it if you do not wish to keep it after you've merged the cells together.

Reasons for merging cells together can vary widely, but the most common reason is to use a heading or category to label a group of connected cells.

Using the list of animals in the spreadsheet you've just opened, how can you rearrange the data in the table so that it has:

- two distinct categories of animals?

- merged cells to label these two categories?

- formatting that emphasises the two categories?

Aligning the contents of cells

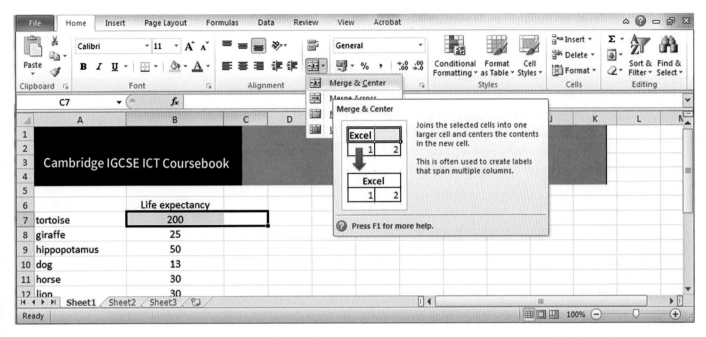

Figure 17.14 Aligning the contents of cells

You can achieve both the actions of merging the highlighted cells together and aligning the contents of the merged cell to the centre if you use the 'Merge & Center' button as shown in Figure 17.14. Aligning cells to the left, centre or right can simply be done by right-clicking on your highlighted cell and selecting the alignment of your choice from the 'Paragraph' options on the 'Home' toolbar (see Figure 17.15).

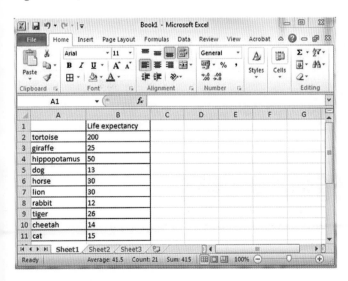

Figure 17.15 Right aligning the contents of a cell horizontally

When you fully justify the contents of a cell horizontally, you are spreading the words out on each line so that you cannot detect that it is aligned to the left or to the right.

There is usually text at the beginning and end of every line of text in a block of text.

When you fully justify the contents of a cell horizontally, you are spreading the words out on each line so that you cannot detect that it is aligned to the left or to the right.	A
When you fully justify the contents of a cell horizontally, you are spreading the words out on each line so that you cannot detect that it is aligned to the left or to the right. There is usually text at the beginning and end of every line of text in a block of text.	B
When you fully justify the contents of a cell horizontally, you are spreading the words out on each line so that you cannot detect that it is aligned to the left or to the right. There is usually text at the beginning and end of every line of text in a block of text.	C
When you fully justify the contents of a cell horizontally, you are spreading the words out on each line so that you cannot detect that it is aligned to the left or to the right. There will be no gaps on either side of the block of text.	D

Table 17.02 Alignment of the contents of a cell horizontally

In row A of Table 17.02, the cell alignment is horizontally centred. The text begins from the centre of the cell and spreads towards the left and right ends in equal measure. No text touches the left- or the right-hand margins. Any line with fewer words or characters will be shorter and further away from the margins at the edges of the cell.

In row B, the horizontal cell alignment is to the left. Text will begin to fill up the space starting from the left-hand margin and spread towards the right-hand margin. Any text that reaches the right-hand margin will flow onto the next line but will always touch the left-hand margin.

In row C, the horizontal cell alignment is to the right. Text starts to spread outwards from the right-hand margin towards the left-hand margin. Any text that reaches the left-hand margin will spill over onto the next line but will always touch the right-hand margin first.

In row D, the horizontal cell alignment is 'justified', which makes all the characters fill the 'block'. Both the left- and right-hand margins will have text touching their sides. The spaces between the words or characters may become uneven as a result of justifying the contents of the cell.

Vertical cell alignment

This refers to fitting all the contents of a cell in such a position that it starts at the top, bottom or from the middle of the cell. If there is too much text in a cell and it cannot be displayed horizontally, it can 'force' the contents to be displayed on the next line, thereby elongating the row to accommodate and make all of a cell's content visible (Figure 17.16).

You can also select the vertical alignment of your choice from the alignment toolbar by choosing one of the three possible options proposed by the Alignment tool in Figure 17.17.

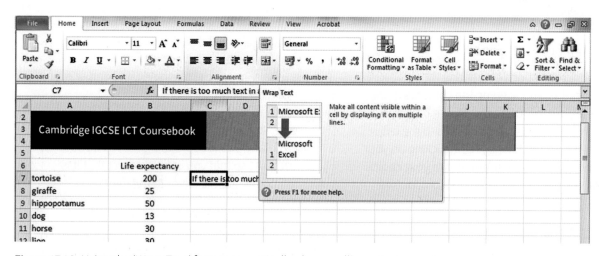

Figure 17.16 Using the 'Wrap Text' feature to vertically align a cell's content

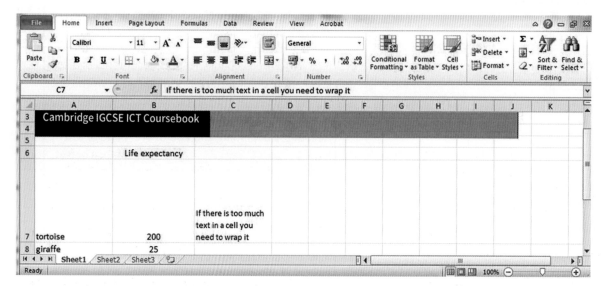

Figure 17.17 The result of using the 'Wrap Text' alignment tool

Formatting cells and cell contents

The 'Print View' of the contents of spreadsheet and database tables looks different from the screen view of the same tables unless you include the **gridlines** to give it a more defined appearance on the printed hard copy (Figure 17.18). However, you would not have to set any gridlines for tables created in any of the other application programs.

KEY TERMS

Gridlines: the visible onscreen lines between cells in a table.

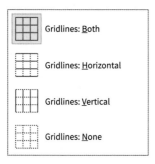

Figure 17.18 Gridlines

The lines seen in the tables onscreen for both spreadsheets and databases are simply part of the program, but will not be visible on paper. You should insert the gridlines to improve the presentation of your printed hard copy version of the same table. If you wish to remove the gridlines from the onscreen version of your table, you should remove the tick from the 'Gridlines' box found on the 'View' tab of your toolbar. Gridlines can be useful when you are creating web pages because the grids allow you to lay out items on your web page in the cells that are visible to you as the creator of the web page. Different web browsers may display your web items differently if you don't use the guides provided by the grids in a table. However, when you are using the website or viewing it, you might not appreciate the gridlines at that stage. It is advisable to use the gridlines onscreen while you are creating your web pages, but it is best to hide the gridlines once you have completed making your web page.

If you use a spreadsheet to make a user interface that will connect you to other worksheets within your spreadsheet file, you will also most probably need to remove the gridlines once you have completed creating your user interface.

Gridlines can make a presentation appear sloppy and can sometimes serve as a slight distraction or annoyance. In order to remove them or hide them, right-click on a gridline and select the 'Format Gridlines' option to either hide or accentuate them.

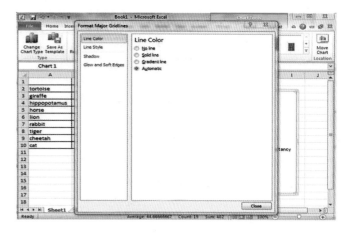

Figure 17.19 Formatting gridlines in charts

Shading and colouring cells

The decision to shade or colour cells usually varies depending on your audience requirements. Besides the most obvious reasons for using colouring or shading in cells, colour is often used for emphasis or to alert users to particular possibilities.

In spreadsheets and database programs, you can use conditional formatting whereby you apply a rule to a set of data to meet certain criteria and then shade it accordingly. The 'traffic light' colour shading scheme can be applied in various scenarios. Teachers can use this system of conditional formatting by applying it to a class's set of results. Students with the lower grades can be shaded red and as the grades progress towards to top grades the shading moves towards green (see Figure 17.20).

213

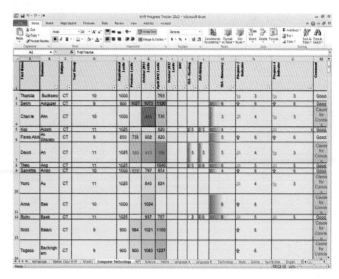

Figure 17.20 Example showing how colouring and shading can be used in cells

In the example in Figure 17.20, column E represents the level students should be working at. If their level drops below that level, their cell will flag up as being closer to the colour red, depending on how far away from the target level they are. The closer they are to their level, the more yellow or pale green their cell gets coloured, and if they are far beyond their target level, their cell will be coloured a brighter green. Furthermore, the last column has an IF statement applied to the values in connected cells and conditional formatting related to those values.

In order to apply conditional formatting to a set of data, you should highlight your set of data before selecting the type of shading you wish to apply. You will then have to create the rule that will stipulate the criteria which you want the set of data to fulfil (see Figure 17.21).

PRACTICAL TASK 17.02

Use the spreadsheet in the file 'Asset 17.01.xlsx' on the CD to carry out the following tasks:

a Create a new rule under 'Conditional Formatting'.

b Use a three-scale colour set to indicate the highest, 50th percentile and lowest values of the animals, life expectancies so that those animals who can live the longest are shown as yellow and those who have the shortest life expectancy are shown up in blue, with those values in between as shades covering the two colours, yellow and blue.

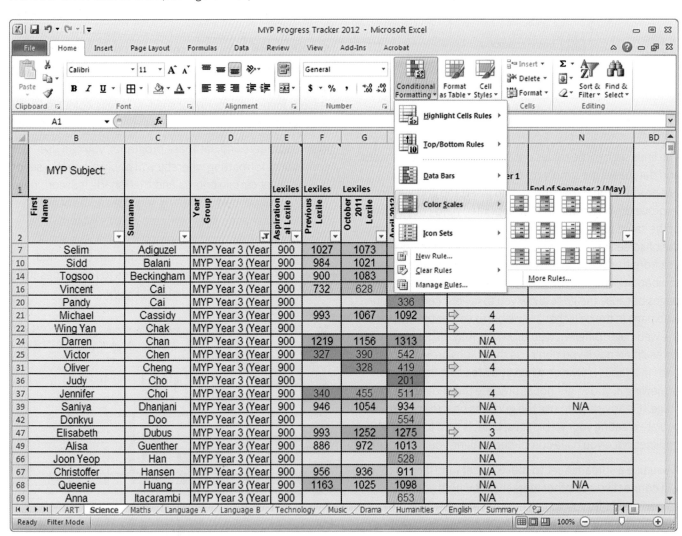

Figure 17.21 Conditional formatting

a

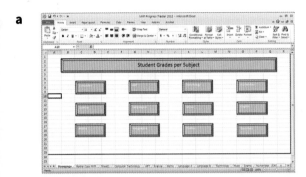

b

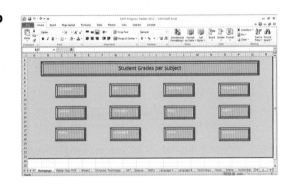

Figure 17.22 (a) Example of a coloured spreadsheet 'homepage' (b) With background colour to hide the gridlines

In the example in Figure 17.22a, colouring has been used on this 'homepage' from which buttons link to subsequent worksheets in this spreadsheet.

In this example, a background colour has been used to distinguish the buttons on the left-hand side. The gridlines disappear when you apply a background colour to a section of cells (Figure 17.22b). This example demonstrates a slightly different use of how colour can be used effectively in cells.

17.03 Mail merge a document with a data source

Mail merged documents are created when you want a set of documents or letters, each of which holds the same information (called a form document), except for the unique data which are the name and address of each separate customer. This means that you could set up your form letter and mark the places on that letter where you will be bringing in a name and address from your data source. It saves a lot of time as you could print 100 or 1000 letters, each with an individual name and address on it, all in one go!

KEY TERMS

Mail merge: combining the data from data sources into other document types in order to make multiple copies of the same document for the purpose of sending it to many different people.

215

PRACTICAL TASK 17.03

Follow these six steps in order to create a mail merge using the files 'Asset 17.02.docx' and 'Asset 17.03.xlsx' from the CD:

1 Set up the form document, in other words type your letter or document that you want to send out. With your word processor open, Mailings>Start Mail Merge, then select Letter if yes (Figure 17.23).

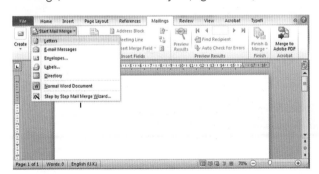

Figure 17.23 Using mail merge tools

2 Click on 'Select recipients' from the 'Mailings' from the menu bar.

3 Select the table you have your recipients listed in and press OK.

4 Click on 'Insert Merge Field' from your toolbar. If you need to insert a special field, such as date, you should place your cursor where you want to insert the 'date' and go to 'Insert' on the menu bar. In the text section, select 'Quick Parts' and then select 'date' from the list of special fields available. Click 'OK' and this should insert the current date into your mail merged documents. (See Figure 17.24 Inserting a special field, such as 'date' in a mail merged document)

Figure 17.24 Inserting a special field, such as 'date' into a mail merged document

5 To insert the usual fields from your data source, position your cursor where you wish to insert each field in your WP document.

6 You can preview your merged documents by clicking on the arrows that take you to the 'next record'.

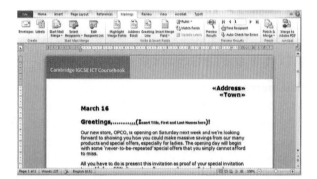

Figure 17.25 BEFORE previewing the mail merged letters

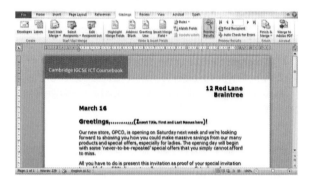

Figure 17.26 AFTER previewing the mail merged letters

7 If you need to edit individual documents, you can choose to 'Edit Individual Documents.

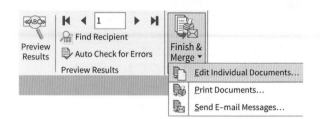

Figure 17.27 Editing individual letters after mail merge

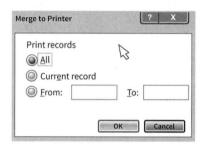

Figure 17.28 Printing individual letters after mail merge

8 Alternatively, you can print all the documents or print only those you wish to print by choosing your selection in the next window.

9 You can save your mail merged letters by selecting the 'Merge to PDF' or by closing the file which will prompt you to save it as a word processing (WP) file in a folder of your choice.

Figure 17.29 Saving mail merged documents

216

QUESTION

You will probably have realised that you can also use mail merge to merge a data source to print out address labels or envelopes.

a Find out what other types of document could be used for the mail merge function in order to save time.

b Other than an 'Amount Due' field that you saw used in the example, discuss what other fields could be useful for a variety of mail merge uses.

PRACTICAL TASK 17.04

You are working as Marketing Manager for a new supermarket chain, with responsibility for ensuring that all the company's documentation reflects the company's standards of professionalism. Follow the instructions in the file 'Asset 17.06.docx' on the CD to complete the task.

Summary

- Although most document types allow you to carry out similar formatting techniques, formatting can be applied in different ways and to different effects within each type of program.

- Presetting the margins, page orientation, column widths, spacing, pagination and so on can make it much easier to create professional-looking documents.

- Using software tools effectively involves knowing how to edit tables to align the content of cells and to format the contents by using colouring and shading effectively.

- Mail merging is a useful tool for businesses because they can use a wide variety of document types together with their customer databases to promote and advertise their products to larger groups more efficiently. Merging data such as contact details by simply pressing a button saves a lot of time, effort and resources for companies.

- Mail merge requires a form document and a data source which are merged once placeholders from the data source have been inserted into the form document.

Chapter 18:
Data manipulation

Learning objectives

When you have completed this chapter, you should be able to:

- design, use and create an appropriate database record structure
- design, use and create a data entry form considering purpose and audience
- use arithmetic operations or numeric functions to perform database calculations
- sort data appropriately in a database
- search a database to select subsets of data
- produce reports to display data appropriately.

Overview

People have been storing items in databases for centuries. There are examples of databases all around you. A typical example is the clothing in your wardrobe. You would usually have different spaces allocated to place the different types of your clothing, such as your coats, trousers, dresses, tops, socks and so forth. They would all go in different parts of your wardrobe and you would probably not leave all your clothing in one big heap or pile on the floor of your wardrobe. If you take the analogy of the clothes in your wardrobe and compare it to a database on your computer, you could liken each type of clothing to a table in a database and the individual item of clothing to a record in a database. The wardrobe would be the database. Each type of shirt would be different colours and styles and these could be likened to the different fields in database terms.

However, it is not all that simplistic because you can get two main types of databases: flat-file or relational databases. Databases on computers all have tables with fields and records. When you set up a database for a particular purpose and for a specific audience, it can be a powerful organiser that can generate excellent efficiencies within companies.

18.01 Creating a database structure

Flat-file databases

A **flat-file** database is a collection of all the data from one organisation in a large table where data is stored in rows. An example of a flat-file database could be for a local hair salon. They would hold records of all their customers containing information such as their names, addresses, telephone numbers, date of birth, hair colour, hair length, hair treatments received, date of last visit and cost of services, and so on. Every time a customer returns for their next haircut, their data is added all over again in another row. This wastes a lot of time and is an inefficient method of handling data compared with using a **relational** database. This method increases the possibility of data input errors that would result in inaccurate and invalid information being produced from such a database. When this happens, it is referred to as 'garbage in, garbage out' (GIGO). The repetition of data in this manner is termed data duplication.

> **KEY TERMS**
>
> **Flat-file database:** data collected about one organisation in one large table.
>
> **Relational database:** a database with several tables that have fields related to each other.

219

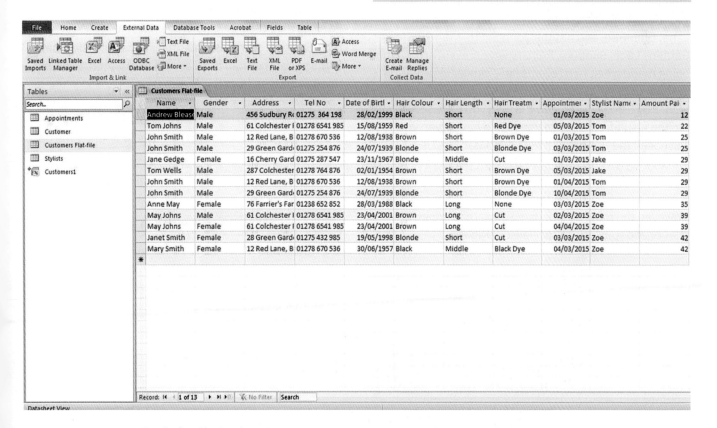

Figure 18.01 An example of a flat-file database

Relational databases

A relational database is made up of different tables to store all the data from a flat-file database in smaller tables that would have **fields** related to each other. In the same example of the hair salon, there could be three different tables, one for the customers, one for the stylist and one for making appointments. In order to know which stylist will be attending the customer for a particular appointment, the tables need to link together. There must be a common field to link the customers to the stylists who style their hair, and another link between either the customers or the stylists and the appointments table so that customers who made appointments with stylists would be linked to their appointments. One problem with flat-file databases is that the same customer could be added to the database as if they were new customers, and customers with the same first names or surnames could be confused with each other. In a relational database this problem is usually prevented by using **primary keys** to identify each customer by a unique identifier. An appropriate primary key could be made by allocating a unique customer ID number for each new customer the first time they visit. Whenever they return for another service, you would simply find their record by using their unique identifier (their customer ID number) to ensure you are talking to the right 'John Smith', from 12 Red Lane, Braintree, and not the 'John Smith' from 29 Green Gardens Lane, Sudbury. Primary keys prevent errors from being made when two records have similar information in some of their fields. If you tried to find John Smith's record by using his name as the field you were searching for, the result from your search would have given you a list of all the 'John Smith's in your database. Using a primary key ensures you have the right person's details. Primary keys are not used in a flat-file database. Flat-file databases can be created using a spreadsheet program. However, the most appropriate software to create a relational database is a specialist database.

KEY TERMS

Primary key: the unique identifier for each record in a database.

Field: a category describing database items (the headings in tables).

Record: all the information from all the fields about one person or object.

QUESTION 18.01

Why is it essential to use a primary key and foreign keys in a relational database?

A relational database is a solution to the chaos that could result if you kept all the data in a flat-file database. The first step is to import the data from the spreadsheet into the database program. The next step is to separate the large table into reasonable tables that would avoid the issue of **data duplication** and getting customers' details muddled up.

KEY TERMS

Data duplication: repeating data by adding data that is already held in the database.

The advantages and disadvantages of using relational tables rather than a flat-file database

Using a relational database is beneficial in the sense that you do not have to duplicate data. An example is when a customer makes a subsequent appointment: you do not have to re-enter their customer details again. You can call up the Appointments table and search for the customer by using their Customer ID. This would give you access to their personal details, such as their name and the name of the stylist they had the last time they visited, because this can be seen from the Stylist ID which is also in the Appointments table. The possibility of making spelling mistakes when you type all the customer's details in again are reduced because you do not have to re-enter the data.

Using a relational database also saves space in your database because you are not repeating data.

QUESTION 18.02

a Define the terms *flat-file database* and *relational database*.

b Give examples of where it would be appropriate to use a flat-file database and where it would be better to use a relational database.

PRACTICAL TASK 18.01 – Extension

a Using the data from the file 'Asset 18.01.xlsx' on the CD, add data to three database tables as follows:

- A Customers table with their details as follows: Customer ID, Customer Name, Address, Telephone Number, Date of Birth, Hair Colour, Hair Length, Hair Treatments.

- A Stylists table with the stylist details: Stylist ID, Stylist Name, Times Available, Stylist Level.

- An Appointments table with the appointment details as follows: Customer ID, Stylist ID, Date of Appointment, Time of Appointment.

Set up primary keys for each table: Customer ID for the Customers table, Stylist ID for the Stylists table and Appointment ID for the Appointments table.

b Populate these three tables with plausible data.

QUESTION 18.03

Explain how the primary keys would work in each of these tables and what kinds of problems they are preventing by being used in this way.

c Once you have set up the three tables in your database program, create the links between the three tables as seen in Figure 18.02.

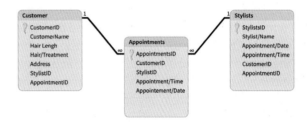

Figure 18.02 Relationships between three tables in database

Data types

Setting up an appropriate relational database requires appropriate **data types** to be selected for each field, such as text, numeric, decimal, currency, date/time or **Boolean**/logical for each linked table.

AutoNumbers are numbers that are allocated automatically as you enter each new entry. Primary keys are usually AutoNumbers. There can only be one primary key in each table. However, when you need to use a primary key in another table it cannot have an AutoNumber as a data type and it is referred to as a **foreign key**. Primary keys used in other tables are termed foreign keys for obvious reasons.

🔑 **KEY TERMS**

Data types: the different types of data that each field can hold, such as date/time, text and so on.

Boolean operators: logical operators like AND, OR and NOT that are used to refine searches by combining field names to exclude or include particular records.

Foreign key: when a primary key from one table is based in another table it is foreign to that table but it is still a unique identifier of a particular record in the database.

Text as a data type can be used as any letters from the alphabet and some numbers. Text as a data type is one of the broadest groups because you can always use text for almost any type of data. It is not as restrictive as some of the other data types. Examples of uses for this data type include customer names, telephone codes and mobile phone numbers; because these numbers begin with a zero, they cannot be accepted as numbers.

Numeric as a data type only includes numbers that begin with numbers greater than zero. They can also be numbers with decimal places, integers or percentages. Examples include customer numbers, stock numbers and so on. However, where numbers are mixed up with letters (alphanumeric) they cannot be accepted as numbers but are classified as text.

Date/time as a data type includes several different formats of dates and times. The different formats of date/time include General, Long, Medium or Short, as seen in Figure 18.03.

Medium Date	
General Date	19/06/2007 17:34:23
Long Date	19 June 2007
Medium Date	**19-June-07**
Short Date	19/06/2007
Long Time	17:34:23
Medium Time	05:34 PM
Short Time	17:34

Figure 18.03 Formats of the date/time data type

221

Once you have selected a particular format as a data type you will not be allowed to enter a date or time entry in any other format. For example, a long time format can only be typed in as any time that shows hours, minutes and seconds: 23:26:36 means the time is 26 minutes and 36 seconds past 11 at night. An error message will appear if you try to enter the time in any other format.

Currency as a data type includes all the currency symbols in the world. The procedure is that you would have to change the Region and Language settings in the control panel of your computer first, as shown in Figure 18.05.

Once you have selected the country, you should click on 'Additional settings…' in the first window and then select the 'Currency' tab at the top in the second. You can then edit the currency symbol by pressing 'Reset' and agreeing to remove any previous settings on your computer. These regional settings will work in any application and should not reflect only USA dollars as a currency option. When you type in the amount of money your customers have paid, the currency symbol will fill in automatically. This is another way to reduce any possible input errors.

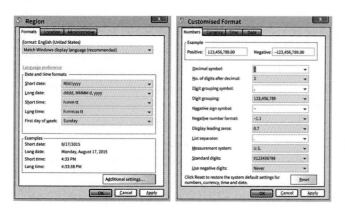

Figure 18.04 Editing the currency symbol on your computer

Boolean/logical (1/0, yes/no, true/false) as a data type can be useful for saving a lot of space in your database because a question could be posed and the answer needn't be a long wordy answer for every record but a simple 1 or 0, true or false. An example could be 'Male or female?'.

PRACTICAL TASK 18.02

Follow the advice given above to ensure that the currency symbol on your computer reflects the currency of your own country and not USA dollars as the currency option.

QUESTION 18.04

Make a list of any other possible Boolean or logical data types.

Placeholders for media items in a database

Commercial endeavours often require media items such as images, video or sound bites to be included in their databases. You can achieve this by using the 'Object Linking and Embedding' (OLE) data type. OLE data types include almost any file format you may wish to embed in your database.

KEY TERMS

Placeholders: 'frames' or 'empty boxes' to insert items of text, images, sound, video and so on.

QUESTION 18.05

a Replacing Table 18.01 on a separate sheet, identify the different data types that can be used in a database and give an example of each one.

Data type	Example

Table 18.01 Database data types

b On a separate sheet reproduce Table 18.02 and refer to Asset 18.02.accdb to complete it.

	Customer table	Stylist table	Appointments table
Primary key			
Foreign keys			

Table 18.02 Primary and foreign keys

Figure 18.05 Data types

The different data types are shown in Figure 18.05.

Field properties

Field names in tables should be meaningful and short, such as DOB for date of birth or CustID for Customer ID, because they can be easily identified by the database user and shorter field names means you can save more space in very large databases.

Fields you have selected can be formatted more specifically by editing the subtypes. If you select a numeric field and require the number to hold two decimal places, you can edit the subtype as shown in Figure 18.06.

The default setting for decimal places in numeric fields is set to 'auto'. This means it will automatically follow how data is entered initially. Alternatively, if the auto setting does not suit your requirements, you can reset it as shown in Figure 18.06.

The field size can also be set for each field. Text fields are allowed a maximum of 255 characters. Most fields do not require that much space. An example of a reasonable field size for a customer's name could be between 25 to 30 characters. Boolean data types, such as 1 or 0, only require one space in the field size box. Some date data types, such as 08/07/2015, only require a field size of 10.

External data

Before external data is imported into a database file, its structure should be identified. Databases do accept different file format types, such as .csv, .txt and .rtf.

.CSV

CSV (comma separated variables) is a file format where each record is stored on one row and each field is separated by a comma. An example of a record in a .csv file could be John Smith,12 Red Lane Braintree,01278 670 536,12/08/1938,Brown. This can be interpreted in the context of our example to mean that the first field is the customer name (John Smith), the next field is his address, followed by his telephone number and so on. Each successive comma signifies the next field in the database table.

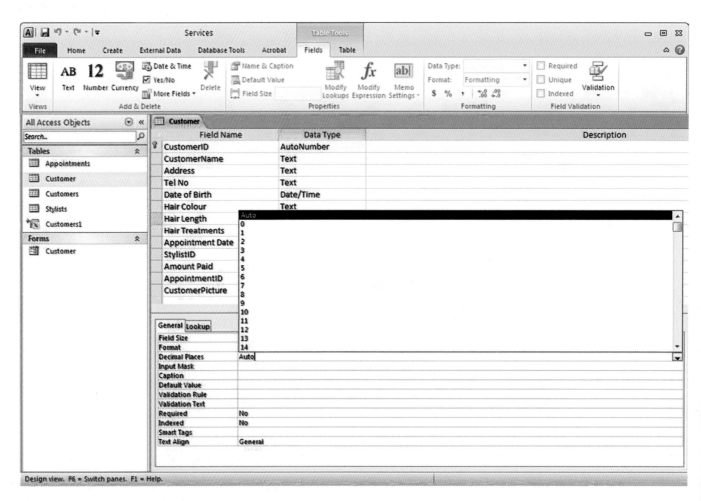

Figure 18.06 Formatting subtypes

PRACTICAL TASK 18.03

Compile a CSV file in a spreadsheet program with just two rows of data and with about five different fields. Save this as a .csv file using an appropriate file name.

.txt

External data can also come in the .txt file format. This is because a plain text file (.txt) has no formatting such as bold or italics and can be read by almost any text editor.

.rtf

Rich text files (.rtf) are also text files but have limited formatting attributes, such as bold or italics.

Locating, opening and importing data from an existing file

Importing data from an existing file can occur from within the program that you want to import data into, or you can export it to the program you want it to go to. If you use a database program to import data from a spreadsheet, then you have to locate and open the database file first and then import the data from the spreadsheet into the database as shown in Figure 18.07.

There are more than ten different types of sources of external data that can be linked or imported into a database.

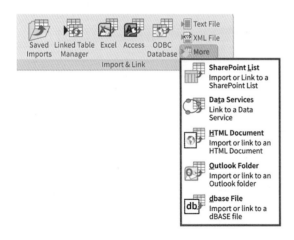

Figure 18.07 Different types of data sources that can be imported and linked to a database

The 'Saved Imports' source is basically a data file that you have previously created and stored on your computer or somewhere sensible.

Data sources can also be stored in remote SQL databases from which you can retrieve records by using the special ODBC drivers. One example of such data sources might be the records of an online shop. If you need to view the items in an online shop, they are connected to an SQL database which is connected to the website you are using to see all the shopping items before you select the ones you wish to purchase.

If you are building your own database and wish to link to another database that is remote (on the internet) or on a local server, you can do so by selecting from the various options available from the 'External Data' toolbar (see Figure 18.07).

The role of primary and foreign keys in a relational database

Primary keys serve to attach a unique code to each new record in a relational database so that records that hold the same field names are not confused with each other. There can only be one primary key in a table. Foreign keys are also primary keys but they are the primary keys found in tables other than where they are the primary key. They are foreign because they are actually the primary keys in other tables. An example that clarifies the difference between primary and foreign keys is shown in Figure 18.02, where the CustomerID is the primary key in the Customer table, but when it appears in the Stylists table or the Appointments table, it is referred to as a foreign key.

QUESTION 18.06

a Identify the primary keys in the Stylist table and the Appointments table.

b Identify the foreign keys in the Stylist table and the Appointments table.

PRACTICAL TASK 18.04

Using the relational database found in the file 'Asset 18.02. accdb' on the CD:

a Add a few more entries to the three tables in the database.

b Create suitable primary keys for each table.

c Create suitable **relationships** between each table.

KEY TERMS

Relationship: the links between the various tables in a database.

Creating a data entry form

Once you have created your tables using the correct data types and linked them together through relationships, you are ready to enter your data into the tables. When you enter data into a database there is always a strong possibility that you can make a few data entry errors, especially if you are using a table format because transferring data line by line can sometimes be confusing to the human eye. There are a number of different ways to enter data into a database.

PRACTICAL TASK 18.05

a   Using the spreadsheet in the file 'Asset17.01.xlsx' on the CD to import a table that already contains data from another source into a new database application.

b   Enter half of the data by copying it line by line into your database.

In addition, the database software tools allow you to create forms by using the built-in formats, as shown in Figure 18.08.

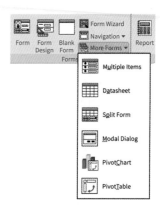

Figure 18.08 Using software tools to create forms

Using the forms option will insert any data you already hold in your tables directly into the default form and you can simply add more records by navigating to the last record that was entered (see Figure 18.09).

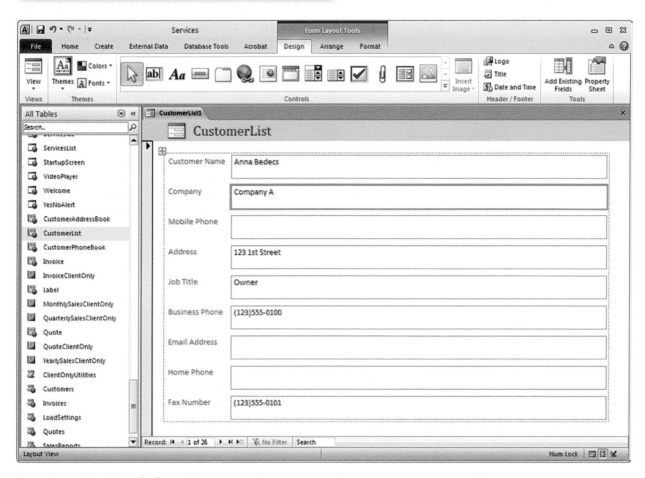

Figure 18.09 Features of a form

226

Key features of form design

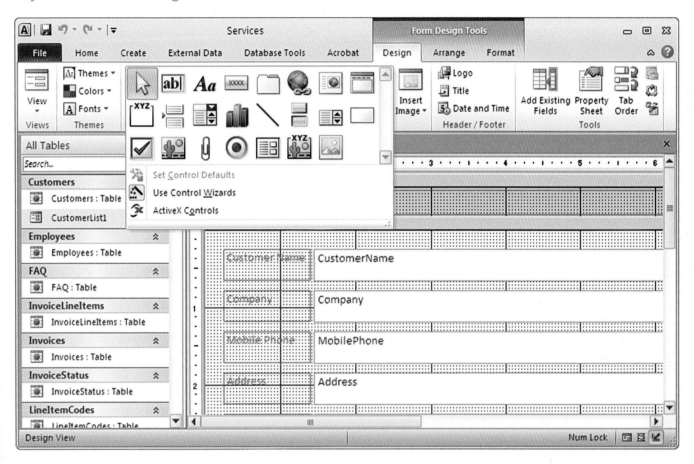

Figure 18.10 Design features for the design view of a form

Design features	Functionality
Select	Selects shapes that you already have in order to edit them.
Text Box	Inserts a rectangular text box of the size you require for users to write text into.
Label	A label is usually used to name an object on your form, e.g. you can write the label 'Name' next to the text box for the field 'Name'.
Button	Buttons can be assigned functions to use a dialogue box or choose an action, e.g. an acknowledgement. Actions are associated with different categories and can include opening and closing forms, etc. (see Figure 18.11).

Figure 18.11 Assigning buttons to functions

Design features	Functionality
Tab Control	Tabs are labels at the top of a subform and help to organise data into sensible categories on a form (see Figure 18.12). 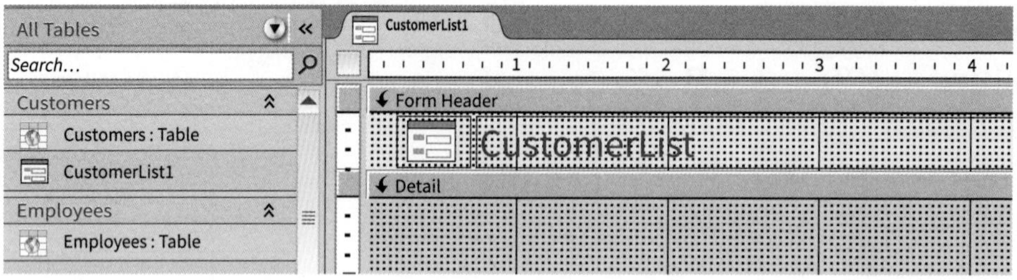 Figure 18.12 Tabs in a form
Hyperlink	Linking to web pages, or other files held elsewhere.
Web Browser Control	If, for example, you want to add an address field showing a map of that place on a form, you can add a web browser control feature. A web browser control feature allows you to add web content to a form.
Navigation Control	The navigation control feature allows you to select action buttons to navigate around the database.
Insert Page Break	Inserts a page break in the form.
Combo Box	If you want to have a drop-down box for users to select from a list of options based on one particular field, this feature is useful.
Toggle Button	A toggle button allows you to choose between two options only.
List Box	A list box is similar to a combo box in that it allows the user to choose from a list of options. It looks up the values from a values list.
Check Box	This is similar to an options button because users can check all the options that apply to them.
Unbound Object Frame	This is similar to a placeholder or frame to insert charts, images, etc. into a form.
Attachment	If you have a file you would like the user to view but not on the form itself, you could include it by attaching the file to the form.
Option Button	An option button allows you to choose only one option from several options available.
Bound Object Frame	This is similar to a placeholder or frame to insert charts, images, etc. into a form from another database table.
Image	This is like a placeholder that allows you to insert images into a form.

Table 18.01 Design features for creating forms

Unbound object frames display any chart, image or other OLE object that is not stored in a table, while bound object frames display charts, images or any other OLE objects that are stored in a database table. When you use bound object frames to fill in idata in a form, you only need to write the label name and the corresponding field and the different records will be filled in automatically from the records you have stored in the table. Unbound object frames allow you to fill in the records manually from their source. Some of the features shown in Figure 18.10 and Table 18.01 can be used as bound or unbound object frames.

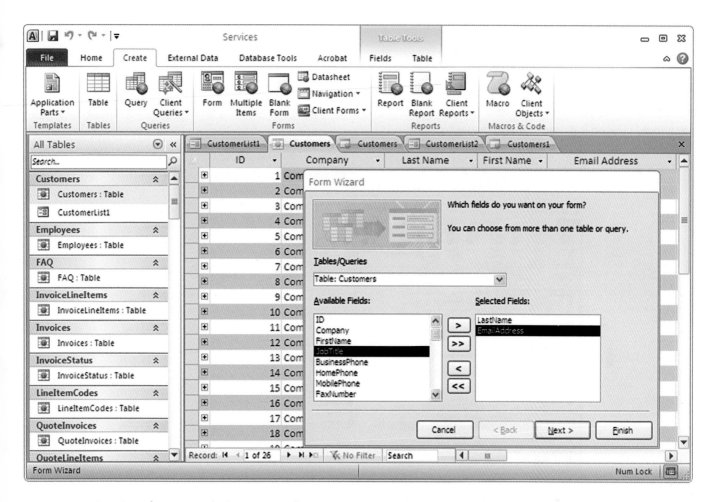

Figure 18.13 Creating a form using the 'Form Wizard'

Creating a data entry form

When you create a form, you could begin by using the 'Form Wizard' (Figure 18.13) to make a reasonably professional-looking form very quickly. It has a set of designs from which you can select and styles you can use. However, if these styles do not suit the user's requirements, you still have the option of further developing your form in the 'Design View'. Some of the features you could use to customise your form are listed in Table 18.01.

PRACTICAL TASK 18.06

a   Using the database in the file 'Asset 18.01.accdb', create a form to fill in new customers' details, following the structure shown in Figure 18.02.

b   Change the following aspects of the data entry form:
   i   Use an appropriate font type, style, size, colour.
   ii   Change the spacing between the fields.
   iii Change the character spacing of individual fields.
   iv   Include radio buttons and drop-downs.
   v   Highlight key fields.

18.02 Manipulating data

Manipulating data involves changing the data that is input and stored in your database in some way within the database program. This can be done if you:

- use arithmetic operations or numeric functions to perform calculations or sort data in a database

- search a database to select subsets of data.

Using arithmetic operations to perform calculations within a database

Scenarios where arithmetic operations might be used can include calculating profit for a business or adding and subtracting stock in a shop, converting currencies, creating invoices and so on. To do this, you need to create a **calculated field** in the database. A calculated field is a special type of database field that allows the information in it to change when the data changes in other fields in that record. The data stored in the calculated field is not stored in the database field but is calculated based on values in other fields within that record by using a particular formula or function. Calculated fields are useful when you need to calculate an answer based on a number of variables.

In the table where you want to create a calculated field you should click on the drop-down in the last column, 'Click to Add', and choose 'Calculated Field' and the data type you wish to use. In the example database in the file 'Asset 18.02.accdb' on the CD, in the table called 'Customers', select 'Currency' as your data type (see Figure 18.14).

In this 'Calculated Field' you will be able to build your arithmetic operation by following the prompts accordingly.

To calculate the 'Total Cost' of each item in this table, you would need to multiply the 'Quantity' by the 'Cost per unit' for each item (see Figure 18.15).

Figure 18.14 Adding a 'Calculated Field' into a table

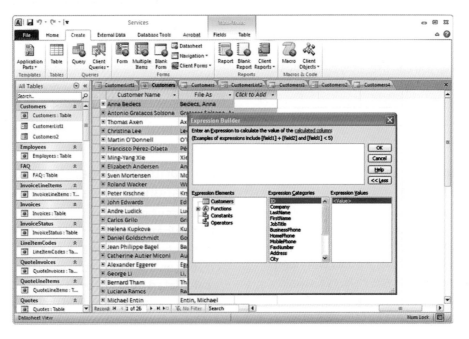

Figure 18.15 Building an arithmetic expression in a calculated field

In the example in Figure 18.15 you will notice that it doesn't store any data in the calculated field, but changes according to any changes you have made in the fields linked to it through the arithmetic expression.

In the Customer table of the J Zee Hair Salon database, there are three calculated fields showing 'Cost', 'VAT' and 'Total Cost'. To calculate the VAT, you should multiply the 'Cost' by the VAT rate (17.5% in this case) to give you the amount of VAT that has to be added to the 'Cost' (see Figure 18.16).

Customer Picture	OLE Object
VAT	Calculated ▼
Total Cost	Calculated

Figure 18.16   Calculating the VAT field

To calculate the 'Total Cost', you should add the 'Cost' to the 'VAT' by going to the 'Datasheet' view of your table and going to the far right-hand tab. Use the drop-down to select the 'Calculated Field' and then follow the instructions from the 'Expression Builder' (Figure 18.17).

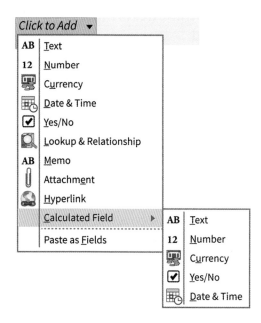

Figure 18.17   Using 'Calculated Field'

Select the 'Expression Element' from the Customer table and double-click on the field you want to use in your calculated field. Next, you should select the 'Operators'

from the 'Expression Element' and complete your calculation by going back to the 'Expression Element' to choose the next part of your calculation.

QUESTION 18.07

a   Discuss how radio buttons and drop-down menus can be useful in a database. Give examples.

b   Explain how performing calculations in a 'calculated' field in a database differs from performing calculations in a spreadsheet cell.

PRACTICAL TASK 18.07

1   Change some of the data in the fields 'Quantity' and 'Cost per item', and notice how it changes the data in the 'Total Cost' field.

2   Use screenshots to explain how you created the "calculated field" that calculates and what it does as a result.

3   Add in another calculation that will work out a discount of 10% on all total costs exceeding $20.00. Show your answer by using annotated screenshots

EXTENSION ACTIVITY 18.01

Create another table of your own choice that would allow you to build a function into it and test it by changing the data in the fields linked to the calculated field. Discuss the implications for uses in ICT systems where databases are used.

When you create a calculated field in a database you will need to add the calculated field within an existing query. Refer to the database, Asset 18.03, found on the CD. Use the query already in this database, "Amounts Customers Paid". In a new column, insert a new calculation for 'VAT' and another new calculation to add the 'VAT' to the original 'Cost' which will give you the 'Total Cost'. (See screenshot below). Click on 'RUN' (in the menu bar) when you have finished setting all your calculations. This will open in the window which will show you all the results of your calculations. (see Figure 18.19).

231

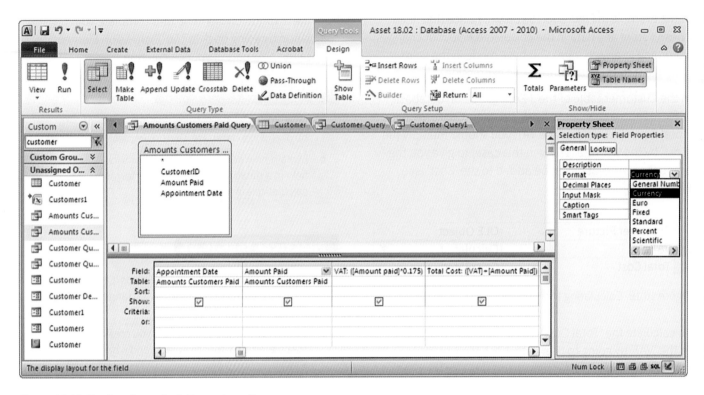

Figure 18.18 Performing calculations at run time

You can see examples in Figure 18.18 of multiplication and addition; division and subtraction would be treated in the same way.

The results of your calculations can be seen below

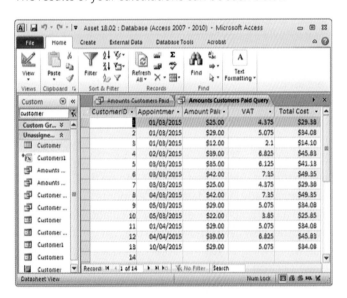

Figure 18.19 The results of performing calculations at run time

Using other arithmetic formulas in a calculated field

If you want to use the remaining two arithmetic formulas to calculate in some fields, you should insert a relevant field in your query. Refer to the database for the JZee Hair Salon (Asset 18.02) and follow the instructions below:

Add a field and label it, 'Discount'. This field will be a percentage (5 divided by 100) and will represent the amount of discount that needs to be applied to the 'Total Cost' of each sale.

Add another field that will subtract the amount of 'Discount' away from the 'Total Cost'. Label this field 'Final Total to Pay'

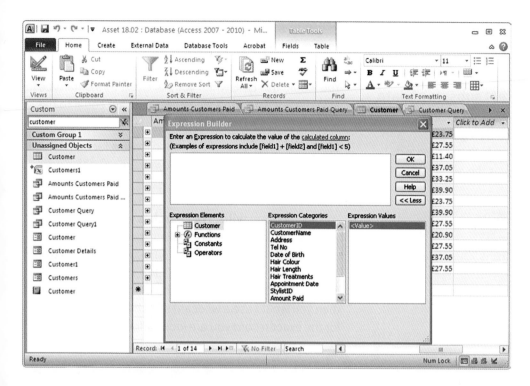

Fig 18.20 Using 'Division' in a calculated field

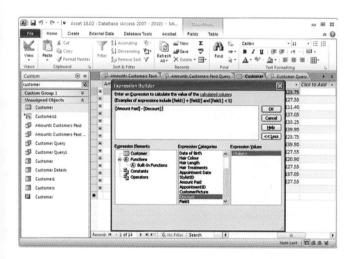

Fig 18.21 Using 'Subtraction' in a calculated field

In both instances the calculated figures appear in the table as soon as you have completed using the expression builder which allows you to select which operators, functions or formulas you want to use to do your calculations.

Sorting data

You can sort data on a single field, such as sorting the 'Quantity' field in order from the items that sold the most to the least (descending), or from the least to the most (ascending); see Figure 18.22.

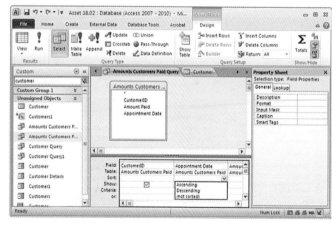

Figure 18.22 Sorting a field into ascending or descending order

In order to sort a field you would have to create a query and select the table first, then the file you want to sort. In the row 'Sort' use the drop-down to select your preference. 'Run!' your query to see the result of your sort (see Figure 18.23).

CustomerName	Cost
Andrew Blease	$12.00
Anne May	$35.00
Jane Gedge	$29.00
Janet Smith	$42.00
John Smith	$29.00

CustomerName	Cost
Tom Wells	$29.00
Tom Johns	$22.00
May Johns	$39.00
May Jones	$39.00
MarySmith	$42.00

Figure 18.23 The results of 'sorting' in ascending and descending order in a query

In order to refine a sort you could sort on multiple criteria, such as sorting into alphabetical order as well (see the second screenshot in Figure 18.23).

Searching a database to select subsets of data

To find information on different field types, such as alphanumeric or Boolean, you should create a query and fill in the 'Criteria' and the row beneath that, called 'or'; the query shown in Figure 18.24 gives the result shown in Figure 18.25.

Figure 18.24 Using Boolean search criteria

EXTENSION ACTIVITY 18.02

Discuss the different types of questions you could ask of your database and create suitable queries to find answers to your questions from your database.

Searching using a variety of operators

You could also use other operators, such as LIKE, AND, NOT, OR, >, <, =, >=, <= and <>.

You would use LIKE when you have text as a data type in a field but wish to find all records that are equal to the text word.

You would use the equal sign when looking for equal values with numeric data types in a field you are searching on.

Wildcards

You can perform **wildcard searches** when you have a vague idea of what you are looking for and do not know the exact details. If you know a particular client has paid in an amount of money with a '2' in it but can't remember if they paid $12, $20 or some other number with a '2' in it, then you would use a wildcard search to help you search for the exact record you are looking for (Figure 18.26).

KEY TERMS

Wildcard searches: a substitute to represent part of a word that you are uncertain about when searching for a similar word.

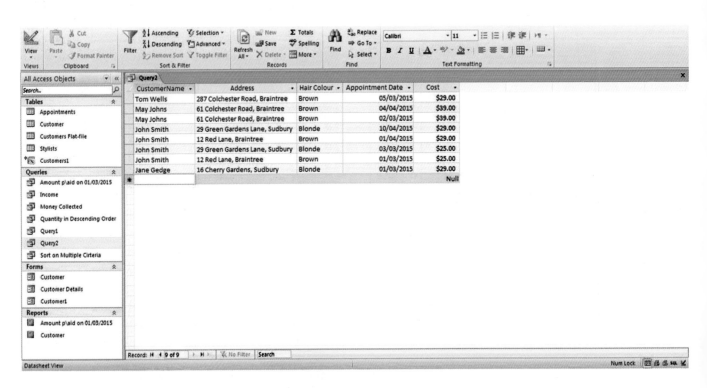

Figure 18.25 The results of the query in Figure 18.24

Field:	CustomerName	Address	Hair Colour	Appointment Date	Amount Paid
Table:	Customer	Customer	Customer	Customer	Customer
Sort:					
Show:	☑	☑	☑	☑	☑
Criteria:					Like '*2'
or:					

Figure 18.26 Using wildcards to search

The results of such a search would yield all the amounts paid that have a '2' as the second digit. The result would be any number ending with a '2'. The position of the '*' could be any other digit in that number. If you placed the '*' in the second position, 'Like "2*"', you would yield a different result. The result would be all the amounts paid starting with a '2' (see Figure 18.27).

a

Query2	
CustomerName ▼	Cost ▼
Andrew Blease	$12.00
Janet Smith	$42.00
Mary Smith	$42.00

b

Query2	
CustomerName ▼	Cost ▼
John Smith	$25.00
Jane Gedge	$29.00
John Smith	$25.00

Figure 18.27 The results of using wildcard searches:
(a) Like *2 (b) Like 2*

The results are quite different depending on the position of the '*' in a wildcard search.

PRACTICAL TASK 18.08

Use a wildcard search on the CustomerName field to find all customers whose name begins with the letter 'J'.

18.03 Presenting data

Once you have searched for data from your database, you would need to present or display it in some format. This is usually presented in a report. You can generate a report which will display the results of your query according to the design style you select when you use the 'Report Wizard'.

A report can also be created to simply display the contents of any table. You could sort some of the fields in the table into ascending or descending order and present this data in a professional-looking report. Reports can take various formats, such as product labels or mailing labels created from data you have stored in your database or imported from other sources, like a spreadsheet or a contacts list from your email program. You can create a report in the database program and then 'merge' this with a word processor to make labels ready for printing. The 'Label Wizard' is usually very useful because it helps you to format the data from your report to fit onto your labels. When you want to print out mailing lists the report first gets the addresses from your tables or a query so that when you print the 'report' you get the labels.

Displaying the required data and labels in reports

When you create a report, you can use the data from any of your tables or from your queries. However, you may not wish to display all the fields' data in a particular table, only some of it. This can easily be done by ticking the 'Show' box and leaving the tick out if you do not wish to use the data in a particular field (see Figure 18.28).

In the example in Figure 18.28 you may not wish to include the company contacts or the home phone number on a mailing label created using a database report. The resulting label will only include those fields for which you have placed a tick in the row 'Show'.

Hiding details can be useful at times when you only wish to display some data and not everything for a particular reason.

235

Field:	LastName	FirstName	Address	City	StateProvince	ZIPPostal	CountryRegion	Company	HomePhone
Table:	Contacts	Contacts	Contacts	Contacts	Contacts	Contacts	Contacts	Contacts	Contacts
Sort:									
Show:	☑	☑	☑	☑	☑	☑	☑	☐	☐
Criteria:									
or:									

Figure 18.28 Displaying only data you need in a report

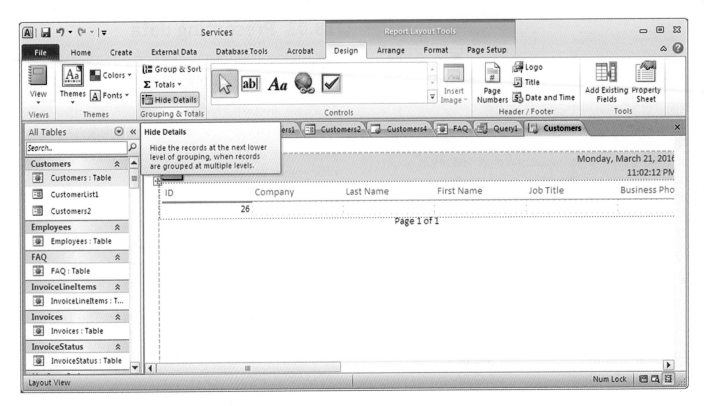

Figure 18.29 Hiding and showing data and labels in a report

You can hide the details by selecting the data or labels you wish to hide and then clicking on the 'Hide Details' button found in the 'Grouping and Totals' section of the toolbar. If you click on the button for the second time the data will reappear (see Figure 18.29). 'Hide Details' refers to hiding the records at the next lower level of grouping, when records are grouped at multiple levels. This is done after you have created your query and are about to display (show) the results in a report. When you use the 'Hide Details' button from the report design view section, you have the choice of hiding only those fields of a record you wish to hide and not all the unselected fields for all the records as you would if you only used the 'Hide' butto not ticking the 'Show' button when creating a query).

Report headers and footers and page headers and footers

These two sets of items are not the same. Report headers and footers do not have a set area on a report where they appear regularly. The items making up a report header are those that appear at the top of the main body of the report as part of the design style of the report. It only appears just that once and is not the

same as a page header that contains information that is repeated on every page in the document.

Page headers and footers contain information that is constantly updated, like page numbers, dates and times, and so on.

Report footers contain information at the end of the report and usually only appear just that once. Similarly, it is not repeated as information in page footers would be.

Setting report titles

Figure 18.30 Displaying a title in a report

Double-click on the 'Title' icon to insert the title for your report. You can format it according to your own requirements (see Figure 18.30).

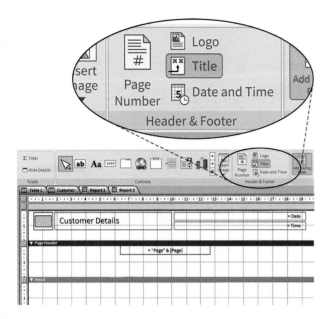

Figure 18.31 Building the report header and page header

If you double-click the various items from the 'Header/ Footer' toolbar, the items will position themselves on your report page. The report title, logo, date and time positions itself in the report header section of your report, while the page number positions itself on the page header section of your report. You will notice that items that can be updated automatically go in the page header section, but items that will only appear once go in the report header section of your report.

Different report layouts

You can choose from different report layouts when you use the Report Wizard (see Figure 18.32):

- tabular layout: looks similar to a table, with the labels running horizontally across the top and each of the records appearing in successive rows below the first row of labels
- columnar: there are a number of columns on the report and the labels appear next to the text box where the user will fill in the data
- datasheet: this is similar to the tabular layout except that there are both row and column labels
- justified: fields can be next to each other and of different sizes, in order to accommodate longer and shorter fields.

PRACTICAL TASK 18.09

Use the data from the customer table in the Asset 18.02 JZee Hair Salon database on the CD to create labels to stick on each customer's hardcopy file. Each label should contain the customer's name, the colour of their hair and whether their hair is long, middle or short.

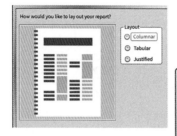

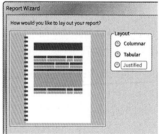

Figure 18.32 Report layouts

237

Formatting numeric data

If you wish to align numeric data in a cell so that the decimals increase or decrease, you should first select the Format tab and then choose the number option's 'increase' or 'decrease' decimals to shift the decimal place to the left or the right accordingly (see Figure 18.33).

Figure 18.33 Aligning the decimal places of numeric data

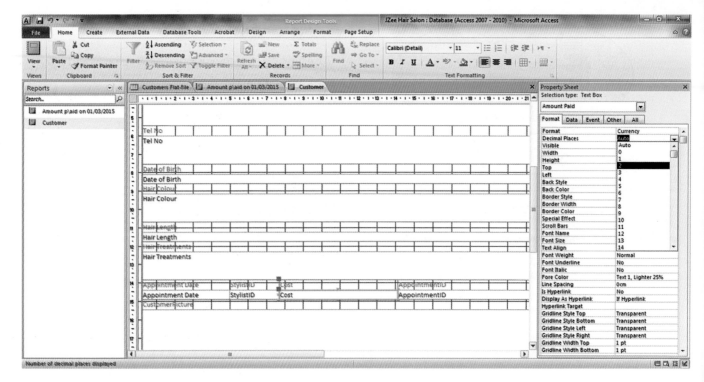

Figure 18.34 Formatting numeric fields in a database report to reflect the correct number of decimal places

At times you may wish to format numeric data as a percentage or a particular currency, as required by your task. Choose these from the formatting tab above the decimal formatting icon in the number section.

At other times, you may wish to align data and labels appropriately, such as, right-aligning numeric data and decimal alignment.

Open your database report in 'Design View' and select and highlight the field in which you wish to change the alignment of the numeric data. Go to the 'Home' toolbar and select 'Text Formatting' and again select 'right-aligned' to move the numeric data to become right-aligned. Close the database report and save it accordingly. When you re-open the database either in 'Report View' or 'Design View' it will show as such.

Furthermore, increasing or decreasing the number of decimal places in numeric data can be done in the following way:

In the report, highlight the field in 'Design View' and right-click on it. Select 'Properties' and again select 'Format'. Choose 'Decimal Places' and if it refers to currency, choose '2' decimal places. Alternatively if it is a percentage to one decimal place, select '1' decimal place. Close the report and save it accordingly. When you re-open it it should show you that your chosen field will reflect the number of decimal places you had formatted it to be.

Export data for use in another application

Reports created in a database are often required for use within other application programs. In order to display such data, you should export it. However, there are many different target applications to export data to, as can be seen in Figure 18.35.

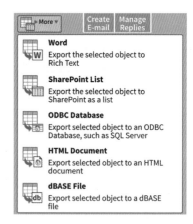

Figure 18.35 Exporting data to a variety of applications

Databases and the ways that the data can be manipulated support some very important services in everyday life. When you shop online the items you browse through before making your purchase are stored in a database on a remote server, such as a Structured Query Language (SQL) Server. SQL statements are used to update data onto remote servers in order to carry out tasks, such as transaction processing. This is just one example of the important tasks that you can conduct with databases. Online bookings, e-commerce, online banking and so forth are other examples of tasks that are supported by the ability to export data from database programs.

You can also export data to SharePoint lists and emails in order to send data on to several others in a more efficient manner. Many tedious tasks of copying and pasting contact details for customers, clients and so on can be avoided in this way.

PDF and XPS files allow users to share information with others without granting them permission to edit that information easily. The ability to export information directly into PDF and XPS file types has saved users from having to copy and paste information from and to many different applications before being able to create a PDF or XPS document. Previously, you would have had to copy and paste your information from the database into a text file and then transferred it into a PDF document, because earlier versions of database software didn't have the built-in functionality to export information directly into a PDF or XPS document type.

Mail merge has been used in many businesses and this is where databases have become very important sources of information. Collecting and selling databases with contact details of individuals has become a major business in recent years and this has led to many problems relating to privacy issues and the misuse of computers. Businesses buy databases with individuals' contact details and send them lots of advertisements via email as spam, and through the post as junk mail.

EXTENSION ACTIVITY 18.03

Discuss the extent to which databases can have an impact on an individual's privacy in today's world.

PRACTICAL TASK 18.10

You work for a holiday letting company, Happy Holidays, and you are going to do some clerical work for them. The files for this task are stored on the CD under Chapter 18 and you should save them to your own computer before you start. Open 'Asset 18.04.docx' to find out more.

239

Summary

- There are two types of database you could use: flat-file and relational databases. Relational databases can be large and complex but have the potential to streamline large business operations substantially.

- It is important to use the correct data types to represent the different fields because you can impose validation rules on particular fields to help reduce input errors, thereby avoiding GIGO.

- Data can be imported in various formats, such as .csv, .txt and .rtf, from various other applications like spreadsheets, databases or even email contact lists. Similarly, data can be exported to various other applications, such as other spreadsheets, databases, SQL servers and so on.

- Data in databases can be manipulated in different ways: by sorting the fields in ascending or descending order, or by searching using queries that incorporate single or multiple criteria and use arithmetic, Boolean operators or wildcard searches.

- Data can be presented in reports that can fit all sizes of documents, including labels.

- Reports can take the format of being tabular, columnar, datasheet or justified, or you can customise them yourself by using the design view method to create your report.

Chapter 19:
Presentation

Learning objectives

When you have completed this chapter, you should be able to:

- use a master slide to appropriately place objects and set suitable styles to meet the needs of the audience
- use suitable software tools to create presentation slides to meet the needs of the audience
- use suitable software tools to display the presentation in a variety of formats.

Overview

In the past, presentations would have been delivered by a presenter who would have been speaking (usually from cue cards) using posters, pictures, books, writing boards and possibly sounds or musical interludes accordingly. Nowadays, you can deliver presentations by speaking and using on-screen prompts in the form of a slide show with pictures, sounds and videos. There are several versions of presentation software available for installation onto your computer, or you could create a presentation online and then download it onto your computer.

The needs of presenters have changed dramatically over time as more sophisticated presentation software and the associated video, image and sound editing software options flood the market. Presentation software is now being demanded for other needs, such as photography and advertising, not just for aiding a person doing a speech or presentation. The demarcation between the use of presentation software and video, animation, sound and image editing software is being blurred as each successive piece of software attempts to improve on its ability to present video, animation, images, sound and text in increasingly more impressive ways.

19.01 Placing objects appropriately

Presentation is an important aspect in all spheres of life, and just as it is important for you to be presentable in the way you dress and speak, so is it important to place objects appropriately according to the type of document you are presenting and to consider your target audience in your presentations. However, objects such as a text box, an image or a media object are placed in a document in the order that you place them, and in an invisible frame, called a layer. If you place a text box in the shape of a rectangle over all the other objects you already have in your document, they will not be visible unless you use 'Send to Back' or make it transparent. The different layers of objects can be moved around and positioned wherever you wish to move them to by using the 'Wrapping' tool. When you plan to place objects in the most appropriate places in a document this is referred to as planning the layout of your document.

Master slides

Master slides can be used to create a style template that you can use as the basis for all the slides in your presentation. The house style is where you set up the size of your fonts for the headings and normal text, the colour schemes, background colours and borders that will be the same on all the slides you apply the master slide to.

A master slide can be used to place objects, such as images, text, logos, slide footers, automated slide numbering and so on as a placeholder on each slide (Figure 19.01).

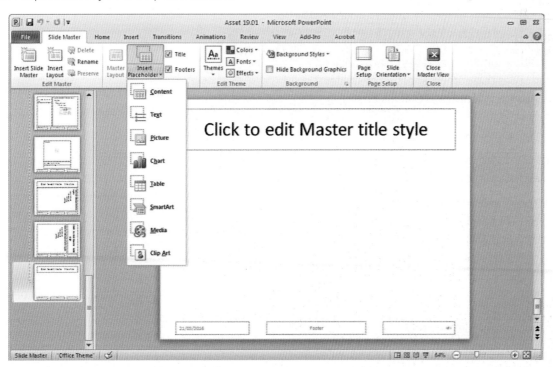

Figure 19.01 Creating a master slide using place holders

242

PRACTICAL TASK 19.01

Create a master slide to place the following objects in placeholders: images, text, logos, slide footers and automated slide numbering. Including an image placeholder on a master slide will make it appear on each of the other slides as well. The master slide serves the same purpose as a template. The placeholders allow you to place different images in the placeholders for that particular type of object on the different slides in your presentation. There can be placeholders for images, text, media (video, sound and so on), content, charts, tables, smart art and so forth.

QUESTION 19.01

Explain what it means to insert a custom slide in your master slide layout. Discuss the reasons why you might want to carry out this action when you already have a master slide layout in place for your presentation.

Consistency of styles, colour schemes, transitions and animations

Professional-looking presentations usually have a consistent style and display carefully selected colours that do not clash, font and image sizes that show a degree of proportion in comparison to the whole slide, and transitions and animations that are used at appropriate times and serve to entertain or inform and not to distract the audience.

Most presentation software packages offer a range of preset design styles that combine colours or shades together with different font styles that match those colours. The font types and sizes are also preset so that all similar heading types have the same size, type and colour.

This enables you to ensure that your presentation has a more professional look about it.

The look of a presentation is not all that matters. Presentations must be effective. This means that the presentation should serve its intended purpose, irrespective of what it looks like. The main reasons why presentations are used include:

- To help a speaker to remember all the main points of the speech. This means that presentations should not have a lot of sentences and text; a slide can only accommodate a limited amount of text and if the audience are expected to read a lot of the text from

QUESTION 19.02

Compare the two presentation slides in Figure 19.02 and list all the aspects that would classify them as created by either a professional or an amateur.

Figure 19.02 Presentations for comparison

each slide, they would struggle to listen to what the speaker is saying at the same time.

- To highlight relevant information from a chart, graph or picture during a presentation.

- To use as a teaching tool during interactive Flash presentations where students can drag and drop items into the correct blocks and receive immediate feedback regarding their responses.

- To display on a loop where information can be presented automatically without stopping and without a real-time speaker, such as in off-line digital advertisements.

In the first example in Figure 19.02, the colour scheme is a preset one; the selection available is shown in Figure 19.03.

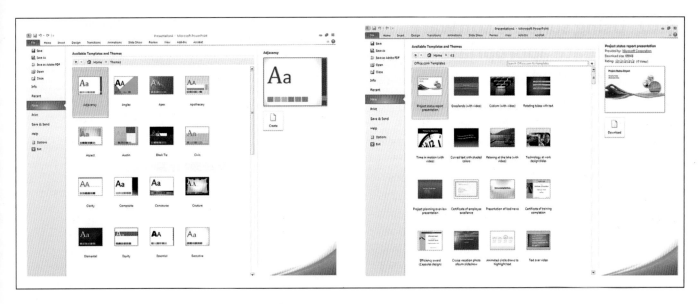

Figure 19.03 Preset designs in presentation software packages

Preset colour schemes and designs make it easier for you to concentrate on the content of your presentation instead of wasting a significant proportion of your time creating a suitable design for each slide and then ensuring that all your slides have a consistent style.

Transitions refer to the effects that occur as you move from one slide to the next slide, such as the next slide flying in from the bottom left-hand side of the screen. Figure 19.04 shows the various transitions available in a presentation package.

If a presenter is delivering a long speech, a set of transitions can serve to provide interesting movements between slides to liven up a presentation. You can include sound if you think it is appropriate for your audience, but it should not serve as a point of distraction for your audience where they become amused or focus more on the sound instead of on the essence of your presentation or speech. You can apply your transition to all your slides for consistency or to only a select few slides, whichever is more appropriate.

At times, you may wish to move to the next slide without having to move towards the mouse in order to click it to get to your next slide. In such a case, it is advisable to set the slides to move to the next slide automatically after a few minutes or seconds. However, this can sometimes not work very well in practice because if you are delivering a presentation, you may have interruptions that will extend the time to more than you have allowed. This could also cause you to rush through your speech so that it matches your slides more closely. If you think this is likely to happen, it might be better to use the 'On Mouse Click' option. This allows you to move to the next slide when you are ready to move and not after a preset time; this avoids confusing your audience if you rush through your slides and do not leave enough time for them to think about what you have said during your presentation. You may not always know beforehand how much time you will need to stay on each slide and therefore a set time is probably not always the best option to use.

Animations are typically used to inject some humour into your presentation and to make it more interesting for the audience. However, that will depend largely on the presentation's purpose and the effectiveness of the animation for explaining or clarifying a particular point in your speech or presentation. Also, too many animations or inappropriate animations can serve to distract your audience from the main purpose of your presentation. Their precise purpose should be carefully considered if they are used together with other media in a presentation.

243

Figure 19.04 Presentation slide transitions

19.02 Using suitable software tools to create appropriate presentation slides

Nowadays, presentations require more sophisticated objects in order to effectively meet the needs of the various target audiences. An example of different audience needs includes those of a photographer. Typically, a photographer would want to display their photographs within a presentation mode, showing some photographs and some text describing the context of the photographs. There are various ways you could make a presentation to display these. The photographs could first be edited in an image-editing piece of software before being transferred to the presentation slides. Suitable house style designs could be selected to maintain consistency for the whole presentation. Photographs could be displayed in various layouts on each slide, or many could be laid out in creative styles on one slide by using suitable software tools to rotate, flip, resize, layer, insert borders and so on. If you only wished to show photos you could insert a photo album or photo gallery, depending on the presentation software you are using. Likewise, other media, such as sound, animations or videos, can also be edited in appropriate software and then transferred to the slides in your presentation.

If you are using one of the online presentation packages you can collaborate on a group project where the different groups can create different parts of the whole presentation; anyone in the group can access the presentation at any time and be able to gauge the progress of the presentation, add their contributions and edit the presentation according to the group's needs.

Manipulate specified areas of a presentation

Headings and subheadings can be preset by using the master slide as a template to determine their layout. Headings typically use a larger font size than subheadings. Bullets are an important feature in presentations because speakers and presenters use the bullet points to remind them of the points they wish to speak about during their presentation or speech. Ideally, you should avoid using too many whole sentences or large blocks of text, because the audience could be distracted from what you are saying when they try to read every word on the slide. In order to assist your audience with any notes, you can always provide them with a printed 'Notes Page', which will include any speaker's notes you would be using.

Access to the speaker's notes page is via the 'View' toolbar, as shown in Figure 19.05.

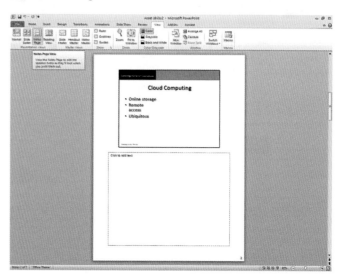

Figure 19.05 Notes page in a presentation printout

Text and notes about your bullet points can be expanded in the speaker's notes section of your printouts (Figure 19.05). In certain instances, the audience may wish to make notes as the speaker delivers the presentation. In this case, you could print out the outline of your presentation because it provides spaces with lines for the audience to write their own short notes about what you might be saying at that time (see Figure 19.07).

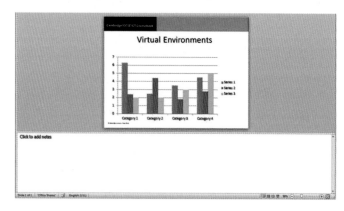

Figure 19.06 Notes pages for speaker to make their own notes during presentations

In certain instances, the audience may wish to make notes as the speaker delivers the presentation. In this case, you would select print, then in the 'Print what?' box, select 'Handouts (3 slides per page)', then click on 'Print'. See Figure 19.07.

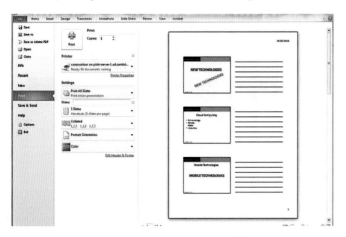

Figure 19.07   Showing space for members of the audience to make their own notes during the presentation.

PRACTICAL TASK 19.02

a   Open the MS PowerPoint file 'Asset 19.01.pptx' and the MS Word file Asset 19.02. Now create a new presentation of 6 slides containing the words in the Word file, and follow the instructions below to make your presentation look exactly like the one in the pptx file 'Asset 19.01.pptx'.

b   Select the layout that has a main title and a subheading below it.

c   Use the text 'New Technologies' as the main heading, and in the subheading space add the text 'Report by: *Your Full Name*'.

d   Use these as headings for each of the next six slides in your presentation: Cloud Computing, Mobile Technologies, Collaboration Technologies, Virtual Environments, Web 3.0 Technologies, 3D and 4D Technologies.

e   Use the text in the file 'Asset 19.02.docx' on the CD to arrange the appropriate text on each slide.

f   Place a suitable image from the folder with the images onto each slide.

g   Use the data from the spreadsheet in the file 'Asset 19.03.xlsx' to create a chart showing the popularity of each type of technology. Create the chart in a spreadsheet application program and import it into slide 7 of your presentation. Add text that summarises the data in the chart using a few bullet points for each point you make.

h   Create some speaker notes for each slide. Include comments that will remind you to hand out the printout or notes pages to the audience, or comments that will remind you to smile and greet your audience at the start. This is to indicate that you understand that you are the audience for your presenter or speaker's notes and that these are not really meant for the audience but serve to remind you of things you may wish to do during your presentation or other cues you will need to help you deliver your presentation to the best of your ability.

i   Change the background colours on all the slides to suit the theme of new technologies.

j   Use the text in the file 'Asset 19.02.docx' appropriate for the slide on 'Collaboration technologies'. Underline the subheadings and use italics for every instance of the word 'collaboration' in the text.

Using software tools to meet audience needs

All the different presentation software packages have a selection of slide layouts to suit different needs. The first slide is typically for communicating the purpose of the whole presentation by inserting the main title and a subtitle suggesting a brief summary of the presentations aims, including the name of the presenter in an appropriate font size.

The layout of subsequent slides will depend on different needs. For example, if you wish to compare two items, you could select the layout with two text boxes and one common text box at the head to insert the text about the items that are to be compared. There are other layouts you can choose from, as indicated in Figure 19.08.

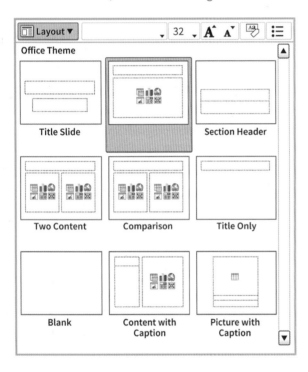

Figure 19.08 Using different slide layouts

If none of the preset slide layouts suit your requirements, you can create your own layout by using the placeholders found in the 'View' toolbar. You can choose from the various options available, such as text, images, media and so on.

Text enhancement

This is another word for formatting text. Besides the usual selection of font types, sizes and colours, you could also use WordArt to enhance the text in a presentation. You can enhance your text by placing it at different angles using the 'Rotate' and 'Flip' tools. The 'Rotate' tool allows you to position your text at any angle. The 'Flip' tool allows you

to make your image face itself. If it was facing left, it would face in the opposite direction after you had 'flipped' your text (see Figure 19.09).

Figure 19.09 Rotating text

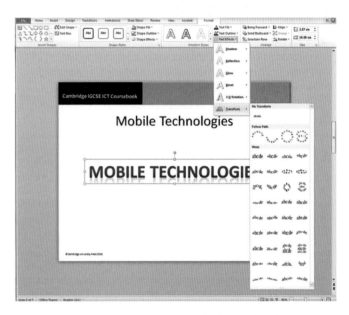

Figure 19.10 Formatting text using the 'Transform' tool

The 'Transform' tool allows you to create a shape out of your text (Figure 19.10). The shape is then treated like an image and it can be reshaped and resized accordingly. Other presentation packages also have similar tools, which can also be found in all drawing and image editing software programs. Once you have created your text according to the shape, size and colours that are appropriate for your audience, you can import it from the other program into your presentation. You do not need to be limited to the range of tools available within one presentation package. There are several text and image editing tools within the various software packages to choose from. However, each program will save the text or image file in a different file format and some of these may not be compatible with the one you choose to import it into. In this case, you should use a file format converter in order to convert your text or image into a file format acceptable to the presentation package you will be using. There are several free online file format converters available to choose from.

Placing appropriate images on slides

There is a range of images that can be placed on presentation slides: still images, video clips and animated images.

Still images include ClipArt, logos, drawings, sketches and photographs; even text which is in the form of WordArt is classified as an image. ClipArt has a bank of small images on some of the most common topics. They are accessible by using appropriate keywords. You can resize ClipArt in the same way that other images can be resized. Existing logos can be found on the internet and can be imported into a relevant folder before being imported as images into your presentation.

Video clips are short videos and these can be placed in presentations in different ways: either from a file you have previously stored on your computer, from another website or from the ClipArt video bank. If you select a video clip from one that was stored on your computer, you can insert it directly into your presentation slide and when you view your presentation in slide mode, you can press the 'Play' button in order to start viewing the video clip. However, the video may need to be resized to the size of your slide unless you prefer to see it in a smaller shape.

Video clips on slides can also be formatted so that they can have borders, shapes and video effects (Figure 19.11).

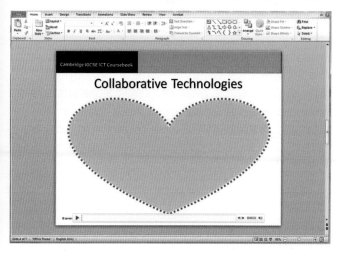

Figure 19.11 Video clip shapes and border patterns on a slide

Animated images can be used to make your presentation interesting and to inject some humour at times. You could create your own animated image using a specialist piece of software or you could import animations from the internet or ClipArt as well. You can save animated images in many different file formats; the most common is as a .gif file format or file extension. Other animated image file formats are included in Table 19.01.

File extension/ format	Description
.ani	MS Windows Cursor
.png	Animated Portable Network Graphics
.eva	Extended Vector Animation
.fla	Adobe (Macromedia) Flash
.flc	FLC
.fli	FLI
.gif	Graphics Interchange Format
.mng	Multi-image Network Graphics
.swf	Small Web Format
.swi	SWiSH Project File
.webp	WebP

Table 19.01 Animated image file formats/extensions

EXTENSION ACTIVITY 19.01

Some animations are bitmap and others are vector images. Research these file types and discuss the differences between them. Discuss the most appropriate use of each.

Placing sound within a slide

Sound in a presentation is one of those elements that you should consider most carefully before using, because when a speaker is talking, background sounds could be very distracting to the audience. Likewise, sounds used together with transitions can also be distracting for your audience if there is a clicking or bell sound after every bullet point appears on a slide. If the target audience are young children and your intention is to draw their attention to your next bullet point then sound might be a sensible option to choose. However, it may not always be appropriate to include sound too frequently in your slides.

Placing charts imported from a spreadsheet onto slides

Charts are very useful in delivering high quality presentations because numerical data can be displayed graphically and speakers can use charts to emphasise certain points more clearly than if they did not have a chart to refer to during their speech or explanation. Even if you used data displayed in a table, it would not be as easy for the human brain to process many numbers as easily as it is when the same information is displayed graphically in a chart or graph.

There is more than one procedure to import charts from the spreadsheet program where they are made into your slide presentation. The simplest method to follow is to copy the chart from the spreadsheet and then paste it directly onto the appropriate slide in your presentation. An alternative method is to 'Insert' a chart from the toolbar in your presentation program. This will automatically open as a split screen showing you both your presentation window and the spreadsheet window. You can then edit the data in your spreadsheet in order to create your chart and it will automatically change in your presentation program as soon as you have completed your editing of the data in the spreadsheet (see Figures 19.12 and 19.13). If the type of chart that opens in the spreadsheet is different from the type of chart you wish to create, you can change it to the appropriate chart type accordingly.

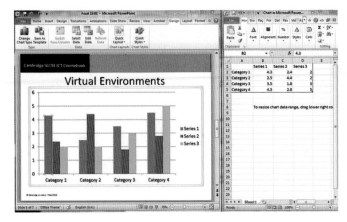

Figure 19.13 After editing the data in cell B2 of the spreadsheet

QUESTION 19.03

By referring to the spreadsheet skills you learnt in Chapters 17 or 18, discuss how you would format the data series so that they display stacked bars representative of the series name. (Hint: if series 1 was about apples, then the bars in category 1 should have columns of stacked apples, and so on.)

You can format the data series, add categories or data series, delete unnecessary categories and data series, rename categories and data series. This way of importing a chart into your slide is much better because you can see how the chart looks as you are creating it and you will simultaneously be able to gauge whether it is suitable for your audience.

Placing objects such as symbols, lines, arrows and call out boxes on slides

Symbols

At times, you will need to use symbols that are not represented on your keyboard in a slide. Examples of these are symbols such as the degree or the copyright symbols. All the Arabic, Asian and Cyrillic alphabets are included, as are mathematical and statistical symbols not found on your standard keyboard. These symbols can be inserted into your text by clicking on the 'Insert' toolbar, as shown in Figure 19.14.

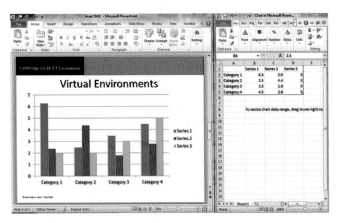

Figure 19.12 Before changing the data in cell B2 of the spreadsheet

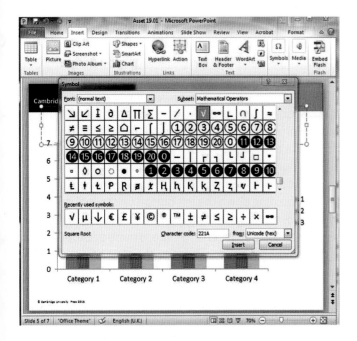

Figure 19.14 Inserting symbols not represented on a standard keyboard

Lines, arrows and call out boxes

Lines, arrows and call out boxes serve to label items in sketches and diagrams. You can annotate your diagrams by using call out boxes and provide short explanations about the items or labels that the pointer from the call out box points to. However, when you edit any other text that precedes these objects, they will not move together with your text or images and will therefore be misplaced in the document. In order to solve this problem, you could screenshot an image of the arrows, lines or call out boxes before you attempt to edit any text preceding it and paste the image together with its arrows, lines or call out boxes as a single image that will move as a normal image would shift its position accordingly when a document is being edited.

Lines, arrows and call out boxes can be found by clicking on the 'Shapes' option in the 'Insert' toolbar. There are many different types of lines, arrows and call out boxes to choose from. An interesting tool is the 'Scribble' line tool which can be used as a pen/pencil. You can scribble freehand on your slide if you use this tool. If you only have a mouse or a touchpad, creating a steady line or path can be challenging. You should only choose this option if there are no other preset options suitable for you to use and edit according to your needs.

'Action Buttons' are basically icons that are already hyperlinked according to their name. An example is the icon with a picture of a house on it, which represents a 'Home' button. If you insert this home icon onto any slide it will take you to your first slide, which it assumes is similar to a web page's home page. If you wish to move to the next slide you could insert the icon with the arrow that points towards the right. The last action button is a button that is not hyperlinked to anything. You can customise it and hyperlink it according to your needs.

Creating consistent transitions between slides

Consistent transitions between slides in presentations serve to focus the minds of the audience rather than distracting them with transitions that are different each time, which might cause them to wonder about what transitions might be coming up. Transitions should be seamless and unobtrusive for mature or serious-natured adult audiences. Younger audiences may enjoy the more glitzy transitions such as the 'vortex' style. It also depends on the occasion at which the presentation is being delivered. An example where glitzy transitions may be appropriate could at an end-of-year school prom party where a slide presentation could be looping photographs of students throughout the evening. However, a similar style of transition between slides would not be appropriate for a finance manager presenting his annual budget at a board meeting.

Creating consistent animation facilities on text, images and other objects

After creating a slide presentation, you may have to create consistent animation on text, images and or media objects depending on what the user's requirements are. Animations on text are useful when you need to reveal each bullet point one at a time whilst you are delivering your presentation. You could select an entrance type of animation that emphasises each point and in such a case you may wish to use an animation, such as, the 'grow shrink' or 'teeter'. There are several others you could also choose from depending on your target audience.

You could also apply similar animations to images and other objects. It is worth noting that using animations in this way can be highly distractive for a more serious or mature audience and you will need to exercise caution when deciding when it is most appropriate to use animations. Younger audiences tend to enjoy more animations and in some cases it can serve to keep their attention rather than distract them. At times, using too many different types of animations can be distractive and it may be that only the younger more playful age groups will appreciate the use a variety of different types of animations in any one presentation. The more professional types of presentations tend to stick to a consistent type and use animations more sparingly than those used for a younger audience.

PRACTICAL TASK 19.03

Refer to the presentation Asset 19.04 Using consistent animations on text, images and media objects and answer the questions below:

1   What type of animation is used on the first slide? Is it 'fade-in' or 'wheel'?

2   What other type of animation could you use if your target audience was for children under 8 years old? Explain your reasons for your choices?

3   If your target audience was sixth form students, do you think the animations would be suitable for them? State reasons for your answer.

4   How would change this slide to make it more appropriate for sixthform students? What are reasons for your choices?

5   On slide 3 add suitable animations to make it relevant for high school students.

6   Do you think it is a good idea to add an animation to a video in a presentation slide?

7   What could be a suitable animation to add to media objects in a presentation? Give the advantages and disadvantages of using animations in media objects.

Displaying a presentation in a variety of formats

The format that you should display your presentation in will depend on the purpose and aims of your whole presentation and on who your target audience is. If your presentation will be used for entertainment or marketing purposes, you could choose to loop it on-screen for the duration of the time you will need it to be displayed. When you loop your presentation on-screen, you can set how long each slide should be displayed and for how long you want to loop it. A presentation can be looped on-screen in one of three different modes. Some features will be disabled depending on which of these options you choose. If you are presenting as a speaker, a full screen will be displayed. This way of displaying a presentation is usually when a speaker is addressing an audience. The option to loop is not available for this type of show, but the presenter has the option of manually advancing from slide to slide or setting the timings in advance. The 'pen colour' option is also not available but the 'laser pointer' option is available by holding down the 'Ctrl' key and holding down the left button on the mouse or touchpad. Although using a laser pointer can be useful for highlighting key aspects on a slide, a more appropriate laser pointer is a handheld device that can be used when the presenter is positioned away from the computer. This gives the speaker the advantage of having their hands free to interact and physically engage more with the audience during the presentation. The on-screen laser pointer requires the speaker to be standing at the computer during the presentation and this implies that the speaker's full attention will not be on speaking but on fiddling with the computer. This could cause the presentation to be of a lower quality than if a handheld laser were to be used.

In the kiosk show style, the presentation can be looped only to end when you next press the 'Esc' key.

In a controlled presentation the presenter or speaker will manually control movement between the slides by clicking with the mouse.

You can also use presenter notes and audience notes as described earlier in this chapter.

QUESTION 19.04

Discuss the differences between displaying a presentation in each of the show styles. Give examples of typical scenarios which would be suitable for each type of display.

Summary

- Determining the aims and purposes of a presentation will determine the design style, layout, use of multimedia, objects and the final type of display to use.

- Presentations can include many interactive and multimedia objects to make them interesting and engaging for the target audience.

- Objects prepared in other software packages are commonly imported into slides in a presentation and are not necessarily developed within the presentation software itself.

- Consistency is a key element of good quality presentations where the features used in the presentation do not distract the audience but are used effectively to engage and focus the minds of the target audience more sharply on the message within the presentation.

Chapter 20:
Data analysis

Learning objectives

When you have completed this chapter, you should be able to:

- create and edit a data model
- understand how to use complex formulas and functions
- devise suitable test plans and test the data to demonstrate that the model works
- use search tools in spreadsheet software to select subsets of data
- sort data using single and multiple criteria
- use software tools to adjust the display features in a spreadsheet.

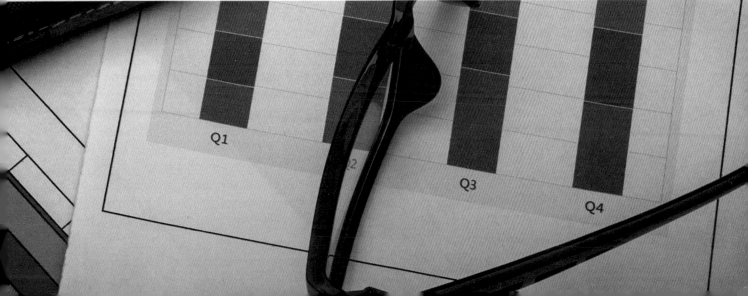

Overview

When we make decisions about things, we are actually analysing data and information all the time. This is much easier to do when our minds have small amounts of data or information to sift through. However, when large amounts of data need to be considered in making important decisions, it is best to use computer-based data analysis tools, such as those found in spreadsheets and databases.

There are many IT applications with data models at the core of their main function, and there are also many different angles to approach this topic:

- You could be presented with a scenario or problem and asked to solve this problem or find the best solution. For example, for the awards day at school, the teacher would like to know which student deserves the award for the most effort based on the number of homework tasks, assignments, questions answered in class and so on by the student. This information is recorded in the teacher's spreadsheet on their computer. In order to be fair to all the students the teacher should analyse this data carefully instead of choosing her favourite students by guessing.

- You could be presented with a data model and asked to interrogate it to find the answers to complex problems, such as those already found on the internet. For example, suppose your family wants to fly for your graduation ceremony to another country. Your grandparents might also be travelling with them and they might not like to travel for very long periods of time. In addition, your family may have a limited budget so they may want the least expensive flights possible. In this case you would use a web-based database or spreadsheet set up in such a way that they have all the data available already and you would have to interrogate this data to find the best solution for this particular problem. These types of data models are termed 'booking systems', but they operate as web-based data models which are online.

- You could be asked to create a new data model based on a particular scenario, such as keeping data on your finances. If you constantly updated the figures in your data model, it would help you to know what your financial state was at any particular time, and help you to predict what your financial status would be in the future based on 'what if?' scenarios; you could present your data graphically using **charts** or **graphs**.

252

KEY TERMS

Chart/graph: data taken from spreadsheets can be represented by creating a graph or chart, such as a bar, pie or line graph. You can use different colours, lines and patterns for more visual clarity.

QUESTION 20.01

Ask your friends or family a few of the following questions and match the type of IT application where the data could be analysed to give them the best data-driven solutions to their problems:

a What goal(s) would you like to achieve in the next year?

b What would you need in order to achieve this goal?

c What information/data do you have to tell you that this is the best way to achieve your goal?

d Match an ideal IT application or data model that they could use to help them make a more informed data-driven decision rather than a vague guess without analysing the data more closely.

20.01 Creating a data model

In this section, you will be asked to work on practical tasks using a spreadsheet as a data model.

Accurate data entry

Data entry has to be 100% accurate, because if there are any mistakes with data entry the information extrapolated from the processed data will also be inaccurate. The GIGO acronym means 'garbage in, garbage out': if you put any rubbish data into your data model you can only expect rubbish results from it. For example, if you accidentally type someone's data of birth incorrectly and you update your data model automatically, you may end up with information that says someone is 200 years old, which is not possible (yet!).

In addition, data is often shared between organisations, and even bought and sold by many others. This is the main reason why data protection legislation stipulates that data must be accurate and up to date. Organisations share information about you; sometimes you are aware of it, and sometimes they gain your permission in a way whereby you believe your data is safer than it actually is. An example of how things can go wrong is when a credit card was sent to a pet cat through the post. This could have happened in a number of different ways: data from the veterinarian was either sold or stolen (through hacking) from their database and then scanned in remotely without verification by humans. The sheer volume of data in some databases would be too cumbersome to check every single one as to its authenticity.

QUESTION 20.02

Do some research to find out what kind of data protection exists in your country.

EXTENSION ACTIVITY 20.01

Evaluate the seriousness of data being entered incorrectly in a data model where people's lives may be endangered as a result of incorrect data entry. Explore methods that could be used to reduce the number of data entry errors.

Using formulas and functions

Both **formulas** and **functions** carry out calculations in a spreadsheet. Some calculations can be done using either a formula or a function to yield the same result, such as adding up some numbers. If you add numbers that are adjacent to each other you could use a function, such as SUM. An example could be =SUM(A1:D1). This would add the numbers in the cell **range** from A1 to D1. Alternatively, one could add these same numbers by using =A1+B1+C1+D1 to get the same result. If you have hundreds of **cells** to add and the cells are all adjacent to each other, then it would be more efficient to use the function, SUM, rather than take a long time to key in each and every one

of the hundreds of cells into the formula. Functions like AVERAGE or COUNTIF make it easier for those who find working with mathematical operations difficult to use because the functionality is built in to the function. In addition, the '*fx*' wizard allows you to edit the formula by choosing the functions and editing the arguments you require for your calculations.

 KEY TERMS

Formula: arithmetical or mathematical operations carried out on cells even when they do not form part of a range of cells; for example, you can add cells together where you cannot use the function SUM because the cells being added up are not adjacent to each other.

Function: arithmetical or mathematical operations that are carried out on groups of cells, ranges, columns or rows and are very specific, for example AVERAGE or SUM.

Range: a group of cells in a spreadsheet that consist of more than one row and column and where the cells are all adjacent to each other; for example, a range could include cells starting from A1 across the rows to F1 and vertically down from A1 towards A9. The last point in the range would be F9, so: top left = A1, top right = F1, bottom left = A9 and bottom right = F9.

Named cell or range: each cell in a spreadsheet has a name by default, for example E7 is the cell in column 'E' and in row '7'. If you use some functions and formulas, you may need to rename a cell or a group of cells, for example if you have range of cells about shoe sizes and are creating a spreadsheet to work out prices of certain sizes, you may need to use the LOOKUP function but will have to refer to a named cell or named range of cells. In this case you could name these cells 'Shoe Sizes'.

Cells: the small rectangular sections on spreadsheets used to enter data such as text, numbers or symbols and to perform calculations using formulas and functions.

PRACTICAL TASK 20.01

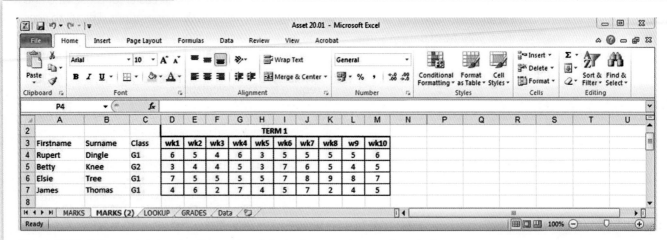

Figure 20.01 Data model showing the marks of students over a ten-week period

Use the data model (spreadsheet) in the file 'Asset.xlsx' from the CD to do the practical tasks in this chapter.

a Create a model similar to the one in Figure 20.01 which will grade the marks that students attain in their tests throughout the term and produce a comment about their final result.

b Insert a few of your friends' names and enter marks (dummy data) for them for the ten weeks.

c Insert a **column** to indicate which class the students were in (see Figure 20.02).

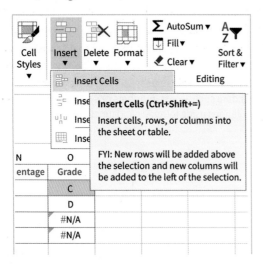

Figure 20.02 Inserting a column

d Insert a column for Percentage next to the 'Total Marks' column.

e Delete the columns 'Total Marks' and 'Grade'.

f Delete row 4 with the data relating to George Gonk, as he has left the school now.

g Insert data for a student, James Thomas in class G1, who was transferred from another class. His marks are 4, 6, 2, 7, 4, 5, 7, 2, 4, 5 (remember to enter the data accurately).

h Insert a row above row 1 to indicate Term 1.

i Merge the cells from D1 to N1 and format the resulting cell as bold and centre-aligned.

j Format the whole spreadsheet so that all the text is blacK.

KEY TERMS

Columns: made up of cells that are adjacent to each other and go from top to bottom or bottom to top vertically.

Mathematical operators

Mathematical operations should follow a particular order, and brackets must be used correctly in order to get the correct answer. All the numbers with addition signs and

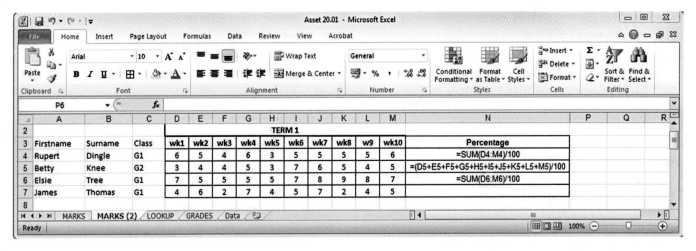

Figure 20.03 Using brackets in formulas and functions

subtraction signs that are next to each other should be enclosed in brackets first and then their sum or difference can be multiplied or divided in that order. The addition and subtraction must be carried out first and then the multiplication and division should be carried out last.

In row 4, no brackets were used (Figure 20.03) and only the last cell was divided by 100, whereas we really wanted to divide the sum of all the numbers before that in the whole row by 100 as was done in row 5. You must add the brackets around all the numbers you want to add up if you want it to be all divided by the number outside the brackets, for example by the 100 (see row 5). Alternately you could use a function such as SUM which will use brackets to include all the numbers it wants to add up before dividing by the 100 (see row 4).

PRACTICAL TASK 20.02

Correct the formula in row 4. Explain why it was incorrect.

QUESTION 20.03

a   Which of the rows is using a formula and which is using a function to calculate the percentages?

b   Explain the difference between a formula and a function.

Relative and absolute referencing

If you are working on a large data model, it can be cumbersome to have to add formulas and functions for each and every case. In this case, you could replicate or copy the formula or function down as long as you enter the first one in yourself. The spreadsheet program will assume you want to use the next set of data in each row or column and will refer to this set of data when applying the formula or function. This is done by what is called relative referencing (Figure 20.04).

255

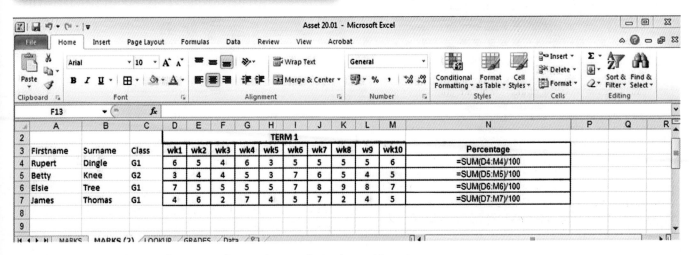

Figure 20.04 Using relative referencing when replicating formulas and functions

However, there are times when you do not wish to use **relative references** and need to use one set formula for all your data subjects. In this case you will have to prevent the spreadsheet program from assuming you want to use the relative referencing style by using '$' in front of each part of the formula or function you want to use, so that that specific part does not change according to the row or column you are referring to; in other words, it is an **absolute reference**.

KEY TERMS

Relative reference: if you had to apply a formula to many cells, you would usually have to write a new formula in each cell. However, spreadsheets allow you to replicate such formulas by making a formula refer to each set of cells across the adjacent cells you want to refer to by using relative cell references.

For example, if you want to refer to the same cell for all the **rows**, see the result of using the relative referencing method in Figure 20.04.

KEY TERMS

Absolute reference: If you had to apply a formula to many cells but did not need to refer to relative cell references as you replicate the formula, you could stop the formula from referring to relative cells by using absolute cell references. Simply insert the '$' sign in front of each part of the absolute cell you wish to use.

Rows: made up of cells that are adjacent to each other and go from left to right or right to left horizontally.

Figure 20.06 uses absolute cell referencing for cell I6. Note the '$' sign in front of the '6' in cell I6 (I$6).

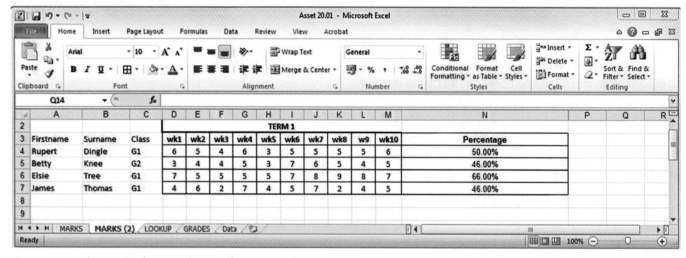

Figure 20.05 The result of using relative referencing in formulas/functions

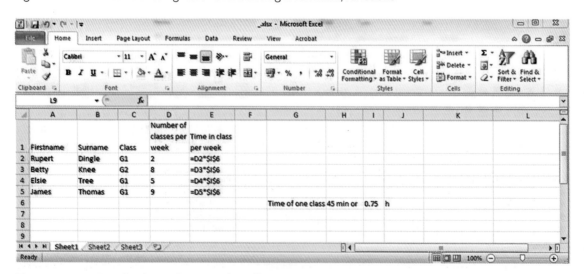

Figure 20.06 Using absolute referencing for cell I6

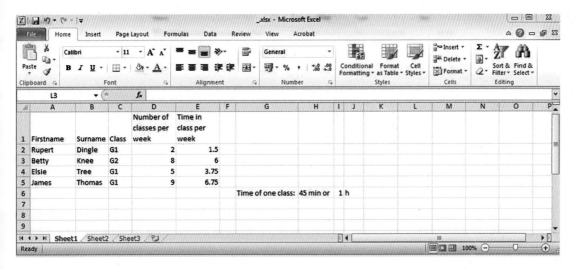

Figure 20.07 The result of using absolute referencing of cell I6

This is using an **absolute reference** to cell I6 when replicating the formula down the rows. Notice that all the references for column I refer to the same cell I6 and do not change to row 3, 4, 5 and so on as it would if you were using relative cell referencing. The result of this is shown in Figure 20.07.

Cells or a range of cells can also be named; for example, if you wish to refer to a particular cell or a range of cells when using formulas and functions, it is easier to remember their name instead of the actual range, say B2:G15. You can give it a relevant name, such as 'Grades'.

Nested functions

When you insert one function inside another function in a spreadsheet cell, it is called a **nested function**.

If you want to record the grade of a student next to the score, you could use a nested IF function because it can compare the scores to a range of grades and select the appropriate one for each student as you replicate the function for each student.

257

a

This is the first condition that must be met.

=IF(M2>=80,"A",IF(M2>=70,"B",IF(M2>=60,"C",IF(M2>=50,"D",IF(M2>=40,"E","U")))))

b

Figure 20.08 (a) Using the IF function. (b) The results

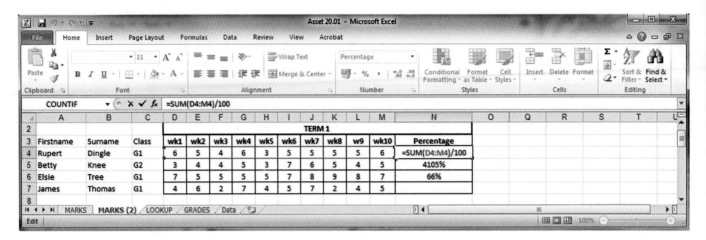

Figure 20.9 Using the SUM function

KEY TERMS

Nested formula/function: you can 'nest' a formula or function inside another formula or function in one cell of a spreadsheet.

As the function works its way through each condition, it will record the relevant grade. For example, if the student's score is between 80 and 100, it will record the grade 'A'; if it's between 70 and 80, it will record a 'B' and so on. However, if all the conditions are not met, it will record the last option in the nested function: in this case, a 'U'.

EXTENSION ACTIVITY 20.02

Think of how nested functions could be used in different scenarios.

Using functions

The SUM function adds up all the numbers which are listed in the row or column. They have to be adjacent to each other for you to be able to use the SUM function to add the numbers in those cells (Figure 20.09).

The AVERAGE function works in a similar way to SUM, except that it works out the average of the numbers in the listed range of cells (Figure 20.10).

The MAXIMUM and MINIMUM functions will give you the highest and the lowest numbers in a range of numbers.

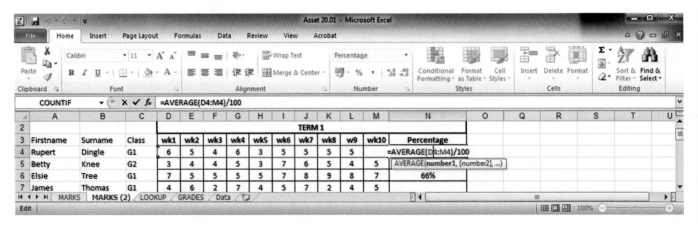

Figure 20.10 Using the AVERAGE function

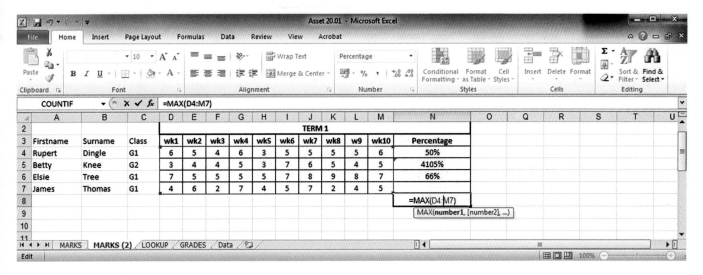

Figure 20.11 Using the MAX function

The INT function changes all real numbers by removing all the decimal points and giving you the rounded up/down integer only. This is often used for rounding down money, for example $46.89 will be rounded up to $47, without the 89 cents part of it.

The ROUND function allows you to control how many decimal points you want a number with lots of decimal places to be rounded to. If you have the numbers 2.512789 in cell C4 and 2.4912137 in cell C5 to round to 2 decimal places, you should use the function '=ROUND(C4, 2)' and replicate the function in all the cells in which you need to use it. It should give you 2.51 and 2.49 in the cells where the function is located.

The COUNT function is used to count the number of data entries in a range of cells. This function looks like this '=COUNT(C3:G4)'; if there is data in all of the cells in this range, you should get an answer of 10 (see Figure 20.12).

In order to create a named cell or a named range, you should highlight the cell or the rage of cells you wish to name and click on the ringed area shown in the screenshot below and then press 'ENTER' on your keyboard. This is one way of naming a cell or a range of cells. When you use the named range in a function, such as, VLOOKUP, you can refer to the named range which will be available from the list of all your named cells and ranges.

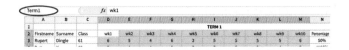

Figure 20.13 Naming a range of cells

The LOOKUP function looks up the values in a named range and refers to them for your calculations. If a student achieves a score of 47% this would be equivalent to a

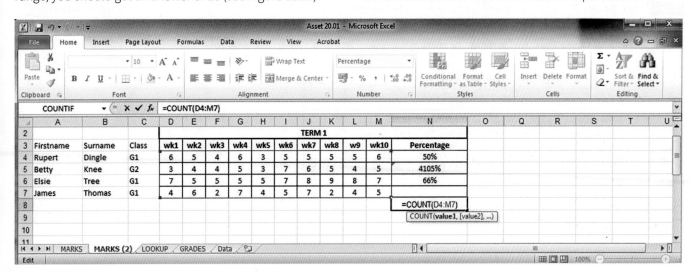

Figure 20.12 Using the COUNT function

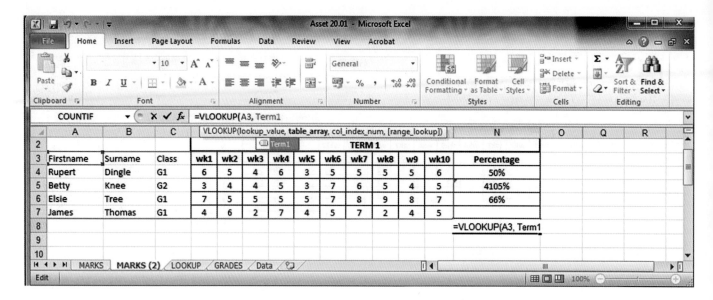

Figure 20.14 The named cell being recalled for use in a function

grade E. It could take you a very long time if you had to manually fill in the grades for hundreds of students' scores. The LOOKUP function will refer to the grades that match each student's scores and fill these in automatically for you (see Figure 20.14). VLOOKUP refers to data that is looked up in a column (which is Vertical), and HLOOKUP refers to data that is looked up in a row (which would be Horizontal).

In the example in Figure 20.15, the function looks up the grade matching the score for cell M2 by referring to the range of grades in the LOOKUP **sheet** and then records it where you want it to go.

KEY TERMS

Sheets: in spreadsheets, the sheets are like the different pages of a book. You can rename each sheet to whatever you prefer and add as many sheets as you need to.

Essentially, the scores and grades of the students in one table are compared with the scores and grades in another table.

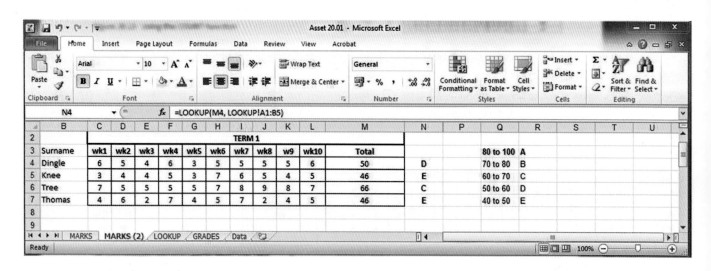

Figure 20.15 Using the LOOKUP function

20.02 Test the data model

Once you have created your data model, you should test that it works as you intend it to work. Sometimes data is entered incorrectly into a system and the results can then not be trusted as being reliable or valid. Sometimes the formulas or functions you used may be inappropriate or not work properly. In order to ensure that your data model is as robust as it possibly can be, you should start by developing a test plan.

Test plan

A test plan should include the following items.

Test data

The test data has to include all the possible data types that users might enter into your data model, for example normal data (this is the data you expect users to enter); extreme data (data outside the boundaries of the normal data you'd expect users to enter; for percentages, for example, users shouldn't enter a percentage above 100 or below 0); erroneous data (simply careless mistakes that users often make, for example instead of $12.00 users may enter $12,00).

Expected outcome

This is the correct answer that should be displayed if the test data were entered correctly and the system was working as intended.

Actual outcome

This is the actual result that was returned from the data model after the test data was entered.

'What if?'

This is a powerful aspect of using data models by asking 'what if?' you entered data 'x' or 'what if?' you rather chose to enter data 'y'; what would be the outcome? You could go one step further and make more informed choices depending on the result of a 'what if?' decision.

There are two main ways to test a data model: first, you should test whether you have entered all the data into your data model accurately; secondly, do all the formulas and functions allow you to use your data model for the purpose it was intended?

Verification and validation

Testing the data involves different types of checks, e.g. verification and validation. Verification is a process whereby the data is checked either by someone else by visual verification (visually checking the data entered against the original source of the data) or by using a method called double-data entry. When you use the double-data entry method, someone else can enter the same data and any differences between those entered by the two different people could suggest a possible data entry error. Verification is usually done by humans. Validation is a way of ensuring that the right type of data has been entered, and although this method is not as effective as the human verification method, if both methods are used they serve to reduce the number of data entry errors.

There are a few different validation methods that can be used. A presence check alerts you to the fact that data has not been entered into your system, which might affect the quality of your results. A range check allows data to stay within the upper and lower boundaries of its range. A type check ensures that the data type is correct, for example a date data type has to be a valid date. Another common validation check is the length check, for example postal codes have a certain number of characters, and if your data exceeds or is less than the prescribed length, then it is possible that there is a data entry error.

Selecting your data and justifying your choice

When testing the data model itself, ask the questions that users may ask when they are using the data model. In the example above, a typical question might be: How can I find out which student got the highest or lowest score for any week? For an answer, see Figure 20.16. If it works, then your data model passes this test.

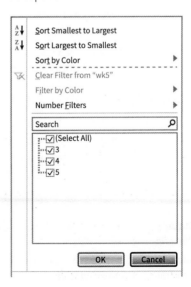

Figure 20.16 Sorting data

In order to work out the average mark for each student, you'd have to enter a string of data for a student and check if the result you get from your data model is the same as you would get if you calculated the average manually. If it works for one student, you could safely assume it would work for all the students in your data model because the replication of a function or formula is normally accurate.

You must check all the formulas and functions by using the different types of data, if relevant. You must always justify your reasons for your choice of test data. The different types of data would be normal, abnormal and extreme data.

Normal data

This is the type of data you expect users to enter into your spreadsheet system. This would usually be within the expected range, although users could still enter incorrect data which a validation check might not be able to pick up. Testing that a spreadsheet's formulas and functions return the correct answers when users type in normal expected data is the best way to ensure that your system works as expected.

Extreme data

This refers to data that is still acceptable by your system but at the very top or bottom end of the range of data that your system can accept. Beyond these extreme points, your system should reject the data from being entered. It is another way to ensure that the validation rules applied to your spreadsheet are working properly.

Abnormal data

This is testing your spreadsheet system with data that is outside of the normal range, such as numbers or types of data that are not compatible with the validation rules set up in the spreadsheet system. Common types of abnormal data could be trying to enter text instead of a number, or a date in the incorrect format. Usually, testing will reveal what the problem is. Sometimes you could be unaware of case sensitivity when entering data, such as passwords and login details, and a system will reject the entry.

> **KEY TERMS**
>
> **Abnormal data:** test data that is completely unexpected and not within the range of expected data.
>
> **Extreme data:** data that is just on the boundary and close to the limits of the range of data being tested.

Calculate your expected outcomes

The expected outcomes must always be worked out before you carry out the actual tests, so that you can compare your expected outcomes with the actual outcomes. If there is a difference, then you must look further into where the problem might lie in order to correct any errors. It is wise to also retest once you have corrected any errors to ensure that your data model is as robust as it possibly can be.

What if?

In order to make your data model a more effective modelling tool you should also test it by using 'what if?' questions. These allow you to change the values in cells in a spreadsheet in order to see how it changes the outcomes of the formulas in the worksheet. In the data model being used in this section, it would be useful to know how many more marks students would need to shift up to the next grade boundary. If it was only a few more marks, students could be motivated to work just a bit more diligently and be able to achieve a higher grade. In this way, the data model has also served as a motivational tool for teachers and students. In spreadsheets you can use a 'what if?' scenario to answer such questions. To create a 'what if?' scenario, you must go to the 'Data' **tab**, choose the 'What if Analysis' tool and follow the on-screen directions.

> **KEY TERMS**
>
> **Tabs:** small buttons typically placed at the bottom of a spreadsheet and serve to navigate between the different sheets.

You can use best case and worst case scenarios by changing some values to see what outcomes could result for each case. An example could be when you want to find out how much the total value of a property portfolio will change if house values drop by a certain percentage, or how much it would rise if the values rose by a certain percentage. It allows the user to ask 'what if?' types of questions. You can also use a different method to answer 'what if?' questions by manually changing the values in certain cells and watching how it changes in the cells where the results are displayed. In more complex spreadsheet systems, this method is best avoided in favour of the method explained above. In the previously worked example, before the 'what if?', Rupert Dingle had

50 marks and a grade D, and Betty Knee has a score of 54 and also a grade D, as shown in Figure 20.17.

		TERM 1										
Firstname	Surname	wk1	wk2	wk3	wk4	wk5	wk6	wk7	wk8	wk9	wk10	Total
Rupert	Dingle	6	5	4	6	3	5	5	5	5	6	50
Betty	Knee	3	4	4	5	3	7	6	5	4	5	46

Figure 20.17 Data before applying a 'what if?' scenario

After the 'what if?', if each student could work hard enough to get another 7 marks, how many of them could move up one whole grade?

Figure 20.18 shows that only two of the four students would move to a higher grade. However, if each student got 10 marks more, three students would have a higher grade. You can then make further decisions based on the results of 'what if?' tests. This is the crux of modelling tools and systems used on computers.

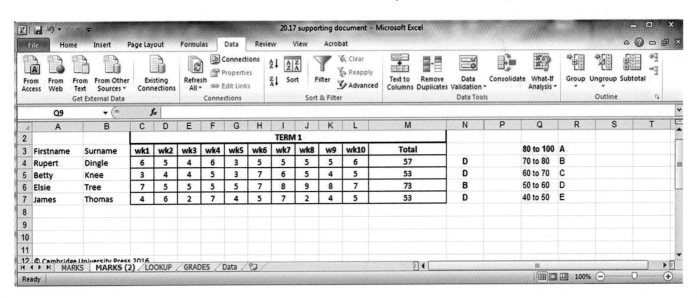

Figure 20.18 The outcome of the 'what if?' scenario

PRACTICAL TASK 20.03

In this practical task, refer to the data model used above. Create a test plan to check that your data model works properly. Use Table 20.01 as a guide.

Test number	Type of test data	Type of test	Test data	Expected outcome	Actual outcome
1					
2					
3					

Table 20.01 Test plan

For a test plan such as the one illustrated in Table 20.01, the first five columns would be completed before testing takes place; in fact, they would probably be completed at the design stage as they need to represent the success criteria.

Once the tests have been carried out, and the 'Actual Outcomes' recorded for each test, the expected and actual outcomes are compared. Where there is a difference,

the changes needed to meet the expected outcomes are recorded in the final column of the test table.

The types of changes that may be required will vary but could include: correcting a formula or selecting the correct required columns for a report or query; it could be that the data in a report does not line up under the column heading.

Once the changes needed have been addressed, the tests will be carried out again. This is called re-testing.

20.03 Manipulating data

This can be done by using search tools and by sorting data using selected criteria and the operators AND, OR, NOT, LIKE, >, <, =, >=, <=.

The AND operator allows you to use other logical functions more effectively to expand the number of conditions they can test. The AND operator will give you a TRUE answer if all the arguments to the function work out to be TRUE, but if one of them works out to be FALSE, then it will give the answer FALSE. When you use the logical argument of an IF function, it will return one answer if the condition works out to be TRUE and another answer if the condition works out to be FALSE. However, if you used the AND function as the logical part of the IF function, you can greatly expand the number of conditions you want to test (see Table 20.02).

Function or formula	What it does	Result or outcome
=AND(TRUE, TRUE) e.g. =AND(5+2=7,3+3=6)	All of the arguments are true.	TRUE
=AND(TRUE, FALSE) e.g. =AND(5+2=7, 3+3=5)	One of the arguments is false.	FALSE

Table 20.02 Use of AND

When used in conjunction with another logical function, such as the IF statement, the AND function has more potential to expand the number of conditions that can be tested. Use these four sets of data as an example to learn how to use the AND operator: 57 (in cell M2), 62 (in cell M3), 71 (in cell M4) and 88 (in cell M5). Trying the tests in Table 20.03 gives the results in Figure 20.19.

Function or formula	What it does	Result or outcome
=AND(1<M2,M2<60)	It tests that M2 is between 1 and 60. Both arguments are true.	TRUE
=AND(1<M3,M3<60)	It tests that M3 is between 1 and 60. One argument is false.	FALSE

Table 20.03 Example AND tests

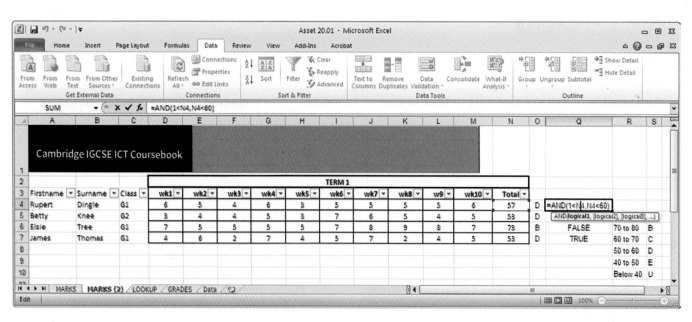

Figure 20.19 Using the AND logic function

Using the AND operator together with IF is shown in Table 20.03 and Figure 20.20.

Function or formula	What it does	Result or outcome
=IF(AND(40<M2,M2<100),M2, "This student must work harder")	It tests whether M2 is between 40 and 100; if both the AND arguments are true, it will display the value in cell M2.	57
=IF(AND(40<M3,M3<100), M3, "This student must work harder")	It tests whether M3 is between 40 and 100; if one of the arguments of the AND operator is false, it will display the statement "This student must work harder".	"This student must work harder"

Table 20.04 Using AND and IF

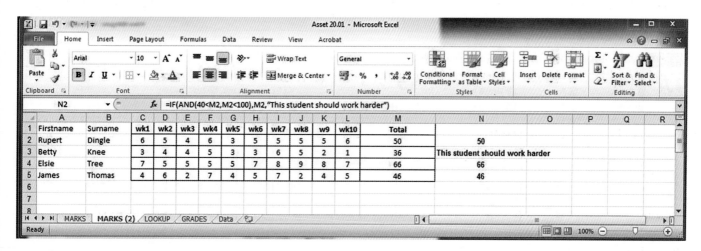

Figure 20.20 Using the AND logic function together with nested IF statements

Using the OR operator is slightly different from using the AND operator, as shown in Table 20.05.

The function or formula	The result
=OR(TRUE) e.g. =OR(2+3=5)	TRUE
=OR(TRUE, FALSE, TRUE) e.g. =OR(2+3=5, 3+4=6, 4+2=6)	TRUE
=OR(FALSE, FALSE, FALSE) e.g. =OR(2+1=2, 3+4=5, 6+1=6)	FALSE

Table 20.05 Using the OR operator

If students must pass test 2, test 4 or test 6 with a score of over 60 in order to pass the final examination, then we can use the OR operator.

An operator in this sense is similar to those used in mathematical calculations but does not necessarily mean the same thing. An '=' in mathematical terms always means equal in value on both sides of this sign. In spreadsheets, an '=' sign is used at the beginning of all formulas and functions. Spreadsheet operators include those that carry out addition, subtraction, multiplication, division and the power operators. Power operators take the highest precedence in calculations, followed by the multiplication and division operators. The addition and subtraction operators take the lowest precedence in calculations.

An example of how they work can be seen in the following case: without precedence rules, $2*3^2 = 36$; if you followed the correct precedence rules as stated above then your answer should be $2*(3^2) = 18$. Similarly, compare $2+3^2 = 25$ versus $2+(3^2) = 11$. The results are substantially different if you do not follow the precedence rules of the operators in a spreadsheet.

PRACTICAL TASK 20.04

Using the data model in the file 'Asset 20.02.xlsx' on the CD, work out the results for the students if it was compulsory for them to pass tests 1, 3 and 5.

The NOT operator will give the opposite of a logically true statement, as shown in Table 20.06 and Figure 20.21 with the results shown in Figure 20.22.

The function or formula	The result
=NOT(TRUE) e.g. =NOT(2+3=5)	FALSE

Table 20.06 The NOT operator

Usually, if the grades for test 2 in column D are greater than 6, then the students will not pass, i.e. the 'Final Examination' should be 'FALSE' not 'TRUE', but by using the NOT operator, it changes the result into the opposite of what it should be logically.

When you use the LIKE operator you should use VBA code. It will search through all your data to find entries that are 'like' what you have in your LIKE search parameters. For example, if you would like to find all the students who have the same overall grades, or if you are have a list of addresses and need to find all the people living in a particular street, you could use a few letters from that

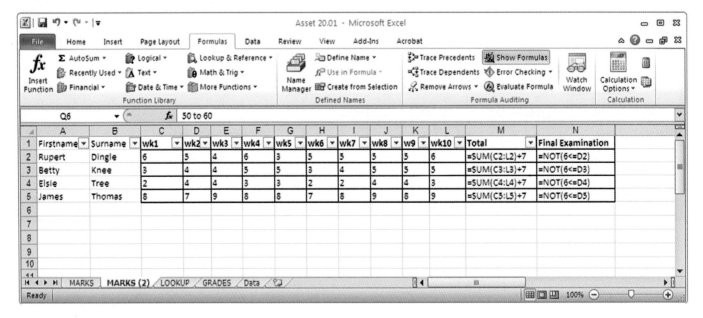

Figure 20.21 Using the NOT logic function

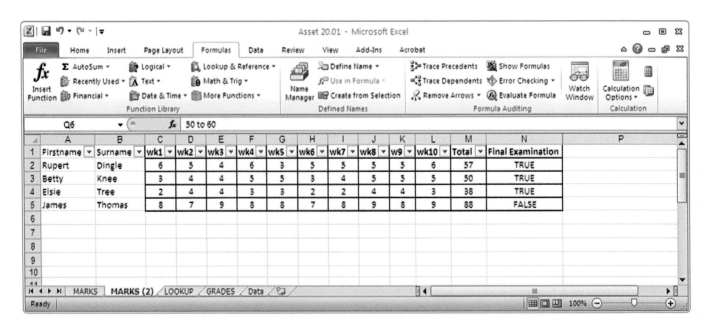

Figure 20.22 The result of using the NOT logic function

street's name in your LIKE operator and it should find them for you.

Using the >, <, =, >= and <= operators is very similar to the way they are used in mathematics or other computer applications; they mean the same things. However, you will mostly use these operators when you use validation techniques, for example if you want to allow numbers greater than a certain value to be entered into a cell, you can use it as shown in Figure 20.23.

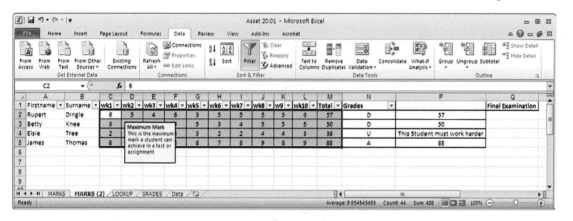

Figure 20.23 Using data validation

PRACTICAL TASK 20.05

a In your copy of the 'Mark grader' spreadsheet, set up a validation rule so that marks for each test cannot be higher than 10 or lower than 1 by following the instructions in Figures 20.24, 20.25 and 20.26.

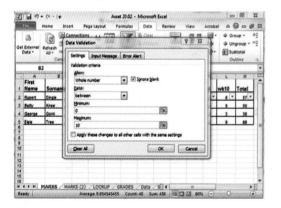

Figure 20.24 Setting up a validation rule

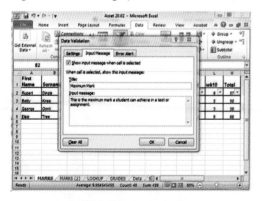

Figure 20.25 Inputting a message for the user during the setup process for a validation rule

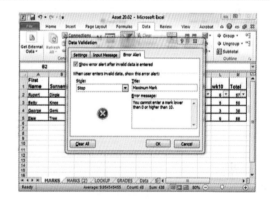

Figure 20.26 Setting up the error message when setting up the validation rule

b Test your validation rule by entering test marks that are outside the range you stipulated in your validation rule.

c Use the other logic operators, such as <=, >= and so on, and test them using many different possibilities.

d Explain how the BETWEEN operator works as a combination of other logic operators.

You can also search for data in your data set by using **wildcards**. The wildcard symbols are '*' or '?', and they represent literally anything after you have stated the characters or values you do know. If you know the beginning or the end of something you are searching for but can't remember all of it, you can use a wildcard to help you search for what you are looking for. In our example spreadsheet, if you wanted to find a student with a name that begins with a 'G' and you can't remember what the name was, you could use a wildcard search like '=G*' and this would give you all the student names beginning with the letter 'G', such as George.

If you use '?' as a wildcard it will give you all the entries that have the same number of characters as '?'s that you use. For example, if you use six '?'s, you will get all the entries that have six characters, such as Rupert and George.

QUESTION 20.04

a If you use these wildcard searches what answers would you get?

- G*   • *e   • *e*

b Think of other ways you could use wildcards to narrow your searches.

Sorting data

Sorting data involves placing the data you have in order from the largest to smallest values or vice versa, or in alphabetical order from A to Z or from Z to A. You can also sort by using either a single criterion or multiple criteria. This can be achieved as shown in Figure 20.27.

You can also use filters to sort data using a single criterion, as shown in Figure 20.28.

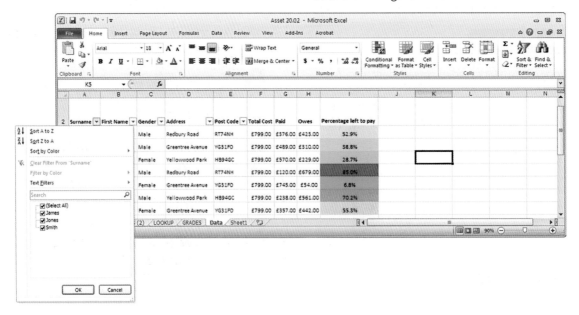

Figure 20.27 Sorting data into alphabetical order

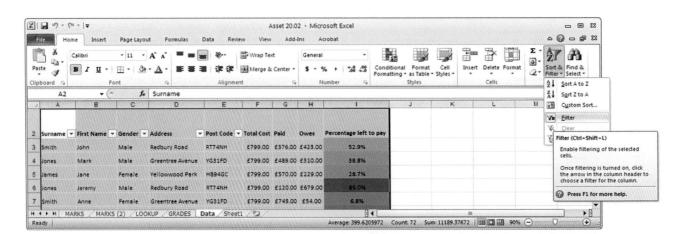

Figure 20.28 Sorting data using filters

PRACTICAL TASK 20.06

Use the Data worksheet Asset 20.02.xls to carry out these instructions:

- Select the filter icon.
- In the Surname column, tick only the 'Smith' box. What is the result of this sort?
- Discuss the usefulness of being able to sort in this way.

You can also conduct a sort within a sort. This means you will be using multiple criteria to sort your data. For example, if you want to find out where a particular person with the surname Smith lives and you also know Smith is male not female, you would need to filter out all the 'Smith's from your Surname field and then filter under the gender field for all 'females' within your 'Smith' results from the Surname field (see Figure 20.29).

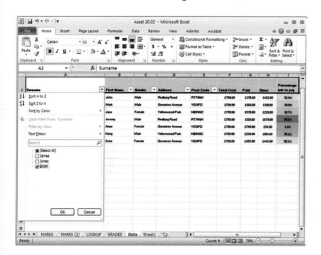

Figure 20.29 Sorting using multiple criteria

The result is shown in Figure 20.30.

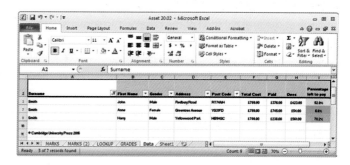

Figure 20.30 The result of using multiple criteria as in the above spreadsheet

If you filter out only the males, the result will be as shown in Figure 20.31.

EXTENSION ACTIVITY 20.03

Discuss the pros and cons of using filters and multiple criteria to sort larger amounts of data.

20.04 Presenting data

Once you have created your spreadsheet system, tested your system and manipulated the data to suit you, you may need to present your findings to persuade your target audience or to include it in a report.

If you need to display features on one page, you may need to adjust the column width, row height or cell sizes so that all your data, labels and formulas are visible.

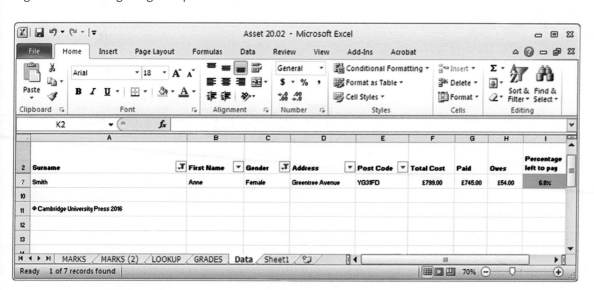

Figure 20.31 The result of the above 'sort within a sort' technique

269

PRACTICAL TASK 20.07

Look at the presentation of the data on the spreadsheet in Figure 20.32 and compare it with the spreadsheet in Figure 20.33. List all the differences.

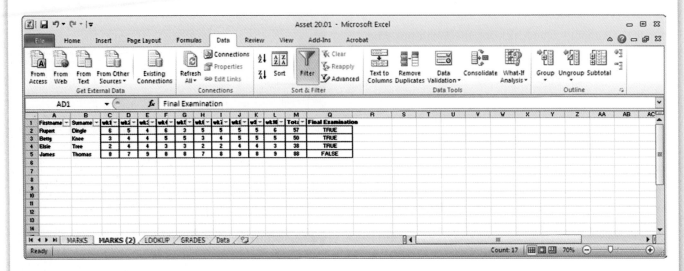

Figure 20.32 Unclear spreadsheet for presenting data

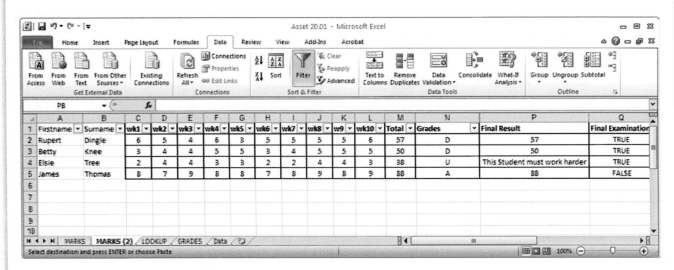

Figure 20.33 A more presentable spreadsheet for presenting data

Text wrapping and hiding text

Text wrapping allows you to fit all your words in one cell on more lines vertically to save space horizontally.

In the example shown in Figure 20.34, cells A1 and Q1 have had their text wrapped.

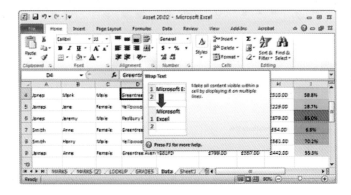

Figure 20.34 Wrapping text to narrow the column

When you display formulas which take up a lot of space horizontally, you may also need to wrap your text.

In order to display your formulas, you should select the 'Formulas' tab and then 'Show Formulas', as shown in Figure 20.35.

If you do not need to show all your columns, you can 'Hide' some as shown in Figure 20.36.

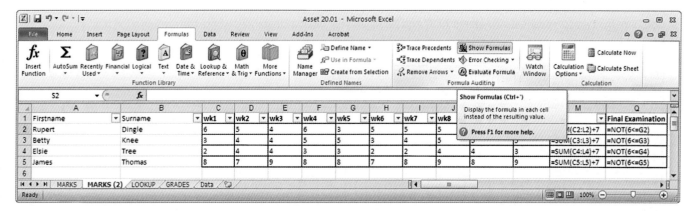

Figure 20.35 Showing formulas

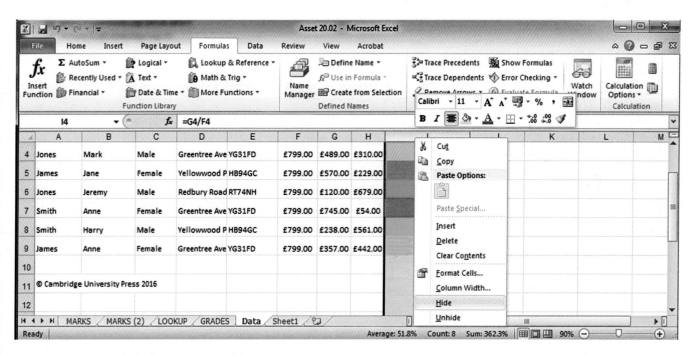

Figure 20.36 How to hide data on a spreadsheet

Enhancing your spreadsheet

At times, it might be appropriate to enhance the
presentation of your spreadsheet according to the target
audience's needs.

PRACTICAL TASK 20.08

Compare the two spreadsheets in Figures 20.37 and 20.38, and highlight all instances where the presentation has
been enhanced.

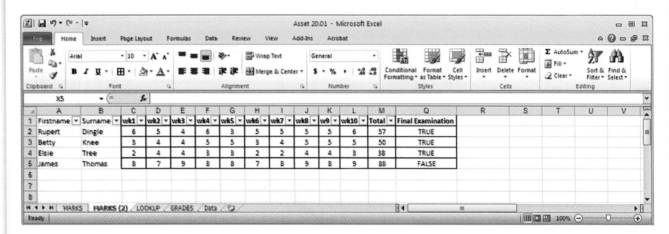

Figure 20.37 A spreadsheet without any text enhancements

272

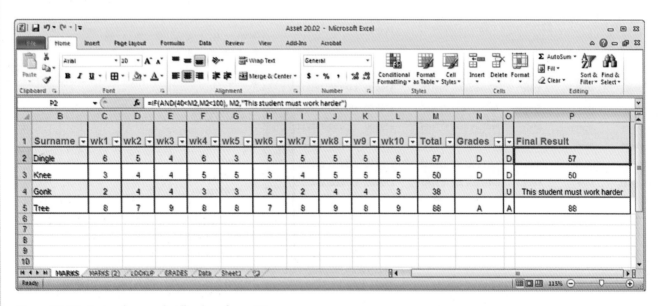

Figure 20.38 Text colour and cell colour formatting

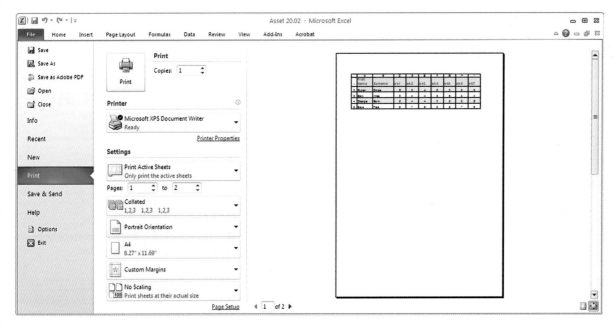

Figure 20.39 Adjusting the page orientation in 'Print Preview' mode

If you tried to print this page as it is now, the print preview in Figure 20.39 is what it would look like.

KEY TERMS

Pages: these are the same as spreadsheet sheets.

It spreads out over two pages in 'Portrait' orientation. It might be better to change the 'Page Setup' to make it more presentable and visible on one page only. In order to do this, you can use the 'Page Setup' tab as shown in Figure 20.40.

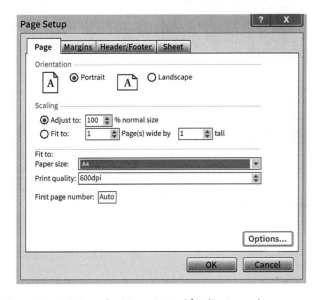

Figure 20.40 Using the 'Page Setup' facility to make your page more visually presentable

This enables you to have more control over the layout and presentation of the data on the page on which you wish to present your data. If you adjust the page orientation to 'Landscape' and fit it to one page, it should look like Figure 20.41.

273

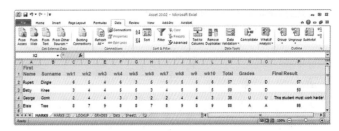

Figure 20.41 A more presentable page

You can further enhance your presentation by including 'Gridlines' and 'Row and Column Headings' from the 'Sheet' tab in the 'Page Setup' section of the 'Print Preview', as shown in Figure 20.42.

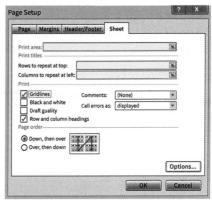

Figure 20.42 Using gridlines

Figure 20.43 shows how your page will look now.

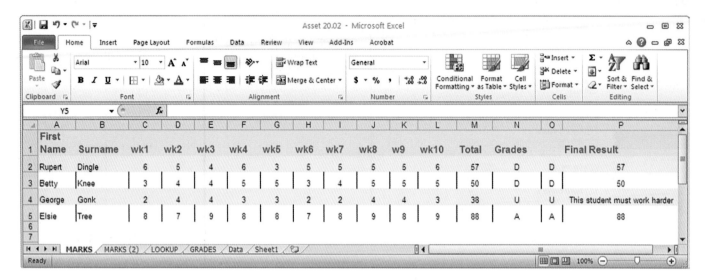

Figure 20.43 The results of using gridlines

PRACTICAL TASK 20.09

Use the Data worksheet in the 'Mark grader' spreadsheet to further enhance the presentation of this spreadsheet.

274

Formatting numerical data

Look at the spreadsheet shown in Figure 20.44.

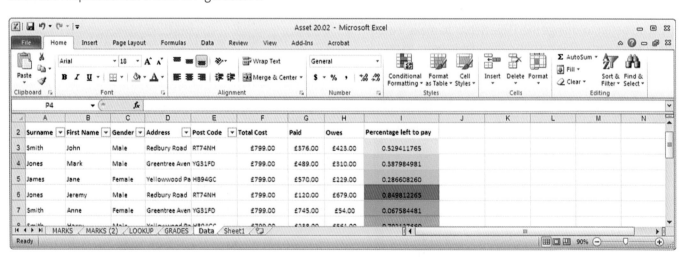

Figure 20.44 Formatting cells for currency

Columns F, G and H refer to a currency, and column I refers to a percentage. In order to reflect that in each cell, you would have to highlight the columns and change the format of the data type as shown in Figure 20.45.

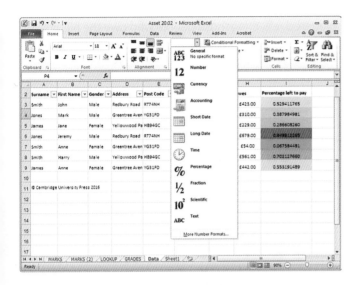

Figure 20.45 Using the currency formatting tool

The result of selecting 'Currency' is to open a window offering the choice of various currencies from different countries (see Figure 20.46).

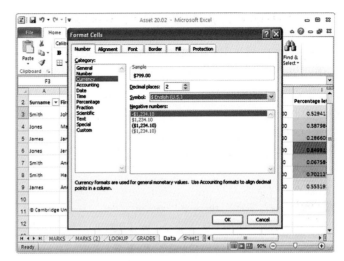

Figure 20.46 Selecting different types of currencies from different countries

The result of selecting the American Dollars currency can be seen in Figure 20.47.

The column with the percentages doesn't look good enough to present in a report or anywhere else. In order to enhance it for presentation, you should ensure that it has the % symbol and doesn't have too many decimal places if they are not really required.

275

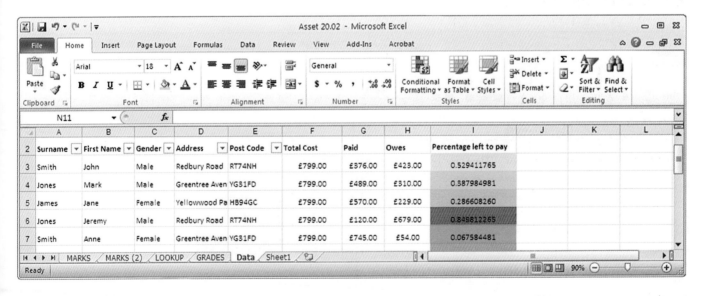

Figure 20.47 Currency set to '$'

In order to work out the percentage that each person still has to pay, you should use a formula that would divide the amount paid by the total cost and then use the % formatting tool to display your answer as a percentage, as shown in Figure 20.48.

Sometimes, you may need to display a few decimal places in your data. This can be done by using the 'Increase Decimal' tab to suit your requirements (see Figure 20.49).

Using conditional formatting

If you wish to find out which people have the most and least to pay by using a colour coding system you can apply conditional formatting to your data. You could use a three-colour scheme similar to the traffic light system with the colour red reflecting those people who owe the highest percentage and the colour green representing those who

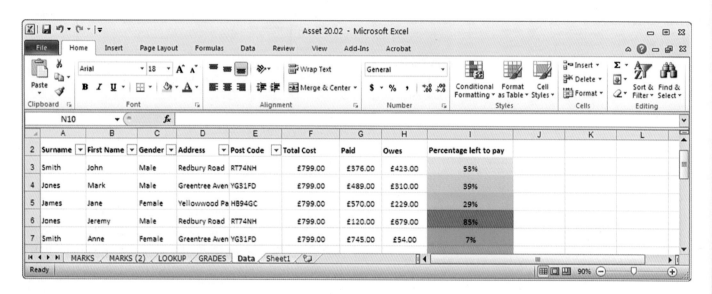

Figure 20.48 Using the percentage symbol

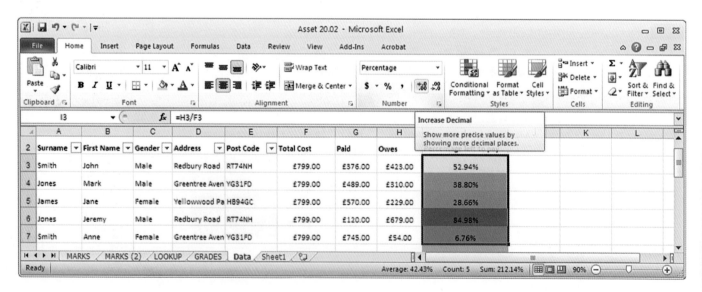

Figure 20.49 Using the 'Decimal Places' tool

owe the lowest percentage. The yellow colours show those in between (see Figure 20.50).

In a spreadsheet you can use conditional formatting to highlight cells with a certain value in a different colour for each value. This can be useful if you use the 'traffic light' colours, where red signifies some kind of alert or danger, the colour green indicates the opposite of the colour red, and orange or yellow indicate an approximate middle point somewhere in between the red and green values. An example where conditional formatting is used often is when teachers apply it to students' grades to indicate how far off their target grades they might be. If a student has a grade coloured red, it could indicate that the student has failed to achieve their target, and if it is green then they would have exceeded their target; if orange or yellow, they may have just achieved their target grade.

EXTENSION ACTIVITY 20.04

Discuss the implications of using conditional formatting as in the situation above.

PRACTICAL TASK 20.10

You work for a company that sells educational toys online and are going to perform some clerical tasks for this company. (Apply formatting for currency according to the local currency in your country.) Use the file 'Asset 20.04. docx' from the CD and complete the tasks.

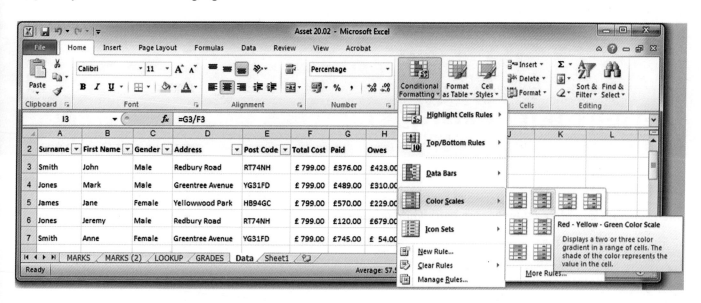

Figure 20.50 Using conditional formatting

277

Summary

- Spreadsheet models can use formulas and functions to solve real-life problems.
- Data models need to be tested with normal, abnormal and extreme data to be robust.
- Spreadsheets are good for testing 'what if?' questions.
- Data in spreadsheet models can be searched using single and multiple criteria.
- The use of wildcards helps to refine searches significantly.
- Data can also be sorted into ascending or descending order.
- The results from manipulating data in a spreadsheet model can be presented using various formats to make the results fully visible and clear using page orientation, conditional formatting and colour.

Chapter 21:
Website authoring

Learning objectives

When you have completed this chapter, you should be able to:

- identify and describe the three web development layers
- understand the function of the content layer to enter the content and create the structure of a web page
- understand the function of the presentation layer to display and format elements within a web page
- understand the function of the behaviour layer to add scripting language to elements within a web page
- use software tools to create the content layer of a web page to meet the needs of the audience
- use software tools to appropriately place the content in a web page
- use software tools to create navigation within a web page and between web pages
- use software tools to create the presentation layer of a web page
- know how to publish a website
- test a website.

Overview

Creating a website can be done in several ways. Factors to consider when deciding upon an appropriate method to use to build your website include your own level of computer skills, whether your website is a static or dynamic website and how large it will be. If your website is going to be a static website that excludes interactive or multimedia web objects, you could probably attempt to create it using HTML in a text editor, which are found on all computers, especially if you have reasonably good skills in using HTML. Alternatively, you should use either an online content management system (CMS) or a generic web authoring software package, which are available in most computer shops. This will have to be downloaded and installed on your computer, whereas using an online CMS website doesn't require you to install anything on your computer because it is cloud-based.

Web authoring software allows you to develop a website in a desktop format. The software will generate the required HTML coding for the layout of the web pages based on what you design. Usually, you can toggle back and forth between the graphical design and the HTML code to make changes to the design of the web page through the accompanying HTML code. In addition, web pages have interactive elements, such as rollovers, drag-and-drop features and things that you can click on. These require writing scripts in computer programming languages like JavaScript to create these.

> **KEY TERMS**
>
> **World Wide Web:** an information system that operates over the internet. It lets documents connect to other documents using hyperlinks, so that the user can search for information by moving from one document to another.
>
> **Script:** a set of instructions for a computer.
>
> **Scripting language:** a programming language, such as JavaScript, used to create a script.

A CMS is usually an online website-building website that allows you to drag and drop web objects onto web pages and include a host of complicated web objects without having to understand the programming code or HTML behind the making of each web page. Another method to create a website would be to use HTML code and any other necessary programming language. This method gives you the greatest autonomy over the designs and functionality you can build into your website, but requires you to have a higher degree of computer skills than if you choose to use a CMS or web authoring package to build your website.

In this chapter you will explore these different methods to develop web pages. However, web development involves the consideration of its three layers: content, style and behaviour.

> **KEY TERMS**
>
> **Browser:** a type of software that allows you to go on the internet. All websites have two different ways you can access them: either by their URL, for example http://www.weather.com, or by their IP address, which is a string of numbers, e.g. 162.209.40.58. These can be difficult to remember compared to URLs. A browser obtains the correct IP address from the DNS (Domain Name System) servers for the domain name of your URL and then connects you to the URL you typed.
>
> **URL:** Uniform Resource Locator is another term for the name of a website.
>
> **Syntax:** every language has a set of rules that govern the ways its words combine to form phrases, clauses and sentences. Similarly, in computer programming languages, syntax defines the combinations of symbols that are considered to be a correctly structured document or fragment in that language.

21.01 What are the three layers of web development?

Web development involves three separate layers:

Content layer

The content or structure layer is the information that people see when they look at a web page. Content can consist of text or images and includes the pointers that are needed to navigate around your website. The function of the content layer is to enter the content and create the structure of a web page.

Presentation layer

This layer refers to the style of the web pages, the layout and formatting and how it is presented to its users. Often it is the CSS in the HTML tags that will dictate the way the web pages are presented. The function of the presentation layer is to display and format elements within a web page.

Behaviour layer

This layer, sometimes also called the scripting layer, refers to how web elements will behave when users interact with them. The behaviour layer enters scripting language to elements in the web page.

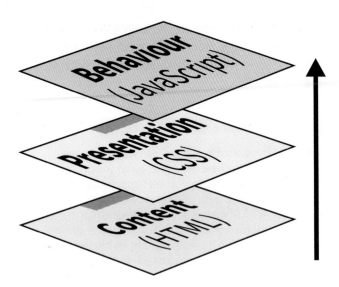

Figure 21.01 The three layers of web development

QUESTION 21.01

Match these terms into pairs and explain the link between them:

JavaScript	Content layer	Presentation layer
HTML	CSS	Behaviour layer

🔑 **KEY TERMS**

CSS: Cascading Style Sheets allow you to control the layout and look of your web pages easily and without the use of tables, as explained in the examples in Section 21.03. CSS also creates the look and formatting of a document written in HTML. In other words, CSS is a simple way to add style such as fonts, colours or spacing to web pages.

HTML: Hyper Text Markup Language is the code you use to create web pages. It uses tags that allow you to have much more control over the design and layout of your web pages than if you used any other method that has predesigned web pages and templates for you to use.

EXTENSION ACTIVITY 21.01

Describe the benefits of using the different ways to create web pages and explain how the three layers of web development fit together.

21.02 Creating a web page

Different ways of creating a web page

To summarise, a web page can be created in three main ways.

Using a CMS

When you use a CMS to create a website it manages everything for you, such as the design, layout, navigation and so on. You do not need to repeat the styles, layout and navigation for every web page in your website. At the beginning you will need to select the style, layout and navigation and these will be managed by the CMS across all the web pages of your website. Thereafter, all you need to do is to populate your web page with the content you want to go on it.

Using HTML

You will need to know the HTML tags to code each page of your website. You will have to select the style, use tables to organise the layout for each item you wish to place on your web page and if you have more web pages, you will also need to use HTML code for your navigation.

Using software application programs

Some software application programs in the Office suite can also be used to create a web page. They are already installed on your computer and saving the file as an HTML file format effectively makes it a web page.

This section will give you explanations from all of these three ways interchangeably as we proceed through the topics.

PRACTICAL TASK 21.01

a   Find an example of a CMS and a software application program in which you can create a web page.

b   Make a list of the similarities and differences between using these three different ways of creating web pages by completing Tables 21.01 and 21.02.

Similarities	CMS	HTML	Application software
Style			
Layout			
Navigation			
Adding media			
Other elements			

Table 21.01 Similarities between web page creation methods

Differences	CMS	HTML	Application software
Style			
Layout			
Navigation			
Adding media			
Other elements			

Table 21.02 Differences between web page creation methods

If you choose to use HTML to create your web page, you must use tags enclosed by '< >' and you should also use the correct syntax in each tag. All new HTML documents begin with these tags:

```
<!DOCTYPE html>
<html>
```

The head and body sections of a web page

There are two parts to an HTML document: the head and the body. The contents of the 'head' are not displayed on your web page; the 'body' of your HTML document contains what will be displayed on your web page.

In the head, you can expect to find the title of the page, for example `<title>`My Web Page`</title>`. This will be visible in the browser as a tab title, but not on the page itself.

You might also find metatags, JavaScript and CSS code. Most of these aspects are for the more advanced website creators. You will cover how to attach stylesheets (CSS) to the header in Section 21.03.

The body contains all the information that will be visible on your web page, including any tables, text, images and sound. You will learn how to place these elements below.

Why tables are used to structure elements within a web page

Tables allow for greater control over the layout of a page, and for the creation of more visually interesting pages. Pages with a grid layout (often invisible) use tables to control that layout. You can also use tables to divide the page into sections, so that sidebars, navigation bars or framed images with their titles and captions are set apart.

Tables allow you to organise information on your web page and help to keep all the sections in their places. Each cell of a table can have its own formatting: the data in it can be aligned to the left, centre or right. Tables also have header-data cells in which the column headings can be placed.

A table header is usually the top row that contains information that helps identify the content of a particular column.

Inserting a table and specifying attributes

Tables should be placed in the body of your web page. In HTML, you will need to use opening and closing tags around each piece of text for it to sit correctly in the table.

Using the following HTML code, the result will be as shown in Figure 21.02.

```
<table>
    <tr>
        <th>Team A</th>
        <th>Team B</th>
        <th>TOTAL POINTS</th>
    </tr>
    <tr>
        <td>40 points</td>
        <td>38 points</td>
        <td>78 points</td>
    </tr>
    <tr>
        <td>67 points</td>
        <td>54 points</td>
        <td>121 points</td>
    </tr>
</table>
```

Team A	Team B	TOTAL POINTS
40 points	38 points	78 points
67 points	54 points	121 points

Figure 21.02 An HTML table

Here's what each part of the HTML code does:

- `<table>`: Each table must begin with a `<table>` tag.
- The `<tr>`, `</tr>` tags are the tags for table rows.
- The `<th>`, `</th>` tags are the tags for table headers. All table headers are formatted to be centre aligned and bold automatically, so you don't need to add extra tags to do so.
- The `<td>`, `</td>` tags are the tags for data items to go in the cells of the table.
- As no borders are specified for the table, they are invisible.

PRACTICAL TASK 21.02

a Use similar HTML tags to those used above in an online HTML tutorial of your choice to create a table with four columns and five rows.

b Make the first row a header row, with labels 'Blue team' 'Red team' 'Yellow team' and 'Total'

c Now add data in column 1: 32, 34, 12, 36

d Now add data in column 2: 16, 38, 10, 26

e Now add data in column 3: 46, 4, 18, 16

f Calculate the total points and add these into the final column.

When inserting tables into the body of your page, you might want to add **attributes** to the table tag. An attribute is an additional piece of information about an HTML element.

Attributes you can specify within a table include adjusting cells to span more than one row or column and setting table and cell sizes in terms of pixels or % values.

If you used the following HTML, the result would be as shown in Figure 21.03.

```
<table border="5">
  <tr>
      <th colspan="2">TABLE TITLE</th>
  </tr>
  <tr>
      <td>Column A</td>
      <td>Column B</td>
  </tr>
</table>
```

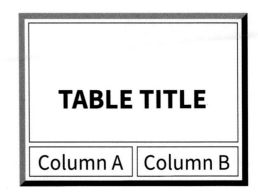

Figure 21.03 Table resulting from the HTML code above

Looking at the above HTML:

- The BORDER part of the tag is an attribute of the table and the number refers to how many pixels wide you want the border around the table to be.
- The COLSPAN="…" attribute specifies how many columns you would like a cell to span across, which is useful for headers. If you want it to span five columns, you should write COLSPAN="5".

PRACTICAL TASK 21.03

a How can you create invisible borders?

b Add another column to your table. In what way should you adjust the 'COLSPAN' attribute for the table title to make it span the whole table?

The following code produces the result shown in Figure 21.04.

```
<table border="5" width="50%" cellpadding="4"
cellspacing="3">
    <tr>
        <th colspan="2">
            TABLE TITLE
        </th>
    </tr>
    <tr>
        <th>Column A</th>
        <th>Column B</th>
    </tr>
    <tr align="center">
        <td>Data 1</td>
        <td>Data 2</td>
    </tr>
    <tr align="center">
        <td>Data 3</td>
```

```
        <td>Data 4</td>
    </tr>
    <tr align="center">
        <td>Data 5</td>
        <td>Data 6</td>
    </tr>
</table>
```

TABLE TITLE	
Column A	Column B
Data 1	Data 2
Data 3	Data 4
Data 5	Data 6

Figure 21.04 Table resulting from the HTML code above

Looking at the HTML above:

- The WIDTH="…%" will determine the size of your table (or individual cells, depending on where you specify the attribute) as a percentage of your screen. If you want your table to be half the size of your screen you should use WIDTH="50%" at the beginning of your table tag.

- CELLPADDING refers to the distance between the edge of a cell in your table and its contents. You can use a number to indicate this value, for example CELLPADDING="3".

- CELLSPACING refers to the space or border around each cell in your table. You can also use a number to indicate the size of this, for example CELLSPACING="4" represents a bigger space around each cell compared to CELLSPACING="2".

PRACTICAL TASK 21.04

Use the HTML code above and make this table three quarters the size of your screen. Include two more columns, Columns C and D, and add 'Data 7' and 'Data 8' into two more rows. Make the cells shorter and have less space around each cell. Make sure your table header spans the additional columns.

You can learn about how to apply further styles to tables to make them fit the design of your page in section 21.03.

Inserting text into a web page and applying styles

When you insert text in the body of your web page, you will need to make sure you tag it correctly so that it displays properly. As you learnt when inserting tables, you need to remember to use opening and closing tags around all your text.

In HTML, <h1>, <h2> and <h3> tags refer to the sizes of the text in the headings, h1 being the largest size and h6 the smallest.

The <p> tag refers to the beginning of a new paragraph and the </p> refers to the end of a paragraph.

If you want to leave a blank line between each paragraph, you should use the <br> tag. This tag comes as a single tag and doesn't require a closing </br> tag, because there is nothing in between the tags, just one blank line, so only one single tag needs to be used.

If you want to format your text to bold or italics, you can use , for bold or <i>, </i> for italics.

The <li> tag refers to a list. There are two types of lists you can create using HTML tags. There are unordered lists, <ul>, and there are ordered lists, <ol>. Unordered lists will appear with bullets for each list item and ordered lists will have either numbers or letters for each list item. Each list of items needs to have the type of list tag first, followed by the <li>item1</li>,<li>item2</li>, etc. you want to use. An example could be:

```
<ol>
<li>red</li>
<li>blue</li>
<li>green</li>
</ol>
```

You could try to create an unordered list using a similar format in HTML.

PRACTICAL TASK 21.05

Study the HTML below and then answer the two questions that follow.

```
<!DOCTYPE html>
<html>
<head><title>Mo's Music Page</title>
</head>
<body>
<h2>Types of Music</h2>
<p>There are many different types of
music that are enjoyed by people all
over the world. Some types of music
are very old and can be traced back
to centuries ago, such as<i>classical</
i> music. On the other hand, <i>rap</
i> music is a very modern type of
music dating back to the last 40
years.</p>
<br>
<p>Some of the more <i>traditional</
i> types of music, dating back even
further, use no musical instruments,
yet can be very pleasant to listen
to. Yet other types of music use
very primitive styled instruments and
are very important in a <i>cultural
sense.</i></p>
</body>
</html>
```

1 Refer to the HTML above and highlight all the invisible sections of this web page.

2 Draw boxes around each section of the web page to indicate the structure of this web page. Label the following parts clearly: head, body, paragraphs, headings and the title.

Inserting images, moving images and sound into a web page

If you use HTML tags to insert an image into your web page you must use the tag <img>, but this won't show any image by itself, as you have to tell the browser which image to show. You need the URL of the image so the browser knows the address of that image. You don't only have to use images that are on your own computer.

You supply the image URL by adding an attribute called source to the image tag, written as 'src'. Add an '=' sign and a pair of quotes to place the attribute values in.

So it should look like this now:

```
<img src="https://media.istockphoto.com/
photos/pet-cat-sign-picture-id464523952">
```

Inside the quotes is the URL of the image you want to use from the internet. If for some reason the image is not displayed because of server failure or something else, or to help those with sight problems who use a screen reader, it is best to add some alternate text to explain what the image is by adding another attribute to the image tag, like this:

```
<img src="https://media.istockphoto.com/
photos/pet-cat-sign-picture-id464523952"
alt="Ginger cat">
```

Height and width are attributes you can use to change the size of the image.

```
<img src="https://media.istockphoto.com/
photos/pet-cat-sign-picture-id464523952"
alt="Ginger cat" width="90%">
```

PRACTICAL TASK 21.06

In a text editor of your own choice, write HTML tags to create a web page about what your dream holiday would look like. Include suitable headings, paragraphs containing some text, and some still images.

If you want to add a moving image to your web page, you can add an animated GIF in place of a still image. Use the 'src' attribute as above and remember to include alternate text:

```
<img src="https://media.giphy.com/media/
onsxwAbM8xUNa/giphy.gif" alt="happy dog"
width="500" height="280">
```

There are some points to note about the HTML above:

- The <img src="…"> part of the image tag explains where to find the image by listing its URL inside quotation marks.

- The width="500" height="280" part of the image tag states the size you want to make this image on your web page in pixels.

Aspect ratio

When you resize an image, be careful to reduce or increase its height and width by the same percentage, so that the image retains its aspect ratio. This means it will not be distorted by becoming either taller or fatter. For example, the happy dog could be resized to three times bigger while maintaining its aspect ratio (although it might look more pixelated). The new size attributes would be width="1500" and height="840". In effect, the old ratio 500:280 is the same as the new one, 1500:840. If you only specify width or height, then the other will resize automatically to maintain the correct aspect ratio.

QUESTION 21.02

a   When you compare the HTML code for the GIF with the previous <img> tag, what has been added?

b   What is the purpose of including 'alt text' next to an image?

c   Rewrite the HTML code by changing the values of the size attributes so that the moving image is 300 pixels wide. Make sure the image maintains its aspect ratio. Include a second image in your code and make it slightly smaller in size compared to the image described above.

When you add sound files into a web page, it is best to have controls, such as play, pause and volume buttons, together with the sound file. This is different from trying to insert text or an image into a web page and can be achieved by using the following types of tags:

```
<audio controls>
<source src="Song1.mpeg-4" type="audio/
mpeg">
</audio>
```

Hyperlinks, bookmarks and anchors

A **hyperlink** is any image, icon, text or item that when clicked on takes the user to another web page, an email link or a file on their computer. The user does not need to know the exact URL of each web page you want to see; the hyperlink has this web address in the background and will take you there if you click on it.

All hyperlinks have a source (where it will go from) and a destination (the place it will take you to).

Hyperlink sources can start on documents, such as a word processing document or a presentation you are working on, and take you to a destination within the same document or to somewhere on the web. Alternatively, they can start from the web and refer you to other documents.

A **bookmark** is a type of hyperlink. It is a quick link to another location on the same web page (especially if you have a very long web page that is not all visible onscreen at the time you might wish to view it). It can also link to another web page or to another file saved somewhere other than the same web page.

An **anchor** is a tag within a page's HTML that you can create a link to. You usually use anchors if you want a user to go to a graphic or link halfway down the page without having to read through all the text to get to the part they're interested in. If the object has an id attribute, you do not need to create a new anchor on the page as you can link the bookmark directly to the object.

 KEY TERMS

Hyperlink: either text, an image or part of an image that is a link to another item or web page. Text links are usually coloured and underlined, and when you roll over them using a mouse your pointer will often turn into a small hand.

Anchor: a type of hyperlink that will take you to a specific part of a web page.

Bookmark: a named anchor which operates and is created in a similar way to the way that you'd create an anchor.

PRACTICAL TASK 21.07

Creating anchors within a web page

If you have a web page with some sections that might not be relevant to all users, it might be useful to allow them to skip those parts and go straight to a specific spot further down on your web page. This can be done using anchors.

There are two aspects to consider. First, you should name the spot, and second, you should create the link to that spot.

You are skipping to a heading for a section called 'Bookings'. Insert named <a> tags near the heading, like this:

```
<a name="Bookings"></a>
<h2>Bookings></h2>
```

You can now link directly to the <a> tags on the page.

At the spot from which you want to start skipping some parts of the web page, you should insert HTML like this:

```
<a href="#Bookings">How to book your
tickets</a>
```

'Bookings' is the exact spot on the web page you are going to skip to FROM this location, and the text you will see for your clickable bookmark says 'How to book your tickets'.

Use an object's id attribute to create a bookmark

If you are using newer versions of HTML like HTML5, you can name an element using an id attribute rather than creating an additional anchor. For example, if you have a heading for your bookings section:

```
<h2>Bookings</h2>
```

you can give this heading an individual label.

```
<h2 id="Bookings">Bookings</h2>
```

You can then use the same bookmark HTML to link to the heading, rather than <a> tags near it.

Creating hyperlinks to locally stored web pages

You can use the same procedure as in the last task. You will need a FROM link and a TO anchor. The only difference is that the bookmark at the FROM spot has to have the location of a web page as well as the name of the anchor.

As the web page is 'local' (because it's part of the same website you are linking from) you do not need to add the 'http…' part of the address and only need to specify the page itself. This is known as a **relative file path**.

At the FROM spot use this type of HTML code:

```
<a href="page23.html#Bookings">How to
book your tickets</a>
```

'Bookings' on page 23 of the website is the exact spot on the web page you can skip TO, and the text you will see at this spot is 'How to book your tickets'.

At the TO spot which will be on page 23 of your website you can name your element with an id attribute called 'Bookings', or insert this HTML code:

```
<a name="Bookings"></a>
```

On page 23 of your website is where you will find the spot called 'Bookings' and it will have a link to it from the first HTML code.

Creating hyperlinks to a website using the URL

If you wish to link to a completely different site from the one your bookmark will be on, you will need to enter the whole URL. This is known as an **absolute file path**. For example, you could use:

```
<a href="https://en.wikipedia.org/wiki/
Ticket_(admission)">Tickets you can
buy</a>
```

to take users away from your site by opening the new page in the same window.

Creating hyperlinks from images

You have already created a hyperlink from text, by using <a> tags with an href inside:

```
<a href="Bookings">How to book your
tickets</a>
```

Instead of using clickable text (in this case 'How to book your tickets'), you could instead create a clickable image. To do this, you need to add your image reference (and some alternate text) inside the hyperlink tag, instead of adding text:

```
<a href= "Bookings">
<img src="https://media.istockphoto.com/
photos/book-now-business-concept-for-
reservation-booking-written-on-sticky-
picture-id913207718" alt="Book tickets now"
height="100">
</a>
```

Creating hyperlinks to send mail to a specified email address

Websites often have a 'Contact Us' section. In addition to a postal address, telephone and fax numbers there is usually an email address available, which is often clickable. A 'mailto:' link can be added to your usual hyperlink HTML code along with the email address you want to use, as in this example:

```
<a href="mailto:office@bookings.com">
Email Us</a>
```

When you click on the visible 'Email Us' link, your email program will open ready for you to write an email to the address written after 'mailto:'.

> **PRACTICAL TASK 21.08**
>
> Write the HTML code that creates a link on your web page for users to email you. This link should look like an icon and not be text that the user should click on.

PRACTICAL TASK 21.09 ⊙

Creating hyperlinks to open in a specified location

Links can be opened in a variety of ways, including:

* in the current window
* in a new window
* in a window with a specified name.

a If you already have your web page or website set up, try to create a hyperlink that will open in the same window as the web page by using the example HTML code as a guide. This procedure works in exactly the same way as you would create anchors to open a link on the same web page.

b Now try to create a hyperlink that will open in a new window in your browser by using the example HTML code as a guide:

```
<a href="http://www.[choose any website
you wish and fill it in here] "target="
_blank ">This goes to a new window in
the browser</a>
```

This is what the link should look like on the web page:

This goes to a new window in the browser.

c If your page has lots of links and you don't want them each to open a new window every time, you can create hyperlinks that will open in a window with a specified name in your browser. Instead of calling your window '_blank', if you specify a name, for example 'new_window' then each link the user clicks on will open in that same window, rather than opening a new one each time. Try this using the following example HTML code to start:

```
Here is a link to <a href= "http://www.
yahoo.com">Yahoo</a>.
Here is a link to <a href="http://www.
wikipedia.com ">Wikipedia</a>.
Here is a link to <a href="http://www.
google.com ">Google</a>.
```

First try adapting the code so that each link opens in a new window each time.

Now try adapting the code so that each link opens in the same new window, one on top of the other.

d Create an image hyperlink for the Yahoo URL and place it next to the text link.

Absolute and relative file paths

When you start creating your website, you should create a main (root) folder to store all your files. Sometimes you might wish to store the different types of data, such as images, audio or video files, in separate folders (possibly within the main folder). When files are placed in different folders you need to specify the file location or path so that browsers can find them. HTML supports two kinds of paths: relative and absolute file paths.

Absolute file path

An absolute file path specifies a file's precise location within a computer's entire folder structure; for example, if you wish to link to a URL on the web (outside of your site), use the http protocol, for example http://wikipedia.com.

Relative file path

A relative file path will refer you to a file in another place in relation to the file you are working on. If the file is in the same place as your current file you are working in then it is not necessary to specify the folder name, unless it is inside another folder.

If you want to go up one level in the folder hierarchy you must state the relative file path by starting with two full stops ('..') and a slash, followed by the file name, for example '../filename'.

If you want to go down one level in the folder hierarchy you must start with the name of the subfolder followed by a slash, for example 'subfolder/filename'.

If you want to refer to a different folder within the same folder (this is called a sibling folder), you must first move up the folder hierarchy (using '..') then move down the folder hierarchy by using the name of the sibling folder.

It is best practice to use relative file paths creating hyperlinks to local web pages because it makes it much easier to do something like change your domain name without having to change every hyperlink. It also means you can test your website while it's still saved on your own computer before you upload it to a server. If you use relative file paths, your site structure and all the links within it can remain the same, even if you decide you'd like to change the name or location of the site itself.

21.03 Using stylesheets

What is CSS?

CSS stands for Cascading Style Sheets. Styles define how to display HTML elements. Styles can be inline, which means they are usually placed right next to the text you want to apply a particular style to, and apply to a single HTML element; whereas stylesheets enable you to change the appearance and layout of all elements on a web page and on your website by just editing one single file. It is not necessary to change the formatting on every page of a whole website. The style you create in your stylesheet cascades throughout your website, web page or unique element.

The hierarchy of attaching multiple stylesheets and using in-line styling

If you are using CSS stylesheets and HTML formatting on the same page, it gets applied in a hierarchical way. The HTML formatting overrides any formatting styles that are declared in stylesheets, whether those stylesheets are embedded in the document or are saved in external files.

Inline styling

Inline styling is used to apply a unique style to a single HTML element in the body of the web page using the style attribute, for example:

```
<h1 style="color:pink">This is a Pink
Heading</h1>
```

This inline styling changes the text colour for a single heading and will not be applied to any other part of the web page. (Note that you need to use the American spelling "color".)

Inline styling overrides any CSS instructions found in the head of the web page, because your browser will always use the style it reads last.

Internal stylesheets

Figure 21.05 shows how internal stylesheets are attached. All the CSS rules should be placed in the head of the HTML document, in between the <style>. . .</style> tags.

```
<!DOCTYPE html>
<html>
<head>
<style>
    body    {background-color:lightgrey;}
    h1      {color: blue;}
    p       {color: green;}
</style>
</head>

<body>
<h1>This is a heading</h1>
<p>This is a paragraph.</p>
</body>
</html>
```

Figure 21.05 HTML code used for internal styling

External stylesheets

External CSS is a completely separate file (with an extension file name .css) that will apply the style to your whole website. If you want to change the style of your website you will not have to re-write each web page all over again. You could simply change the instructions in your external CSS and the new style will be cascaded across all the web pages of your whole website.

External stylesheets are defined in the <head> section of an HTML page, in the <link> element (see Figure 21.06).

```
<!DOCTYPE html>
<html>
<head>
<link rel="stylesheet" href="styles.css">
</head>

<body>
<h1>This is a heading</h1>
<p>This is a paragraph.</p>
</body>
</html>
```

Figure 21.06 HTML code showing how external styling is applied

---

EXTENSION ACTIVITY 21.02

What is different in this HTML code in Figure 21.06 from that in Figure 21.05? What differences can you expect to see on this web page compared to the previous web page?

Creating CSS HTML code

CSS is linked to the presentation layer in web development.

A CSS rule set consists of a selector and a declaration block:

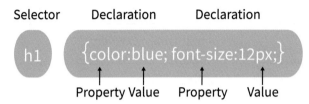

The selector points to the HTML element you want to style.

The declaration block contains one or more declarations separated by semicolons.

Each declaration includes a property name and a value, separated by a colon.

Figure 21.07 CSS HTML code requires you to create CSS rules like this

A CSS rule consists of two main parts: a **selector** and a set of **declarations** which are enclosed in curly brackets; each declaration is separated by semicolons (see Figure 21.07). Each declaration is also made up of two parts: the property name (for example 'color' or 'font-size') and its value. The property name and its value are separated by a colon, as seen in the following example of internal styling:

```
<!DOCTYPE html>
<html>
    <head>
    <style>
        body {background-color: yellow;}
        h1 {color: orange; text-align: center;}
        p {font-family: "Times New Roman";
        font-size: 20px;}
    </style>
    </head>
    <body>
        <h1>My First CSS Example</h1>
        <p>This is a paragraph.</p>
    </body>
</html>
```

The CSS rule is placed in the head of the HTML document, and you must make reference to which style you want to apply in the body of your HTML document, as shown in the example above.

Examples of selectors are <h1>, <p> or <table>. The declarations for the <h1> selector are 'color' and 'text-align', and the declarations for the <p> selector are 'font-family' and 'font-size'. You can change the values of each declaration and apply these formatting styles to any section of your web pages in the body of your HTML document by referring to the selectors you declared in the head of your HTML document.

Selectors you might want to use include:

- types of elements; for example, to select everything in <p> tags and make it red and centred, use p {text-align:center; color:red;}

- unique element ids on a page; for example to select and style an element with the attribute id="para1", use #para1 {text-align:center; color:red; background:blue;}

- **class**, for elements you have grouped together; for example to select and style a class with the attribute class="posh", use .posh { text-align:center; color:red; background:blue; font-family:"Comic Sans MS";}.

289

QUESTION 21.03

In each of the examples above, a new style declaration has been added to each selector. Identify the new declarations and explain what the 'para1' element and 'posh' class will look like.

KEY TERMS

Selectors: when using CSS to create stylesheets, the CSS rules require you to specify the selectors (HTML elements) to which you wish the styles to apply before defining the declarations. The declarations are applied to the selectors.

Declarations: when using CSS to create stylesheets, the CSS rules require you to define the properties and the values for each selector you wish to use by using declarations.

Class: a group of elements to which a style can be applied. This can be quicker and less confusing than selecting the id attribute of each individual element.

The types of styles that you can define in a web page include, but are not limited to, those in Table 21.03:

	Property	Specifies	Example
Background	colour	The background colour of an element	background-color: yellow;
	image	The image to use as the background of an element	background-image: url("mypic.gif")
Font	style	styles such as bold or italics	font-style: bold;
	typeface, or fontface	typeface such as Courier or Times etc.	font-family: Courier;

Table 21.03 Types of background properties for web pages

QUESTION 21.04

If you change the values of a declaration for a particular selector, explain how it affects the website. Give an example to show your understanding.

PRACTICAL TASK 21.10

Open the CSS file (Practical Task 21.10.css) and change the properties and values of each selector as follows:

Selector: h1
- The font set to the default serif font on your computer
- Font size to 18px
- Font colour to red
- Text aligned to the centre
- Text set to bold

Selector: h2
- The font set to the default serif font on your computer
- Font size to 14px
- Font colour to blue
- Text aligned to the left
- Text set to italics

Selector: h3
- The font set to the default serif font on your computer
- Font size to 10px
- Font colour to brown
- Text aligned to the right
- Text set to underlined

Selector: p
- The font set to the default serif font on your computer
- Font size to 14px
- Font colour to red
- Text aligned to the left

Selector: li
- The font set to the default serif font on your computer
- Font size to 14px
- Font colour to red
- Text aligned to the left
- Text set to bullets

Save the file as a CSS stylesheet, called STYLESHEET_1

In your own web page, import this file as a link into your web page. Follow the explanation in section 21.03 (subheading "External stylesheets"). When you have saved your new style in your web page, refresh the web page and the new style should have cascaded throughout your web page. This is making use of a relative file path because the external file you are referring to is not in the same place you are working in. Follow the convention for the different levels of hierarchy of where your file is located.

Attaching styles to tables

When you use HTML5, you must use CSS styles for tables. This includes:

- Background colour
- Horizontal alignment
- Vertical alignment
- Spacing

- Padding
- Borders (collapsed, border thickness and visible/invisible)

Most code works the same way; simply write your code to apply to the table elements you would like to style. For example if you want your table, header and data (cells) to all have black borders one pixel wide, write:

```
table, th, td {
border: 1px solid black;
}
```

Column 1	**Column 2**
Data 1	Data 2
Data 3	Data 4

Or for the borders to be made invisible, write:

```
table, th, td {
border: 0;
}
```

Column 1	**Column 2**
Data 1	Data 2
Data 3	Data 4

To collapse the borders of each cell together to one pixel wide, write:

```
table {
border-collapse: collapse;
}
table, td, th {
border: 1px solid black;
}
```

Column 1	**Column 2**
Data 1	Data 2
Data 3	Data 4

Table headings in HTML are formatted to be bold and centred by default. If you want to have a left-aligned or right-aligned heading you can use the CSS 'text-align' property. Here is an example:

```
th {
    text-align: right;
}
```

Border spacing in HTML determines how much space there is between the cells in a table. In CSS, you can use the 'border-spacing' property. Here is an example:

```
table {
    border-spacing: 10px;
}
```

PRACTICAL TASK 21.11

1 In the HTML below, find and highlight the declarations that describe:

- background colour
- horizontal alignment
- vertical alignment
- padding
- spacing
- borders

in a table.

2 Next, find and highlight which parts of the page body each declaration will style.

```
<html>
<head>
<style>
table {
    width:100%;
}
th, td {
    padding: 5px;
    text-align: left;
}
table#t01, th, td {
    border: 1px solid black;
    border-collapse: collapse;
}
table#t01 th {
    background-color: black;
    color: white;
}
```

```
table#t01 tr {
    background-color: #eee;
}
table#t02, th, td {
    border-collapse: separate;
    border-spacing: 15px;
}
table#t02 th {
    background-color: blue;
    color: yellow;
}
table#t02 td {
    height: 50px;
    vertical-align: bottom;
}
table#t02 tr{
    background-color: green;
}
</style>
</head>


<body>
<table id="t01">
<tr>
<th>First Name</th>
<th>Last Name</th>
<th>Age</th>
</tr>
<tr>
<td>Jenny</td>
<td>Taylor</td>
<td>23</td>
</tr>
<tr>
<td>Yasmin</td>
<td>Joourh</td>
<td>49</td>
</tr>
<tr>
<td>Sun</td>
<td>Park</td>
<td>18</td>
</tr>
</table>
<br>
<table id="t02">
<tr>
<th>First Name</th>
<th>Last Name</th>
<th>Age</th>
```

```
</tr>
<tr>
<td>Lucy</td>
<td>Chan</td>
<td>32</td>
</tr>
<tr>
<td>Ali</td>
<td>Masood</td>
<td>16</td>
</tr>
<tr>
<td>James</td>
<td>Green</td>
<td>27</td>
</tr>
</table>

</body>
</html>
```

3 Now change the HTML code above to:
   - change the background colours from those already used to colours of your choice
   - change the horizontal and vertical alignment
   - decrease the padding
   - increase the spacing between the cells in table t02.

Saving, attaching and commenting on CSS files

Saving external CSS files is similar to saving any other file type. When you are ready to save a CSS file you should use .css after the file name.

Your external CSS file should be written in a text editor, such as MS Notepad. It should not contain any other HTML. Selectors and declarations are usually written on different lines as follows:

```
body {    background-color: green;
}
h2 {
    color: red;
}
p {
    color: purple;
}
```

PRACTICAL TASK 21.12

Create a cascading stylesheet where:

- the background colour is a pale green colour
- the heading is size h1 and bold with font type Arial Black
- sub-headings for each paragraph are size h3 and in italics with font type Arial
- the text colour in each paragraph is red
- any tables have collapsed borders and 10 pixels of padding in the cells.

Save this stylesheet as a .css file to be used as an external stylesheet.

When you are attaching your stylesheet it is best practice to use a relative file path. This is because your stylesheet will be stored in the same place as the rest of your website. If you need to move or rename the website, your css file can move with it and any links to it will still work. If you want to edit any of the styles, you can edit the css file and the whole site will change with it.

If you were to use an absolute file path, the styles on every page would 'break' as soon as you change the name of the folder the css is stored in.

When you want to attach the stylesheet to your page you must use the <link> tag in the head part of your HTML file. Use the name of the css document that you created in a text editor.

Here is an example:

```
<head>
<title>My Web Page</title>
<link rel="stylesheet"
href="webpagestyle.css">
</head>
```

The browser will be able to find your css file as it will be saved in the same directory as all your other HTML files.

PRACTICAL TASK 21.13

Attach your external CSS file to one of the web pages you have created, or place it appropriately in one of the free online HTML tutorials to observe the effects of your HTML.

You can add comments to an external stylesheet to help explain what each section of the document is meant to be doing by using CSS comment tags. In the stylesheet, your comment will look like this:

```
/*This is a comment about my stylesheet*/
```

Any comments placed between these tags will not be interpreted as CSS by a web browser. Comments are very helpful in long CSS documents as they help to explain what each section of the code is designed to do.

21.04 Test and publish a website

Testing your website is the last stage before making your website go live. The level of testing will depend on the method you used to build your website. If you used HTML code to create your whole website, you will have more tests to conduct before publishing your website. However, if you used a CMS or web authoring package then you may have fewer tests to carry out because these methods allow novice website creators to create websites without needing any programming skills.

You could design your own test plan according to the web elements you used to create your website; you could also use one of the many online website testing checklists available; or you could use an online automatic website checker that will give you a report with recommendations to improve your website.

How to upload and publish the content of a website using ftp

If you're using a CMS or web authoring software package you will not need to use ftp to upload and publish your website because these provide 'non-technical' ways to accomplish uploading and publishing a website.

When you publish a website you upload web pages from your computer to your hosting account. This is called 'ftp'ing because you're using the File Transfer Protocol. It's similar to moving files from one folder to another on your computer. The main difference is that when you move files to your hosting account, they are transferred over the internet.

Before you get started you should have the domain name of your website pointed to your hosting account. You will also need three pieces of information to proceed: your domain name, your username (created when you set up your hosting account) and your password. In addition, you will need an ftp client. There are many ftp clients available online. You should download ftp client software onto your computer and then follow the instructions below in order to upload your files using ftp.

The interfaces of most ftp clients are divided into two sections: the left-hand side will show all the files on your computer and on the right-hand side those that you want to upload onto the internet. Simply drag and drop those from your computer on the left-hand side to the right-hand side and click connect. Your files should then be published to the internet.

Creating a test plan for a website

Any test plans should test the following aspects:

- suitability for target audience
- purpose of website
- use of consistent house style
- navigation system
- use of different components
- interactive elements
- hyperlinks
- user forms
- ease of use.

The main aspects that should be checked are:

- Functionality
    ○ Does the site work as you wanted it to work?
    ○ Does it work in the most common browsers (for example Internet Explorer, Chrome, Firefox and so on)? Which is the most popular web browser?
    ○ Do all the links, hyperlinks and anchors work?
    ○ Can you look at every page, document or file you have included?

- Usability
    ○ Does the index or home page load first when you open the website/go to the URL?
    ○ Can you find the main navigation method as soon as you open the index page?
    ○ Can you get back from every page without using the browser's 'back' button?
    ○ Can you get to all the other pages in the site from every page?
    ○ Is the navigation method consistent throughout the site?
    ○ Can you use the whole site without getting frustrated?

- Effectiveness
    ○ Does the site present all the relevant information in the best format?
    ○ How quickly do the multimedia objects load?
    ○ Can you read each page without having to scroll too far (up/down or sideways)?
    ○ Is all the content of a good enough quality? (Check all the images, video, audio and so on.)

A typical website test plan for the functional tests would look like Table 21.04 on the following page.

PRACTICAL TASK 21.14

Use Tables 21.04 and 21.05 to test the usability and effectiveness of a specific website.

Web page	Small screenshot of page	What did you test?	What was it supposed to do?	What did it do?	What did you change as a result of this test?

Table 21.04 Website functional testing

For the usability tests, the plan might look like Table 21.05.

Web page	Your opinion	Feedback from your reviewers	What needs changing?	How you would do this?

Table 21.05 Website usability testing

How to justify your choice of a test plan for your website

There are many different ways to test a website. These will depend on the method you used to create your website. If you created your website using an online website creator, you will not have to test the functionality of the navigation because these will have been arranged to work properly without you having to create the links from scratch. However, if you used HTML code to create the links manually, you will need to check that they work as you intended them to work.

On the other hand, it is always better to test the functionality of the navigation system regardless of how the website was created. Functionality should include checking that the flow of content is appropriate, and that it matches the client's intentions; that the pages are in the intended order; that there is not too much text on any single page (it is best, where appropriate, not to have more text on a page than can be seen at one time, as users will sometimes assume that what they see is all there is and not attempt to scroll further down the page). If such items are checked, the functioning of the website should run smoothly and not intrude upon the user's experience on the site.

It is likely that the navigation system will have been customised in some way and this could introduce errors.

If you created a website for a client you will need to check how satisfied with its effectiveness your client is and whether the users are also satisfied with the website.

You would need to explain why you chose to include certain web elements and why you chose not to use some.

Justifying your choice of a testing plan should include why certain tests have to be included and why some tests would not be necessary.

EXTENSION ACTIVITY 21.03

Evaluate the two test plans in Figures 21.08 and 21.09, explaining your reasons clearly.

Ronny's website

Test plan

No mistakes on pages	✓
All images OK	✓
All links working	✓
All links go to the right pages	✓
All text can be read	✓

Figure 21.08 First test plan example

Test plan for Trentliz version 1

Test			Expected Result	Actual Result	Action required	Successful? Y/N
FUNCTIONALITY TESTING						
Buttons and icon links	Home page	ILC1-Programme button	Goes to the ILC1-Programme page	It downloads the programme and guide.	It should open on the ILC1-Programme page	Yes
		ILC1-Documents button	Goes to the ILC1-Documents page			
		ILC2-Programme button	ILC2-Programme page			
		ILC2-Documents button	ILC2-Documents page			
		Facebook icon button	Goes to the NIS Education Facebook page			
		Twitter icon button	Goes to the NIS Kazakhstan Twitter page	It goes to the NIS Kazakhstan Twitter page	None	Yes
		LinkedIn icon button	Goes to the NIS LinkedIn page			
	ILC1-Programme Page	ILC1-Programme button	Goes to the ILC1-Programme page			
		ILC1-Documents button	Goes to the ILC1-Documents page			
		ILC2-Programme button	ILC2-Programme page			
		ILC2-Documents button	ILC2-Documents page			
	ILC1-Documents Page	ILC1-Programme button	Goes to the ILC1-Programme page			
		ILC1-Documents button	Goes to the ILC1-Documents page			
		ILC2-Programme button	ILC2-Programme page			
		ILC2-Documents button	ILC2-Documents page			
	ILC2-Programme Page	ILC1-Programme button	Goes to the ILC1-Programme page			
		ILC1-Documents button	Goes to the ILC1-Documents page			
		ILC2-Programme button	ILC2-Programme page			
		ILC2-Documents button	ILC2-Documents page			
	ILC2-Documents Page	ILC1-Programme button	Goes to the ILC1-Programme page			
		ILC1-Documents button	Goes to the ILC1-Documents page			
		ILC2-Programme button	ILC2-Programme page			
		ILC2-Documents button	ILC2-Documents page			

Figure 21.09 Second test plan example

Summary

- There are three web development layers: content, presentation and behaviour.

- These three layers are linked together as follows: content layer with HTML, presentation layer with CSS and the behaviour layer with scripts, for example using JavaScript.

- Tables are widely used for the purposes of structuring the web elements on a web page because different browsers will open them differently if they are not placed in table grids when designed.

- When setting up the table grids to create the content layer, you have to consider the attributes within a table, such as width in terms of pixels and % values, borders (should they be visible or invisible? How thick should they be?), background colour, horizontal and vertical alignment, all in order to meet the needs of the user.

- HTML code can be used to create CSS files that will cascade a style throughout the whole website by simply changing one file.

- Relative file paths must be used when attaching stylesheets because a relative file path specifies a file location in relation to the location of the current document.

- Absolute file paths must be used when attaching an external stylesheet to a web page.

- The main aspects of testing a website are functionality, usability and effectiveness.

- Once you have created your website and finished testing it you can publish it by signing up to a website hosting facility, which should guide you through the process of publishing it. Many web hosting services include ftp services, which means transferring files from one host to another over the internet.

Glossary

®Bluetooth   A wireless technology for exchanging data over short distances.

3G   3G 'third generation'. A standard for access technology enabling connection to the internet using mobile.

4G   4G 'fourth generation'. A much faster standard for connection to the internet than 3G.

Abnormal data   Invalid data used when testing a system; this is data that should not be accepted.

Absolute file path   Shows the whole of the path to the file from the root directory.

Absolute reference   In a spreadsheet, an absolute cell will always point to the exact cell described if it has a dollar sign ($) in the row or column coordinate, or in both. For example, =A5/A2.

Actuator   Device used to carry out the physical requirements of a computer.

Analogue data   Data in its original, physical form. Typically output from a sensor.

Analogue-to-digital converter   Device that changes analogue.data to digital data so that it can be stored on a computer system.

Anchor   a type of hyperlink that will take you specifically to a different part of the web page you are on.

Animation (in presentation software)   An effect used on individual elements on one slide.

Animation using computers   Sequence of different pictures which project movement. CGI (computer-generated imagery) is the application of computer graphics to special effects in films and television programmes.

ANPR   Automatic number plate recognition.

Applets   A small program that is designed to be executed from inside another program, not from the operating system.

Applications program   a type of software that allows you to create many different types of documents, such as letters, invoices, presentations, web pages and so on.

Application software   Sets of instructions to the computer that allow the user to do something useful.

Apps.   Short for application.

Artificial intelligence   An expert system that can change the rules by which it works according to experience of what has happened in previous occurrences.

Aspect ratio   The proportional relationship between the width and height of an image, expressed in numbers as in 14:6.

Audio-conferencing   A telephone meeting between multiple callers in separate locations.

Automated objects   Objects that update automatically every time your page is updated, for example date and time, page numbering, and so on.

Automated teller machine (ATM)   Cash point machine used to withdraw cash or manage a bank account.

Backing store   a secondary storage device for data.

Backup file   A copy of a file of information which is stored somewhere away from the computer and can be used to restore the file if the data is lost.

Bandwidth   A measurement of how much data can be sent along a communications channel in a given time, usually per second.

Bar code   A series of black and white lines representing a code number, used in a variety of applications.

Bar code reader   Device used to read bar codes – can be fixed or hand-held.

Batch processing   The data to be processed is collected together in batches and is then run at some later more convenient time. The data must not be time sensitive.

Binary code   The representation of a number in the binary system, which comprises only the digits 0 and 1.

Binary number system   The base-2 numeral system which represents numeric values using only two symbols, 0 and 1.

Biometric data   records that are used to identify people by a physical attribute that doesn't change. An example of this would be a database of fingerprints of known criminals.

Biometrics   The technologies that measure and analyse human body characteristics for the purpose of authentication. Typically used are fingerprints, eye retinas and irises, voice and face patterns.

Blog   Short for 'web log' – a website with regular entries of commentary, descriptions of events, or other material such as graphics or video.

Boolean   Data that can only take two states and hence can be represented by 0 or 1.

Botnets   Describes a number of internet computers set up to forward transmissions (including spam or viruses) to other computers on the internet.

Browser   A software application for searching and retrieving information resources on the world wide web.

CAD/CAM   Software which allows for the design of an item and then for its automatic manufacture.

Cascading style sheets (CSS)   A style sheet language used for describing the presentation of a document written in a markup language such as HTML.

CD ROM   Compact disk read only memory – optical storage media.

CD ROM drive   Device used to read CD ROM, CD-R and CD-RW media.

Cells   the small rectangular sections on spreadsheets used to enter data such as text, numbers or symbols and to perform calculations using formulas and functions.

CGI   Computer-generated imagery software for creating cartoons.

Changeover   The planning of how the new system is to replace the old system. Should include training/ file construction and hardware and software implementation. Typical methods are direct/phased/parallel/ pilot.

Chart/graph   data taken from spreadsheets can be represented by creating a graph or chart, such as a bar, pie or line graph. You can use different colours, lines and patterns for more visual clarity.

Chip-and-pin   Microchip built into debit/credit cards to provide security when purchasing.

Cloud we sometimes refer to something being 'in the cloud'. It refers to software applications and data that are stored online and used through the internet. Cloud computing means that we don't have to think about where our data is, because with cloud computing it will be wherever we are.

Coded data Data that has been changed in some way so that entry and storage in the computer are simplified, e.g. M instead of male and F instead of female.

Columns made up of cells that are adjacent to each other and go from top to bottom or bottom to top vertically.

Comma separated values (CSV) A simple structured format for data; used to exchange data between programs of different types.

Command-line interface Interface between the computer and the user which requires the user to type commands at a prompt supplied by the operating system.

Compiler A computer program that transforms source code written in a programming language into another computer language.

Compressed hours When employees work the same number of hours but over fewer days.

Computer assisted learning (CAL) Using computers to teach students facts about a particular topic. Would also be used for testing and producing results.

Concept keyboard A computer input device. They have a flat surface and are used with a prepared paper or plastic overlay to indicate what will be input when the board is pressed.

Consistent style the style on all of a company's promotional materials, with the same colours and logo position on all documents, using the same images and there being a 'sameness' in the look of all their materials.

Contactless payment Devices, including smartphones that use radio-frequency identification (RFID) or near field communication (NFC) to make secure payments.

Content management system (CMS) A system used to manage the content of a website.

Contiguous data Data stored in a solid uninterrupted block; usually in spreadsheets or memory.

Contrast the difference between how dull or bright an image and how it appears in reality or as can be seen by the human eye.

Cookie A small amount of data sent from a website when the user is browsing that site; it is stored in a user's web browser.

Copyright the exclusive and assignable protection of intellectual property by law.

Corporate branding the promotion of a particular company or organisation through the advertising style it uses. The more people see the style the more they associate it with that particular company or organisation.

Crop cutting out a part of an image that is not required for the intended purpose.

CSS Cascading Style Sheets allow you to control the layout and look of your web pages easily and without the use of tables, as explained in the examples in Section 21.03. CSS also creates the look and formatting of a document written in HTML. In other words, CSS is a simple way to add style such as fonts, colours or spacing to web pages.

Custom written software Software that is specially commissioned to carry out a particular task.

Data Material that is stored in the computer.

Data capture form Form designed to collect data and then to allow easy entry of the data to the computer.

Data duplication repeating data by adding data that is already held in the database.

Data logging Collection of data for future processing.

Data manipulation The process of changing data to make it easier to read or to make it more organised.

Data packets When data is transmitted, it is broken down into small, similar blocks of data which are reassembled once they reach their destination.

Data table Table which lists and defines the purpose and type of each variable used in a computer program.

Database A collection of data. It normally has more than one file (table) which can interact with other files so that the need for duplication of data is reduced.

De-skilling The effect on workers who no longer need a particular skill because it is done by new technology.

Declarations when using CSS to create stylesheets, the CSS rules require you to define the properties and the values for each selector you wish to use by using declarations.

Dedicated Something that is designed to do only one thing. A dedicated microprocessor is used to control a washing machine, a job that it does very well, but it can't do anything else.

Design Producing the parameters of the solution to a problem. Done in the order: output/input/ storage/ processing. Design can be done on paper or directly to the computer.

Desktop publisher (DTP) Application that allows the import of text and graphics to the computer and can then be used to arrange it on a page.

Device driver A program to control a device that is attached to your computer, such as a printer.

Digital camera Camera which uses memory to store photographs instead of film. Can be used as an input device.

Digital certificate An electronic certificate similar to a passport to allow the exchange of information securely over the internet using the public key infrastructure (PKI).

Digital data Data in electronic form, suitable for storage on a computer.

Digital-to-analogue converter Device that changes digital data to analogue data so that it can be transmitted via telecommunications or used to drive an actuator.

Direct access File where the data is indexed making access to a specific piece of data very fast.

Direct data entry When input devices transfer data into a computerised information system. E.g. RFID, MICR.

DNS server Domain name system server. DNS turns the userfriendly version of a domain name, such as www.thisismysite.com, into numbers such as 60.22.161.42. This set of numbers is called an Internet Protocol (IP) address and is used to route you to your requested site. DNS works through a massive distributed database that stores domain names and their IP addresses so that it can find the domain name you want.

Double data entry a proofing technique that uses the COUNTIF spreadsheet function together with conditional formatting to highlight the differences in two lists of items.

Drone Unmanned aircraft or flying robot.

Duplex a feature of printers that enables automatic printing on both sides of a sheet of paper.

Electrical overload electrical circuit overloads are when too many electrical items are plugged into one socket causing more current to be put across an electrical wire or circuit than it can handle.

Electronic conferencing Use of electronic communications to allow people to hold meetings without actually meeting. These links could be voice only or more often would now include live video, then known as video conferencing.

Electronic funds transfer (EFT) Transfer of money from one bank account to another by computers.

Electronic funds transfer at point of sale (EFTPos) Money is transferred, by computer, from the customer's bank account to the shop's bank account to pay for goods.

Encryption Making data difficult to read by scrambling mathematically. Before reading, the contents must be decrypted.

Ethernet the most common standard defining the wiring and signalling in a LAN.

Expert system A computer system that stores facts about a particular topic and can search the facts for sensible information according to a set of rules.

External storage device data storage that is separate from the computer, it usually plugs into a USB port on the computer.

Extracting a pie chart sector when a section of a pie chart is extracted out of the pie chart in order to highlight or emphasise a point.

Extreme data Values at the extreme ends of normal data used in testing a system; this is data that should be accepted.

Facimile (fax) An exact copy of a document that is scanned transmitted as data by telecommunications links.

Field An area of a record in a file which stores a specific piece of data.

File A collection of data covering a particular topic.

File directory An index which allows fast access to the files.

File extension a way to identify the type of file.

File name a way to identify a file.

Firewall A stand-alone machine or an application through which external messages must be filtered. This stops viruses and unauthorised access to the system.

Flash memory cards Used in mobile phones (cell phones), MP3 players and digital cameras as storage.

Flat file Database held as a table and stored in a single file.

Flexible working A working schedule different from normal working patterns when working hours can be varied instead of fixed.

Foreign key A field in one table of a relational database that is linked to the primary key in another table.

Formatting The preparation of the surface of a storage medium so that it is ready to accept data. The process results in the previous data being erased.

Formatting text using the font type, font size, font colours, etc. that you prefer for your text.

Formula arithmetical or mathematical operations carried out on cells even when they do not form part of a range of cells; for example, you can add cells together where you cannot use the function SUM because the cells being added up are not adjacent to each other.

Function arithmetical or mathematical operations that are carried out on groups of cells, ranges, columns or rows and are very specific, for example AVERAGE or SUM.

Geographic information systems (GIS) For capturing, storing, checking and displaying data related to the surface of the Earth as a map.

Graphical user interface (GUI) Uses windows (W) to create a border to the information, icons (I) to represent files, menus (M) to allow user to make choices and a pointer (P) to select choices. Hence, sometimes called a WIMP.

Graphics Pictorial representation and manipulation of data.

Graphics tablet Device to input designs as they are being drawn by hand; also used in editing graphics/photographs.

Gridlines the visible onscreen lines between cells in a table.

Gutter margin A typographical term meaning an addition to the margins on the inside of two facing pages in a book. It compensates for the part of the paper made unusable by the binding process.

Hacking Unauthorised access to computer systems.

Handshake When the computer wants to communicate with a device it is important that rules are established for the communication. This must be done before communicating and is known as handshaking.

Hanging paragraph indentation of the second and subsequent lines of a paragraph that is different from the first indentation of the paragraph.

Hard disk Magnetic storage device.

Hardware The physical parts of a computer system.

HCI Human computer interface.

House style Sometimes called 'branding', it is a set of rules to keep all written communications of an organisation in the same format throughout that organisation.

Horizontal flip if an image faces the left-hand side before it has been flipped, it will face the right-hand side after it has been flipped.

HTML Hypertext markup language.

HTTP Hypertext transfer protocol.

Hub Central node of a network or sub-network to which each computer is connected. Data transmitted by one computer is passed to all ports of the hub.

Hyperlink A link from a hypertext document that takes you to another location when you click on a highlighted word or an image.

HyperText Transfer Protocol (HTTP) Used by the World Wide Web to define how a web page is formatted and transferred.

HyperText Transfer Protocol secure variant (HTTPS) HTTP using a secure encrypted link.

Icon Pictorial representation of a specific file, directory, window, option, or program.

Indented paragraph a paragraph that begins its first line of text a few spaces away from the left-hand margin.

In-plane switching (Ips) A screen technology allowing greater viewing angles and colour reproduction.

Inference engine A processing program which is the part of an expert system that derives conclusions from facts in the knowledge base of the expert system.

Information assets valuable data that you wouldn't want to be stolen or corrupted.

Input device transfers data into a computer so that it can be processed.

Intellectual property the ideas and skills of other people that belong to them.

Integration of software Pieces of software that can communicate with one another and share data without changing its form.

Interface The hardware and software that create the connection between the user and the computer or the software being used.

Internet A public, worldwide WAN whose contents are not controlled.

Internet café Where customers can pay to use computer systems and usually coffee is available.

Internet connection sharing ICS is a way of connecting more than one computer in a LAN to the internet using only one connection and IP address.

Internet Service Provider (ISP) ISPs allow a connection to the internet (usually with a price attached to different levels of service).

Intranet A privately operated WAN, like the Internet, except that the data content is controlled and access to it is also controlled.

ISBN International Standard Book Number, which consists of 13 digits. ISBNs include a check digit calculated using a mathematical formula to validate the number.

Item Item of data stored in a field.

Iteration Process of repeating a sequence of steps.

Joystick An input device used in games, simulations and control applications to move an object.

Key (field) The field that is used to identify the record within the file.

The item within the key field must be unique.

Keyboard Input device used to input characters.

Landscape the wider, shorter orientation of a page compared to the narrower, taller version of a page with a portrait orientation.

Laptop Portable computer, able to operate from internal battery power, also known as a notebook.

Layout the way objects are arranged in the space provided on the page of a document.

Legend a key at the side of a chart or graph that indicates what the symbols or colours and patterns represent in the chart or graph.

Linker A computer program to combine files generated by a compiler into single executable file, or another object file.

Local area network (LAN) Network that is physically close together. The machines are close enough to be hard wired.

Lossless A form of file compression that allows all original data to be recovered when the file is uncompressed.

Lossy Lossy compression reduces a file by permanently eliminating some information so when the file is uncompressed, not all of the original information is still there (although you may not be able to notice it).

Machine code Set of programming instructions to match the electronic design of a particular computer. An example of a low-level language.

Magnetic disk Storage medium that can store large amounts of data in a way that allows direct access to the data.

Magnetic ink Special ink used to print characters so that they are in both computer- and human-readable form.

Magnetic stripes Magnetic material which stores information about the holder, typically on the back of a credit card/debit card.

Magnetic tape Storage medium which is now a bit out of date but is still used to keep backup files on some systems.

Mail merge A time-saving method of sending the same letter to many people with the automatic addition

of individual names and addresses from a database to each letter.

Mainframe computer Large-scale computer typically used in a large organisation to be the processing power for all the terminals in a multi-user system.

Master slide the main slide where you can create the design you want to use across all the other slides in a presentation.

Memory sticks Pen drives used to store files (up to many gigabytes) or transport files from one computer to another.

Microcomputer Term no longer in use to describe a PC – personal computer.

Microphone Device used for input of sound to a computer system.

Microprocessor A dedicated device that incorporates all the parts of a computer processor on a single chip (also known as CPU – central processing unit).

Minicomputer A larger computer than a PC but smaller than a mainframe. Called a mini because when they were invented they were the smallest computer. Typically used to control the checkouts in a supermarket.

Mirror when you look in the mirror your actual left-hand side becomes your right-hand side in the mirror image.

Modem An abbreviation of 'modulator/demodulator' – hardware device to connect a computer to the telephone network; needed because the computer produces digital signals and the telephone network uses analogue.

Module Smaller components after a problem has been broken down by the use of top-down design.

Monitor Device that shows computer output in picture form. TFT monitors may be used for a PC system or be an integral part of a laptop.

Motherboard A motherboard contains a computer's basic circuitry and sockets to plug in components.

Mouse Input device used to control a pointer in a graphical user interface.

Multi-access (operating system) Operating system which allows the resources of a computer to be used by a number of users at terminals. The processing is centralised.

Multi-tasking (operating system) Operating system which can do a number of different things simultaneously. Microsoft Windows is a typical multi-tasking OS.

Multimedia Combination of more than one of: text, graphics, photographs, sound, animation, video.

Multimedia package Set of software which uses many different media to convey or manipulate information.

Multimedia projector Output device used for presentations.

Musical instrument digital interface (MIDI) A communications link between an electronic instrument and a computer. Each device must have midi hardware.

Named cell or range each cell in a spreadsheet has a name by default, for example E7 is the cell in column 'E' and in row '7'.

Nested formula/function you can 'nest' a formula or function inside another formula or function in one cell of a spreadsheet.

Netbook Small notebook, often used simply to send emails or access the internet.

Network Linked set of computer systems, allowing the sharing of resources.

Network operating system Operating system which allows a number of machines to be in communication with each other and to share data and resources.

Non-contiguous data Data that is not stored in a solid uninterrupted block; usually in spreadsheets or memory.

Notebook Portable computer, able to operate from internal battery power, also known as a laptop.

Objectives of a solution List of things that a solution should do, that has been agreed between the analyst and the user and will be used during the testing of the solution to decide whether or not the solution works.

OCR Optical character recognition.

Off-line This is a way of using the computer where the user or device is not directly connected to the processor.

Off-the-shelf software Ready-for-use software.

OMR Optical mark reader.

On-line Using the computer where the user or the device is directly connected up to the processor.

Online processing Processing which allows the user to interact directly with the main computer.

Operating system Set of software which controls the hardware and applications of the computer and provides an interface with the outside world.

Optical disk Storage device that stores large amounts of data in a way that can be accessed directly. The data is stored and read using lasers, rather than magnetically.

Optical mark form Form used to record optical marks which are then read by OMR.

Page orientation the way you position your page having the narrower width across the top of the page is called 'portrait' orientation; having the wider width across the top of the page is called 'landscape' orientation.

Pages these are the same as spreadsheet sheets.

Pagination the numbering of pages in a document.

Part-time working working fewer hours per week than people usually do.

Password Secret code that gives the user access to the computer, file or folder.

Pharming A cyber attack that redirects a website's traffic to another, fake site.

Phishing Phishing attempts to acquire sensitive information for malicious reasons whilst masquerading as a trustworthy entity in an email or other electronic communication.

Physical data Data that exists in the physical world like length, area, weight. This data is analogue and is not in the right form for a digital computer.

Pixel The smallest part of a computer graphic image. A large number of pixels are put together to form the whole image. The pixel is so small that it cannot be seen.

Placeholders 'frames' or 'empty boxes' to insert items of text, images, sound, video and so on.

Plotter Device used to produce hard copy output of line drawings from a computer.

Point of sale (POS) The cash register/till in the shop where customers pay for their purchases.

Pointer device Used for input to the computer by pointing at a particular output on the screen. Typically the pointer is a mouse.

Presentation software Software that allows a presentation to be produced using linked screens (or frames) that can be followed in an order. Allows use of animation and sound as well as standard outputs.

Preview a tool that allows you to see what your document will look like before you either print it out, save it or send it somewhere else

Primary key In a relational database it is a key field that is unique for each record. It is a unique identifier, such as a passport number. A relational database must always have one primary key.

Printer Device used to produce hard-copy output from a computer.

Privacy of data Some data is confidential and methods need to be used to ensure that the wrong people do not see it. Methods used include passwords and encryption.

Privacy settings Settings in your software to control who is allowed who is authorised to view your postings.

Private key Used in cryptography, it is an encryption/decryption key known only to the people exchanging. It is shared by the communicators so that each could encrypt and decrypt messages.

Process control (operating system) An operating system which allows a processor to control the use of sensors and actuators.

Processor called CPU, short for central processing unit.

Proofing Reading a copy of a publication to find and correct errors in text or art.

Protocol Guidelines or procedures to follow for the format of data transmitted between two devices, for example: FTP, HTTP.

Prototyping Producing a partial solution to a problem so that that area of the problem can be tested without reference to the rest of the solution.

Proxy server Controls the access of authorised users to data on a different network and prevents external users gaining control of the system.

Pseudo-code A method of describing the design of a system in the user's own language. Looks like programming code but cannot be run or compiled.

Public key In cryptography it is a value provided as an encryption key, when, if combined with a private key can be used to encrypt messages and digital signatures.

Radio-Frequency Identification (RFID) A RFID reader will typically consist of a small chip and an antenna.

Random access memory (RAM) That part of the computer's memory that is used to store programs and files that are being used by the computer at that time. The contents of RAM are lost when the power is turned off.

Range a group of cells in a spreadsheet that consist of more than one row and column and where the cells are all adjacent to each other.

Re-skilling When a worker with a particular skill that is no longer needed learns and uses a different skill.

Read only memory (ROM) That part of the computer's memory that is not erased when the power is turned off. Contains code used when the computer is turned on.

Real-time processing Operating system that processes an input and produces output immediately.

Record Part of a file which stores data about a particular entity. All records in the file store the same type of data.

Reflect producing a mirror image of the original image.

Relational table Complex database structure stored in more than one table, which are linked together (by foreign keys).

Relative file path A path specifies a unique location in a file system. A relative path starts from a given working directory, not from the root directory. Avoiding the need to provide the full absolute path.

Relative reference When a relative reference is replicated to other rows or columns, the cell reference will automatically update itself accordingly, unlike the absolute cell reference which always points to an exact cell.

Repetitive strain injury (RSI) Injury caused by the constant use of certain muscles, mainly fingers or joints in the arms, as a result of typing for long periods of time.

Requirement specification List of the necessary hardware and software to put a solution into practice and a list of the wishes of the proposed user of the solution.

Resize changing the width and/or height of an image to fit its intended purpose.

Resolution Measurement of the clarity of an image based on the number of pixels used to create the image.

Robotics Study, design and use of robots for use in automated industrial processes.

Rotate turning an image around from its original position.

Router Complex hub which contains the network addresses of the attached computers and can forward data to the correct location, often used where a LAN connects to a WAN.

Routkits A malicious program to allow an unauthorised user to control a computer system undetected.

Rows made up of cells that are adjacent to each other and go from left to right or right to left horizontally.

Sans-serif font font types that do not have any serifs or 'tails' at the ends of characters.

Scales the units of measurement used on the axes of a chart or graph.

Scanner Device that reads an image on paper into the computer.

Script a set of instructions for a computer.

Scripting language a fairly simple programming language, such as JavaScript, used to create a script.

Search engine A computer program that searches for and identifies items in a database that correspond to keywords entered by the user for finding particular sites on the world wide web.

Secondary storage device sometimes called external memory, this is non-volatile memory (does not lose stored data when the computer is switched off).

Secure socket layer (SSL) Layer that allows an encrypted connection between your web server and the web browser of visitors to it enabling private information to be transmitted without problems such as eavesdropping, data tampering or message forgery.

Security of data Data that is being stored is necessary otherwise it would not be stored. The security of the data is how it is looked after to make sure that it is not destroyed, typically by making backups of the data.

Security settings Settings you can change to protect your computer from harm.

Selectors when using CSS to create stylesheets, the CSS rules require you to specify the selectors (HTML elements) to which you wish the styles to apply before defining the declarations. The declarations are applied to the selectors.

Sensors Input devices that capture physical data.

Sequential file File where the data is stored in a logical order, e.g. Alphabetic.

Serial file File where the data is stored in the order in which it was received.

Sheets in spreadsheets, the sheets are like the different pages of a book. You can rename each sheet to whatever you prefer and add as many sheets as you need to.

Slogan a phrase or a string of words (not necessarily a sentence) that are representative of a company or organisation.

Smartcard A plastic card such as a credit or debit card with a built-in microprocessor that are used to carry out financial transactions.

Smartphone A mobile phone that can perform many of the functions that a computer performs.

Smishing A security attack where a user is tricked into downloading a virus or malware onto a cellular phone or mobile device.

Social networking People use a website to talk, share ideas and images and to make new friends.

Software A general term for instructions to a computer to perform a variety of tasks.

Solid-state media storage media with no moving parts, based on electronic circuits and using flash memory.

Solid-state memory Similar to RAM only the data is persistent (non-volatile). Used as a replacement for hard disks.

Sound card this enables the computer to send audio information to an audio device, such speakers or headphones.

Spam When multiple copies of the same message are sent over the internet to try to force the message on people who would not otherwise choose to receive it.

Speakers Electro-mechanical device producing sound output from electricity input.

Spreadsheet Application designed to handle numbers and calculations in a grid formation. Is also used for predicting future trends according to rules that govern the numerical data input.

Spyware A program that can secretly record what you do on computer. It usually tries to capture passwords, banking and credit card details for fraudulent purposes.

Stepwise refinement The breaking down of a large problem into smaller sub-problems (see top-down design).

Storage media something onto which data is written for safe keeping, like a tape or a disk.

Supercomputer Most powerful type of computer. The extremely fast processing speeds make it useful for applications requiring large amounts of calculation like weather forecasting.

Switch Similar to hub but only sends data to devices that are addressed, rather than all devices. Used to cut down traffic on complicated networks.

Syntax every language has a set of rules that govern the ways their words combine to form phrases, clauses and sentences. Similarly, in computer programming languages, syntax defines the combinations of symbols that are considered to be a correctly structured document or fragment in that language.

System flowchart Diagrammatic representation of the way the hardware and software operate in the system and the way that the files are stored.

Systems analysis Standardised set of steps that can be used to analyse a problem and design and implement a solution to the problem.

Systems analyst Person responsible for carrying out the stages of systems analysis on a project.

Systems life cycle the different stages in the process of producing a new IT system.

Systems software Software that operates the computer hardware and provides a platform for running application software.

Tablet A small, wireless, portable, personal computer which has a touch screen interface.

Tabs small buttons typically placed at the bottom of a spreadsheet and serve to navigate between the different sheets.

Tabulation refers to how far to the left or right text is indented.

Technical documentation Set of detailed descriptions about how the solution was arrived at and how it works. Intended for someone who needs to maintain the system.

Tele-conferencing A conference between two or more people in separate locations using computer networks to transmit audio and video data.

Template a frame upon which to build a document by simply copying the same style or filling in your own relevant information in the spaces provided

Test plan Set of test instructions designed to test specific parts of the solution.

Test strategy Decision made by the systems analyst about who/where/ when and how the eventual solution is to be tested.

Tethering Using a mobile device that's connected to the internet as a modem for another device, such as a laptop or a WiFi-only tablet.

Thermistor Semiconductor device that is used to read temperature (its resistance varies with temperature).

Time dependent Data which must be used immediately otherwise it becomes useless is said to be time dependent.

Top-down design The breaking down of a large problem into smaller sub-problems (see stepwise refinement).

Touch screen Screen that allows input as well as output. Input is accomplished by pointing at an area of the screen.

Touchpad Used in laptops as an alternative to a mouse as an input device.

Trackerball An input device used to control pointers; may be used in older laptops. Very similar to a mouse.

Transitions (in presentation software) An effect used to make a slide appear or disappear, such as fade or blinds.

Trilateration A technique to find the user's position, speed, and elevation by constantly receiving and analysing radio signals from GPS satellites.

Universal resource locator (URL) Unique reference for each resource on the internet.

URL Uniform Resource Locator is another term for the name of a website.

User documentation Detailed descriptions of how to use the system.

Utilities A small program that provides an addition to the capabilities provided by the operating system such as: antivirus, disk repair, file management, etc.

Validation Checking data input to a system to ensure that it follows certain rules and is sensible.

Variable Symbolic name, often in programming code, that can take different values.

Verification Checking of data input to ensure that is correct.

Vertical flip if an image is upright in the original image, after it has been vertically flipped, it will appear upside down.

Video card this is an internal circuit board for displaying images from a computer onto a screen.

Video conferencing Electronic meeting where all physically separated participants can be seen as well as heard.

Virus Computer code that is maliciously placed on a computer system with the aim of damaging the system.

Virus protection Software which identifies viruses and deals with them by not allowing access or erasing them.

Vishing A fraudulent phone call from someone, for example, posing as a bank representative who tries to persuade victims to reveal financial information.

Visual verification a proofing technique whereby you visually check a document for accuracy and correctness.

VOIP Voice Over Internet Protocol.

Watermark A very faint design visible behind the main text.

Web 2.0 Use of the internet that aims to enhance communications, secure information sharing and other forms of collaboration. Web 2.0 concepts have led to the development of social-networking sites, file-sharing sites, wikis and blogs.

Website authoring Application that enables the user to create a website.

Wide area network (WAN) Machines on the network are so far apart that they cannot be hard-wired. Interconnected by satellite, radio or fibre-optic cable.

Widow / orphan A term used for the lines at the beginning or end of a paragraph, which are split between the top or bottom of a page or column, separated from the rest of the paragraph.

WiFi Wireless technology to connect devices with each other without the use of cables or wires.

WIKI Web page(s) designed so anyone who accesses it can contribute or modify the content.

Wild card search A search for multiple words using wildcard characters such as an asterisk (*) wildcard character to search for a string of characters e.g. *chair, would find, wheelchair, armchair, easychair, or any words ending in chair.

WLAN a Wireless Local Area Network covers short distances, using radio or infrared signals.

Word processor Application dedicated to the production of text-based documents.

World Wide Web an information system that operates over the internet. It lets documents connect to other documents using hyperlinks, so that the user can search for information by moving from one document to another.

Worms A program that self-replicates; it penetrates an operating system with the intent of spreading malicious code.

XML Extensible markup language designed to store and transport data to be both human- and machine-readable.

Index

abnormal data 97, 262
absolute file paths 293
absolute references 256, 257
actuators 31
AI (artificial intelligence) 10, 12, 85
analogue data 71, 72
analogue to digital converter 73
anchors 285–287
animation 67, 68, 242, 243, 249–250
ANPR (automatic number plate recognition) 87
anti-spyware software 51
applets 6
applications programs 163
applications software 4, 280
area charts/graphs 198
arrows 249
artificial intelligence (AI) 10, 12, 85
aspect ratio 152–154
ATMs (Automated Teller Machines) 81
audience appreciation 122–128
audio-conferences 52
automated objects 172–173
automatic number plate recognition (ANPR) 87

backing stores 7
banking 80–81, 119
bar charts/graphs 195, 198
bar code readers 26, 28, 83, 85
batch processing 81
behaviour layers 279, 280
binary number system 3–4
biometric data 12, 114
blogs 135
blu-ray devices 36, 37–38, 39
bluetooth 45, 46
booking systems 79–80
Boolean operators 221, 222
botnets 111
bridges 44
browsers 47, 48, 67, 135, 279
bulleted lists 208, 209
buzzers 31

CAD (computer aided design) 30, 83
CAL (computer assisted learning) 67
calculated fields 229–233
call out boxes 249
capacitive touch screens 20
cascading style sheets 280, 288–293
case, consistency of 191
CAT (computer-assisted translation) 11
CD ROMs 37
CD Rs 37
CD RWs 37
CDs (compact disks) 36, 37, 39
cells 210–215, 253
central processing units (CPUs) 3, 6

CGI (computer-generated imagery software) 68
changeover 98, 99–100
character spacing 191
charts 170, 194–203, 248, 252
chip and PIN readers 27, 28
CLIs (command line interfaces) 5, 8
cloud computing 119
CMS (content management systems) 279, 280, 293–294
colour, changing in image 155–157
colour schemes, consistency of 242, 243
column breaks 206
column charts/graphs 197
columns 205–206, 254
comma separated values (CSVs) 141, 224
command line interfaces (CLIs) 5, 8
communication
    email 51, 118, 131–133
    internet 133–137
    range of applications 65–69
compact disks (CDs) 36, 37, 39
compilers 5
compressed hours 60
compressing files 143–144
computer aided design (CAD) 30, 83
computer assisted learning (CAL) 67
computer-assisted translation (CAT) 11
computer-generated imagery software (CGI) 68
computer modelling applications 77–78
computers
    physical safety of 106
    types 9–10
concept keyboards 18
conditional formatting 276–277
consistent styles 176, 178–179, 242
contactless card payments 27
content layers 279, 280
content management systems (CMS) 279, 280, 293–294
contiguous data 196–197
contrast 157
control applications 31, 74–77
control devices 31
cookies 87, 88, 110
copyright 124, 125
corporate branding 176
CPUs (central processing units) 3, 6
cropping images 148, 153
CRT monitors 28
CSS (cascading style sheets) 280, 288–293
CSVs (comma separated values) 141, 224

data
    duplication 220
    exporting 238–239
    importing from an existing file 225
    manipulation 229–235

presentation of 235–239
    search for subsets 234–235
    sorting 233–234
    types 221–222
data analysis 251–277
data capture forms 69, 95
data entry forms 226–229
data/file structure 96
data handling 69–71
data models
    creating 252–260
    manipulating 264–269
    presenting data 269–277
    testing 261–263
data packets 42, 43
data protection legislation 51
data security 111–121
database structures 219–229
DDE (direct data entry) 17, 24–28
declarations 289, 292
designs, systems 94–96
deskilling 57, 58
desktop computers 2, 9, 10, 49
desktop publishing packages (DTPs) 6, 65, 66, 178
development and testing 96–98
device drivers 4–5
digital cameras 23
digital certificates 114, 115, 116
digital versatile disks (DVDs) 36, 37, 39
direct access to data 35
direct data entry (DDE) 17, 24–28
display screens 28–29
DNS servers 117
documents 160–174, 204–217
domestic devices 60–61
dot matrix printers 30
double data entry 192
driverless cars 10–11
drives 4, 34, 35, 36, 38, 39
drones 13–14
drum plotters 30–31
DTPs (desktop publishing packages) 6, 65, 66, 178
duplex printing 66
duplication of data 220
DVD RAMs 37, 39
DVD ROMs 37, 39
DVD Rs 37, 39
DVD RWs 37, 39
DVDs (digital versatile disks) 36, 37, 39

e-safety 108–111
EFTPOS terminals 85
electrical overload 106–107
electronic funds transfer (EFT) 80, 81, 85
email communication 51, 118, 131–133
employment, effects of IT 56–60
encryption 116

environmental issues 125–126
ethernet 43
ethical issues 126–127, 128
evaluation of systems 102–103
expert systems 84–85
exporting data 238–239
extensible markup language (XML) 142
external storage devices 7
external styling 288
extreme data 97, 262

facsimile communication 51
factual errors 191
fields 220, 224
file extensions 140
file management 139–144
file names 140
file transfer protocol (ftp) 134, 293
firewalls 120
fixed hard disks 34, 39
flash memory cards 38, 39
flat-file databases 219
flatbed plotters 30
flexible working 60
font styles 179
footers 172–173, 236
foreign keys 221, 223, 225
formatting
    numerical data 237–238, 274–277
    text 163, 205–209
formulas, spreadsheets 253
4G 69
ftp (file transfer protocol) 134, 293
functions, spreadsheets 253, 258–260

GIS (geographic information systems) 89
grammar, checking 188
graphical user interfaces (GUIs) 5, 8
graphics tablets 21
graphs 194–203, 252
GUIs (graphical user interfaces) 5, 8
gutter margins 205

hacking 112–113
hanging indentation 208
hanging paragraphs 207
hard copy material 22–23
hard disk drives 4
hardware, components 2–4
HCI (human-computer interface) 8
HD DVDs 39
headers 172–173, 236
headphones 31
health problems, and IT equipment 61
heaters 31
hiding text 270, 271
holographic imaging 11
home 60–61
house style 68, 124, 176
HTML (HyperText Markup Language) 279,
    280, 281
HTTP (HyperText Transfer Protocol) 134

HTTPS (HyperText Transfer Protocol secure
    variant) 134
hubs 43
human-computer interface (HCI) 8
hyperlinks 134, 285, 286
HyperText Markup Language (HTML) 279,
    280, 281
HyperText Transfer Protocol (HTTP) 134
HyperText Transfer Protocol secure variant
    (HTTPS) 134

icons 8
images 146–159, 247
implementation, systems 98–100
in-line styling 288
indented paragraphs 207
inference engines 82
information assets 112
inkjet printers 29
input designs 95
input devices 6, 17–28
intellectual property 124
interfaces 172, 173
internal styling 288
internet 48, 126–127, 133–137
internet cafés 50
internet service providers (ISPs) 45, 46, 134
intranet 48–49, 134
IPS monitors 29
ISBNs (International Standard Book
    Numbers) 70, 71, 84
ISPs (internet service providers) 45, 46, 134
iteration 92

job sharing 60
joysticks 19

key fields 96
keyboards 17

lamps 31
LAN (Local Area Network) 42, 43, 45, 60
landscape orientation 161
laptop computers 2, 9, 10, 49
laser printers 29
layout of documents 160–174
LCD monitors 29
legal appreciation 124–125
legends 199
libraries 83–84
life cycles 91–104
light sensors 22
lights 31
line graphs 198
line spacing 180, 192, 206–207
lines 249
linkers 5
Local Area Network (LAN) 42, 43, 45, 60
lossless compression 143
lossy compression 143–144

magnetic disks 35
magnetic ink character recognition (MICR)
    25–26, 28, 86

magnetic storage media 34, 35–36, 39
magnetic stripe readers 26–27, 28, 39
magnetic tape drives 35, 39
mail merge 162–163, 215–216, 239
malware 111, 118
manual input devices 17
manufacturing industries 78
margins, pages 205
master slides 177–179, 241–242
measurement applications 71–74
medicine 82–83
memory sticks 38, 39
MICR (magnetic ink character recognition)
    25–26, 28, 86
microphones 24
microprocessors 6, 60–61
MIDI keyboards 24
mobile phones 49, 68–69
modelling applications 77–78
modems 43, 44
modules 5, 96, 97
monitoring systems 87–88
monitors 28–29
motherboards 2
motors 31
mouse/mice 18
multimedia presentations 67–68
multimedia projectors 29
music scores 68

named cells/range 253
nested functions 257–258
networks 41–53
newsletters 65–66
non-contiguous data 196
normal data 262
numbered lists 208, 209
numbers, entering 166–167, 168, 169
numeric keypads 18
numerical data, formatting 237–238,
    274–277

OCR (optical character recognition) 23,
    24–25, 28, 86
OMR (optical mark reading) 23, 25, 28, 86
operating systems 8
optical storage media 34, 36–38
orphans 183, 206
output designs 94
output devices 6, 28–31

page breaks 206
page layout 205
page orientation 161, 205
pagination 207
paragraph marks 180
paragraph styles 181, 207–208
part-time working 60
passive infrared (PIR) sensors 77
passwords 113–114
pen drives 38, 39
personal computers 10

personal data 108–109
pharming 116, 117
phishing 116, 117
pie charts 198, 202
PIR (passive infrared) sensors 77
pixels 23
placeholders 222
placing images 151
plain text files (txt) 225
plotters 30
point of sale (POS) terminals 81, 85
policing the internet 126–127
portable hard disks 35, 39
portrait orientation 161
POS (point of sale) terminals 81, 85
power supplies 4
presentation layers 279, 280
presentations 240–250
pressure sensors 22
preview tool 162
primary keys 220, 223, 225
printing files 142–143
privacy of data 112, 119
privacy settings 109, 110
private keys 114
processors 3, 6–7
proofing 185–193
protocols 47
prototypes 77, 94, 95
public keys 114
publicity 66–67

quantum cryptography 12–13
Quick Parts tool 163

radio frequency identification (RFID)
   readers 26, 86
RAM (random access memory) 6
range, spreadsheets 253
read-only memory (ROM) 7
read/write heads 34
real-time processes 79, 81, 85, 87
recognition systems 86–87
records 220
reflecting images 155
relational databases 219, 220–221
relative file paths 287
relative references 256
remote controls 24
removable hard disks 35
repetitive strain injury (RSI) 56, 61
Replace tool 187–188
reports 236–237
requirements specification 93–94
resistive touch screens 20
resizing images 147, 151–152
reskilling 56
resolution 157
retail industry 85–86
RFID readers 26, 86
rich text files (rtf) 225
robotics 12, 78

ROM (read-only memory) 7
rotating images 154–155
routers 42, 43
rows, spreadsheets 256
RSI (repetitive strain injury) 56, 61
rtf (rich text files) 225

safety 105–121
satellite systems 88–89
scales 199
scanners 22–23
scatter charts/graphs 198
school management systems 78–79
scripting language 279
scripts 279
search engines 108, 135
secondary storage devices 7
section breaks 206
secure sockets layers (SSLs) 115–116
security
   computer networks 50–51
   data 111–121
   emails 132–133
selectors 289, 292
sensors 21–22
sequential storage 36
serial storage 36
sheets, spreadsheets 260
signature lines 165
simple mail transfer protocol (SMTP) 134
slogans 178
smart cards 27
smartphones 9, 10, 49
smishing 117
SMTP (simple mail transfer protocol) 134
social networking sites 109–111, 136
software, components 4–6
software copyright 125
solid state storage 34, 38
sorting data 233–234
sound 4, 247–248
spacing 191, 192
spam mail 133
speakers 31
spell check software 186–187
spreadsheets 168–169, 172, 248
spyware 118
SSLs (secure sockets layers) 115–116
storage devices 7, 34–39
styles, corporate 175–184
sustainability 125–126
switches 44
symbols, presentation slides 248
systems analysts 92
systems life cycles 91–104
systems software 4
sytems implementation 98–100

tables 171, 209–215, 281–283
tablet computers 9, 10, 49
tabs 262
tabulation 207

technical documentation 100–101
teleconferencing 89
temperature sensors 21–22
templates 162
test plans 97, 98, 261, 263, 294–296
test strategies 97
tethering 50
text boxes 163
text encoding 144
text enhancement 246–247
text, entering 163–166, 167–168, 171
text messages 69
text wrapping 270, 271
TFT monitors 28–29
third party proofreading 190
3D imaging 11
3D printers 13, 83
3G 69
touch screens 19–20
touchpads 18–19
trackerballs 19
tracking systems 87–88
transitions, consistency of 242, 243, 249
transposition techniques 190
trilateration 88
txt (plain text files) 225

URLs (uniform resource locators) 47, 134,
   279
user documentation 100, 101–102
user interfaces 8
utilities 5

validation techniques 188–190, 192
verification 192
video cameras 23
video cards 4
video conferences 23, 52, 58
virtual reality 14
viruses 118–119
vishing 117
vision enhancement 11
visual verification 192
VOIP (Voice Over Internet Protocol) 58, 69

WAN (Wide Area Network) 42, 43
waterfall models 92–103
watermarks 165
web browsers 47, 48, 67, 135, 279
web-conferences 52
webcams 23
websites 67, 279–296
Wide Area Network (WAN) 42, 43
widows and orphans 183, 206
WiFi 43, 45–46, 50
wildcard searches 234, 268
WLAN (Wireless Local Area Network) 42, 44
WordArt tool 165
World Wide Web 134
worms 118

XML (extensible markup language) 142

Acknowledgements

The authors and publishers acknowledge the following sources of copyright material and are grateful for the permissions granted. While every effort has been made, it has not always been possible to identify the sources of all the material used, or to trace all copyright holders. If any omissions are brought to our notice, we will be happy to include the appropriate acknowledgements on reprinting.

Thanks to the following for permission to reproduce images:

Chapter 1 Robert Lucian Crusitu/Shutterstock; Fig 1.01 Luisa Leal Photography/Shutterstock; Figure 1.02 Niels Pulson DK/Alamy; Figure 1.03 Peter Kotoff/Shutterstock; Figure 1.04 Dennis Golov/Alamy; Figure 1.06 Oleksiy Maksymenko Photography/Alamy; Figure 1.07a ifong/Shutterstock; Figure 1.07b MacFormat Magazine/Getty Images; Figure 1.08 Bloomberg/Getty Images; Figure 10.09 ImageBROKER/Alamy; Figure 1.12 Zonan Milch/Getty Images; Figure 1.13 (l) BSIP SA/Alamy; Figure 1.13 (r) Zonan Milch/Getty Images; Figure 1.13 (b) Bloomberg/Getty Images; Figure 1.14 (l) Arterra Picture Library/Alamy; Figure 1.14 (r)funkyfrog tock/Shutterstock; Chapter 2 Rawpixel.com/Shutterstock; Figure 2.02 ojovago/Alamy; Figure 2.03 lumen-digital/Shutterstock; Figure 2.04 Ulrich Doering/Alamy; Figure 2.05 aydinmutlu/Getty Images; Figure 2.07 36clicks/Shutterstock; Figure 2.08 Zoonar GmbH/Alamy; Figure 2.10 Jim DeLillo/Getty Images; Figure 2.11 Dragomer Maria/Shutterstock; Figure 2.12 Palis Michalis/Shutterstock; Figure 2.13 Brian A Jackson/Shutterstock; Figure 2.14 (tl) Zoonbar GmbH/Alamy; Figure 2.14 (bl) macbrianmun/Getty Images; Figure 2.14 (tr) James Leynse/Corbis/ Figure 2.14 (tc) burner/Shutterstock; Figure 2.14 (br) Moreno Soppelsa/Shutterstock; Figure 2.15 (l) Moreno Soppelsa/Shutterstock; Figure 2.15 (r) James Davies; Chapter 3 Delpixel/Shutterstock; Figure 3.01 Gregory Gerber/Shutterstock; Figure 3.02 BeGood/Shutterstock; Figure 3.03 Trial/Shutterstock Figure 3.05 (l) Ragnor Schmuk/Getty Images; Figure 3.05 (c) Kevin Wheal/Alamy; Figure 3.05 (r) Shaun Finch - Coyote-Photography.co.uk/Alamy; Figure 3.06 (l) ffolas/Shutterstock; Figure 3.06 (r) Coprid/Shutterstock; Chapter 4 silkwayrain/Getty Images; Figure 4.05 laurentiu iordache/Alamy; Figure 4.08 Look die Bildgentur der Fotografen GmbH/Alamy; Figure 4.09 Rocketclips,Inc/Shutterstock; Chapter 5 Monty Rakusen/Getty Images; Figure 5.01 (l) Bert Hardy/Getty Images; Figure 5.01 (r) Pressmaster/Shutterstock; Figure 5.02 (a) Hoda Bogdan/Fotolia; Figure 5.02 (b) Monty Rakusen/Getty Images; Figure 5.03 Culture RM/Alamy; Figure 5.04 Tom Merton/Getty Images; Figure 5.05 JazzIRT/Getty Images; Figure 5.06 ClassicStock/Alamy Stock Photo; Figure 5.07 (l) StephenBarnesBowline Images/Alamy; Figure 5.07 (r) Ulrich Baumgarten/Getty Images; Figure 5.07 (c) endopack/Getty Images; Chapter 6 RGB Ventures SuperStock/Alamy; Figure 6.04 DvdArts/Getty Images; Figure 6.05 Lebrecht Music Library; Figure 6.10 ssuaphotos/Shutterstock; Chapter 7 PaulPaladin/Shutterstock; Figure 7.02 Stuart Jenner/Alamy; Figure 7.07 Artur Marciniec/Alamy; Figure 7.08 ONOKY Photononstop/Alamy; Figure 7.09 J R Bale/Alamy; Chapter 8 wk1003mike/Shutterstock; Figure 8.01 Nikki Bidgood/Getty Images; Figure 8.03 (l) Mike Goldwater/Alamy; Figure 8.03 (r) Paul Thompson Images/Alamy; Figure 8.04 Chaikom/Shutterstock; Chapter 9 MBI/Alamy; Figure 9.01 (l,r) Christian Bertran/Shutterstock; Figure 9.01 (c) Rawpixel.com/Shutterstock; Figure 9.05 Icatnews/Shutterstock; Figure 9.06 Antonio Guillem Fernández/Alamy; Chapter 10 derrek/Getty Images; Figure 10.03 Dejan Stanisavljevic/Shutterstock; Figure 10.06 TACStock1/Shutterstock; Chapter 11 vaniato/Fotolia; Chapter 12 red150770/Fotolia; 12.09 (Dubai) Shutterstock/Subbotina-Kononchuk Anna; Figure 12.13 (kingfisher) Menno Schaefer/Shutterstock; Chapter 13 psdesign1/Fotolia; Chapter 14 Bruce Parrot/Getty Images; Chapter 15 madgooch/Fotolia; Chapter 16 kay/Getty Images; Chapter 17 Reservoir Dots/Fotolia; Chapter 18 z_amir/Fotolia; Chapter 19 sheelamohanachandran/Fotolia; Chapter 20 cacaroot/Fotolia; Chapter 21 kreizihorse/Fotolia; Asset 12.02 Squaredpixels/Getty Images; Asset 12.05 1000 words/Shutterstock; Asset 12.06 Elena Elisseeva/Shutterstock; Asset 13.02, p2 Robert Kneschke/Fotolia; p3 Monkey Business/Fotolia; p4 szeyuen/Fotolia; p5 panmaule/Fotolia; Asset 14.03 Zarianlk/Getty Images.

Thanks to Belmeier Raymond for his help reviewing content.

The screenshots of Microsoft products were used with permission from Microsoft.